Lecturing the Atlantic

Lecturing the Atlantic

SPEECH, PRINT, AND AN ANGLO-AMERICAN
COMMONS 1830–1870

Tom F. Wright

OXFORD
UNIVERSITY PRESS

Oxford University Press is a department of the University of Oxford. It furthers
the University's objective of excellence in research, scholarship, and education
by publishing worldwide. Oxford is a registered trade mark of Oxford University
Press in the UK and certain other countries.

Published in the United States of America by Oxford University Press
198 Madison Avenue, New York, NY 10016, United States of America.

CIP data is on file at the Library of Congress
ISBN 978–0–19–049679–1

1 3 5 7 9 8 6 4 2
Printed by Sheridan Books, Inc., United States of America

{ CONTENTS }

{ LIST OF FIGURES }

{ ACKNOWLEDGMENTS }

The book you hold in your hands is the product of its own journey through trans-atlantic circuits of co-operation, and has amassed many debts of gratitude. It began at the University of Cambridge, where I was fortunate enough to bene-fit from the counsel and scholarly example of Sarah Meer, David Trotter, and Michael O'Brien, among many others. My lengthy long-distance correspondence with Angela Ray helped energize and transform the project, and culminated in our eventual meeting at the American Antiquarian Society at the event that resulted in the publication of the edited collection *The Cosmopolitan Lyceum* in 2013. What I learnt from the group of scholars assembled there in Worcester helped catalyze and strengthen the ideas that run through the chapters that follow.

Archival work for the book was completed thanks to the award of a Mary C. Mooney Fellowship at the Boston Athenaeum; a British Association for American Studies Ambassador's Award for research at Harvard University; a Newby Postdoctoral Fellowship at the Institute for Advanced Study in the Humanities at the University of Edinburgh; and a Fulbright Early Career Fellowship at Northwestern University and the Newberry Library. Sections of this work were presented at meetings of the American Literature Association, American Studies Association, British Association of American Studies, C19, SHARP, and Symbiosis, across both Europe and North America.

The research process was made as smooth as possible by the excellent staff of, among other places, Cambridge's University Library and the Lee Library, Wolfson College; the American Antiquarian Society, the Massachusetts Historical Society, Harvard Houghton and Widener Libraries, New York Public Library, the New York Historical Society, the Cooper Union Library the National Library of Scotland; and Northwestern University Libraries. During my long periods in New England, the hospitality and *joie de vivre* of Murray Wheeler Jr., Barbara and Eugene McCarthy, Kathryn Douglas, and the *céad míle fáilte* of my American cousins re-affirmed my faith in Atlantic exchange.

Many people have enriched this book through advice, suggestions, and cautions against wrong turns. In addition to those listed before, the most important of these include Thomas Augst, Michael J. Collins, Simon Cooke, Wai Chee Dimmock, Carolyn Eastman Hilary Emmett, James Emmott, Paul Erickson, Linda Freedman, Huston Gilmore, Sandra Gustafson, Thomas Jones, Michael Jonik, Susan Manning, Donald Pease, Clare Pettitt, Peter Riley, Matt Rubery, Becca Weir, Mary Saracino, and Ronald J. Zboray. Brendan O'Neill and his successors at Oxford University

Press, and the anonymous readers of the manuscript, helped me feel my way toward the shape this book now takes. Rav Casley Gera gets his own sentence for remaining an inspiration and an insightful critical friend throughout. The completion of this book would not have been very different without the surprise late appearance and miraculously eager involvement of my most valued reader, and my soulmate, Ursula Sagar. Above all, this book would not exist without the support, encouragement, and example of my parents Fiona Fitzpatrick and Paul Wright, for whom it is dedicated.

An earlier version of Chapter 3 was published as "Listening to Emerson's 'England' at Clinton Hall, 22 January 1850," *Journal of American Studies* 14.3 (August 2012). Parts of Chapter 6 were published as "The Transatlantic Larynx in Wartime: John Gough's London Voices," in *Traffic and (Mis)Translations: New England in the World 1600–1900*, ed. Robin Peel (University of New England Press, 2012).

{ NOTE ON THE TERMINOLOGY
OF "ENGLAND" AND "BRITAIN" }

Throughout this book slippage will be noted in sources between the nomenclature of "British" and "English."[1] Recent historiography has described the emergence during the long eighteenth century of an internationally recognized concept of "Englishness," independent of the more abstract political signification of "Britishness."[2] However, the great majority of foreign commentators, and a number of English writers, continued to use the two as synonyms throughout the nineteenth century. Paul Langford locates one origin of this slippage in the reluctance of Romance languages "to coin a precise translation for 'British' or at least to use it once coined," noting that "even Americans, with no linguistic barrier to surmount, did not necessarily show more discrimination."[3] While allowing for this discursive slippage in my sources, I have attempted throughout to use "England" as a geographic designator, and "Britain" and "British" for political and imperial institutions.

Lecturing the Atlantic

Intro — "performative conception of authorship"

↳ a flashpoint of "modernity"
   ↳ immersion in "the local moment" meets a "media ecology" of transnational movements
      ↳ This has created a prob of
method: how to approach one of the period's key 1-3
"fundamentally expressive form[s]" → this answer is transnational + transmedia creation of an "Anglo-Am commons"

3 - "a distinct category of civic orality" in discussion of Br — performing + competing over the terms of a public sphere → uneven (not ideal)

4-5 - Corrective to view of lecture as a national form (association of pub sphere + N·E literary nationalist acts of nation building). → "dialectic of fascination w/ + rejection of such models"
      ↳ lectures perform fascination w/ performance of the exotic.

5 - Examining not so much as materiality but discourse + performance of imagined community — a cul practice. A means of creating an (often uneasily) idealized pub sphere. → "a matter as much of print as performance" 6 "a cul of display"
      ↳ "new categories of text at the boundaries of voice + print."

6 - Orality as "resurgent" rather than "residual" in its cross pollenation w/ print!
   ↳ "new textual forms" of the talking mind" (a more intriguing one perhaps than the pub sphere one).
7 - What we miss in forgetting that writers composed — on intervention into the print model of modernity for ear as well as eye.

7 - Method, intriguing — reconstructing orality + its cul through close readings of both performance + differing receptions (which were part of the design of lecture cul)
      ↳ How it would be reperformed / re-read.

------

ch 1

- 11 - Performing Britishness to perform the apparently neutral inclusivity of rep. not ideal.
- Rise of Scottish model of oral edu + dem pub dissemination. In Am, church meets theatre.
   ↳ He is interested in its move from edu to a more copious cul form — an entertainment. Performance cul. Combining church + theatre in a moral / civic endeavor. "theatricalized pedagogy"
      ↳ charting its emergence as central to the idea of a nation building public sphere in the press of the NE (notes the regional specificity).
      ↳ "secondary field of reception" - 20 But this was not submission to print, a hybrid form.

23 - Emergence of cul of reportage as a contested sphere.
   ↳ methodological protest.
   ↳ views for the process of social construction of a lecture cul + its meanings (multiply mediated e.g. editors interests) 24. Challenge notion of public neutrality — they were always contested texts.

Neutrality as a form of political regulation - shaping a version of cul + civic performance around a series of exclusionary + largely unspoken pol norms / hierarchies. - 32
   ↳ Growth of a pretense of critical public sphere. → "performances of neutrality"
33 - His analysis is devoted to finding behind neutrality the forms of indirection that allowed pol expression + evidence of a critical public. ▷ Indirect pol. "a theatrical or performative commons" 34
      argues this is the basis of a certain kind of pol double-voicedness a form of Lyceum language game used to negotiates demands of civic neutrality + pol expression. Is his idea that it could be dangerous knowledge convincing? Es. of early Emerson + aphorism. [producing wholeness but also revealing ↑ tensions]

37 - Dev of Br themes lectures — means of smuggling pol into an idea of Ang-Am neutral commons. → Anglo - Saxon ethnic ideal [The balancing as obfuscating the Lyceums' about race — circuits of nationalism + revival of pol division of]
      ↳ "Irish-Am counterpublic" as challenge
45-47 - Reporters police the performance + cul meaning of manners that go into shaping of the balancing of Br + Am cultural traits to make up an Ang-Am continuous.

{ Introduction }

The popular lecture was a paradoxical icon of nineteenth-century modernity. On both sides of the Atlantic, audiences and performers transformed a cultural practice with origins in the medieval cloister into an unexpected flashpoint medium of public life. It was an educational form that began to flourish amid the educational fervor of the late Scottish Enlightenment. But it burst into life most powerfully in the United States in the decades leading up to the Civil War, where it was often known as the "lyceum movement." As it grew, this phenomenon sat at the confluence of at least three major transformations in American life. First, it helped shape a revolution in oratory, fashioning a space for educational speech and rational debate that promised to float free of creed or party. Second, it embodied new ideals of republican education, democratizing the habits of elite collegiate pedagogy for the masses, and forging new economies of knowledge and cultural consumption. Third, it set in motion a lasting transformation in the relationship between the public and American literature, providing both the necessary conditions for the modern public intellectual and a powerful new performative conception of authorship. The aspirations of the public lecture form remain with us, conceived anew through book festivals and televangelist performances, lurking in the background of every TED talk video upon which we click.

Lecture culture was a phenomenon often baffling in scope and marked by internal contradictions. The array of spaces both grand and humble that nineteenth-century Americans called "lecture halls" (see Figures I.1 and I.2) were equal parts academy, church, and theater: symbols of both Enlightenment educational ambitions and an Evangelical cult of presence. Attendance was a formative practice of class and civic identity, yet also a market transaction. Lecturing was often presented as a proudly "neutral" forum and yet, as one of the most powerful means of being "public" in the midcentury republic, soon began to play a key role in controversial social movements. For the lecture-goer, attendance was a crucial means of immersing oneself fully in the local moment, and of performing that participation to one's peers. Yet feverish newspaper coverage of the circuit held out the promise of shared national experience through a media ecology

FIGURE I.1 *Lecture Room of the First Methodist Church, Elmira, New York, circa 1870*

FIGURE I.2 *The Broadway Tabernacle, December 1847*

linking village, town, and metropolis, allowing diverse actors to hear, read, and debate about the same message. It is perhaps these interdisciplinary tensions that have contributed to the form's strange critical neglect. Even as contemporary scholarship has consolidated our understanding of multiple modes of nineteenth-century public culture, orality, new media, and reform, uncertainty about how *prob of* to approach the scope and conflicts of lecture culture has helped perpetuate a *method* continuing scholarly disregard for a fundamental expressive form of the period.[1]

Lecturing the Atlantic argues for a new interpretation of this neglected institution. It reorients our understanding of the lyceum by seeing it as an international and cross-media phenomenon patterned by an intellectual and cultural investment in what I term an "Anglo-American commons." This occurred in two related senses: first, as the traditions, practices, or heritage of a diasporic people; second, more abstractly, as a recognition of shared resources of culture, language, and history.[2] As Elisa Tamarkin and Christopher Hanlon have recently shown, a surprisingly large proportion of antebellum cultural production can be understood in terms of a "contest over transatlantic connection."[3] This book hails the lyceum as an arena for such contests of unique power and immediacy. As I reveal, the lyceums of the republic satisfied a voracious popular appetite for discussion of Britain through multifaceted performances that reflected on the problems and potentials of transatlantic history, literature, politics, manners, and shared cultures of reform. The complexity of lecture hall performances stems from their fascinating role as a metarhetorical meditation on the comparative nature of the discursive arena itself. Utterances from the lyceum stage, I argue, must be understood as a distinct category of civic orality that enacted key ideals of an enlarged but unevenly integrated public sphere; one with a productively ambivalent relationship to nationalism, cosmopolitanism, and empire. Lyceum discussions of Anglo-American themes therefore helped define the very nature of this evolving American speech ritual and the notion of a democratic character.

This book explores the ways in which some of the midcentury North Atlantic world's most enduring cultural figures, such as Frederick Douglass, William Makepeace Thackeray, and Ralph Waldo Emerson, as well as some of the more fascinating marginal voices such as Lola Montez and John B. Gough, brought such topics to the platform. I will show how their performances helped address fundamental questions about the condition of the transatlantic world: the public spheres of republic and monarchy; the meanings of emerging social, physical, and linguistic distinctions; and the lessons of Old World modernity and imperial destiny for a republic embroiled in national crisis. By unraveling the meanings of these debates, I interrogate the lyceum's idealized rhetoric of classless democratic unity and its modeling of public interaction, to suggest how the diverse and often fraught discourses of an Anglo-American commons provided an ideal symbolic site for these negotiations.[4] My analysis of an Anglo-American performative commons connects the transatlantic turn in cultural studies to important debates in media theory and public sphere scholarship. In doing so, *Lecturing the Atlantic* make a case for the world of the antebellum platform as a material network that helped shape the nature of midcentury US public culture through its reimagining of Anglo-American commonality.[5]

Lecture Culture

In embarking from this viewpoint, this book offers an enlarged conception of lecture culture that challenges a still widely accepted narrative inherited from influential nineteenth-century commentators. One strand of this narrative was the emphasis on its sheer novelty. To Douglass the figure of the public lecturer was "a modern invention called forth by the increasing demands of restless human nature."[6] For Emerson, the new mass form of the spoken essay promised "a new literature, which leaves aside all tradition, time and place and circumstance."[7] Implicit in these assessments was also the promise of national distinction. For *Harper's Monthly* editor George William Curtis in 1855, "The popular lecture [was] an American and a Yankee institution" with "nothing corresponding" in the societies of Europe.[8] To Henry David Thoreau, it was the institution "from which a New Era will be dated to New England, as from the games of Greece."[9] In such ways, midcentury northern cultural nationalists of various stripes were apt to present lecture culture as a national metonym, a superstructure of federated listening spaces whose emphasis on internal self-reflection helped to forge a distinctive literary culture and national public. This view was codified several generations later by the lyceum's elegists who idealized the midcentury platform as an arena that had forced the issue of women's rights and antislavery, secured the triumph of liberal principles, and had become synonymous with the flowering of an indigenous public culture.[10]

In what little recent work exists on the lecture circuit, Americanist scholarship has often appeared to follow the lead provided by views such as these.[11] They set the tone for foundational modern accounts of the lyceum, a movement that for Donald Scott "not only expressed a national culture; it was one of the central institutions within and by which the public had its existence."[12] Similarly, for its most recent historian, Angela Ray, the movement was a "culture-making rhetorical practice" whose nation-building agency depended on a collective turn inward.[13] Broader accounts of nineteenth-century literary and reform movements have long recognized the importance of lecture culture, but have still tended to invoke a consciously "national" lyceum.[14] This narrative was sustained by F. O. Matthiessen's classic act of canon formation in *American Renaissance* (1941), which held up the popular lecture as the solution to Emerson's "quest for a form," and an engine of native literary emergence.[15] Even where more recent accounts of oratorical culture have been increasingly attuned to lecturing as part of what Lawrence Buell calls transatlantic "proliferation of media," the sense still remains of a domestic forum whose role in forging the consciousness of the new republic was made possible by turning its back on European influence and models.[16] However, as the essays in the recent collection *The Cosmopolitan Lyceum* (2013) have revealed, an uneasy dialectic of fascination with and rejection of such models was in fact a vital component of lecture culture. As I argue in the introduction to that volume, the historical archive shows us that nineteenth-century audiences were in thrall to both the vocal and the exotic, and that lecture culture played on the often contradictory interaction between cosmopolitan and nationalist impulses.[17]

Print and Orality

Beyond calling for an enlargement of lecturing's geographic and thematic scope, this book also re-examines the boundaries of its communicative context. The first gesture involves a reassessment of terminology. Though I follow nineteenth-century usage in treating the terms "lyceum" and "lecture circuit" interchangeably, the latter was in fact merely the most visible part of a broader civic institution of the lyceum movement. Even pushing beyond this to the key term "lecture" only gets us so far. The origins of the Latin word *lectura* ("reading") take us back to the monastic dictation practices of an age of scarce print, and only in the sixteenth century does the verb "to lecture" enlarge its meaning in English to refer to instructive oral discourse.[18] Come the period covered in this book, the term had enlarged once again to embrace a new and diverse mass form, confined not only to sacred or collegiate contexts but now brought before a heterogeneous audience, and embracing matters far more diverse. This was still a form centered on a lone figure delivering a discourse forty-five minutes to two hours in length, often read aloud from a text, but it was now also a category of performance strangely located somewhere between the playhouse and pulpit. Popular lecturing married intellectual stimulation with a structure of display, and was as much a part of show culture as any other staged ritual. Given such breadth, it makes little sense to speak of a unified form of "the popular lecture." I prefer to embrace the looser but more instructive concept of "lecture culture": a cluster of practices and habits that constellated around a particular type of vocal performance event.[19]

A key claim of what follows is that lecture culture's significance as a discursive construct demands weight equal to that of its material reality. In the words of the subtitle of the first modern study of this phenomenon, lectures represented a "town meeting of the mind," a phrase Carl Bode intended to suggest parity and continuity with the New England collectivist tradition.[20] This book takes a literal reading of that phrase in arguing that lecture culture was an arena that was constructed as much *in the mind* as in front of the lectern, as an imagined or projected community and process, and as something framed by contemporaries eager to inflect and condition the meanings of a cultural phenomenon. As Thomas Augst has argued, lecture halls were "not simply another source of knowledge, they were engines of civil society, ritual spaces that mobilised communities around the symbolic value of education as a democratic good."[21] I build upon this sense of "symbolic value," and upon the arguments of print studies put forward by Trish Loughran and others, to argue for the popular lecture as a form whose value lies in its idealized construction of a public sphere centered uneasily on concepts of tolerance, liberality, gentility.[22]

This is most clearly evidenced in the constant process of conditioning of the lecture circuit through its contact with and reliance on rival media. Thanks to a proliferating culture of reportage, transcription, and commentary, the lyceum was a matter as much of print as of performance—a culture of display that was experienced and conditioned far more through newspaper reportage as by first-hand encounter. The American press was invariably present at prominent lectures to capture details for broadcast in the next day's paper. From the 1840s onward it was customary for some local and city newspapers to report on the previous day's lectures as newsworthy events. Throwing one's voice into a lecture hall meant engaging what Thackeray called the "reflecting medium" of the American press, setting words loose on a national circuit of transmission and reception, and speakers could not predict upon whose ears or pages they might fall, nor the nature of their contingent effects.[23]

These dynamics helped generate what we now perceive as new categories of text at the boundaries of voice and print. In their accounts of the rise of print-based cultures, Walter Ong and Jack Goody both point to the long nineteenth century as a moment of irreversible transition between oral and print paradigms.[24] Ong speaks of the "tenaciousness of orality" in post-oral cultures by which verbal features retained a "residual" presence in an increasingly "chiro-graphic" landscape.[25] However, as the New England editor and public speaker George William Curtis acknowledged in 1856, such claims for the demise of the oral may have been premature:

> A few years since, when the steam-engine was harnessed into the service of the printing-press, we were ready to conclude that oral instruction would have to yield the palm, to written literature ... but we forgot, in our hasty generalization, how the law of compensation rules everywhere ... so the new motor, in the service of newspapers and books, would call out other forms of the talking mind.[26]

We might think of this law of compensation as a governing process of nineteenth-century media life: that is to say, nineteenth-century orality can be viewed more valuably as resurgent than as residual. Opportunities for live speech multiplied. Oratory resounded from the pages of the antebellum media: turning its densely packed pages, the auditory sense is still repeatedly assailed by elaborate transcriptions of speeches, debates, toasts, commemorations, and lyceum talks.[27] The steam-driven press of the 1830s, we might say, did not extinguish the oral or render it obsolete, but catalyzed greater prominence for the verbal, generating new textual *forms* of the talking mind in which print is called in to reinforce, not replace, the spoken word. Lecture reports lie at this fault line of communication history among several forms of intermedial overlap, reliant on a complex reciprocity between speech and print events, helping to reconfigure hierarchies of literacy and textual knowledge in a number of ways.[28]

These were speech texts most obviously because they had captured words spoken in a given context. To some, the very orality of the lecture form suggested a new intermediary creativity between text and voice—in this vein, *Putnam's* magazine argued in 1854 that "the greatest achievements in poetry are the plays which were never intended for print; and doubtless the best additions to our literature will be the lectures which were only written to amuse an audience, and not intended for publication."[29] This status lay in the plausible fact that many pieces were composed for the ear, and we lose sight—or more, appropriately, miss the sound—of this fact when we treat them as straightforwardly written texts. To take only the most obvious example, lyceum orators such as Emerson, aware of the intertwined nature of oral and print, wrote with both the ear and the eye in mind, always aware of multiple possible scenes of listening and sensual reading. Their sonic appeal was a cardinal element of their nineteenth-century meaning and literary function. The orator's initial rendition was understood as merely one of many potential reimaginings of an aural composition, and speech texts were understood as demanding oral reanimation to establish the word's true meanings and confer upon the reciter some public ethos of the original speaker.

My analysis involves immersion in a deep archive of newspaper and periodical sources as rhetorical artifacts in their own right, which projected oratorical events outside the lecture hall into the hands of an atomized reading public. Lecturing was a material and textual network of knowledge whose role in the antebellum imaginary consisted of discursive contests over the meanings of public speech.[30] Since such reports frequently allow us to trace a number of divergent responses to a single oratorical event, they enable critics to perceive the processes by which socially agreed-upon interpretations were formulated, meanings contested, and the authority of speakers challenged.[31] I suggest that tracing an original speech act, in all of its ambiguities, through a series of transformations and scenes of reception allows for a fuller appreciation of the multiple textualities and new media modalities of lecture culture.[32] My focus is therefore on close reading of both performances and their reception, exploring the use that performers made of the lecture form and the use that media interests made of their utterances as complementary forms of what Kenneth Burke's rhetorical analysis asks us to think of as dramatic action.[33]

Book Outline

An introductory chapter helps to flesh out the arguments made above. In it, I trace the roots of modern lecture culture to the civic institution-building of late eighteenth-century Glasgow, before sketching the emergence and evolution of the American lyceum movement in the 1830s. I also explore the ways in which practitioners and observers struggled with one of the key claims for the early lyceum: that it was a space of dispassionate, bipartisan neutrality. Since lecture culture was conceived from the outset as an unaffiliated arena, distinct from the stump and the pulpit, disagreements over its usefulness amounted to debates over the function and viability of nonpartisan speech in a democracy, and over how orality and performance might be controlled, co-opted, and understood. As I make clear, lectures on Anglo-American ideas and themes provide a useful testing ground for such ideas, not simply because of the often indirect politics and assimilationist agenda of such events, but because an intense culture of visual scrutiny meant that "Englishness" and "Americanness" became politically charged categories for performance analysis.

Lecturing the Atlantic then turns to four case studies that illustrate these dynamics in action between 1830 and 1870. Since much has already been written about the American tours of Charles Dickens (1867–68) and Oscar Wilde (1882), I made the decision to go beyond these well-known cultural flashpoints, to explore a series of lesser-understood instances of performers who took Anglo-America as their theme.[34] Chapter 2 begins this work by thinking about the role of British imagery in the lecturing campaign against slavery. It explores the multiple uses that Frederick Douglass found for British liberalism, tolerance, and Anglo-Saxonism in his transition from "lecturing agent" to cosmopolitan intellectual. Chapter 3 takes the example of Emerson's high-profile 1850 lecture on England in New York and Ohio, and reveals the ways in which his reimagining of industrial Britain in terms of "order" was understood in terms of wider theatrical culture and crises of Anglophobia. In chapter 4, I explore what I term the "choreography of reform" by turning to the examples of Whig activists Horace Greeley and Horace Mann. Both the educational reformer Mann and the legendary campaigning news editor Greeley drew upon spatial and temporal prophetic rhetoric in the service of subtly contradictory visions of Anglo-American futurity.

Chapter 5 pursues the global literary celebrity Thackeray on his two tours of the United States during 1853 and 1855. It charts the media controversies that attended his discussion of themes of monarchy, humor, and global "Englishness," and the ways in which his brand of genial humor was by turns celebrated as a signature mode of Anglophone culture and an imperial affront. The final chapter concludes the book's discussion by turning to the Irish "spider dancer" Lola Montez and the British-American temperance reformer John B. Gough. Exploring the transition that these two unlikely figures made from the worlds of reform and theater to that of mainstream lecturing, I reveal the surprising means by which both attempted to serve as guarantors of transatlantic unity during the strains of the Civil War. Through these reconstructed rhetorical contexts, *Lecturing the Atlantic* tells a story about the ways in which midcentury Americans thought about Britain, how they articulated these views to their fellow countrymen, and how the strange media journey of such ideas helped shape public culture.

The American Lecture Hall and
an Anglo-American Commons

In March 1857, the New York–based *Putnam's Monthly* magazine offered its verdict on an iconic national pastime. "The lyceum," its article began, "is the American theater. It is the one institution in which we take our nose out of the hands of our English prototypes—the English whom we are always ridiculing and always following—and go alone."[1] By 1857, it was possible for organs of cultural nationalism such as *Putnam's* to point with pride to this nation-building endeavor as one that, once and for all, marked the public sphere of the republic as distinct from its European counterparts: more democratic, egalitarian, and possessed of its own unique dignity.[2] And at the close of its affectionate survey of this still-new world's characteristics and foremost speakers, the magazine concluded that lecturing was "the American amusement which is most congenial to our habits and tastes," and a performance culture that seemed in these antebellum years to be "the great exchange of the world."[3] It is an assessment whose wry subtleties continue to resonate for modern scholars seeking to understand the world it describes. Imagining lecture attendance in terms of taking one's "nose" from the books of tradition, it encourages reflection on the medium's contradictory relationship to more static print-centric scenes of reading. In presenting the phenomenon as "theater," it invites us into an expansive understanding of lecture halls as spaces of license and spectacle, a pragmatic compromise between educational and dramatic impulses.

Moreover, the emphasis on the lecture hall as a "great exchange" and its discourse as "congenial" underscores the importance of self-proclaimed neutrality to how this milieu preferred to see itself. In one of the most influential modern readings of the phenomenon, Donald Scott has argued that the popular lecture of the period was "expected to incorporate the public, to embrace all members of the community, whatever their occupation, social standing or political and religious affiliation. Useful to all and offensive to none, the lecture was an oratorical form deliberately and carefully separated from all partisan and sectarian discourse."[4] This aspiration for the lyceum as "great exchange" dominates many contemporary accounts. Its cultural arbiters, that is to say, saw its function as an ecumenical cultural commons, and its usefulness defined by its ability to find "congenial" discursive ground whose propriety might mediate the tenser forces of midcentury life.

This idea of commons must be read as closely related to the issue of nation. In defining the lyceum through its democratic opposition to "English prototypes," it captures American lecture culture's self-conscious and richly generative simultaneous disavowal and embrace of Old World models. British literature, history, reform, and social developments and the health of Anglo-American culture were some of the most prevalent themes on the circuit. Far from removing its "nose" from Old World influences, the midcentury lecture hall was one of the most revealing contexts through which Americans could reflect on the challenges and legacies of British social and intellectual "prototypes," as a form of resistance to and reciprocity with transatlantic habits of congregation, display, debate, and commentary. As Christopher Hanlon has recently argued, a surprisingly large swathe of antebellum cultural production can be understood anew when viewed in terms of a "contest over transatlantic connection, an American competition over English history, culture and politics."[5] The "great exchange" of the lecture hall was at the heart of such contests, most importantly because discussions of an Anglo-American imaginary were seen by many to provide just the kind of "congenial" subjects whose unifying appeal might transcend the contending forces of midcentury national life.

Contests over the purposes and uses of the nation's lecture halls provide a route into a renewed understanding of some of the most pressing debates of the period: debates about the necessary conditions of a rational society and the role of performance and speech within that. But even further, these disputes were about the attempt to fashion and construct an idealized public through habits of congregation, scrutiny, listening, and reflection. Lecture hall disputes over the relevance and purchase of British "prototypes" were central to this endeavor, in part because it is through lecture culture's own transatlantic origin myth, and its handling of its debts and affinities to its inheritances from the British public sphere, that we can best know it. These performances were likewise a key medium through which midcentury Americans forged and modeled concepts of their own national character.

This introductory chapter illustrates these themes through a survey of lecture culture during the 1830s–1860s. It draws upon a wide archive of articles, editorials, letters, journal entries, public commentaries, and reminiscences in order to develop and nuance the claims of multiple generations of historians and critics. The discussion falls into two parts. The first surveys the transition of "lyceum" into "lecture culture" and the shifting values that this involved. It explores the role of ideas of civic speech, and the influence of the experiments of Scottish educationalists such as John Anderson and George Birkbeck on what many participants in the lyceum saw as its laudable values of liberal neutrality, independence, and civic duty. The tension between such (often unattainable) ideals and the demands of individualist republicanism, I proceed to argue, was one of the catalyzing dynamics of lecture culture.

The second part of this chapter argues that we can read the American lecture circuit's obsession with a transatlantic imaginary as a complex, and problematic, means of securing this neutrality. Lectures on British history, literature, travel, and reform, I maintain, provided a shared referential field of what *Putnam's* called the "English prototypes." Performances on these themes helped to legitimate an ascendant national identity based on a sustaining dialogue with the "manners" and institutions of the British public sphere. As I show, this category of performances embraced key lecture by groups—such as Native Americans or Irish nationalists—whose rhetoric challenged the meanings of the Anglo-American commons. But more often, it was a medium by which the mainstream lecture platform could model a form of transcendental whiteness, using Anglocentric manners as a cultural adhesive.

Civic Speech from Glasgow to Massachusetts

The delivery of educational and entertaining talks to public audiences was not an entirely unknown practice in the early American republic. In the decades following the Revolution, enterprising itinerants began to carve out a living as traveling independent speakers. What the nation lacked, however, was any means of cohering such efforts. The first meaningful attempt at orchestrating lectures into regular courses was provided by Josiah Holbrook, a pioneering educationalist. Holbrook founded an organization in Milbury, Massachusetts, in late 1826, opting for the moniker "lyceum," deriving from Aristotle's teaching ground, to refer to a body devoted to community learning. In a manifesto published in the *American Journal of Education* in October of that year, he outlined the goals for what he called a "society for mutual instruction," with a diktat to "check the progress of that monster, intemperance" and "diffuse rational and useful information through the community generally."[6] While lacking in specifics about how this goal might be achieved, Holbrook proposed "regular courses of instruction by lectures or otherwise" as an arrangement that might "do more for the general diffusion of knowledge, and for raising the moral and intellectual taste of our countrymen, than any other expedient which can possibly be devised."[7] In this sense the lyceum can be viewed both as a social institution and as a crusade, conceived from the outset as a discrete arena, distinct from the political stump and the pulpit, in which communities could speak to and learn from each other.

Catalyzed by the self-improvement spirit of the Jacksonian period, sister organizations proliferated during the 1830s through areas settled by the New England diaspora, notably the northern Midwest.[8] As this spread of lyceums continued

into the following decade, the loosely connected debating society model gave way
to a more static and spectatorial system based on the hosting of talks by visiting speakers. In the major cities in particular, the lyceum became associated
overwhelmingly with lecture courses rather than other forms of discussion. By
the 1837–38 season there were already twenty-six annual lecture courses offered
in Boston, and the nation soon boasted hundreds of lecture-sponsoring organizations under guises such as Young Men's Associations, Mercantile Libraries,
Philomathean Societies, and Athenaeums, which hosted lectures in regularized
winter seasons running from midautumn through spring.[9] By the mid-1840s, the
transition from "lyceum" proper to "lecture circuit" was clearly visible.

After weathering a slight downturn in the late 1840s, this circuit saw a significant resurgence during the next decade. By 1855 a Boston paper observed that
"every town or village of any sort of enterprise or pretentions has its annual
course of popular lectures, while the cities support several courses."[10] Across
the country, such courses now included comparable specialist interest lecture
organizations, including German-American lyceums from the mid-1830s in
Pennsylvania and a number of African-American equivalents. "Originally casual and irregular," observed another Massachusetts paper in 1860, lecturing
had by now entirely "matured into a definite system, which may be regarded as
having passed the stage of experiment. It is now an institution, a fixed fact."[11]
In Bode's terms this was "now a lyceum from which most of the early elements
except the lecture had disappeared, but the lecture proved it not an ailing attraction."[12] Central to this transition was a general trajectory of lyceum as education
to entertainment.

This shift from debating lyceum to speaking circuit gave birth to the short-
lived profession of the "public lecturer." The 1840s in particular were the heyday
of semiprofessional freelance speakers, entrepreneurial young men who began to
forge careers and precarious livelihoods by touring an increasingly thickly popu-
lated local network as largely independent actors in a knowledge economy. From
the early 1850s onward, this loose system consolidated further into what contemporaries knew as the "star system": rather than serving local or amateur speaking talent, this mature cultural economy was now dominated by a small number
of eminent names (largely drawn from the metropolitan elites of Boston and
New York who toured the country lucratively each winter.[13] Every September, the
membership of what was termed the "Lecturing Fraternity" announced itself in
the form of listings of available lecturers in the editorial column of the *New York
Tribune*, with over a hundred speakers from all walks of professional life ready to
bring their spoken thoughts to the market. They were what *Putnam's* magazine
in 1857 termed "the intellectual leaders of intelligent progress in the country."[14]

Contrary to the assertions of many of the American lecture circuit's most
impassioned commentators, a number of parallel activities across the Atlantic
can be read as important precedents for these advances. In England, educational
public talks of some form had been a feature of London life for centuries through

institutions such as the Gresham or Blackfriars series, and through the periodic ventures of fellows from Cambridge and Oxford. By 1800, lectures were being delivered across the country from Newcastle to Bristol, and in 1815 the *Times* of London spoke of "peripatetic philosophers who give lectures for a guinea each course, in every village near London."[15] Some of these were devoted to new urban audiences of the industrial cities. The prevailing model of these English events, however, was the engagement by private arrangement of enterprising professors or graduates, squarely aimed at middle-class audiences and the metropolitan discursive elite, and generally focused exclusively on belletristic subject matter or scientific demonstrations. Especially in London, this model of the occasional lecture as something approaching a society event flourished during the early nineteenth century, and was one of the public arenas of scientists such as Michael Faraday and writers from William Hazlitt to Thomas Carlyle. By midcentury, the American lecture system resembled this model in tone and composition. But it was a version of lecturing from north of the Scottish border, and the ideas upon which it was based, that was to prove particularly influential on the tone and self-image of the American context.

At the very outset, when educationalists such as Holbrook began to feel their way toward the lyceum movement they were often explicit about one particular point of inspiration. Of the new Franklin Institute of Philadelphia, an 1827 chronicler observed that "the plan is unquestionably of Scotch origin ... the first among the universally instructed nations of Christendom."[16] Opening the Boston Mechanics' Institution the same year, the inaugural speaker claimed that such lyceums "owe their first establishment to that country ... which has long been distinguished for its anxious attention to the education of its children."[17] To many of the founders of the organizations that would evolve into the lecture circuit, the most inspirational models for institutions of civic education were Scottish, and in particular those pioneered at the turn of the century in the colleges of Glasgow, dedicated to bringing education to the new industrial populace and allowing the free circulation of information through Scotland's growing industrial cities.[18] American lecturing thus drew upon and transformed a generation of debate within Scottish social thought over the possibility of independent spaces of free reflection and nonpartisan debate separate from the noise of industrial society.[19]

By the 1780s, the emphasis on lectures had grown into a phenomenon notable enough to attract the ire of Samuel Johnson, whom James Boswell records as remarking,

> Lectures were once useful; but now, when all can read, and books are so numerous, lectures are unnecessary. .... People have nowadays got a strange opinion that everything should be taught by lectures. Now, I cannot see that lectures can do as much good as reading the books from which the lectures are taken. I know nothing that can be best taught by lectures, except where experiments are to be shown.[20]

Whereas this classic teleology of orality and literacy took lectures to be a pre-modern mode belonging to a time of scarce literacy, this "strange opinion" was very much a feature of Scottish pedagogy. The distinction with more print-based English practice was sharp enough for later observers to point to "the two great modes of university teaching" in the two nations: public lecturing in Glasgow, Edinburgh, and St. Andrews, versus private tutoring at Oxbridge:

> The English tutor exhibits a local picture of a magnificent castle and princely domain, describes minutely all the parts of the building, and all the beauties of the grounds: the Scottish professor holds up the panorama of an extensive and diversified country, gives the name, the distance, and magnitude of any thing which meets the eye, and concludes by bestowing a map of its roads, with directions for traveling over it to advantage.[21]

As encapsulated here, it is a duality rich in symbolism: between analytic and synthetic knowledge; taxonomic breadth and intensive depth; aesthetic judgment and utilitarian survey; above all, between attitudes to the correct orientation of speech: English private exchange over Scottish sociability, hermetic Socratic engagement over utterances aimed at a broader audience.

This predilection for oral training went in tandem with a more public under-standing of the duties of universities. Scottish academia of the period combined belief in the civic function of effective public speech with an emphasis on freedom of educational access and the duties and obligations of learned men to share their expertise. From the mid-eighteenth century onward, it was customary for college lectures to be advertised in the press and for urban publics to attend. Professors at Glasgow and Edinburgh such as Adam Smith, Thomas Sheridan, and Hugh Blair were professionally obliged to give public courses known as "anti-toga" lec-tures, named for the lack of academic robes worn on such occasions.[22] Education in Scotland therefore retained a distinct attitude to discursive public orality as a civic act, and Smith was shocked by the more sparse attendance at the lec-tures he delivered while in post at Oxford.[23] In the 1790s, John Anderson, pro-fessor of natural philosophy at Glasgow, developed this impulse and pioneered newly expanded courses of lectures tailored specifically for mixed public audi-ences. This new, specifically public form of lecture was adopted by a sophisti-cated, middle-class, mixed-gender audience, but also succeeded in attracting and retaining more modest sections of Glaswegian society. One memorialist recalls that "within the walls of the College of Glasgow, there was a large class of opera-tive mechanics and artizans, receiving instruction in science, which hitherto had been to them quite inaccessible as the pages of a sealed book."[24]

Upon his death in 1796, Anderson left his estate to found a civic body known as the Andersonian Institute, where his endeavors were continued and expanded by his influential successor, George Birkbeck.[25] Developing the idea of loosely institu-tionalized local adult education venues for the common man, Birkbeck founded the Glasgow Mechanics Institute in 1821 (see Figure 1.1) before taking these Scottish

FIGURE 1.1 *"Rival Lectures: Mechanics' Institution," Northern Looking Glass, 1825*

ideas to London, where he formed a London counterpart in November 1823, the precursor of the university college that now bears his name. By this point, comparable institutions had already become a fixed feature across southern Scotland, and with Birkbeck's help such initiatives spread throughout England's industrial regions, a mechanic's institute phenomenon that rose in tandem with the lyceum movement. The adult education experiments of Anderson and Birkbeck had not been entirely unprecedented, but they were marked out by their regularity, by the way that accessible lecture halls became distinct and permanent features of urban settings, and in the new types of public they helped to create.

The model of Scottish public lecturing rested on a series of ideas of key importance for their American transfer. One of the clearest was a paternalistic emphasis on the duty of elites both to diffuse useful knowledge and to model a form of learned disposition. The Edinburgh periodical *Blackwood's* advised in 1819 that lecturing should be a selfless act in several senses:

> The man who stands up to instruct his countrymen on such subjects—not in books, which are open to all consideration—but by a public appointment as a half-professor, ought especially to be a *sound* teacher. His hearers are not, at least not ought to, be assembled to hear speculations and fancies however acute and amusing.... He stands there as a sort of literary representative of his lettered countrymen, and ought, therefore, to speak authentic knowledge and belief, that which is held, and avouched and avowed by literary and intellectual authorities.[26]

In this conception, Scottish lecturing was as much about cultivating taste and sensibility as it was about explaining the world. The motivation to combat urban idleness and the perils of unrest also underpinned the rhetoric of inclusivity. Of equal importance for later developments in the United States was the way in which the new habits of congregation seemed to fuse social, sacred, and peda-gogic elements. Scottish educators figured this new space of the lecture hall in terms of a devotional register of removal and sanctuary, sacred enclosures in which communities could dedicate a quiet hour. Writing in 1825, one prominent protagonist of the early institutes, Reverend Bennie of Stirling, captures how this quasi-ecclesiastical spirit was understood as both communion and withdrawal:

> We withdraw from the turbulent and noisy scene to meditate on the mys-teries of nature, and enrich our minds with the treasure of knowledge. In the august temple of science the sounds of violence are never heard; there a perpetual stillness reigns; and whosoever would enter that temple to wor-ship must leave behind him the bitterness, the scorn, and the petty resent-ments of life.[27]

Here, lecture attendance is an act of civic attention and orality at one remove from the excess of both religious and political "violence." The unprecedented conceptual and social space opened up by what Thomas Love Peacock, in his satire on such institutions, called "steam intellect" was understood by many to represent a malleable opportunity for unclassifiable new varieties of social performance.[28]

Creation of an American Circuit

As Bode is careful to note, there was no "exact chain of events to connect the first American lyceum to British predecessors."[29] However, the documentation of early lecturing pioneers suggests that Scottish forebears and models were more significant than Bode maintains, particularly in the ideas they offered about the conduct of the public sphere. For one thing, there was a greater general emphasis upon the virtue of public speech in Scottish education.[30] The "elocutionary revo-lution" that formed part of the Scottish Enlightenment placed new emphasis on the performance dimensions of oratory, celebrating gesture, facial expression, and vocal tone as primary bearers of meaning, confirming the importance of the role of public orality, and the means through which it ought to be taught.[31] The main route by which these educational values and institutional "prototypes" crossed the Atlantic was through the wide influence of a prominent 1824 *Edinburgh Review* article, "Scientific Education of the People," by prominent Scottish Tory Henry Brougham. Taking up the mantle from Birkbeck, he offered a reforming manifesto that celebrated the rise of lecture-hosting organizations and called for the foundation of a new wave of democratically controlled institutions. "Let no

[handwritten margin note: "ib idea of demo was also of distinction"]

one assume any such [philanthropic] titles," he counseled, "if he has done nothing in his own neighbourhood to found a popular lecture course."[32] The piece was widely recirculated and reprinted throughout the United States, and struck fertile ground among northern and southern educationalists with enduring mutual traditions of looking to Scotland for practical inspiration.[33] Brougham's call was met with even greater enthusiasm here than among his original British audience, and the rise of the lyceum as a forum of public speech can justifiably be seen as part of a larger story of Caledonian pedagogic exchange whose influence on the values of public life was manifested in various ways in this new lecture culture.

A number of factors explain this tradition's rapid uptake in the United States, and none more so than the wider strength of the American oratorical tradition. Public speech has always been seen inordinately central to definitions of American public life.[34] As Daniel Boorstin put it, "As the nation struggled into self-consciousness, the orator—the man standing to or for or with his community— acquired a mythic role."[35] In this unprecedentedly literate early republic, verbal arts retained a central place; oratorical performance was respected as both a socially useful art form and an aesthetic experience. It persisted as a commonplace that oratory was a mode of expression native to republics; as one reviewer for the *North American Review* put it in 1852, "As the government becomes more and more democratic ... the occasions for popular eloquence multiply," in the form of celebrations, commemorations, civic ceremonies, and recitations.[36] More than simply a key source of information, education, and inspiration, in the early republic speech was a public office and a diagnostic indicator of national progress.

The form of the lecture also suited the emerging national predilection for utilitarian entertainment. Lecture attendance provided a space for the performance of democratic civic participation, the forging of civic identity through communal dialogue, and the forms of voluntary affiliation that struck French observer Alexis de Tocqueville as so extraordinary in his seminal writings on the young republic. The localized franchise structure provided an outlet for the multiple groups of community elders to arrange entertainments suited to their own tastes. It sat well with both Congregationalist forms of church governance, and with a republican conviction that representative democracy hinged on the creation of an informed citizenry, promoting what the *New World* magazine saw in 1843 as "the most striking tendencies of the age; disseminating and equalizing knowledge, approximating the unlearned and the learned."[37] Furthermore, central to the success of the lecture hall's outreach ambitions was the sheer eclecticism of the topics it covered, which might range from astronomy or botany through history and literary criticism to accounts of exotic lands in one course. This promise of something for everyone was central to the values of a mixed denominational culture's magnanimous acceptance of a democratic mixture of concerns that spoke to multiple tastes, and the existence of a site of exposure to shared knowledge encouraged aspirations of community cohesion.

As much as this, the nascent lecture form also succeeded because it forged a powerful synthesis between the performative and ritualistic qualities of the theatrical and the churchgoing public worlds. At its midcentury height, lecturing stood at the productive confluence of Enlightenment educational ambitions and an Evangelical cult of presence, providing an ethically aware audience with a reassuringly improving and often explicitly moral discourse that based itself on many of the patterns of devotional life. The debts that the lecture form owed to the sermonic tradition, and the fact that many local rural and indeed metropolitan lyceums met in church buildings, contributed immensely to what many saw as a form of "lay preaching."[38] Its buildings and auditoriums straddled the boundaries between these worlds, with lectures hosted here in prominent churches, there in spartan meeting rooms, and elsewhere in venues configured toward theatrical performance. The existence of a "Lecture Room" at the heart of Barnum's American Museum in New York provides a fitting symbol of lecturing's fluid cultural status.

This marriage of academy, church, and playhouse was particularly attractive to the performance-oriented impulses of the midcentury republic. As early as 1838, a Boston reporter had observed that "it has been discovered that the two objects of entertainment and improvement may be united in one pursuit."[39] Yet this might also be a simple question of public rectitude. As one 1850 magazine editorial conceived it, part of the eagerness with which national community authorities had supported lecture culture was as "a protest against the theater," arising from a "desire to substitute something more wholesome in [its] place" while ultimately fulfilling a role "somewhat in the same line."[40] Writing a generation later, Charles Dickens Jr. noted in similar fashion that lecture halls persisted as "a substitute for the drama ... to be found in hundreds of places where theaters are impossible. They afford a means of entertainment to that large class which still clings to the Puritan notion that theaters are ... immoral."[41]

The theatricalized pedagogy of the public lecture duly affected the texture of literary life. The self-conscious relationship of oratory to the development of American letters has long been acknowledged, and the critical consensus since F. O. Matthiessen has been alive to the role of the oral in the evolution of the dominant strands of nineteenth-century aesthetics. Even Walter Ong's foundational survey of spoken and written cultures, for example, finds time to reflect on the commonplace that "orality echoes, sometimes hauntingly, in the style of early American writers."[42] Speaking of the Revolutionary period, Christopher Looby has celebrated a "distinct countercurrent in the literature of the period that valorizes the grain of the voice in addition to, or instead of, the silence of print."[43] The same can be said of the antebellum literary moment, with the atmosphere of the lecture hall permeating not only the obvious locations of literary culture such as the pages of Emerson, Thoreau, Douglass, and Twain, but also the frenzied eclecticism of *Moby-Dick*, and the ironic intellectual soliloquies of Poe's narrators.

Reportage and a Nation of Listeners

Having found such fertile soil in which to set its roots, the lecture circuit began to shape an unprecedentedly national shared culture of performance. As Ray points out, the unique reach of the circuit meant that countless "people, from Maine to Michigan and Minnesota to Maryland," would have heard the same lecturer give "roughly the same speech."[44] Lecturing was in this sense at once a profoundly local phenomenon and a national experience—part of what Ronald Zboray characterizes as the Jacksonian era's "unprecedented constancy of communications throughout the country."[45] The medium was thereby an ideal tool of Jacksonian nation-building, and was championed in particular by East Coast elites of Whiggish infrastructural leanings. In a lyrical account for a British reading audience in 1868, for example, one such cultural arbiter, Thomas Wentworth Higginson, told the story of lecturing's growth as the capstone of a continent-wide infrastructure-building mission:

> Across the prairies of the American continent, five hundred miles west of the Missouri river, and about midway between the Atlantic and Pacific shores, there moves westward into the wilderness a railway construction train of eighty vans. There is no house within a hundred miles, nor sign of human existence, save that connected with the new railway itself.... It is the measured footstep of advancing civilization. With each day's sunset more than two additional miles of this habitable globe have been permanently girdled and possessed by man. These iron rails once laid, all else follows, all the signs and appliances of American social order: the farm, the workshop, the village, the church, the school-house, the *New York Tribune*, the *Atlantic Monthly*, and the popular Lecture-system.[46]

In this way, the nineteenth-century lecture hall was frequently idealized as fundamental to a certain view of midcentury northern national identity, and the means by which "social order" could be achieved and acquired.

Crucially, however, lecture culture could never truly be called a national institution since it made a far greater impression in the North than in the South.[47] Public speech was as central to southern cultural self-definition as it was to northern, and southern debating and conversational clubs emerged in tandem with the lyceum movement, some sponsoring lectures in comparable fashion. Southern intellectuals and educationalists such as Thomas Grimké of South Carolina admired Holbrook's efforts and corresponded with him, and institutions such as the Virginia Lyceum and the New Orleans Lyceum hosted major lectures during the peak antebellum years. However, unlike much of the North, there was no clearly defined system in the South for traveling lecturers, far less infrastructure. In 1856 the *Charleston Courier* noted with regret that, the example of "occasional lecturers" aside,

> we can hardly be called a lecture hearing community, as that simple and yet potent means and instrument of mingled instruction and delight has not established itself as yet permanently and statedly in our calculations of social resources and advantages.[48]

With some notable exceptions, traditions in the South tended toward the closed form of the formal membership club and debating society. As Michael O'Brien has noted, public orality took second place to the private training of future members of the southern oligarchy.[49]

Crucial to lecture culture's aspirations to national coverage was the role of the press. The remarkable reach of prominent papers such as the *New York Weekly Tribune*, combined with a feverish culture of reprinting, generated a remarkable secondary field of reception. The editorial of one Pennsylvania newspaper observed in 1842 that "the most popular lecturer seldom speaks to more than 1000 persons [whereas] a paper may be read—often is read—by one hundred thousand. We give half a dollar to hear a lecture ... for the papers, containing much more valuable matter, we give from one to six cents; and it passes from hand to hand."[50] Yet lecture reports were an apparatus of storage and transmission that complicated hierarchies of voice and print, reinserting language conceived for performance into the world of the written word. As Mary Saracino and Ronald Zboray have shown, such newspaper texts would be passed by "hand to hand" throughout a reading public far broader than the audience for any given lecture series.[51]

Nineteenth-century oratory therefore worked upon dual audiences: a primary crowd of live auditors and a vast potential secondary readership for accounts and transcriptions of speeches. These were texts whose formulaic nature concealed their serious cultural work. More than just another means of filling newspaper columns, they formed an essential part of the envelope of communication events: they represented processes of meaning-creation, transmitted the experience of participation, and helped fashion a range of imagined publics. Lecture reports were textually validated and relied for their intelligibility on the sense of a community of listeners and readers. Attending lectures held the promise of a shared experience: a form of literary consumption that linked village, town, and metropolis, in which diverse peoples could hear, read, and argue about the same topics and concerns. Since lecture reportage was promiscuously reprinted from one end of the republic to the other, reading speech texts fostered a sense of far-flung democratic kinship that McGill, following Benedict Anderson, asks us to conceive in terms of "a sense of near-simultaneity that was crucial to the imagination of the federal form of the nation."[52] Furthermore, the very combination of voice and print generates its own temporality, since fusing speech and text allows for what Carey calls "the space-binding potential of communication" to engage and exchange with "the time-binding power of oral speech and discourse."[53]

More often than not, the accounts that readers discovered by picking up their paper in Ohio, Maine, or Texas were brief and straightforward. But these sat alongside far more elaborate "portraits" with ambitions to capture the rich sensory experience of the oratorical moment, including the physicality and vocal qualities of the orator and the social texture of audience response. Lectures were, of course, far more than just words and language—indeed, there was a sense in which they were less about listening than a more wholly immersive visual and theatrical spectacle. As George William Curtis asked in *Harper's Monthly* in 1860, of "the living speaker, commanding subject and audience by fullness of knowledge and potency of will—every muscle and nerve in the service of thought and emotion, every pulse obedient to the intellect—what is like it?"[54] A defining aspiration of lecture culture was to offer readers something *like* that experience of human presence. *presence in print.*

Some of the most valuable lecture reports extant also highlight a concern with documenting audience behavior, assuming the duty of assessing the health of the movement by gauging and projecting public response. Creative techniques used to this end might involve represented voices of the crowd, capturing atmosphere and audience tensions at work. Following the model of communication theorists such as James Carey, we can read into these illustrations of audience response what he terms the "projection of community ideals."[55] By depicting social relations at work and by mediating between different publics, they were one among many textual forms that Isabelle Lehuu's work has encouraged us to see as the "staging" of town and city life.[56] Just as scrutiny of performers often amounted to an attempt to define and promote the ideal of republican civic conduct, these reports' focus on audiences acted to project ideals of citizenship. One example of this might be newswriters' reflections on turnout. The "large proportion" of clergymen in the audience at one of Unitarian minister Orville Dewey's 1855 performances was taken as "a gratifying vindication" for the *Charleston Courier* "of the reputation of our city in literary culture and hospitality."[57] The "respectable attendance" at a lecture by Frederick Douglass in Peoria, Illinois, in 1859 was read as "highly creditable to the good sense and candor of this community—It shows clearly that a spirit of toleration ... prevails extensively among the great body politic of our city, judging the popular sentiment by appearances."[58]

On the other hand, observations of audience conduct could also be read as a more critical commentary revealing certain truths about public life. Sometimes this might strike a comic note, as when a reporter from Alexandria, Virginia, in 1854 lamented the "severe reflection upon the literary and patriotic character of our community" signified by the widespread snoring and sleeping at lectures; or when a counterpart for the *Cambridge Chronicle* in 1851 made similar complaints about student behavior in an appearance from Emerson.[59] Newspaper representations of less benign forms of response offer pointed commentaries on issues of public dialogue, autonomy, and group responsibility. The "tone and tenor" of the heckling of an 1849 abolitionist lecture in Flushing, New York, for example, led to the editorial conclusion that a "more disgraceful affair had never occurred in this village."[60] Attentive spectatorship was in itself a form of public spectacle; a medium of self-representation by which a respectable public made visible its respectability.

In this way, scouring newspaper columns was a chief means by which a national public—both urban and rural—not only "read" but also "heard" the character and mood of its own civic life. Sometimes, likewise, it was the only means by which the lecturers themselves could gain a sense of their own success or failure in otherwise inscrutable audience environments. As Thomas Wentworth Higginson recalled in his memoirs late in the century, "In some of the older towns, especially, the lecturer found himself confronted with what seemed a solid body of somewhat recusant and distrustful hearers, and went home discouraged, only to be assured in the next morning's local newspaper that his hearers had been greatly pleased."[61] Such instances of textually translated response allowed not just performers but all citizens to take the temperature of their own public sphere.

Remediation and "Crooked Witchcraft"

The relationship of these transcription processes to speakers' intentions was rarely straightforward. From the age of Cicero onward, resistance to textual summation has run hand in hand with oratorical culture, but by the nineteenth century, preachers, politicians, and lecturers had largely come to accept that orations would transcend their original live context to reach the masses through print in the days after delivery.[62] For popular lecturers, however, transcription posed a different kind of problem. Once their material had been transcribed and reported in regional or national papers, lectures might prove a hard sell in other nearby towns. In a metatextual 1853 lecture entitled "The Audience," Oliver Wendell Holmes reflected on this fact, but lamented that "in a very great city, you must add a row of Reporters to the rest. They are generally a lean and sober class of people, who sit ready to drain your brain dry as fast as it is opened to them."[63]

Such attention was not merely distracting but also a source of financial injury. Speech events were among the many victims of the lack of copyright infrastructure in the antebellum literary marketplace, proving that the republican understanding of print as public property explored in McGill's work also extended to voice, since papers tended to base their arguments for transcription on the view that the spoken sounds of the republic represent a justifiable common weal.[64] Contrary to Holmes's assertion, moreover, this attitude was not only the preserve of the urban media: in April 1849, one rural Maine newspaper justified its

intensive coverage of a lecture by Horace Greeley on the basis that he was "a public man, and therefore 'public property.' "[65] As the lecture circuit began to take
on a distinct form in the early 1840s, a debate over these practices raged in the
national press, with the ethical merits of transcription hotly debated.[66] Assuming
the negative position, the *New York Evening Post* argued in late 1841 that

> the practice which certain newspapers have recently adopted, of reporting
> the lectures made before the different societies of the city, strikes us as one
> which does great injustice to the lecturers . . . for a newspaper to take up the
> words of a man, as far as they fall from his mouth, and spread them before
> some ten or twenty-thousand readers, is to do him a great wrong.[67]

The *New York Commercial Advertiser* agreed that this was "a rank injustice,"
whereas the *New York Express* took a contrary view, announcing its intention "to
continue the practice we have commenced at great labor and expense," arguing
that "the world should know abroad what is said or done in the world at home."[68]

This complicated dialectic of reciprocity and resistance between lecturers and
reporters was a key dynamic of midcentury lecture culture. Performers frequently
enthusiastically encouraged transcriptions:[69] instances abound of lectures transcribed with the assistance of performers, and performers such as Greeley and
Twain would customarily provide newspapers with copies of their finished script.
However, as the case studies of this book reveal, elsewhere performers would
attempt to stave off direct capture of their words with equal fervor. As one might
expect from his horror of "American inquisitiveness," for example, Thackeray
explicitly forbade reportage of his speeches, and Emerson became somewhat
notorious for his apparent attempts to thwart such efforts.[70]

In an 1855 editorial on lecture culture, the *Boston Atlas* boasted of its possession of "one of the best phonographers" in the city, and wryly characterized
the act of transcription as "crooked witchcraft."[71] The aesthetics and values of
nineteenth-century reporting were rarely straightforward, and reportage was seldom transparent in its capture of oral events. This complex response, and the
relish with which such interpretive work was undertaken by newspapers, was a
defining feature of lecture culture, and one of which lecturers were only too well
aware. Even the most apparently authoritative of cultural figures were often at
the mercy of a print media that framed and altered the meanings of their performances in ways beyond their control. Unraveling the subtleties of this "crookedness" is a central process of this book, raising a set of methodological problems,
and fusing the tasks of archival cultural history and the textual insights of literary criticism.

Different constituencies hovered between various modes of response, rereading, altering, accommodating, and distorting elements of performances, submitting the meanings of live speech to productive flux. One starting point for
conceptualizing these processes is Stuart Hall's formulation of transparent,
negotiated, and oppositional readings.[72] These three modes are necessarily

schematic but nonetheless instructive. A "transparent" reading accepts and channels the mode and message of the speaker's appraisal, broadly unchanged and faithfully rendered. By contrast, through a range of stylistic, rhetorical, or editorial means, "negotiated" readings attempt to mediate the appraisal of the speaker, presenting a partially modified or inflected encoding of their message and lessons. "Oppositional" readings "recode" the performance and its drama of appraisal, consciously undermining, amplifying, or radically revising the speaker's intended meanings.

In what we might call a form of "crooked" mediation, editorial decisions impacted the received understanding of lecture performances in a number of key ways. Even when advertised as "phonographic reports," reporters might lend a misleading form to inchoate utterances. Newspaper accounts were also frequently of necessarily ambiguous authorship, and reportage was in practice a corporate expression of a particular reading community that, as James Machor argues of the parallel culture of book reviewing, represented "not merely individual responses but expressions whose content was corporate and communal."[73] Accounts of lectures certainly posed as communal, fusing the newspaper and reporter's values. More conceptually, they also recoded meaning by removing spoken language from the site of its enunciation, collapsing different models of communication and media into each other. The very act of remediation necessitates a creative distortion, and our prevailing modern understandings of this process helps us recognize redeployments whose competition with prior media results in an inevitable yet productive antagonism.[74]

In this way, the problematic "crookedness" of coverage might lie outside of the text itself, notably through random infelicitous juxtapositions, a menace of reprinting that Dickens felt to be almost as injurious to intended meaning as intellectual property theft itself. Dickens wrote to Henry Brougham in 1842 in despair at how an author was "diffused all over this enormous Continent, but cannot even choose his company. Any wretched halfpenny newspaper can print him at its pleasure—place him side by side with productions which disgust his common sense."[75] Machor's insights can also shed light on the regulatory function of reviewers in antebellum reception contexts. As in other processes of mediated reception, reports often either subtly or explicitly advised readers about how to consume the text in their hands. The cumulative effect of textual features helped model a response, consciously or unconsciously promoting an often implicit partisan ideology. By allowing us to trace a number of divergent responses to a single oratorical event, such reports enable critics to better understand the processes by which socially agreed upon interpretations were formulated, meanings contested, and the authority of speakers challenged.

As one paper in Albany put it in 1853, the result was often a relationship of explicit hostility: "The reporters, editors and other gentlemen of the press keep the strictest watch over [the lecturer] and are ready to pounce on him at the slightest provocation."[76] For *Putnam's*, commenting in 1857, public lecturing was an adversarial "literary tribunal" with the celebrity orator merely a caged animal: "Lecturing is the manner in which the Yankee hunts lions.... They hire a large room, for a trap, and hang fifty dollars over the desk ... watching him carefully as he is consuming the bait."[77] Looking back from 1870, George William Curtis recalled:

> A dozen years ago many of the newspapers poured volleys of contempt upon the peripatetic gentry who infest the country with superficial essays written out of cyclopedias and other sources of information, and who humbug the innocent rural populations (of Albany, say, and Philadelphia and Boston and Buffalo) into paying extravagant sums for an hour's reading of the performance. Alas! Man's inhumanity to man![78]

On one level such antagonisms emerged from a debate about media forms, and the proper role of print as a monopoly medium of public life. But they also expressed wider social skepticism about a milieu that was seen as the self-indulgent realm of charlatans and metropolitan condescension. It reminds us that even across the northern states, lecture culture was by no means a universally cherished new cultural force.

The opposition between the lecturing and reporting worlds often had an implicit political basis. Key Democrat-leaning papers opposed lecture culture from the outset because they saw within it, not without reason, a more or less overt form of Whig propaganda. The most prominent such opponent was the *New York Herald*, which for much of the 1840s and 1850s persistently lambasted what it called the "Humbug Lecture System." In 1859 it complained,

> Of all the humbugs practiced upon the credulity of the American people the lecture system is the greatest and most hollow.... This sort of business is not in our line. We deliver our lectures in the HERALD seven times a week and several of them together, short and to the point, to ninety thousand subscriptions and half a million readers, at the small charge of two cents, giving more information in each copy than is contained in a thousand of lectures ... the inundation of trash rises higher and spreads more widely over the country.

"The lecturers," it concluded with some satisfaction in 1859, "are continually at the mercy of the newspapers" and tended to "beg hard of the reporters not to publish them in full, but only to 'give just a little notice of them'—a very unnecessary request on their part, and which they would never make if they only knew in what contempt their performances are held both by reporters and editors."[79] This form of adversarial response, based as it was on opposition to the presumption of an elite, metropolitan, and often patrician form of public display and show of power, often took on a generalized antagonism that went beyond the critique of individual lecturers, undermining the legitimacy of middle-class forms such as the lyceum and the very notion of civic orality. The position of the *Herald* represented a key node in a debate about the quality and size of the public sphere, and about the problems underpinning lecture culture's self-image of disinterested neutrality.

The Limits of "Neutral Ground"

To some lecturers, the transition from lyceum to national lecture circuit seemed to carry with it unprecedented creative freedoms. Most famous of these was Emerson. In the full rush of his initial discovery of a congenial secular oral mode, he had migrated from the ministerial pulpit to the lectern, filled with hope for the promise of this nonaligned discursive space. His early remarks on his initial forays into the lyceums of Boston and Concord are characteristically rhapsodic. Even as late as 1846, writing to Carlyle in one of several failed attempts to persuade the Scot to cross the Atlantic and share in the rewards of lecture culture, he remains passionately convinced of the freedoms of its sheer miscellany:

> In New England the Lyceum, as we call it, is already a great institution. Beside the more elaborate courses of lectures in the cities, every country town has its weekly evening meeting, called a Lyceum, and every professional man in the place is called upon, in the course of the winter, to entertain his fellow-citizens with a discourse on whatever topic.... In the Lyceum nothing is presupposed. The orator is only responsible for what his lips articulate. Then what scope it allows! You may handle every member and relation of humanity. What could Homer, Socrates, or St. Paul say that cannot be said here? The audience is of all classes, and its character will be determined always by the name of the lecturer. Why may you not give the reins to your wit, your pathos, your philosophy, and become that good despot which the virtuous orator is?[80]

For Emerson the lecture hall of the mid-1840s was a space of discursive freedom that allowed the speaker to perform as an institutionally independent intellectual free agent. He was to look back on this as the high point of lyceum freedom: a moment in which it retained its early civic function, and before the crystallization of lecture hall orthodoxy imposed its own distinct "shackles" on free expression—constraints that were often cloaked behind a self-conscious rhetoric of neutrality.

As we have seen, ideals of disinterest and separation were among the central balustrades around which midcentury lecture culture was constructed, and lay at the very heart of its self-image. At the midcentury height of the circuit's success, its practitioners repeatedly harked back to these core tenets. One Philadelphia newspaper celebrated how the circuit of 1846 "affirmed common ground where distinctions in politics and religion are to be merged."[81] In a piece on "Places of Public Amusement," *Putnam's* argued in 1854 that "the lecture-room has now become a kind of compromise between the theater and the Church, it is a neutral ground, upon which all parties and conditions may, and do meet."[82] Writing in 1862, Curtis similarly argued that "the Lyceum is a common ground for all fair and capable men."[83] This is certainly the sense behind Scott's reading of the phenomenon as being "expected to incorporate the public, to embrace all members of the community, whatever their occupation, social standing or political and religious affiliation. Useful to all and offensive to none, the lecture was an oratorical form deliberately and carefully separated from all partisan and sectarian discourse."[84] As with many other incipient features of industrial cultural economies, claims for the value of the lecture hall rested on its reputation as an extraterritorial space of withdrawal; an independent nonstate entity that mediates discussion between private subjects in a controlled manner. These claims to a form of commonality drawn from the conscious avoidance of any kind of cultural partisanship pervaded the language around antebellum lecture culture, understood by different participants in different ways, and resting on a series of often contradictory ideas.

Neutrality as contra

Part of this view of lecture hall neutrality was the notion that the lyceum was directed toward the good of audience and society. As we have seen, the ideas of objectivity and nonaffiliation were of key importance to the early lyceum and its Scottish forebears, and even well into the antebellum period, lecturers were expected to be free from commercial or egotistical motivations. Holbrook had prided the early lyceum on refusing to "descend to party strife or sectarian jealousy"; and this tradition of nonpartisanship meant that labels such as Federalist, Democrat, Whig, Unitarian, or Calvinist were left unspoken, and outré ideas ranging from vegetarianism to women's rights were discouraged. Two pressures in particular aided in this self-regulation: an emphasis on mannered inoffensiveness that directed the discourse away from controversy; and a parallel utilitarian emphasis on "useful knowledge" that directed it toward potentially mundane practicality.

Promoters and participants alike eagerly engaged with the vision of lecture halls as spaces of civic equality where all classes could interact. Talks typically took place in a nonaffiliated public space or auditorium such as a town hall, even when a church was promoted as neutral in denominational terms. One common theme was the notion of the auditorium as idealized social microcosm, as expressed in an 1853 editorial in Greeley's *New York Tribune*:

> One of the good results of popular lecturing is its tendency to assemble the entire movable population of a village, or rural township, and make them better acquainted with, and more kindly disposed to, each other ... our division into religious sects, tends to alienate and estrange us from each other. The lecture-room must become the Social Exchange—the place where acquaintances are made and friendships cemented.[85]

Cities or towns might offer more varied opportunities for entertainment and cultural exposure than rural communities, so accordingly here the emphasis rests on the greater potential for smaller communities to sustain themselves through attendance on a regular basis. This was viewed, with some justification, as a marked distinction from the British model. In a postbellum survey of lecturing in England, Moses Coit Tyler reflected back on the stratified nature of a bifurcated model of middle-class urban lectures separated from the demotic talks at mechanic's institutes. Unlike this "vicious basis," he argued, "the precious attributes of our American system of lecturers is, that they are for the American people, and not for any particular fragment of the American people."[86]

Hand in hand with this idea of a truly democratic forum went the view of the public lecture as shared reference point. For Holbrook, the ideal lyceum event was one that allowed audiences to find "a subject and object in which they could unite with unanimity and with spirit."[87] Since the lyceum or lecture hall was supposedly a space where all walks of life met and interacted, observers enthusiastically prized its role in provoking conversation and productive discussion. "It frequently occurs," remarked a magazine commentator in 1843,

> that several members of a family attend a lecture, or courses of lectures, together; when this happens, the subject of the lecturer, and the suggestions which have been awakened, furnish agreeable and instructive tropes of conversation for the domestic circle, and "evenings at home" are thus rendered more attractive.[88]

Margaret Fuller attests to this role of lecture culture as a precursor of what we might call water-cooler discourse even within the major cities, where one could easily "listen in an omnibus, or at the boarding house, to the conversation suggested by last night's lecture."[89] "Lectures often spawned enough conversation afterward," note Mary and Ronald Zboray, "that one did not have to attend to learn of them," and their work on diary records has also furnished copious evidence of immediate responses to lectures in diary form. In such cases, journal writers often adopted a language not dissimilar to that of lecture reporters.[90]

The social inclusivity of the lecture hall was promoted not only by the open nature of the institution but also through its self-conscious eclecticism. Conveners of lecture courses attempted to create programs that would provide something of interest for all listeners. Casting his gaze back in 1865 over the peak years of lecture fever, Josiah Holland addressed a question of definition that continued to face students of nineteenth-century culture, stressing this key element of heterogeneity:

> What is the popular lecture in America? It will not help us in this quest to refer to a dictionary; for it is not necessary that the performance which Americans call a lecture should be an instructive discourse at all. A lecture before the Young Men's Associations and lecture organizations of the country is any characteristic utterance of any man who speaks in their employment ... all the orations, declamations, dissertations, exhortations,

recitations, humorous extravaganzas, narratives of travel, harangues, sermons, semi-sermons, demi-semi-sermons, and lectures proper, which can
be crowded into what is called "a course," but which is properly termed a
bundle.[91]

Historical records confirm that lecture courses offered up a selection of topics
and themes that to us seem bafflingly unsystematic and diverse; a discursive miscellany that Holland considered one of its defining features, and a key condition of its cultural importance. This eclecticism was also marked on the level of
the form of individual pieces, since like other key genres of antebellum literary
life, the popular lecture was an unruly business mixed in register and composite
in form, often ranging between the subjects and modes listed here. Most prevalent, however, were genres of talk that were considered discursively "neutral"
or at least unlikely to offend. Certain general-knowledge topics and intellectual
approaches were therefore legitimized as accepted lyceum mainstays, ranging
from the tamer branches of science, the more staid literary topics, accounts of
international travel, and, above all, the universally popular topics of "great men,"
moral uplift, and self-improvement. Intellectually, claims to neutrality also rested
on offering an accessible and not overbearingly scholarly experience. "Lecturers
should keep clear of the province of books," argued a *New York Times* editor,
and rather "work out the original idea belonging to them, and so create a special
sphere for their own exclusive occupancy as distinct and definite as an embryo in
nature."[92] Neutrality and "diversity" can be seen to have combined as compatible
forms of cultural legitimacy.

We might interpret these aspirations toward lecturing as a "special sphere"
as part of a wider response to the rising temperature of national life in a time
of Jacksonian excess. Lawrence Levine famously located the emergence of
American high/low cultural distinction at turn of the twentieth century, yet a
plausible reading of the lyceum's rise might be that it represented to many a pragmatic middle ground between realms that, as we shall discover in following chapters, were engaged by midcentury in vigorous dispute.[93] Alarm at the increasingly
poisonous nature of pre-lyceum theatrical and oratorical culture, particularly
after flashpoints such as the 1849 Astor Place Riot and the 1856 attack on Charles
Sumner by Preston Brooks on the floor of the Senate, was one factor that lay
behind the desire for something like the lyceum that might offer a more consensual outlet for audience passions. By presenting and conducting itself in terms of
what Fuller dismissively termed a hybrid mode of "Entertaining Knowledge," its
champions can be seen to have attempted to provide just such a form, in part by
sidestepping critical issues of section, party, and reform as part of a wider political agenda conducted in an antipolitical tone.[94]

This ostentatious emphasis on neutrality required a high degree of institutional self-policing, and examples abound of committees vetoing more risky
topics. Among prominent examples, the New Haven Lyceum objected on

numerous occasions during the 1840s to not only reformist speakers such as Wendell Phillips, but also outré ministers such as Henry Ward Beecher, Theodore Parker, and George Cheever.[95] In February 1852, when the Catholic convert and editor Orestes Brownson spoke at the Cincinnati Mercantile Library Association and made unflattering remarks about Hungarian radical Louis Kossuth, he was met with a storm of hissing and accusation that by talking politics he had abused "the confidences of the Association by traveling outside the proprieties of the lecture halls."[96] It was a sign of the extent of this censorship even within major centers that in 1858 Parker felt obliged to start his own independent "Fraternity Course" of lectures in Boston in 1858 devoted to "the great humane subjects of the day, to which the ordinary lyceums in cities seldom tolerate in any direct allusion."[97] As a result, the mainstream lyceum was for the most part an arena of political fence-sitting.

Moreover, the ability to offer a "cool" performance was regarded as a great virtue: a demonstration of rationality above all things. The lecture hall was decisively not a world of eruptive oratorical flashpoints: unlike the freewheeling agonism of the stump, the revival meeting, or even the Senate floor, there were forceful institutional imperatives toward propriety and consensus. "Compared with the fierce heats of summer and autumn oratory," *Putnam's* observed in 1854, the voices resounding from the lecterns of the winter season "will be no more than a gentle warmth . . . a quiet tempering of the high-strung enthusiasm."[98]

In this reading, lecture halls were spaces audiences entered in order to be exposed to a range of admirable middle-class behaviors. Running through many of the self-representations discussed here, the public lecture was not just an occasion for shared exposure to one another, but a crucible in which a mode of citizenship based on collective habits of listening and critical attention might be forged. As Oliver Wendell Holmes argued to a Brooklyn audience in 1853, "In entering a lecture-room a man should bring with him no narrow prejudices, for if he does, out of twelve lectures he will be dissatisfied with just a dozen."[99] By persevering through a diverse series of lectures on disparate subjects, it was argued, listeners might cultivate intellectual and cultural breadth; by mixing with diverse members of their town, village, or city, and by observing what Greiman calls the "spectacle of opinion" of their peers, they might achieve a well-regulated social ease.[100] By observing the controlled performance values of civic worthies, and by participating in decorous habits of appreciative attention, the lyceum posed as a realm in which democratic temperament might be acquired. As the following chapters of this book reveal, the ideas behind these aspirations and the tensions they provoked, over issues of bodily control, race, audience conduct, and modes of attention, formed a surprisingly large part of the meaning of lecture events.

The contradictions inherent in this self-image are interesting in a number of respects. In particular, lecture culture's positioning as a self-regulating, inclusive arena rested on a series of fundamentally unattainable goals. Most obvious is the fact that, rather than being truly diverse, the community that provided the basis of national lecture attendance was in fact rather homogenous. As Lawrence Buell rightly notes, American lecture culture certainly offered a more mixed picture than its British equivalent in terms of economic background, and was notably "less class stratified than what developed in Britain."[101] Augst and Ray also testify to the fact that, despite its domination by middle-class, aspirant Americans, lecture attendance involved a surprising range of different class types, particularly in the major cities. However, accounts of lyceum records and attendance figures all point to an overwhelmingly British-American demographic base, and the texture of the mainstream lecture circuit inescapably marked by the dominant atmospherics of Protestant practice.

Critics of public sphere theory such as Nancy Fraser would recognize this arena as one "constituted by a number of significant exclusions."[102] And the model of public action constructed rhetorically in these spaces through all the staged behaviors of lecture culture might also be described conceptually as an illusion of democratic inclusivity in the place of genuine tolerance and participation. Many of the self-characterizations quoted in this chapter and throughout this book betray more investment in the concept of continual self-construction than in the process of genuine dialogue; indeed, it is hard to argue that messages based on unitary presentation of a discourse from the lectern offer much more than an illusion of dialogue. One might further argue that the eclecticism of the form in fact worked against its ambitions. Rituals of attendance and performance may have brought certain self-conscious publics together, but heterogeneous knowledge always threatened to become less about social tolerance or coherence than individualism. *Dialogue vs. Individualism*

The self-image of lecturing as a separate sphere was also undermined by its relationship to economic imperatives. The typical charge of twenty-five cents for an evening's entertainment during the 1850s made a night at the lyceum a financial decision not to be undertaken lightly. This proudly proclaimed neutral ground was a site of commercial interest and exchange embedded as much as any other discursive arena in the forces of the Jacksonian market, and along with schools and literacy represented part of what Sellers terms the "the cutting edge of the market's cultural conquest."[103] Performers and booking agents were impelled to fulfill commercial duties and conform to economic ideals. Far from the morally impelled, selfless actors imagined by Anderson or Birkbeck, lecturers were profit-driven itinerants for whom talking was a trade as much anything else. In this way, lyceum commonality relied upon financial bonds between people, and economic imperatives conditioned much of its discursive neutrality.

It is important to note, however, that the nation's far-flung array of venues and practices never presented a static picture, and the discursive constraints of lecture culture altered over time. The medium underwent waves of shifting exertion and caution. However schematic, most historical accounts offer a plausible basic trajectory that takes its cue from the views of memoirists and latter-day commentators. This narrative is one of narrow topics during the initial lyceum phase giving way to wider discursive breadth as the 1840s circuit grew, before a calcification of acceptable themes during the heyday of the immediate antebellum years. For understandable reasons, the onset of the Civil War thrust political themes into the spotlight of lecturing life, and the previously barred direct treatment of sectarian and racial topics was now a common feature.[104] As postwar observers such as Higginson, Curtis, and Coit Tyler note, this political emphasis remained for some years, making the circuit appear to more than one observer as an extension of the stump. The drift toward entertainment as the circuit matured into the 1870s, however, once again left the lecture hall free of the partisan sound of political debate.

The limits of neutrality led to what some saw as a tamely frivolous irrelevance and arcane quietism. The "implied contract to keep clear of doubtful matters" represented a regulatory force, creating a forum closed to the representation of a plurality of ideologies and identities. An 1856 satire from the *Washington Reporter* captures this staid image particularly adroitly:

> Wanted—A Lecturer, by the Hyper-Critical Clique of Literary Old Fogies. Said lecturer must be competent at once to satisfy the erudite yearnings of this most querulous and of their fair, dried up favorites ... he must display profound familiarity with all the dim lights of obsolete literature of the past three thousand years.[105]

This toothless antiquarianism was a deliberate product of the discursive constraints imposed by the imperative of neutrality, and an index of the ways in which it often represented a historical reach backward for arcane topics at one remove from modern life outside the lecture hall.

This goes beyond the obvious point that this was a milieu whose value as a commons was fetishized out of all proportion to its actual achievements as a social exchange. Rather, lecture culture's contradictions can be readily understood in terms of an often highly productive tension between cultural politics and creative rhetorical expression. While figures such as Curtis might present the lecture hall of 1862 as a space that "asks and willingly hears candid and considerate opinions of every kind," for much of the antebellum period many forms of true political, social, or cultural candor were consciously prohibited in the name of a neutral separation from politics.[106] Yet the nature of the topics concerned was almost always inescapably political, and certain agendas, notably those of Whig centralizers and elite cosmopolitans, dominated at the cost of alternative politics. Even within the boundaries of ostentatious eclecticism, the lyceum also imposed regulatory force through ideals of hierarchy, of intellectual worthiness, of procedures, and of modes of analysis.

"The Peaceful Games of the Lyceum"

The critique of lecture culture as bland accommodation came to be shared by Henry David Thoreau, one of the most enduring literary personalities associated with the platform, and a peculiarly insightful critic of what he termed in 1849 the "peaceful games of the lyceum."[107] He had been an advocate for the potential of communal lecture culture during that decade, but by the mid-1850s his turbulent relationship with the medium had soured, partly as a result of having weathered a series of censorship controversies at the Concord Lyceum and experienced poor reception at other New England lecterns.[108] "It is no compliment to be invited to the lecture before the rich Institutes and Lyceums," he wrote in 1858:

> The settled lecturers are as tame as the settled ministers. The audiences do not want to hear any prophets; they do not wish to be stimulated and instructed, but entertained. They, their wives and daughters, go to the Lyceum to suck a sugarplum. The little of medicine they get is disguised with sugar. It is never the reformer they hear there, but a faint and timid echo of him only. They seek a pass-time merely.[109]

Recognizing the constraints imposed on the lecture circuit by the imperative of neutrality, and blasting what he termed the "bigotry and moral cowardice of New Englanders," Thoreau scorned the lecture hall culture as pandering to "sluggards that want a lullaby sung to them!"[110] He recognized in particular what Scott has described as the "ostentatious firmness" with which organizers excluded the subject of politics, in a gesture of conservative quietism masquerading as ecumenical non-partisan withdrawal in the interests of a passive and depoliticized public sphere.[111] The lyceum was for the most part quite some way from being a reformist or culturally engaged institution, given its avoidance of progressive, liberal, or radical ideas.[112]

If these critiques strike us as similar to the range of contemporary revisions and critiques of the models of the bourgeois public sphere sketched by Jürgen Habermas, then it is because they, too, recognize the limits of neutrality as an organizing principle for any critical public.[113] These rhetorical constraints meant that those who wanted to say anything of real import on the platform were obliged to engage in strategic indirection. The condition of a self-regulating oratorical arena was therefore one of oblique expression: a cultural field of compromise and ambiguity generating various forms of rhetorical disingenuousness. However, the effort of participants to conform and avoid offense is where much of the value of lyceum rhetoric continues to lie. Some of the most fascinating tensions of the form derive from the ingenuity involved in these creative compromises. The limits that Holmes derided in 1850 as the "laws of the lecture-room" are also responsible for its enduring power, and are memorable to the modern reader as among the defining *indirection* aspects of antebellum oral discourse. Viewing lyceum oratory as a mode of nec- *as weary of poi.* essarily strategic verbal compromise opens up many productive avenues of communicative analysis, whether Habermasian or otherwise.[114] We can often trace the ironies behind the self-image of performers and audiences. We can explore each lyceum piece as a dialogue between constraints of neutral discourse and full practical expression, as speakers obscure "authentic" self-representation and "sincere" communication in the pursuit of disguised practical adjectives. And we can turn the idea of "peaceful games" on its head somewhat, as we recognize again the creativity and depth involved in these elaborate performances of neutrality.

This idea of rhetorical "games" also allows us to reconnect with the concept of a theatrical or performative commons with which this chapter began. Lecturing, through this lens, becomes a fundamentally insincere mode of speech; an arena not of transparency but elaborate role play, centered on a repertoire of performative roles. Rather than sharing knowledge, the lecturer is merely acting the part of knowledge transmission, a key feature of which was the display of disinterestedness as performative identity. A second aspect of this role centered on rhetorical games of affiliation through which a quest for rhetorical common ground guided audiences toward a shared set of group beliefs. An understanding of games of this sort underpinned the live act of performance, since for lyceum participants the structure of citizenship was understood not to be conducted solely through rational exchange, but also through an embodied series of affective desires made apparent through the lecturing body.

Viewing the lyceum in this manner allows us to perceive a number of routes to more explicit political and cultural commentary. One of these was through abstraction and metaphor, the most obvious case in point being the atypical example of Emerson's quiet radicalism. If the conditions of neutrality and useful knowledge rendered the lyceum better suited to the presentation of facts than to speculation or experiment, where did that leave the famous Emersonian lyceum aim to wrong-foot, "unsettle," and challenge audiences?[115] One answer to that question is that the peaceful games of the lyceum underwrote or at least proved highly conducive to the creative and conceptual abstractions of his first great period of Transcendentalist expression. Critics have often traced the origins of Emerson's early aphoristic, compressed aesthetic back to their frequently oral origins. This approach may be extended to illuminate the role of lecture hall "shackles" behind various of his rhetorical hallmarks. The symbolic and metaphoric practices of midcentury oratory can be traced to the mastery of subtlety and double-voicing required to successfully negotiate the compromises, or "games," forced upon speakers by the lecture hall contexts in which they spoke.

Another common approach to the games of the lyceum on the part of lecturers was a commitment to patterns of analogy and refraction. This habitually involved placing ideas with dangerous potential at one remove from their actual targets, and accordingly was particularly effective as a reformist tool for commenting obliquely on the habits of the American people. Lectures that traded in accounts of travel were a straightforward means by which the moral and empirical authority of firsthand experience lent force to a critique of national issues introduced at a cosmopolitan remove, relying for their force on the subtleties of analogic relevance.[116] One of the most popular of all lectures on the pre- and postbellum platforms was Wendell Phillips's "The Lost Arts," a piece that used the strategic potential of analogic critique in just this way. The lecture took aim at what Phillips termed "the national prejudice" and "most prominent characteristic of self-conceit" by outlining at elaborate length the artistic and technological marvels of antiquity and the comparative inferiority of the nineteenth-century equivalents, with many subtle but pointedly controversial political and social barbs along the way.[117] As the evergreen success of such a lecture suggested, lecture audiences were perhaps more willing than sponsoring committees to countenance disruptive ideas when framed in "peaceful" and palatable terms.

Seemingly inoffensive or peaceful genres thus took on a new dangerous potential. Reformers who operated freely in a chosen arena of activism outside the lyceum found ways of exploiting the resources of more neutral, congenial performances within it. In an age when professional roles were more mobile and interchangeable than they were to become, the ill-defined place of men of letters and would-be reforming figures in public life allowed for slippage between different modes of expression. The role of lecture hall reformer is a particular case in point. As T. Gregory Garvey, Amy Hughes, and others point out, the Jacksonian merging of the "sisterhood of reforms" with practices of publicity more familiar to entertainment presented a central contradiction: once reform becomes merged in public consciousness with the grammar and habits of show culture, new avenues open up for expression, while at the same time the role of public acceptance of reform's sincerity diminishes.[118]

This type of indirection can be read productively in terms of Kenneth Burke's account of rhetorical reframing.[119] As Josiah Holland noted in 1865, performances of lyceum intellect were often a case of taxonomy and typology:

Men wish for nothing more than to know how to classify their facts, what to do with them, and how far to be governed by them; and the man who takes the facts . . . and uses them to give direction to the popular life, and does all this with masterful skill, is the man whose houses are never large enough to hear him. This is the popular lecturer *par excellence.*[120]

One cardinal ambition of many popular lecture practitioners was, as we have seen, to help define the correct role and character of democratic knowledge, and to ensure that elites and nonelites understood the world in compatible ways. Acts of hierarchy, classification, and the organization of information—about scientific discovery, geography, global events, classical literature, or simply correctly identifying flora and fauna—were fundamental ways in which this might be achieved. And they worked by providing what Burkean rhetorical analysis calls "terministic screens:" frameworks that license habits of thought or reference points that structure group undestanding.[121] The remainder of this chapter considers one such rich reference point in the shape of lectures on British themes.

Anglo-America and Assimilation

Anglo-American themes appeared on the platform under three main guises, the first of which was popular discussion of British history and literature. From general accounts of the monarchy or the English Reformation to studies of individuals such as Oliver Cromwell or Admiral Nelson, the patchwork narrative of British history was rich in both mass appeal and social application. Even more popular were accounts and discussions of literary history from Shakespeare to Tennyson. During the 1850s alone, James Russell Lowell and Oliver Wendell Holmes both delivered prominent series of lectures under the title "The English Poets," and the literary critic E. P. Whipple spoke to the similar themes under the title "The English Mind."[122] Most prominent of all were the live appearances of contemporary British writers themselves, including Dion Boucicault and William Makepeace Thackeray in the 1850s and, most famous of all, Charles Dickens's triumphant reading tour of 1867–68.

Firsthand testimony of travel in Britain represented a second case. "Travel lectures" were one of the most enduringly popular genres on the circuit, a mode that Donald Scott has understood as "less a travelogue than a kind of comparative ethnography," offering audiences information about the globe while meeting an appetite for narratives of daring exploits.[123] The most eagerly anticipated talks treated audiences to thrilling accounts of exotic locales, including Africa, Asia, and the Arctic. Yet accounts of the more familiar sights and customs of Britain had their own unique appeal, offering listeners the chance to reflect upon subtler and more minute social and cultural distinctions. Many of the speakers discussed in this book brought comparable reflections and observations to the platform: Douglass's account of British racial tolerance, Emerson's and Mann's descriptions of English landscape and industry, Greeley's aural tour of the Great Exhibition, and Gough's unique journey through the gothic spectacle of night-time London. These were only the tip of the iceberg of a wider genre comprised of often straightforwardly touristic entertainments; lectures that, as the period progressed, were increasingly accompanied by visual aids including the vivid precinematic forms of magic lanterns and panoramas.[124]

The third and final strand involved lectures about reform, be it relating to social developments or campaigns in Britain or to transatlantic campaigning efforts themselves. Fourierists such as Henry Clapp lectured on social experiments in Scotland, for example, while Mann condemned British educational standards, and Greeley championed industrial progress.[125] Other lectures considered mutual Anglo-American efforts in the cause of temperance, abolition, or women's suffrage. The role of the lecture hall as global conduit was crucial to the topic in hand. Since lecturing seemed to embody key values intrinsic to the reform impulse—modernity, civic commitment, congregationalism, evangelical earnestness—the act of attendance and participation could help cement a common transatlantic purpose based on reformist values or make clear the limits of shared affinities.

Under these conditions, Anglocentric topics became a reliable crowd-puller on any lecture program. Some committees seemed eager to promote these themes as part of lyceum neutrality: no matter what one's occupation, social standing, political affiliation, or religious beliefs, it was argued, some kind of discussion of

British history and culture could serve as accessible common ground. Listening for an hour to descriptions of the details of British history, analysis of Lancashire industry, or the beauties of English poetry was to provide an imagined point of commonality amid partisan disputes. This was seen as especially true of cultural topics, compatible with the impulse that the lecture platform should be, in Curtis's terms, "one spot free, one platform upon which we will have none but aesthetic and literary differences."[126] To some lecturers, speaking about transatlantic themes did indeed serve as an aestheticized space notionally emptied of politics. However, most knew very well the cultural and ethnic politics inherent in such topics.

For one thing, all three of the above categories offered routes to indirect yet trenchant social commentary. Discussion of transatlantic literature, history, travel, or reform was one of many ways in which orators could work around lyceum constraints over explicit politics, using comparison and analogy to situate domestic controversies at one remove. After all, speakers who rose to their feet to lecture about Britain addressed some of the most pressing questions in the early republic: what to admire and to reject from the Old World social model; which tendencies of modernity to embrace or condemn; whether Britain's imperial methods were a cause for caution or emulation. In the antebellum party political climate, and at a moment of particular diplomatic strain between London and Washington, public attitudes to the former colonial power could sharply inflect one's positions on a range of pressing contemporary issues, and the tone and spirit of public appraisals of British society acquired outsized significance.[127] The body of transatlantic commentary from American writers, reformers, and lecturers was, as Paul Giles rightly suggests, a displaced form of the "condition of England" genre of Thomas Carlyle, Henry Mayhew, and Elizabeth Gaskell "reconceived in transnational terms."[128] The lyceum was one of the sites through which this intense, consequential cultural dialogue with British society was sustained.

Yet these lectures also rested on a much less subtle kind of domestic politics, one far less to do with neutrality than assimilation. To speak about Britain was always to speak about not just power but heritage. Lecture committees enjoyed promoting the ethnic centrality of Anglo-American heritage as a normative and unifying aspect of an increasingly complicated social world. Writing about the early republic, Leonard Tennenhouse has described this prevalence of consciously artificial Englishness as "a model of diaspora that depends less on a specific place of origin than on reinventing a cultural homeland."[129] And as Tamarkin has shown, flamboyant displays of allegiance to "Our Old Home," as Nathaniel Hawthorne called it, were also a surprisingly central theme of antebellum public life.[130] This was particularly marked in the lecture hall. To listen to Mann speak of "the mother country"; to hear Emerson guide listeners through his conception of the global "British family ... expanded not altered"; or to witness Thackeray praise "we candid Anglo-Saxons" was to encounter a rhetoric of kinship that drew power from its collective reception.[131] It offered a space for the claiming of a common culture for citizens of Anglo-Saxon descent, allowing for the assertion of group consciousness and identity around such an imagined homeland.[132] Attending these events was one way of becoming more English, and counterintuitively, thereby more legitimately American.

Lecture culture's Anglo-obsession came to greatest prominence during the demographic upheavals of the 1840s. Rapidly increased immigration, urban diversity, and the newly ambiguous social distinctions caused by the market revolution and Jacksonian democracy meant that assertions of Anglo identity took on a new significance as social markers. Andrew Chamberlin Rieser notes that "the rise of nativism after the lyceum vogue is not entirely coincidental," and the ubiquity of lectures on British themes was one way in which the mainstream platform helped enforce a normative ethnic identity.[133] Though Holbrook had intended a truly diverse audience for the national lyceum, the reality rarely lived up to this ideal, and through the Civil War lecturing largely retained its original Anglo-Saxon cultural imprint in terms of both audience demographics and tastes, not least thanks to the Yankee diaspora into the Midwest. As Higginson had noted, "Foreign immigrants are apt to avoid [the lecture hall] or to taste of it, as they do of any other national dish, with courtesy, but not with relish."[134] We might think of lectures on transatlantic themes as one such paradoxical "national dish." By insisting on the relevance of Britain as the normative point of cultural comparison, these performances helped define the relationship of marginalized peoples to the public sphere, and policed the homogeneity of antebellum citizenship.[135] By placing such topics at the center of a forum defined by its self-improvement ethos, they helped make knowledge about Great Britain a talismanic form of aspirational cultural capital. And by continually stressing English history and heritage, speakers and committees encouraged audiences to merge their own origins within the mythic commons of an imagined cultural homeland.

I have chosen to describe these classes of lecture in terms of an Anglo-American commons because the focus of discussion was always as much about the relationship between the two nations as about an eastward gaze alone. Often, their chief subliminal concern was defining the limits and health of the transatlantic imaginary itself. As could be seen in the reams of travel writing of the period, the governing trope was the measurement of distance and affinity, fixating on the comparative state of society, on language and accent, or on institutional continuities of property, sovereignty, or social contract, as a way of talking about cultural evolution. As might be expected in the domain of oratory, one perennial concern was that of transatlantic voice. Time and again, lecturers romanticized an Anglo-Saxon inheritance based on free public speech. In national life both North and South, but particularly in the New England society from which lecture culture emerged, oratory functioned, as Buell puts it, "not just as a graceful accomplishment, but as a vital sign of the health of the republic," and this was a health that was customarily measured against its transatlantic counterpart.[136] As subsequent chapters of this book show, lecture hall representations of Britain can frequently be read as ways of thinking about the comparative practices of speech, performance, and exchange underpinning notional Anglo-Saxon candor.

The lecture hall was also therefore an ideal place in which ideas about an Anglo-American commons could be challenged. This challenge often took the form of separation. Throughout the nation, dedicated lyceums for individual ethnic groups flourished in tandem with the mainstream platform, from German lyceums in Pittsburgh and Chicago to African-American lecture-hosting organizations in a wide variety of towns and cities, and new research is continuing to uncover the richness of secondary local and national circuits with their own sets of normative themes.[137] But challenges to the exclusionary origin myths of Anglo-America were also an enduring and significant undercurrent in mainstream lecture culture. A range of performers questioned the relevance or importance of British inheritance, overturned historical myths, and revealed the material limits of shared culture. These elements of critique were present through a lot of the key lectures discussed in subsequent chapters, not least for those reformers or statesman who sought to direct the politics of the republic away from that of Westminster, or the ambitions of the British Empire. Perhaps the most interesting were delivered by those who perceived themselves as victims of an overbearing Anglosphere. Two instructive examples will suffice: the case of Irish nationalists, and that of Native American performers.

Challenging an Anglo-American Commons

A number of key Irish nationalists came to the United States following the unsuccessful Young Irelander uprising of 1848, to drum up support among the fast-growing Irish diaspora. Upon their arrival, they were encouraged to turn to the lecture circuit not just as a propaganda and fundraising tool but as a means of cultivating an Irish-American counterpublic and group identity. In doing so they introduced arguments that worked against the Anglo-American commons, promoting a distinct brand of international solidarity based on the progress of global republican ideals, and a cultural worldview that turned away from the hierarchies and symbolism of Britain. Such sentiments arrived at a fortuitous time, with vocal interests north and south ready to express sympathy with the heroes of recent European revolutions as part of an internationalist solidarity that President Franklin Pierce invoked in his 1853 inaugural oration, referring to "the oppressed of the world" who had "turned their eyes hitherwards."[138] The lectures of Irish nationalists during the years that followed argued for a new form of antimonarchical republican kinship between the Unites States and the globe. Yet within the sectional context, their challenges to the Anglo-American commons pushed in two different directions, exemplified by the figures of Thomas Francis

Meagher and his fellow revolutionary John Mitchel, figures who are not part of my discussion in subsequent chapters, but whose cases I shall now briefly discuss.

Upon arriving in the United States in 1852, Meagher was welcomed as a global statesman, and his internationalist republicanism found a popular audience, particularly on northern lecture platforms. Over the course of that year he lectured from New England to St. Louis, toured through the Hibernian association stages of the South, and then on to California in 1853. He initially lectured about his experiences on the British penal colony of Tasmania, from where he had just escaped a life sentence, using the travel lecture format to campaign for what he called the "progress of republicanism in England and throughout the English colonies."[139] As he traveled around the country, however, he developed a wider repertoire, speaking to audiences about "Great Irish Orators" and delivered a strident piece on "Ireland in '48." That lecture used an account of the doomed uprising to make an argument for transatlantic solidarity and an Irish-American freedom coalition. "Those who drag a single star from that sacred constellation of liberty," he urged his audience, "should have the hand of every man against them."[140] As he took these reflections southward, Meagher was denounced from Catholic pulpits and newspaper columns; others bridled at his Anglophobia, with one prominent observer in New Orleans writing that his "lecture was much injured by his abuse of Great Britain."[141] But his reframing of republicanism was influential. In the South in particular many sympathized with Meagher's self-characterization as trapped in a "fatal quarrel with a formidable government."[142] An early memoirist also recalled the "fervid enthusiasm" of an Albany lecture that crossed "distinction of race, creed or class ... equal portions of native and naturalised citizens."[143] Meagher's tours aimed to help forge an aspirational Irish group consciousness, making what he called "the inalienable inheritance of my poor country" part of a shared Atlantic culture of freedom.[144]

John Mitchel exemplified a different direction that these transnational affinities might take. Mitchel's opposition to imperialism and industrialism found a receptive audience in the South, where it dovetailed not just with sectionalist but also proslavery sentiment. Mitchel arrived in America in 1853 having escaped from Bermuda, where he had written the *Jail Journal* (1854), a diary that was to become one of the canonical texts of Irish nationalism. He helped found the New York Irish-American paper the *Citizen,* and translated its anti-British tone to the platform in lecture tours during 1856–57 that took him up and down the eastern seaboard and west to Chicago and Detroit.[145] Like Meagher, Mitchel championed international solidarity based on shared love of liberty and hatred for monarchism, and drew sympathy for the Ireland he had left over which had "settled a deeper and darker pall than ever.... Her children," he said in one lecture in New York, "lay dying by myriads round her coasts, mourned only by the hoarse Atlantic."[146] However, Mitchel led his listeners toward different political conclusions than Meagher had done. Rejecting what he saw as the ineffective "transatlantic philanthropy" of Daniel O'Connell's abolition, he began to argue

*Mitchel –
proslavery,
Irish
nationalism*

for the expansion of slavery, and offered up a vision of an Irish-American commons based upon racial subordination.[147]

There were other more conciliatory voices on the lecture circuit also working toward the goal of a Green Atlantic. One illustrative example was the County Wexford-born dissenting Unitarian minister Henry Giles, who became a successful lecturer during the 1840s, attempting to unify Irish and Anglo-Saxon traditions and to champion Celtic culture with lectures on topics such as "The Spirit of Irish History" and "Irish Character, Mental and Moral."[148] He informed his audiences that he had been "heard with generous interest ... in city halls and in village lyceums" since the early 1840s, but by the end of the decade and the worsening of the Famine, the story of Ireland was "no longer novel. It is now not a story, but a drama; a black and fearful drama."[149] Confronted with the mass immigration resulting from that "drama," and the demonization of the new Irish population, Giles aimed to forge common ground with the American population through shared affection. In the lecture "Irish-Born Citizens," for example, he argued that "America though distant, is not foreign to Ireland and the Irish.... If home is truly where our affections are, where those are to whom our affections attach us, then America must be to the vast numbers of the Irish people most really their home."[150]

During these years, the mythology of the Anglo-American commons was also challenged through the work of Native American lecturers. Indigenous culture was always a feature of the lecture circuit. This was a point at which mainstream culture seemed to be consigning such civilizations to the status of historical curiosity, and they became a popular lecture hall topic that served various agendas. Most prominent were the tours of the painter and amateur ethnologist George Catlin, who lectured from the 1830s onward, accompanying his accounts of living with the "vanishing Indians" of the West with paintings and costumed coperformers. He also lectured in Britain: for example, in 1841 he spoke to the Royal Institution in London in 1841, where he made the case for a preservationist Museum of Mankind and the need for Britain, with its "more than thirty colonies in different quarters of the globe," to send "artists and men of science" to "receive" and "perpetuate" their labors ... thus uniting the "philanthropic world."[151] As Kate Flint has noted of the period, "the notional Indian could be readily adapted, in a number of disparate contexts" to suit the narratives of transatlantic modernity,[152] and here we see Catlin mobilize indigenous culture as a way of unifying the Anglosphere. But this struggle to render the indigenous experience meaningful within an Atlantic world was also expressed in more meaningful ways by Native American orators themselves, whose views about what to reject and embrace in Anglo-Saxon culture clashed now as much as ever before.

Perhaps the most eminent example was William Apess's famous "Eulogy on King Philip," which was delivered at two high-profile appearances in Boston in 1836. A Pequot Indian descended from a white grandfather and Pequot grandmother, Apess took to the lecture circuit to offer a complex argument against assimilation and Indian removal. The figure that the press called the "gentlemanly savage" appeared in the full attire of a New England elite, presenting himself as an embodiment of Anglicized dignity, determined to cement his place as an oratorical authority of Anglo-American history.[153] Yet his task was to undo the master narratives of that shared history. Promising to lay forth the crimes "committed by whites upon Indians before the civilized world," his central grievance was couched in the language of Anglo-American property law:

> In December 1620, the Pilgrims landed at Plymouth, and without asking liberty from anyone they possessed themselves of a portion of the country, and built themselves houses, and then made a treaty, and commanded them to accede to it. This, if now done, it would be called an insult and every white man would be called to go out and act the part of a patriot, to defend their country's rights.[154]

Apess perceived this historical exclusion of Native Americans from the British Empire's systems of justice and civil rights as continuing under the republic. His lecture offered a revisionist account of the history of the wars of early British America, replacing the leaders of the Revolution with a new American hero and stressing indigeneity over *Mayflower* descent as the authentic basis of the nation. As Philip Gura notes, the lecture was concerned with "overturning the filiopietism through which his contemporaries celebrated the achievements of the Pilgrim Fathers," and through which they read the world as an uncomplicated Anglo-American realm of power.[155] Apess wanted to transform white sympathy for an imagined Indian into support for an inclusive democracy. But his message was also progressive in its rejection of the idea that the tangled and troubled past must dictate the future. In closing, he urged audiences to not to remain obsessed with the ills of history, arguing that "we have not to answer for our fathers' crimes; neither shall we do right to charge them one to another. We can only regret it, and flee from it."[156]

For the vast majority of midcentury lectures on the Anglo-American commons, the opposite dynamic was true. Time and again, audiences were encouraged not to flee from but to re-engage and identify with the Anglocentric history of the republic through debate, discussion, and rituals of devotion. During a time in which cultural consumption was being redefined as a public act and identity as performed, attending lectures became a way of enacting a powerful commitment to social participation. Lyceum attendance was intrinsic to the formation of bourgeois class identity but , at a moment in which ethnic hierarchies were coming into being, could also sometimes help create the myth of a distinctively white public.

A way of performing whiteness

Whiteness and Transatlantic Manners

In nineteenth-century culture, Englishness was frequently presented as the paramount form of what Matthew Frye Jacobson and others have called "variegated whiteness."[157] Lecture culture was only one of many contemporary contexts in which this identity was constructed. On the part of audiences, opting to patronize notionally Anglocentric institutions such as the lyceum, and in particular to attend events on Anglo-American topics, might well be interpreted as a way of declaring one's ownership of white heritage and the psychological and material privileges it afforded. But whiteness was also something constructed through the response to details of live performance in print. Once again, the lyceum's status as a medium encoded and recoded by the press allows us to see just how important a set of complementary ideas about whiteness and transatlantic manner were to the meanings of lecture culture.

The mid-century lecture platform was certainly an overwhelmingly white institution. "A lecture by a gentleman of color is sort of a 'rare bird on the earth' and is very like a black swan," observed the *Chicago Tribune* of an 1863 appearance by African-American physician-orator Martin Delany.[158] Most talks by minority performers took place at one remove from the mainstream platform. As chapter 2 explores, before the Civil War only a handful of black Americans, including Douglass, Frances Ellen Watkins Harper, and John Sweat Rock, achieved recognition as speakers on unsegregated lyceum platforms. Similarly, though, there were a handful of well-known Native American orators and campaigners during the period, including Apess and Elias Boudinot, who toured the eastern seaboard making the case against Cherokee removal during 1825–26. Their activities were as much activism as mainstream entertainment, and duly cordoned off.[159] One exception was the success of Ojibway chief George Copway ("Chief Kah-ge-ga-gah-bowh"), who became a platform star at the height of the 1840s circuit. Even when such speakers of color found themselves before what we might loosely think of as mainstream lyceum audiences, they were often constrained by the discursive pressure of speaking on a limited range of subjects.

Such relatively "mainstream" lecture culture was not only exclusionary, but also often played host to those promoting ideas that helped consolidate racial hierarchies. Most notoriously, the high-profile lectures of Swiss-born Harvard zoologist Louis Aggasiz, after his arrival in the United States in the late 1840s, helped lend authority to polygenist theories of scientific racism.[160] Thanks to a raft of science orators, lyceum lectures became an influential means by which pseudoscientific racisms were legitimized and spread through popular culture.[161] There were prominent exceptions that sought to do justice to biological realities, the most consequential of which may have been Massachusetts statesman Charles Sumner's spirited antiracism lectures of the postwar period, which sought to explore the "insult to human nature" offered by the popular elevation of whiteness.[162] From 1869, Douglass also began to tour a lecture extolling the ideas of "Our Composite Nationality." Generally speaking, however, the lecture hall was a space where prejudices were likely to be reinforced, and in which cosmopolitanism was all too readily confused with racial chauvinism.

This was certainly the tone of the many performances that exoticized non-white cultures upon the platform. One of the most prominent exponents of such events was the "Great American Traveller" Bayard Taylor, whose oratorical descriptions of African or Far Eastern scenes often seemed to indulge an appetite for racy orientalist mystification, sometimes delivering his testimony in full national or regional dress.[163] Native Americans were just as likely to be depicted in exoticized fashion at the lectern as they were upon the boards of American playhouses. A number of performers collaborated in this form of display. The tribal leader known as Nicholson Henry Parker, for example, lectured during the early 1850s, offering demonstrations of the "manners and customs" of the Seneca people.[164] Copway was both the best-known figure on this circuit and the most willing to play up to such demands for romantic exoticism. The poet Henry Wadsworth Longfellow recalled attending Copway's Boston lectures in April 1849, describing a "rambling talk, gracefully delivered, with a fine various voice, and a chief's costume, with little bells jangling upon it ... like the pomegranates of the Jewish priests."[165] Advertisements for these appearances captured a cross section of press coverage fixated on similar aspects of Copway's performance: "His gesticulation is graceful and appropriate," reported one Richmond, Virginia paper; the *New York Herald* hailed his "free and fascinating eloquence so peculiar to the Indian."[166]

This fascination with and attentiveness to "manners" was not just a property of performances by nonwhites. A remarkable degree of intensive scrutiny of body and voice was always central to lecture culture. It was one of the chief means by which all lecture events were evaluated during a historical period in which phrenology and other pseudosciences retained widespread popular purchase as methods of reading, assessing, and judging other human beings. Just as speeches by nonwhites were taken as always being *about* the relationship of manners to citizenship, lectures about Anglo-American themes were a vital way of thinking through the implications and symbolism of what Christopher Mulvey has called "transatlantic manners."[167] American observers of midcentury lecturing were fascinated by the supposed properties of "Englishness" and "Americanness." Partly as a result of the oppositions encouraged by the widely read accounts of transatlantic travelers, a popular sense of shifting social identities was very much a preoccupation of the midcentury American imagination.[168] Affect, accent, and physicality were all made part of a series of oppositions between supposedly democratic and aristocratic cultural styles. These dichotomies played out most memorably in the midcentury theater, and in May 1849 the rivalry between contrasting styles of Shakespearean delivery was the immediate cause of the notorious Astor Place Riot in which upwards of twenty protesters lost their lives outside a playhouse in Lower Manhattan. As I reveal in my discussion of Emerson in chapter 4, such tensions over transatlantic manners were also at work in coverage of the seemingly more demure world of the lecture hall.

This dynamic was most obviously at play in coverage of lectures by British performers, in which the body, gesture, and bearing of the foreign visitor were all scoured for their cultural meaning. A few months into his first American tour in late 1852, Thackeray wrote back home to *Fraser's Magazine* in London, marveling at "the ordinary American appetite of inquisitiveness" that had greeted him. For a "lion" of the speaking circuit such as himself, he observed, a typical experience went as follows:

> The lion in America is public property and confiscate to the common weal.... Some learned man is appointed Androcles to the new arrival. One of the familiars of the press is dispatched to attend the latest attraction, and by this reflecting medium the lion is perpetually presented to the popular gaze. The guest's most secret self is exposed by his host. Every action—every word—every gesture—is preserved and proclaimed—a sigh—a nod—a groan—a sneeze—a cough—or a wink—is each written down by this recording minister ... no bloodhound or Bow Street officer can be keener or more exact on the trail than this irresistible and unavoidable spy.[169]

One level this phraseology was merely a typical nineteenth-century trope. *Putnam's* 1857 survey of lecture culture had, for instance, also imagined the celebrity as caged animal before the "literary tribunal" of adversarial reception: "Lecturing is the manner in which the Yankee hunts lions.... They hire a large room, for a trap, and hang fifty dollars over the desk ... watching him carefully as he is consuming the bait."[170] But we can also push this idea of hunting "lions" further, reconnecting it to the iconography of the British state and the Anglophobic rhetorical tradition of "twisting the lion's tail." Reporters covering these lectures often saw their task as policing the meaning of cultural styles. The function of lecture culture was thus repeatedly reduced to a dual movement of attraction and resistance to figures of social and intellectual prestige. Tensions that might be resolved through "careful" submission of the semiotics of manners to an accusatory form of democratic appraisal in the press.

British performance values were sometimes simply idealized or aestheticized. Attempting to capture the meaning of an 1845 Boston lecture by the London-born Transcendentalist reformer Charles Lane, for example, the *New York Tribune* reporter's focus was as much on medium as message, finding himself "charmed by the rich sonorous voice and the elegant enunciation" far more than instructed by Lane's "clear, graphic sketches of the external and internal world of London."[171] The musical charm of the British accent here seems to project its own message, proposing an immersion in elegant Anglophilic gentility as a route to refinement and political consciousness through lecture attendance. In other cases, antagonism toward British performers could also turn on criticisms of their failure to live up to notional standards of manner. For example, another *Tribune* account from its London correspondent, watching the noted Birmingham preacher George Dawson speak in 1856, mediated the performance for readers back home by concluding, "It is not worth crossing the Atlantic to hear [him] ... the plumage of the bird is disproportionate to the body. A more self-conscious speaker, it seemed to me, I had seldom heard, and his intense sympathy with the effects he produced on his audience fairly gurgled at times in his throat or gave his voice the semblance of a *yodel*."[172] Captured lions might thus easily reveal their inadequacy as aspirational symbol.

The level of scrutiny accorded to this discourse of manners was not only evident in coverage of British performers, but was also directed toward Americans returning from Old World voyages. It was part of a two-way modification of what Stephen Fender terms "the rhetoric of emigration": the Atlantic transition as an irrevocable shift of self, body, spirit, and manners.[173] In this Crèvecoeurean conception, the acquisition of American vocality and physicality was a form of personal evolution; thus, quite apart from the matter of content, live details of lyceum performances could be read as implicitly pro- or anti-British in their signs and cultural styles. Primary and secondary audiences alike could gauge returning travelers in terms of the apparent physical or vocal manifestations of their newly acquired intercultural fluency. To appear "British" was to lay oneself open to have undergone a form of degeneration; to betray putatively "English" traits was to harbor potentially sinister, disloyal, antipatriotic intent. As the case studies in subsequent chapters will reveal, part of the fine balancing act of returning lecturers was the opposing imperative to address this issue of assimilation face on, and thus transform it into positive cultural capital.

Party political rhetoric reimagined this putative contrast as a partisan problem of rival political affects: everyman versus nabob; agrarians versus aristocrats. From the late 1830s onward, the Democrat agenda was committed to combating what John O'Sullivan termed "that extensive anti-democratic corruption of sentiment in some portions of our people."[174] Some Democrats went as far as to claim that the activities of Whiggish reform movements had cost them a sense of American selfhood. In Robert Walker's widely published polemic, *Letter on the Annexation of Texas* (1844), he lamented that such reformers "traverse sea and land" to "the capital of England ... and there they join in denunciations of their countrymen, until their hearts are filled with treason; and they return home, Americans in name, but Englishmen in feelings and principles."[175] The archival record suggests that language, accent, and physical traits all became readily available as political shorthand. Body, voice, and manner all became an imprint of cultural loyalties, and national independence was thus seen by some as a revolt against stiffness, polish, and reserve.[176] An effete aristocratic manner was customarily seen as problematically "English," and returning travelers might encounter accusations of reverse engineering back into Europeans. As we shall see, these habits and strategies of print mediation spoke to the inner tension of lecture culture, arbitrating between its role as crucible of brusque nationalism and as symbol of a process that smoothed the rough edges of midcentury cultural divides.]

My reading argues that lectures on Anglo-American themes and their reception need to be understood in two key ways. In one sense, the fixation with transatlantic manners in the lecture hall was about the role of a transcendent form of whiteness during a period of evolving racial stratifications. The idea of whiteness was a shifting marker during this period, and the Anglocentrism of the lecture platform is one forum through which we can valuably gauge these transformations. Yet, as subsequent chapters explore, this evolution in racial consciousness dovetailed with contradictory issues of party politics. The deep archive of lecture response reveals how different constituencies read, accommodated, and recoded details of both content and bodily performance as microverdicts on the state of the Anglo-American commons. This was particularly the case with orators who operated at the boundaries of the medium and of racial respectability. The most famous liminal figure of all was Frederick Douglass, one of the chief orators of the age and an important test case for understanding the limits of lecture culture.

Douglass ch.

— Doug in the lecture trad — pedagog exploiting transatlantic 'voices' to ironically comment on functions + limits of Ang-Am commons + pub speech (seeing him in the trad est. in the intro).

56-7 - Highlighting his move from antislavery circuit to the more 'intellectual' + restrained Lyceum circuit (new audience).

⮡ cross-platform speakers who used these shifts/tensions to reflect on speech itself + its Atlantic connections: made the network of halls + lecture rooms from Cork to Concord part of ab's conceptual + acoustic horizon.

⮡ manipulated an ab discourse of individualist moral suasion (private) into one of public listening. "a social theory of conversion through listening en masse" (60)

⮡ figures his turn away from Garrisonian moral suasion through these ideas of Atlantic speech — takes him also towards broader critique of racial inequality (transition to black press + Lyceum at same time).   ⮡ 'Black cosmopolitanism'

• Uses the Lyceum stage + performance of comparisons + connections not just to interpret Br but to create + embody an image of the non-national subject as a performed 'bodily + vocal ideal' (67)

⮡ Done by his performances of acquired Eng manner + vocalisation in US + performance of racialised traits in Eng. — "transatlantic whiteface" (69)

⮡ forcing audience to face their own conflicted views of an Ang-Am commons - Oing the set of Am dem manners (which subside) + Br haughtiness (which becomes claim of equality).

⮡ charts his post emancipation critique of an Anglo-Saxonism as he initially flirted w/ and his abandonment of Ang Am commons for a "broader form of internationalism" based on 'unity of the global dispossessed' first on stage, but later in print as the dominant form of black cult-ps after mid-C (as the liberal poss of the stage faded).

{ 2 }

Britain and Antislavery

FREDERICK DOUGLASS'S TRANSATLANTIC RHETORIC

At the Broadway Tabernacle on the morning of 11 May 1847, impatient voices had begun to encircle William Lloyd Garrison, master of ceremonies for that year's American Anti-Slavery Society convention. From around the circular stage his voice was repeatedly drowned out as he read from tributes to the event's star speaker, who would be making his eagerly anticipated first major public appearance since returning from a high-profile twenty-month tour of Britain. The renown that the former slave had acquired during this international venture was suddenly palpable; he and Garrison had shared a stage countless times, but the restless atmosphere on this occasion marked a sea change. "The dull comments of Mr. G. were too much for the audience," observed one of the journalists present, "and they called out 'Douglass, Douglass' from all parts of the house."[1] As another had it, Garrison was soon "embarrassed so much that he was compelled to ... bring his remarks abruptly to a close, amid some noise and confusion, by introducing Frederick Douglass to the audience."[2]

As Douglass approached the platform, he faced a mixed audience of delegates from across the northern states, described by one observer as a three thousand-strong "sea of heads ... truly of the 'popular' cast—the bone and sinews rather than the ornamental part of town."[3] The New York and national press were both out in force. "I entered that celebrated edifice," the *Baltimore Sun*'s correspondent wrote, "and soon found myself among a pretty numerous 'corps of reporters.'"[4] These journalists, the *Christian Inquirer* recorded, "were in a phalanx directly in front, busily employed in giving the whole address."[5] Occupying a particularly prominent spot, the *New York Herald* crowed that it had "taken much pains to give our readers daguerreotype reports" of an event that was spreading "bigotry, fanaticism, treason and revolution" throughout the city.[6]

Douglass approached the podium eager to offend. "I am not here to please you with an eloquent speech," he declared, but to offer "sober truths ... a large portion of this audience will be disappointed, both by the manner and the matter of what I shall this day set forth." Amid a mixture of hissing and applause he proceeded to lambast the "bastard democracy" of the United States and denounce its "useless Constitution." His encouraging experiences while traveling, speaking, and campaigning in the British Isles, he explained, had led him to abandon any remaining national sentiment. "I have no patriotism," he declared, defiantly. "I have no country. What country have I? The Institutions of this Country do not know me—do not recognize me as a man." He stood before his audience determined to "defend the Right and Duty of invoking English aid and English sympathy for the overthrow of American Slavery ... and to forward, in every way, the interests of humanity."[7]

This homecoming address was to prove one of the most contentious of his career, and a decisive transitional moment in Douglass's development as activist and intellectual. His 1845–47 speaking tour of Britain and Ireland had transformed him into an international celebrity, permitting his freedom to be bought, and given him a powerful platform from which to speak out as an enemy of slavery. Yet at the Tabernacle, he stood at a career crossroads. To Douglass, remaining an antislavery orator came to represent its own form of servitude and paternalism, circumscribing the limits of his freedom as both speaker and thinker. He came to see voice and vocal expression as a problematic medium for the black intellectual by comparison with the apparently unracialized written word.[8] His appearance beside Garrison on that May morning was part of his move away from his previous role as lecturing agent, and a move toward new challenges as a cosmopolitan public intellectual. As he would at other stages of his career, Douglass cemented this defiance by "invoking" England. During the decades that followed, he would make symbols of and ideas about Britain central to his cause, exploiting the propaganda value of themes including emancipation, Anglo-Saxon history, and traditions of tolerance and free speech, and the complex longings to which they spoke.

This chapter explores the multiple dimensions to Douglass's invocations of Britain at the lectern. It surveys a wide range of his speeches delivered in the United States between the 1840s and 1880s, and during his two British tours, to unravel the creative uses to which he put what Waldo Martin called his attitude of "perplexing duality" toward an Anglo-American commons as part of the struggle for abolition and civil rights.[9] Specifically, I argue that Douglass's transatlantic rhetoric helped underpin three strands of his career.[10] First, the idea of an Atlantic world patterned by institutions of speech allowed him to develop his concepts of moral suasion and public opinion. Second, firsthand testimony of British social relations underwrote his transition from antislavery activist to cosmopolitan intellectual engaged with broader issues of citizenship and racial intolerance. Finally, the complex historical narrative of Britain provided Douglass with a vocabulary and teleology through which to contemplate America's destiny and argue for imagined futures. These strands run like a thread through his speaking career, and were all very much on display in this performance at the

Tabernacle—an event that I will return to in depth in order to unpack both the speech's subtleties and also the intricate ways in which journalistic readings of Douglass's platform "manner" help illuminate debates over racial passing and the theatricality of reform.

Douglass was one of the pivotal figures in the history of American oratory, and his career as speaker took in a diverse range of platforms, most occurring at one remove from the lecture circuit as known to other speakers in this book. This has led critics to separate out distinct aspects of his speaking career; however, for the purposes of this book I will take all of his speeches as *lectures*. Whether delivered at reform conventions, open-air meetings, or under the auspices of conventional lyceum courses, and under whatever label they may have been promoted or reported, his speeches were always marked by a pedagogic rhetoric and civic impulse owing more to Holbrook's lyceum manifesto than to the imperatives of either the stump or even the wider practices of reform activism. Moreover, always attentive to the symbolism of mainstream lecture culture and the reprint pathways of the Anglo-American press, Douglass repeatedly combined the tropes of popular lecturing with those of other oratorical forms. His success and fascination as a performer lay in the potent mixture of individualism with the civic function of what he called the "modern invention" of the lecturer, merging multiple platforms into one continuum of speech.[11] As I show in what follows, his rhetoric turned repeatedly upon the concept of transatlantic "voice," and by doing so offered an evolving and often ironic commentary on the function and limits of not only an Anglo-American commons but the very medium of public speech itself.

Abolition and the Atlantic Lecture Stage

The campaign against slavery was conducted through all available avenues in Jacksonian and antebellum print culture. Petitions and boycotts were promoted through pamphlets and broadsides; published slave narratives helped convert a wider readership; and antislavery newspapers helped sustain local and national communities of activists. This overflow of print of what Robert Fanuzzi has called "abolition's public sphere" helped create a distinctive counterpublic centered on the written word.[12] Yet most accounts of this world of reform have tended to underplay the practical and symbolic role of public speech.[13] The abolition struggle was sustained and defined in part by the metaphors through which it was conducted, and the visual rhetoric of exposure or "lifting the veil" was always at its most powerful when combined with vocal tropes: most famously the totemic declaration ("I will be heard!") that launched Garrison's *Liberator* in 1831, or John Greenleaf Whittier's much-recited poetic hymn to free speech, "Texas: Voice of New England" (1844).[14] In the same way, just as talismanic as the printed slave narrative was the medium of the antislavery lecture, through which white abolitionists, free blacks, and fugitive slaves presented the case against the "peculiar institution" to live audiences, uniting the visual with the vocal in powerful ways.

Though sporadic public addresses and antislavery meetings had long been a contentious feature of northern life, campaigners only began to take their message to public platforms in a concerted fashion in the early 1830s. By the middle of the decade, antislavery activists from Angelina Grimke in Philadelphia to Theodore Weld and Wendell Phillips in Massachusetts were covering growing parts of the North on propaganda tours, and associations such as William Lloyd Garrison's American Anti-Slavery Society had begun to employ "lecturing agents," often ex-slaves, to deliver set-piece speeches. Such events became a controversial yet widespread feature of urban and suburban life throughout the Upper Midwest and North, and periodically brought turmoil in their wake, the most notorious incident being the riot that followed Garrison's and Grimke's speeches at Pennsylvania Hall in Philadelphia in May 1838, in which the building was razed by fire.

Such efforts to publicize this most incendiary of subjects soon sparked international interest. In order to secure financial and moral support for the movement, black and white activists looked to Great Britain, and developed a transatlantic speaking and fundraising network that was to become one of the most crucial and contentious arenas for the antislavery lecture. The aim was to influence international opinion in favor of the cause by giving audiences what once Scottish newspaper in 1851 called "a more vivid idea of the evils of slavery" than that offered in the British press, leading audiences "more forcibly to realise" both the nature of these evils and the need for material support.[15] By the time that Douglass crossed the Atlantic in 1845, this arena had grown into a dense network of sympathetic venues that took in not only northern industrial cities but also small towns and villages from Ulster to Kent, encompassing diverse audiences varying from the genteel and metropolitan to the working class.[16]

Though the abolition movement emerged as a mass force at the same moment as the advent of the lecture phenomenon, it was separate in multiple ways. First, most lyceums and lecture-hosting venues explicitly forbade discussion of such divisive topics, and refused to allow their halls to be used for events with this kind of disruptive potential. This judgment call might be a complicated and unpredictable matter of local tastes. In the very first year of his lecturing career, for example, Garrison found his antislavery lectures barred in his home town of Newburyport, Massachusetts, but permitted just across the Merrimack River at Amesbury.[17] In the Midwest, abolitionists sometimes came to find themselves lecturing in large outdoor tents, a medium Garrison thought of as "a Portable Faneuil Hall."[18] The nature of such performances was also notably distinct from those on the lyceum circuit: events billed as abolition lectures were invariably collaborative affairs, with the main speaker accompanied or introduced by other reformers and activists. Audiences also comprised an atypical section of society, at least initially, and one Philadelphia paper noted that in the 1830s attendance was a largely Quaker phenomenon that comprised "almost exclusively members of the Society of Friends and of colored people."[19] In practice, the overlap of performers and performance spaces was often confusing and imprecise, with key venues used in turn by "mainstream" and "radical" groups, sometimes featuring a similar retinue of speakers. Despite such differences, the rise of the antislavery lecture nonetheless drew upon the prestige, conventions, and even the logistics of popular lecturing. For these reasons it makes sense to speak of the abolitionist and the traditional lecture circuits as existing not simply in opposition but in parallel, with a unified form of the secular spoken address at their heart.

Perhaps the paramount distinction that marked abolition events out from the mainstream lecturing was not a practical but a conceptual and aesthetic one. Holbrook's lyceum had been established in order to diffuse information and knowledge as a form of virtue, typically in a detached manner devoid of overt emotion. Lectures about slavery also centered on the transmission of knowledge, but were inevitably far more directed toward the conscience of listeners, openly geared to influence and manipulate their perception of evil. As such they embodied the most powerful possible means of what antislavery activists called "moral suasion," a theory of propaganda and persuasion based as Frank Kirkland has defined it on "the presupposition that the language of morality directly influences conduct. That is to say, moral suasion requires the belief that it can awaken through rhetoric moral sensibility, and as a consequence, motivate us to do what is good."[20] It was the governing philosophy of the nonviolent Garrisonian wing of the abolition movement, which believed that moral appeals had far greater power than political action.[21] True social change was dependent on the moral autonomy of the individual; reform of self preceded voting or collective action. Since this approach meant standing back from electoral politics and stump meetings, it placed acute importance on the affective, urgent form of the lecture as the most direct means by which to confront audiences with the realities of bondage.

The most powerfully affective lectures were those delivered by black abolitionists, both organized within the African-American community and hired by white antislavery associations. Especially in the latter case, fugitive slaves were conscripted to deliver emotive testimony of the conditions of slavery, to display their scars, recount their successful routes out of bondage, and demonstrate black intellectual and moral capacity. Essentially forms of life-writing, these talks merged personal narratives with outspoken political critique of a type forbidden on the lyceum circuit. During this period, performances by black abolitionists became a transatlantic phenomenon. Free blacks such as James McCune Smith and ex-slaves such as Sarah Parker Remond and William Wells Brown were held up in Europe as living refutations of America's much-trumpeted principles of freedom, and were greeted with welcomes far more sympathetic than those that met their white abolitionist counterparts.[22] European fascination with American ex-slaves was frequently dismissed by antiabolition interests back in the United

States as mere grotesque prurience, with papers such as the *New York Press* lambasting "Britannia's delight in runaway negroes ... all the public places are vocal with them."[23] These performances were gauged to appeal to sensationalist public tastes: audiences were often treated to slave songs, for example, and the showman-like performance of characters such as the six-foot-five fugitive Moses Roper or Henry "Box" Brown, whose "act" recreated the incredible ingenuity of his escape from servitude by means of mailing himself to freedom in a parcel. British audiences consumed such acts as much with the mindset of a theatregoer as a politically engaged seeker of knowledge.[24]

Though transatlantic lecturing provided a major source of publicity for the cause, and a route to financial independence for its protagonists through lecture fees, some black abolitionists found it a limiting platform. Performers frequently felt themselves objectified, and deplored the imperative of incessant sociability involved in constant movement from host to host. Charles Lenox Remond, for example, recounts being forced to stand in the middle of an Edinburgh public hall for over an hour following one 1840 talk, so that all those present could shake his hand.[25] It was also a precarious means of maintaining a living, reliant on a grueling November-to-May season, offering only a moderate likelihood of financial returns at best. Nonetheless, it was ultimately a line of work largely cherished by black abolitionists, and Brown was typical in priding himself on how the circuit had allowed him to support his family via his "own exertions—by his literary labors, and the honourable profession of the public lecturer."[26]

Douglass's Platforms

Douglass was the exemplary figure to emerge from and ultimately transcend this milieu, forging a speaking career that navigated several discursive platforms. Following his escape from captivity in Maryland in 1838 and settlement in Massachusetts, he was initially only the most promising among many black lecturing agents for the cause. In the years following his first speech before a white audience in Nantucket, Massachusetts, in 1841 he was mentored and nurtured by Garrison, soon becoming prolific as a paid lecturer for the Boston Anti-Slavery Society, speaking at thirty Midwestern towns in the fall of 1843 alone.[27] His lecturing crusade was soon to expand internationally: in late 1845, partly to escape the danger to his liberty caused by the publication of his *Narrative*, he sailed from New York to Liverpool to continue the abolition campaign in Great Britain. It was to prove a remarkably prolific tour, and Douglass began his speaking engagements while still at sea, addressing the saloon deck of the *Cambria*, the first of over three hundred talks and lectures he would give during his year and a half stay, in addition to participating in a number of major reform conventions in Ireland and London. His activities attracted fascinated and outraged coverage in both the British and American press, consolidating his twinned public persona as exemplar of African-American potential and critic of US hypocrisy.

To both his supporters and opponents, Douglass's speaking voice became a powerful symbol. In abolitionist pieces written to celebrate his departure, particular tropes of speech were central to how others imagined his influence, captured well in a poem printed in the *Liberator* in November 1846 in which Douglass's mouth is figured as a form of disembodied sacred rapture:

> Thy tongue is loosened—loosened by the ties
> Which held thy brethren in the Western shores;
> Proclaim their wrongs, denounce the nation's lies,
> Where man his brother hates, his God adores.[28]

This vocal fixation was shared by his proslavery detractors, who used an opposing metaphoric register of demonic voice to describe the disruptive force of his activities in Britain.[29] For the *New York Express* in February 1846, his trip was one of a "glib-tongued scoundrel" let loose "in greedy-eared Britain . . . haranguing here and there, he is assaulting his British hearers with tales . . . the meanest kind of calumny is that which speaks through the tongue of a runaway slave."[30] Another upstate New York paper in October the same year complained of "how a thick lipped orator can talk . . . his conceit knows no bounds."[31] In such instances, the very fact of African-American sociability and conversation in the Old World stood as a form of treasonous indulgence. For his own part Douglass shared this own vocal-focused view of what he intended to achieve, writing to Horace Greeley before his departure that his aim was to speak "the sins of one nation in the ear of another."[32]

Upon his return in April 1847, however, Douglass had begun to tire of the paternalistic limitations of his role as Garrison's oratorical subordinate. He saw that the formulaic nature of antislavery lecturing was a trap, felt he had exhausted the potential of a stifling narrative mode, and had grown tired of the lurid stunts that he was expected to indulge, such as the presentations of a blood-stained whip that he told audiences had been used on his cousin.[33] In Britain he had come to share the sense felt by other ex-slaves that, as Audrey Fisch's puts it, "they came as representatives of the transatlantic anti-slavery campaign, but they also took their places in a parade of non-white Others, each displayed in its objectified turn for the English public as an exotic spectacle."[34] Upon his return he therefore took two steps toward greater independence. First was the desire to move into print and remake the press in his own image, and after moving to Rochester, New York, he duly cofounded the *North Star* with Martin Delany, the organ that later became *Frederick Douglass's Paper*. The second step was to attempt to make broader use of such "electricity" by moving beyond the confines of the antislavery speaking circuit.

In between the two distinct abolition and the lyceum circuits existed an intermediary platform: that of African-American literary societies.[35] The middle decades of the century were a moment of flourishing for African-American speech-making.[36] New opportunities for public discussion and new groups devoted to black education helped create a landscape of conventions, church meetings, and looser gatherings at which black voices could be heard and rhetorical training acquired. Speeches from these settings reached a wider public through being carried in specialized publications such as the *Freedman's Journal*, the *Provincial Freedman*, The *Christian Recorder, New York Age and Colored American*, and less frequently in the mainstream press.[37] Whatever the setting, black vocal performance had its own instrumental and symbolic force. Since the early republic prized oratory as one of the paramount achievements of human intellect, proficiency on the public platform was a chief means to refute notions of racial inferiority. As the prominent New York black educator William G. Allen recognized in an 1853 lecture to his African-American congregation, the public voice of performers of color therefore possessed a doubly liberating potential, and he urged his audience that "as ye cultivate the oratorical, do it diligently, and with purpose; remembering that it is by the exercise of this weapon, perhaps more than any other, that America is to be made a free land."[38] Douglass was a prolific orator on this circuit, and devoted much of his career to helping further the interests of Negro institutions.

The narrative of Douglass's rise as orator on both these platforms, his break from Garrison, and emergence as an editor is well known. Less remarked-upon is his movement from abolition lecturing agent to established figure on the integrated lecture circuit, and what that meant for his career and ideas. Some historians and critics have seen his lyceum addresses as watered down in content, and secondary to his efforts on the abolition circuit.[39] However, as Ray has shown, these lectures should "be understood as integral to these efforts, providing the potential for widespread diffusion of his reformist ideas."[40] Douglass saw the lyceum as reform's great weapon, for its wider social reach, and for the subtler forms of enlightenment made possible by the rhetorical ideal of the truly public lecturer. As recently as 1839 he had been unable to join the New Bedford Lyceum due to segregationist policies, and he would have to wait a decade and a half to finally achieve what he termed a "new vocation" as speaker on the mainstream lecture circuit.[41] In January 1854 the Manchester, New Hampshire, lyceum became the first general lecture organization to invite him to speak, under the topic "God's Law Outlawed," a piece in which he found a mutedly objective historical voice to contextualize the 1850 Fugitive Slave Law.[42] In an editorial announcing the invitation, he reflected that "this appearing before Lyceums, is something new ... a cheering sign, this inviting a colored man, who has been a Fugitive slave, to address societies whose purpose is not less intellectual than moral. Such an invitation could never have been given nor complied with a dozen years ago."[43]

With increasing regularity, Douglass began to speak as a paid orator on unsegregated northern lecture stages previously barred to him, and on topics often at one remove from the constraints of a reformist script. He became a sought-after star of the circuit with speeches on such archetypal lyceum themes such as individualist uplift ("Self Made Men," from 1859) and European history ("William the Silent," from 1868) in addition to more obviously reformist themes, including "The Races" (from 1858) and "Our Composite Nationality" (from 1869). By the 1858–59 season, Douglass's name appeared on the list of the *New York Tribune*'s prestigious "Lecturing Fraternity" list of available speakers, foreshadowing his postwar prominence under the support of the Redpath Lyceum Bureau when into the 1870s lyceum performances provided the chief source of his income.[44] The style and tone of his oratory shifted to meet this new platform. His speeches were now delivered with notes, and relied as much upon scholarship and intellectual formality as on force of charisma and autobiographical intensity.

This lucrative work was a key step toward financial independence. But Douglass hailed it more broadly as the beginning of the end for an unofficial quarantine of "contentious" topics on the mainstream platform. Reflecting in a December 1854 editorial, "What Have the Abolitionists Done?," he argued that the growing appreciation of fellow activists "among the Lyceum Lectures of the day" marked "a demand, by the People, for something more than the unnutritious husks, upon which they have been wont to feed."[45] Speaking before the annual meeting of the National Council of Colored People the following year, he proclaimed that the acceptance of black and antislavery lecturers into the "conservative lyceums and other American literary associations" would be "looked to by after-coming generations" as a seminal moment in the history of American free speech.[46] As Douglass put it in 1854, the popular lecturer was a "distinguished and useful functionary,"

> a modern invention called forth by the increasing demands of restless human nature. His office is to communicate knowledge to make men wise, happy and free.—Most honorable work, surely! ... He performs the work of instruction on a grand, yet economical scale, dispensing to thousands, what before was only received by fifties, and doing in one hour what before could only be accomplished in weeks.[47]

This was particularly the case with African-American orators and educators, since the exercise of intellectual display embodied the very self-improvement ethos that the lyceum's bourgeois individualism existed to celebrate. Even in these lyceum performances, however, he was far from uncritical about the institutional constraints of his adopted platform. Quite often his performances turned on ironic critiques of the genteel neutrality of an arena that, in his most famous oration, "The Meaning of July 4th for the Negro," he disparaged as "the grand illuminated temple of knowledge."[48]

Douglass's success in moving between platforms is more important than has been recognized: it not only helped validate him as an intellectual, but his cross-platform status as a speaker changed the meaning of all of his messages. His oratorical career should be seen as a continuum of speech across platforms, a continuation of his goal of moral suasion and consciousness-raising, in which he managed to unify the nature, context, and texture of his utterances as reformist speaker, convention delegate, and lyceum star into a consistent rhetorical project. And across all platforms, he made consistently effective use of the symbolism of mediums of speech. As his speeches of the late 1840s onward demonstrate, even before his official arrival as a mainstream lecturer, Douglass self-consciously positioned himself as part of a broadly conceived Anglo-American culture of speech, repeatedly returning to vocal images and metaphors, and asked audiences in both Britain and the United States to reflect in metarhetorical ways upon habits of speech. Turning now to the imagery of these addresses allows us to trace a shifting attitude to the platform and the tensions between moral suasion and the institutional pressures of the lecture platform itself.

Moral Suasion and the Sonic Atlantic

During his time in Britain, Douglass had been as struck as any of his American contemporaries by the sheer scale of "the reciprocity and interchange going on between the two countries."[49] In this age of shrinking global distance, observers used a repertoire of creative metaphors to help describe the newly complex world of transatlantic connection. Douglass was principally drawn to images of voice. In the first decade of his career, and particularly on his British tour, he continually encouraged his audiences to conceive of international connections and proximity using vocal metaphors. For instance, in front of an audience of three thousand filling London's Finsbury Chapel almost "to suffocation" in May 1846, one moment of Douglass's three-hour speech was particularly eloquent on this effect of discursive immediacy:

> You have been drawn together by the power of steam to a marvelous extent; the distance between London and Boston is now reduced to some twelve or fourteen days, so that the denunciations against slavery, uttered in London this week, may be heard in a fortnight in the streets of Boston, and reverberating amidst the hills of Massachusetts. There is nothing said here against slavery that will not be recorded in the United States.[50]

It was a trope that Douglass was to return to late into his career, noting in similarly faux-intimate terms to an 1887 Washington, DC, audience, "I know England is listening tonight for more indiscreet and revolutionary statements."[51] By conceptualizing Britain and the United States as brought into an almost gothic closeness by the power of speech, he helped transform an interlocking network of venues and speakers into an emblem of the technological sublime. Just as, in Amanda Claybaugh's words, the United States was "part of the imaginative horizon of British reform," Douglass made the network of halls and lecture rooms from Coventry to Concord part of abolition's conceptual and acoustic horizon.⁵² And in its fantasies of intimacy, his rhetoric also helped remind audiences of a shared reform culture made possible by the dynamics of textual travel.

Douglass's lectures of this period reveal an increasingly sophisticated awareness of reprint pathways.⁵³ That is to say, when he raised his voice in Britain he did so in the knowledge that it would "reverberate" on the pages of the American press that were covering his activities overseas with a mixture of fascination and repulsion. He knew that such coverage both prolonged the life span of his words and gave to them greater symbolism. At points he expressed this reprinting process in martial terms. In one further address in his final weeks in London, he promised that he was "determined to be honest with America . . . to denounce her high claims to civilization, and proclaim in her ears the wrongs of those who cry day and night to Heaven, 'How long! how long! O Lord God of Sabbath!' (Loud cheers.)"⁵⁴ This was designed to become a moment of text that would consciously perform its own message upon reappearance in the US press, with the original statement mediated in transcription to incorporate the above applause as a confirmation of British assent. When the Finsbury Chapel speech was later printed as part of *My Bondage and My Freedom* (1855), "loud cheers" duly rang out once again for domestic audiences.⁵⁵

In these British lectures Douglass repeatedly cast himself as a conductor of collective voices, calling upon his audience to proclaim against the evils of the American republic. He asked a Belfast crowd in December 1845 to "speak loud until every slaveholder heard their rebukes and resolved to do justice to the downtrodden slave"; a few months later in Newcastle he urged an audience to "lift up your voices like trumpets and cry aloud against this iniquity. I would have the British press, and the British pulpit, to use their thunders against the slave system of America."⁵⁶ At Finsbury Chapel he impressed upon his listeners that the American slave-owner must feel as if the "voice of the civilized, aye, and the savage, is against him."⁵⁷ Beneath such demands was the theory of mass persuasion at the heart of moral suasion: that conversion through speech could alter the hearts and minds of a people. Far from being a "creature of law," Douglass recalled later in life of his views at this period, "We regarded [slavery] as a creature of public opinion."⁵⁸ Douglass thereby played on and propounded the new eighteenth-century notion of public opinion as an extragovernmental tribunal to which aggrieved groups might seek redress. Abolitionists such as Garrison had seen how representative democracy, growing literacy, and an expanding print media had catalyzed older rhetorical traditions of *vox populi vox Dei* ("the voice of the people is the voice of God"), and regarded such appeals to the abstracted voice of a sovereign public as a symbolic goal of communicative action. The Massachusetts Anti-Slavery Society's 1852 report, for instance, had declared that the "Public Opinion of Christendom is the True Law of Nations, and it is the sense of this truth that makes tyrants . . . whether they sit on thrones or on cotton-bags, tremble when its sentence of condemnation is thundered in their ears. It is the voice that foretells their downfall."[59]

Yet in practice, *opinion publique* was not static but a process. "Public opinion," argued Douglass in Belfast in 1845, was "an aggregate of private opinions."[60] This was the classic individualist model of moral suasion, in which individual conversion led to social change, and is familiar to us through the literary sentimentalism of works such as Harriet Beecher Stowe's *Uncle Tom's Cabin*, a text that as Faye Halpern has argued "makes a case against textuality" by dramatizing the persuasive impact of accumulated speech between husbands, wives, and daughters.[61] Characters within that novel are shown as converted through domestic conversation. Yet in Douglass's lectures, time and again we find not this private model of vocal suasion but one centered on public listening. His was a social theory of conversion through listening en masse. To paraphrase Kwame Anthony Appiah, Douglass saw collective listening as fundamental to "how moral revolutions happen."[62] He repeatedly projected a vision of public opinion formed most powerfully through the combined sway of oratorical charisma, through the contagion of peer response, and crucially, through the symbolic depictions of such acts of collective listening in print. At times this ideal of vocal suasion took the form of the "instrument" of an almost gothic, disembodied national voice. But it found some of its most powerful expression through the imagery of institutions of speech.

Throughout his antebellum lectures and speeches, Douglass was apt to mythologize one such institution in particular: the London venue of Exeter Hall. This grand building on the north side of the Strand was one of the great oratorical arenas of the age and perhaps the most iconic venue of the transatlantic reform circuit (see Figure 2.1). Various benevolent, evangelical, and lecture-sponsoring organizations hosted talks in its vast central hall, and Douglass appeared there himself in 1846 when he was "received and heard with a tempest of applause continually bursting about his ears," according to one account.[63] The building had become shorthand for outspoken liberalism, and to some such as Jerrold's magazine, the philanthropic oratory that filled it acted as a healthy "safety-valve" for British "indignation and scorn and hatred."[64] However, it was far from an uncontentious symbol. The perceived excesses of the words spoken in its hall attracted the skepticism of Dickens, allowed Carlyle to see it as emblematic of a hypocritical midcentury "age of babblement," and drew Emerson to dismiss it a "cave of winds."[65] In the antebellum United States the venue had become particularly associated with the antislavery cause. In 1858, Ohio congressman Samuel S. Cox marveled that "every steamer brings us a lecture from Exeter Hall on our slave propagandist filibusterism."[66] Others went further in lambasting the "sham philanthropy" and "lachrymose sympathy" of the "the noisy negro sympathizers of Exeter Hall."[67] "Exeter Hall Morality" was thus American shorthand for British hypocrisy toward their own social ills,

Exeter Hall.

FIGURE 2.1 *Abolition Fanaticism in New York, 1847*

while, as one Massachusetts observer noted during his time there, "almost every week the walls of Exeter Hall rang with some declamation upon the wrongs of American bondage."[68]

To Douglass, however, the institution held a particularly important role in his imagining of the Anglo-American commons. In an 1848 speech in Rochester, the venue was placed at the culminating head of an encomium to British liberal progress:

> Her passage to freedom is not through rivers of blood; she has discovered a more excellent way. What is bloody revolution in France, is peaceful reformation in England. The friends and enemies of freedom, meet not at the barricades thrown up in the streets of London; but on the broad platform of Exeter Hall. Their weapons are not pointed bayonets, but arguments. Friends of freedom rely not upon brute force but moral power. Their courage is not that of the tiger, but that of the Christian. Their ramparts are right and reason, and can never be stormed! Their Hotel de Ville, is the House of Commons.[69]

Into the next decade, Douglass's speeches continued to invoke the venue, as in 1857 when he recalled how "all England cried out with one accord, through Exeter Hall, through the press, through the pulpit, through parliament, and through the very throne itself."[70] In an idealized conception that we might call the vocal or institutional sublime, the twinned institutions of speech, Parliament and Exeter Hall, are substituted for sites of battle and become part of an institutional iconography of effective collective speech and unity of purpose.

His ideas of a sonic Atlantic were not simply a matter of intimacy but also more subtly of competition. In his speeches and writings, Garrison was apt to wield the name of Boston's Faneuil Hall as quintessential to the democratic ideal of public assembly. But throughout his career, Douglass tended to praise British orators and scenes of speech, comparing the parliamentary tolerance shown to William Wilberforce with that meted out to Charles Sumner in the Senate, while offering lavish firsthand testimony of hearing Daniel O'Connell at Dublin's Conciliation Hall in 1845 and Gladstone in the House of Commons in 1886.[71] We might say that such rhetoric was part of a wider tendency of black abolitionists to defer to British cultural practices, as with Brown's account in *An American Fugitive in Europe* of lecture-going in England.[72] On the one hand, these gestures promoted a form of commonality, urging audiences to avow shared traditions and potential. Yet such implied comparisons also served to cast the American scene in a negative light, marking an estrangement from American institutions. Looking back at the culture of mid-Victorian reform from the end of the century, one British memorialist recalled that "statesmen, weighing one policy against another, have had to ask 'What will Exeter Hall say?'"[73] Douglass's invocations of the venue forced the very same question upon his US audiences. His speeches placed the immediate listeners in his American auditoriums in dialogue with their imagined counterparts assembled in London, playing upon the national honor involved in a comparative assessment of Anglo-American society.

In these antebellum lectures and speeches, therefore, we see Douglass at the height of his conviction that moral revolutions could occur at one remove from politics. Yet they also reveal some growing tension at work, not least of which was a growing belief in the power of institutions, both religious and political. In a muted fashion, we might say, Douglass's continual rhetorical appeals to transatlantic vocal unity, grounded as they often were in British ecclesiastical efforts, were a return to an Anglo-American commons conceived as an international Protestant congregation. But as this emphasis upon institutions in general and on the British Parliament in particular suggests, we can also perceive the growing receptivity toward party-political solutions that would lead to his break with Garrison during the early years of the 1850s. His celebration of icons of British speech and politics placed him at odds with his mentor's antiassociational vision and his concept of individualist moral suasion.[74] As John McKivigan puts it, these years marked a moment when, for many in the abolition movement, "the old techniques of moral suasion to mold 'public sentiment' and free 'the mind of the whole community' seemed increasingly inadequate after 1850."[75] It was a movement mirrored in Douglass's own transition toward the platforms of the black press and the mainstream lyceum, and away from a strict focus on slavery toward a broader critique of racial inequality centered on the individual. As with his earlier speaking career, the symbolism and imagery of the Anglo-American commons was to become a crucial part of his rhetorical agenda. And to see that at its height, we can return to the Broadway Tabernacle scene with which this chapter opened.

Antiprejudice and Black Cosmopolitanism

Douglass arrived back in America that year reaching for a new role and a new rhetorical approach, and saw that he could use his experiences of relative racial tolerance in Britain as a new theme with which to accomplish both. As he had had told an audience in Bristol immediately before his departure, his eagerness to return to the United States was partly based on a desire to make American audiences "acquainted with the fact, that in England the negro was regarded as a man."[76] Now back in the more racially constrained environment of the United States, he was determined to confront Americans with the lessons that London or Dublin might hold for New York or Boston. Just as importantly, he used his experiences of Britain, and his sense of having undergone a fundamental personal transformation, to present a new identity through confrontational rhetorical shifts in his self-presentation and through the embrace of a transformed performance style.

British tolerance was a theme regularly reprised in the months that followed Douglass's return. At a talk on 3 May 1847 in Boston he gave "a narrative of the incidents connected with his visit to England" and, in particular, "his cordial reception in Liverpool, Dublin, and in the numerous places he visited throughout."[77] The following week, he spoke to a mostly black audience at Manhattan's Apollo church about "the various places he visited through England, not omitting his invitation to dine with the Lord Mayor of Dublin and a large number of nobility."[78] "I never knew what freedom was," he told a New York City audience in September, "until I got beyond the limits of the American eagle. When I first rested my head on a British Island ... I was free, at least for a time."[79] Sentiments like these were recurring tropes in the period's slave narratives, in which they sometimes served as rites of passage. They were also a feature of oratory. In an 1842 Boston speech, for instance, Charles Remond recalled how "from the moment I left the American packet ship in Liverpool, up to the moment I came in contact with [America] again, I was never reminded of my complexion."[80] During his own lecture tours in London, William Wells Brown frequently proclaimed himself to be "more free here tonight, in monarchical England, than I should be in my own republican country!," and the social ease of the black man in the English crowd became a defining motif of *An American Fugitive in Europe* (1852).[81]

Such gestures were also related to a common deceptively innocuous technique of mainstream lyceum travel lecturers, by which the accounts of time overseas were used to smuggle in reformist arguments. Perhaps the most prominent example of the genre was Wendell Phillips's highly popular piece "Street Life in Europe," which cataloged comparisons gleaned during his travels, noting in an 1854 rendition that "abroad there is no distinction of color. In the fashionable streets of Paris, black and white walk arm-in-arm and no one notices ... I realized that I was thousands of miles away from America."[82] This was an agenda that an 1860 Brooklyn rendition of Phillips's lecture made clear, counseling audiences that their "consideration" of such differences "would smooth down national prejudices and bridge over the chasm which divides race from race."[83] This subgenre turned the self-improvement ethos of the lyceum upon listeners, forcing audiences to reflect critically upon the social relations of the very rooms in which they sat listening. In the major homecoming lecture with which this chapter began, Douglass repurposed this evergreen lecture hall topic, and made it serve some complex ends.

The crucial passage of the talk comes a couple of minutes in, as Douglass sketches the defining experience of his Old World encounter:

I went to England, Monarchical England, to get rid of Democratic Slavery, and I must confess that, at the very threshold, I was satisfied that I had gone to the right place. Say what you will of England—of the degradation—of the poverty—and there is much of it there—say what you will of the oppression and suffering going on in England at this time, there is Liberty there, there is Freedom there, not only for the white man but for the black man also. The instant that I stepped upon the shore and looked into the faces of the crowd around me, I saw in every man a recognition of my manhood, and an absence, a perfect absence, of everything like that disgusting hate with which we are pursued in this country. [Cheers] I looked around in vain to see in any man's face a token of the slightest aversion to me on account of my complexion. Even the cabmen demeaned themselves to me as they did to other men, and the very dogs and pigs of old England treated me as a man! I cannot, however, my friends, dwell upon this anti-Prejudice, or rather, the many illustrations of the absence of Prejudice against Color in England, but will proceed, at once, to defend the Right and Duty of invoking English aid and English sympathy for the overthrow of American Slavery, for the education of Colored Americans, and to forward, in every way, the interests of humanity; inasmuch as the right of appealing to England for aid in overthrowing Slavery in this country has been called in question, in public meetings and by the press, in this City.[84]

A version of this compelling passage had already formed the basis of one of his widely reprinted public letters home to Garrison, and the material was later to gain even greater prominence through its incorporation into his second auto-biography, *My Bondage and My Freedom* (1855). Yet here in the live moment of performance, the ideas contained in such a gesture and the manner in which it was communicated served intricate purposes both broad and immediate—the opening salvo of a sequence of events that would lead to Douglass's break with his mentor and with his customary rhetorical strategies.

Accounts of Douglass's live reception certainly testify to a varied response. The reliably antislavery *Tribune* emphasized the crowd's approval, noting that "Mr. D took his seat in the midst of the most enthusiasm and overwhelming applause, in which the whole of the vast assembly appeared heartily to join."[85] Other accounts recalled a quite different scene. The *National Era* recorded "the 'hisses' which, from time to time, pierced the eloquence-charmed stillness of the scene" as the meaning of his words unfolded.[86] The *Baltimore Sun*'s circumspect representative conceded that "if I suffered the mortification of hearing it applauded, I enjoyed the pleasure of hearing it visited with merited hisses of indignant disapproba-tion."[87] One New Hampshire paper simply testified to "hisses—almost utterly drowning the applause."[88]

Douglass had in fact preempted such disquiet, promising that "a large portion of this audience will be disappointed, both by the manner and the matter of what I shall this day set forth." His provocation served at least three key purposes. One of the most immediate was to distance himself from the paternalism of those that had invited him, and in the lines following the above passage, he pointedly turned his remarks on the mentor who had just introduced him, remarking, "I cannot agree with my friend Mr. Garrison in relation to my love and attachment to this land. I have no love for America." His mentor's introductory remarks had seemed to aggravate Douglass in their implication that it was patriotism that had brought him home, and his very public declaration of enchantment with England and the sources of support to which Garrison was known to be opposed was a gesture that hastened their separation and licensed Douglass's pivot to con-stitutional antislavery. His increasing distance from Garrison was most clearly implicit in his reference to "English aid and English sympathy," which referred not only to the moral support of like-minded activists but to the specific involve-ment of British churches and the growing importance of figures such as Julia Griffiths, which offended Garrison's anticlericalism.[89]

More broadly, Douglass's rejection of patriotism was clearly intended to drive a rhetorical wedge between himself and other key sections of his audience. By framing this moment as a "confession," Douglass acknowledged the unpalata-ble implications of his ironic discovery that the promise of American equality had been realized in European rather than on American soil. In the lines that followed the above passage, his immoderate praise for Britain transitioned into a rejection of American nationality: "I have no patriotism. I have no country."[90]

This antipatriotism was in part intended as a rebuke to the shrill Anglophobic nationalism that was so much a feature of late 1840s New York cultural life, alluded to in the gesture outward to the "the public meeting of the press, in this city." The press response was indeed instructive. The *New York Sun* was particularly explicit in their accusations of English involvement, lamenting "that a society composed of white men, citizens of our country, residents of our city, should encourage this black, evidently supported by a foreign government, to insist in this outrageous manner ... moves our special wonder."[91] The *Baltimore Sun* was similarly scornful of how "respect and admiration for England, were uttered by the same lips that denounced the American government, laws, church, press, people and character as polluted, rotten[,] corrupt, and every way abominable."[92] This discussion also played out in the South. "The waters of controversy had been violently disturbed by the speech of Frederick Douglass, the fugitive slave," reported the New York correspondent of the *Charleston Courier*, who nonetheless doubted that "his remarks will be reprinted very extensively in the Southern papers. They were quite as ultra as even this meridian will bear."[93]

The third point of provocation lay simply in Douglass's newly cosmopolitan persona.[94] For the first of many times he assumed the position of the archetypal category-spanning cosmopolite, rejecting national ties and labels. It was a stance that Douglass would develop further in coming years in set-piece orations on the revolutions of 1848, or at Burns Night suppers, claiming allegiances far beyond the nation as part of what Greg Crane has called antislavery "constitutional cosmopolitanism."[95] While flaunting his global allegiances, Douglass was nonetheless eager to stress his conscious decision to return, telling a Boston audience, "I could have lived there [Britain]... but I had rather be here now, encountering this feeling, bearing my testimony against it."[96] At such moments, as Giles has argued, Douglass's rhetoric works against indigenous perspectives of all kinds, reducing nationalism to a set of fluctuating and contingent terms.[97] Returned from Britain, he seemed newly eager to explore the complex tensions of self-determination and integration, forcing his countrymen to reimagine African-Americans as global citizens. He positions himself and other transatlantic black abolitionists as having their own "perfect absence" of affiliations, feeling at home only where authorized by nonprejudiced "recognition" of manhood. And at the Tabernacle, this sentiment was expressed through what was essentially a dramatic process.

The scene of British "recognition" that Douglass had described to his audience was one scene rich in class and racial drama. William McFeely and Henry Mayer have both used the model of theater director and actor to describe the relationship between Garrison and his lecturing agents.[98] It is possible to read the moments quoted above as Douglass's rejection of this dynamic, constructing his own drama in the form of a vivid scene of avowal by the British populace in which he is recognized on the basis of mutuality rather than sympathy. The scene he painted was clearly intended to be read as narrative of class, in which slave becomes not just an Englishman, but an English gentleman, "demeaned" to by cabmen and passers-by. Yet Douglass brandished not just his acceptance into English social hierarchy, but a sense of racial passing, in which "complexion" disappears as a factor. Lloyd Pratt has argued that Douglass's career saw him develop a rebuke to the prevailing ideas of sympathetic identification, offering instead a credible experience of strangerhood as rhetorical independence.[99] Lectures such as the Tabernacle performance saw a crucial stage of this persona develop, as Douglass projected not just a new political status, but what seemed to some as a new bodily and vocal identity.

English Manners on Broadway

Ross Posnock has spoken of black American intellectuals always operating under an "unique public glare" and for Douglass this gaze had never been more intense than at the transitional performance at the Tabernacle.[100] Throughout his speaking career, whenever commentators wrote about Douglass's performances, most tended to focus on what Henry Louis Gates Jr. has called the "*homo rhetoricus Africanus*": the paradox of the hyperliterate black orator.[101] Such attention was partly aesthetic, as audiences fixated on his handsome form and imposing leonine bearing. But readings of his performance style were always also freighted with "the silent challenge," as Richard Powell has put it, of "the former slave ... mounted simply by standing at a podium in a three piece suit with all the accessories."[102] Arguments for American citizenship were repeatedly made with reference to Douglass's dignified comportment and apparent cultivation; to his contemporary James Russell Lowell, "his look and bearing are an irresistible logic against the oppression of his race."[103] This pattern of response had suited his Garrisonian supporters well. But upon the stage of the Tabernacle a crucial shift in response to Douglass can be observed, a shift that forced a particular emphasis as much on manner as on matter, as he placed the tensions of transnational racial identity at the fore.

Those reporters present rehearsed some conventional tropes in their coverage, assessing Douglass's speech in terms of conformity to standards of grammar, enunciation, and manner. Several offered generic plaudits to his linguistic and intellectual achievement: one noting that "his speech would have been creditable from anyone"; with another reflecting that "from one who was but a few years since a slave, was truly extraordinary."[104] The *National Era*'s reporter thought that "some of the most eloquent sentences I have ever heard fall from mortal lips ... fell from the lips of a runaway Maryland slave."[105] However, reports also suggest that there was something new afoot that morning at the Tabernacle, as commentators described a performer who seemed corporeally changed by his global experiences. His bearing seemed even more lordly; his bass voice seemed to ring out in a newly Anglicized manner. To listeners that had not been privy to his development over the previous year and a half, the contrast appeared striking.

Just as his narrative of British tolerance was provocative, a new degree of control over body and diction was read as a similar challenge: an explicit appropriation of English physicality and accent.[106]

Such criticism had for some time been part of the wider suspicion around the Anglicization of American abolitionists. The Garrisonians were as concerned as their contemporaries by a perceived declension of manners and virtue, and just as eager to force a revival of politeness and respectability that often seemed at odds with their forceful arguments. Abolition meetings could be models of stilted propriety, seeking to prove the compatibility of radicalism and respectability. The platform style of prominent speakers could also be read as showily foreign. Wendell Phillips's patrician affectations were particularly well known. Speaking alongside Douglass that morning at the Tabernacle, some reports described him in simple terms of "earnest and graceful eloquence," but in other cases observers such as Higginson recalled a performer who "like an Englishman dropped his *g*'s and said 'bein'' and 'doin.'"[107] Traits such as these played into media caricatures of abolition as a movement of self-righteous, rootless fanatics hostile to any love of country. In Robert Walker's widely circulated polemic, *Letter on the Annexation of Texas* (1844), he notoriously lamented that such reformers "traverse sea and land" to "the capital of England ... and there they join in denunciations of their countrymen, until their hearts are filled with treason; and they return home, Americans in name, but Englishmen in feelings and principles."[108]

In the case of African-Americans, needless to say, this malleability became even more contentious and raised troubling questions about the transformative effects of foreign exposure. To the *New York Sun's* reporter in the audience, Douglass's extravagant formality was evidence that he had "lived with white people" in England, "and carried out in extension the doctrine of amalgamation."[109] His affect appeared to go beyond the performance of the bourgeois gentleman toward a form of whiteface mimicry that, in Daphne Brook's terms, threatened to "resist, complicate and undo" pervading racial categories.[110] In this, Douglass was not alone among ex-slaves: as Tamarkin has shown, there existed "within black abolitionism, a rather curious form of individual liberty—the right to stylize one's self as reformed by British manners."[111] Fellow black campaigners such as Sarah Remond were described by attendees at her slavery lectures in terms of the perceived Anglicization of her manner and voice, by which she reimagined herself as a model of English femininity and virtue.[112] The adoption of a mobile accent or transatlantic demeanor served abolitionists well in the Old World, when it was pragmatic to indulge public hierarchies based as much on respectability as skin tone. But equally, Douglass spoke of how he had played the African in England, writing home that "I am hardly black enough for the British taste, but by keeping my hair as wooly as possible—I make out to pass for at least half a Negro at any rate."[113]

His mimetic talents had long been central to his platform style, and impersonating the voices of a range of characters was simply one of his repertoire of tricks to make his oral narratives come alive. Thomas Wentworth Higginson thought him "a perfect mimic. He could reproduce anything," and other accounts speak of him cycling between impersonations from southern slaveholder to northern apologist, "mixing them up, without confusion or mistake, in the puppet show of his imagination, and playing upon them at his pleasure."[114] For his own part, Douglass was often explicit about his conscious shape-shifting, particularly during this crucial period of his career.[115] He spoke frequently of the effort to "improve my mind and deportment ... [to] transform from degradation to respectability," as he put it in his famous letter to his former master Thomas Auld.[116] In his final autobiography, he was especially candid about the costs of accent acquisition, conceding that he "had acquired a style of speaking, which in the South would have been considered tame and spiritless."[117] Douglass's haughtiness and self-possession was legendary, and he had always carried himself with dramatic sartorial dash;[118] one posthumous memorialist recalled his demeanor as possessing the "dignity and grace of a courier, and the bearing of a king."[119] An 1855 report of a speech in Philadelphia spoke of the "true Virginia nonchalance" of his performances, "entirely indifferent to what effects his remarks may have upon his audience."[120] Of course, one man's empowerment was another's insolence. As one New Hampshire observer tellingly complained in 1845, "I was indignant at the insolent tyranny of Frederick Douglass ... his having been a slave—or now being one—does not entitle him to play the master."[121] Yet at this seminal performance at the Tabernacle, Douglass's form of transatlantic whiteface was read as far more worryingly "tyrannical" in its own way.

These associations were central to an image placed at the front of *Abolition Fanaticism in New York*, a pamphlet containing a transcript Douglass's Tabernacle speech, published afterward in Baltimore by defenders of slavery and widely circulated.[122] Its cover depicted the speaker in exaggerated evening dress, effete in gesture and large of lip, brandishing in his left hand a top hat with more than a passing resemblance to a crown (see Figure 2.2). Douglass had been satirized in visual culture before, most often in terms of minstrelsy, as in an 1844 "Fugitive's Song" lithograph.[123] Yet this new image seemed a new departure. An ill-defined audience of white faces peer out from a darkened gloom more closely resembling the atmospherics of playhouse evening than the midmorning daylight of his original performance. It message was complex. By emphasizing his flamboyance, the pamphlet diminished Douglass by placing him back within the racialized milieu of ethnic exhibition. Yet such refinement also left no doubt that the real aim of abolition was the empowerment of the Negro. As Emerson was to discover, the performance culture of late-1840s New York was fixated to a surprising degree upon the use of politicized versions of Englishness. The *Abolition Fanaticism* pamphlet therefore impugned the public cause of antislavery using the same visual language that would fan the flames of the deadly Astor Place riot two years later.

PRICE SIX CENTS.

ABOLITION
FANATICISM
IN NEW YORK.

SPEECH

OF A

RUNAWAY SLAVE FROM BALTIMORE,

AT AN

ABOLITION MEETING IN NEW YORK,

HELD MAY 11, 1847.

1847.

FOR SALE AT ALL THE PERIODICAL AGENCIES.

FIGURE 2.2 *"Exeter Hall, the great anti-slavery meeting," 1841*

Just as in the urban disputes that would erupt on that occasion, the social value of theatricality was also at issue in Douglass's case. In several reports of his Tabernacle performance a broader commentary on the theatricality of reform was implied. To the *Baltimore Sun,* the decorous and artificial elements of Douglass's performance contributed to what the reporter saw as his "false statements," underlining the "fictitious sympathy and false issue" of his arguments.[124] This was also a theme hinted at in an elaborate discussion in the *New York Sun* that drew suggestive parallels with the world of English theatrics:

> As a speaker, Mr. Douglass is chiefly remarkable for the dignity of his man-
> ner and the elegance of his pronunciation, which last, probably by means
> of a considerable sojourn in England, where he associated with well-bred
> people, is nearly faultless. We question whether Mr. Mcready himself, that
> martinet of the English, could find fault with half a dozen words used by
> this escaped slave.[125]

The association drawn here between Douglass and the playhouse *manner* of the English actor Charles Macready points in two directions. Connecting him with the perceived elitism of English theatrical aesthetics placed him within a world of mannered insincerity, with the implicit suggestion that Douglass has become both intoxicated and contaminated by the "well bred" in ways that compromised his effectiveness as authentic bearer of his own experiences. Imagining Douglass as overblown tragedian helped give focus to suspicions about the implications of reform culture, anxieties that went beyond abolition itself. Yet in another sense these attacks also served as a marker of Douglass's success, and through this lens another reading of the theatrical parallel above is possible. When compared, as he routinely was, with the "spread-eagled" style of more emotive American tragedians such as Edwin Forrest, the impassive, controlled rigidity of Macready was already legendary. Given Douglass's repeatedly stated aspiration to present the controlled, dignified black body as an argument against racial intolerance, he might be said to have no more appropriate or relevant points of comparison than "Macready himself, that martinet of the English."

The spectacle of Douglass on Broadway was to serve as a warning and a lesson. Beyond surface appropriation of stylized British manners lay a new cultural stance legitimized by transatlantic exposure. Just as his speech had presented a moment of spectacular recognition and antiprejudice in Britain, his adoption of provocative new manners audibly declared his enlarged sense of self. Just as James McCune Smith's introduction to *My Bondage and My Freedom* would frame the ex-slave's journey to Britain in terms of acquisition of manhood, Douglass's performance affect made a similar case on the platform.[126] By forcing audiences to acknowledge the logic of their own conflicted emotions toward an Anglo-American commons, he obliged his public to consider to whom they would or would not "demean" themselves. His Tabernacle appearance, however, was not the end point, of his engagement with transatlantic rhetoric, and for the remainder of Douglass's career he found continued use for themes and symbols drawn from very different sides of the English national past.

Emancipation and Anglo-Saxonism

The final strand to Douglass's invocation of an Anglo-American commons was his repeated focus on two contradictory aspects of Britain's historical relationship to slavery. The first was the commonplace abolitionist trope of praising Britain's pioneering moral and political fortitude in having abolished the African slave trade in its empire a generation earlier. In Douglass's early speeches and his *Narrative* he had avoided the analogy with British emancipation.[127] However, by the time of his tour to England, he was apt to flatter his hosts by declaring how esteem for this historical example resulted in a powerful affective connection— his "peculiar affection for Englishmen, and a respect for the English character"—and sense of mentorship—"the world is looking to England on this subject. As early as I can remember, I have thought of England in connexion with freedom."[128] This was a posture of tutelage widely embraced by abolitionists abroad; in 1855, for instance, Samuel Ringgold Ward told a Hampshire audience that they were "looked upon by the Negro as his especial friends and guardians."[129] Back at home, Douglass used these expressions of affinity for Britain to frame moments of sublime admiration, observing how the nation had "astonished the world by its grandeur," as well as powerful gestures of absolution.[130] Before a New York City anticolonization meeting in 1849, he declared himself ready to "respect them—for I forgive them what they did in days of yore. I respect them for what they have already done, and what they are still doing in our behalf."[131] This positioning allowed for a form of provocative reconciliation whose echoes of Douglass's famous conciliatory letter to his former master Hugh Auld offered a redemptive reading of an Anglo-American commons centered on exoneration as the solution to moral dilemmas.

Emotionally intricate responses of this nature were folded into the series of ceremonial orations Douglass delivered as part of the annual commemorations of Britain's enactment of emancipation on 1 August 1834. Such performances were a central genre of mid-nineteenth-century African-American oratory; black communities in the North had quickly adopted the August date as a festival day, and these events were adopted by northern abolitionists more broadly as a subversive radical surrogate for the Fourth of July.[132] These "Emancipation Day" fêtes were notably integrated events, with mixed-race audiences sometimes numbering in the thousands carrying banners, joining parades, and listening to readings of parliamentary legislation and set-piece oratorical effusions on freedom. These speeches typically relied upon an elaborate counterintuitive rhetoric of contrasts, upending the traditional opposition of tyrannical Britain and America's republic of liberty, and reframing notions of "American freedom" to include antiracism and an end to slavery. What coverage existed in the mainstream press was often hostile, and opponents routinely pointed to the empty contradictions beneath such rhetorical inversions. Orators at an 1858 Emancipation Day events in Poughkeepsie, New York, for example, encouraged the large mixed audiences to consider this "the standing reproach of the American government that while Old England was doing all she could for freedom, slavery should be the law of the republic," yet to the *New York Herald* journalist in the crowd, the realities of London's "less than-triumphant Africa policy" proved the fallacy of the "trite trash of the orators" that day, "that freedom would benefit either negro or country."[133]

Douglass's contributions to these events exploited the date for various rhetorical purposes, the simplest of which was the rebuke of American institutions. During the year following his return from Britain in 1847, he spoke as part of the festivities in Canandaigua, New York, offering a forthright address whose tone and dualistic structure foreshadowed that of his most famous oration, the "July Fourth for the Negro" in nearby Rochester three years later. He began by celebrating "that magnanimous act of British legislation," and honoring the roll call of names who "early struggled in this glorious cause ... Baxter, Addison, Godwin, Sterne, Adam Smith, Gilbert Wakefield," before turning to chastise the dormant churches and impotent politicians of the republic.[134] Such ceremonial epideictic rhetoric sat well with conventional oratorical hymns to the emulation of models of greatness, with a bifurcated logic whereby highlighting Britain's virtue became a vigorous means of spotlighting America's vice:

> How striking and humiliating is the contrast in respect to slavery, between England and America, the mother and the daughter.... the British monarch, self-moved and self-sustained, emancipated, set free and clothed with the dignity of citizenship, nearly a million slaves at a single stroke of the pen.[135]

These speeches were to prove highly adaptive forms of historical narrative. In subsequent years Douglass would work in references to events such as Nat Turner's rebellion, John Brown's "martyrdom" in 1860, and the freeing of the serfs in Russia, telling a crowd in Geneva, New York, that "England is not the only nation whose conduct stands in marked and striking contrast with our own. There stands Russia."[136] In 1848, amid the turmoil in Europe, he was able to celebrate Britain's apparently unique position of stability, praising her "calm, dignified" immunity from the woes of her neighbors and concluding that "my confidence is reposing on what is passing in England—brave, and strong old England ... the heart of the civilized world!"[137] In perhaps the most grandiose of these flourishes, he reasoned in his 1857 Emancipation Day speech that "if only Englishmen may properly celebrate this great concession to justice and liberty, then, sir, we may claim to be Englishmen."[138]

In working through a comparative historical analysis in these and other speeches, Douglass's rhetoric came to rely on a powerful stadial theory of nationhood. This idea, made prominent in Scottish Enlightenment thought, held that society's might be measured along a teleological continuum from savagery through to commercial civilization.[139] Douglass's continual return to the symbol of Britain as cradle of liberty and tolerance involved positioning both that nation and his own within one such historical teleology of progress, in he saw the republic as clearly lagging behind. In his 1857 address, he informed audiences that liberal, industrial nineteenth-century Britain had "literally shot forward with the speed of steam and lightning." For their dual role as instigator and eliminator of the global slavery, he concluded, the people of Britain "were among the first to do us injury, and the first to try to right that injury."[140] This was a view that helped make sense of Douglass's earlier depiction of British tolerance as expressed at the Broadway Tabernacle. The "perfect absence" of prejudice that he and other abolitionists had commended so lavishly was the result of being several steps further toward an imagined egalitarian state of being. However, the theory of progress he offered his listeners was not straightforwardly encouraging. Comparative historical models had led him to conclude that, just as racial superiorities had emerged from periods of trial, violence, and subjection, such ills would only perish through fire. "Some of the most enlightened and highly civilized states of the world to-day," he told audiences in a key late 1893 lecture on Haiti, had been "deeply depraved in morals, manners and customs.... France, England, Italy and Spain have all ... passed through the period of violence."[141] This notion of liberal tolerance as the fruits of bloodshed was emblematic of Douglass's biblical apocalypticism and ideas of national redemption through bloodshed. It was also an understanding of national evolution that connected back to a second aspect of Britain's relationship with slavery: the apparent existence of the practice on its own ancient shores.

Douglass's engagement with the nineteenth-century discourse of Anglo-Saxonism was an ambivalent one. In his speeches and writings, he frequently paid lip service to the widespread prevailing regard for a reputed Anglo-Saxon genius for republican democracy, as when he extolled a white Baltimore audience in 1864 for belonging "to the Anglo-Saxon branch of the great human family ... to the civilization of the nineteenth century, your race is the main spring."[142] Such emphasis upon fanciful racial reimaginings of ancient English history was a running theme through American abolition; Stowe's *Uncle Tom's Cabin* was only the most prominent of many popular works that helped perpetuate the pseudobiological distinction between the capabilities of the "exotic race" and "the hard and dominant Anglo-Saxon."[143] In one sense, this was a discourse that Douglass spent his career trying to dismantle. In multiple lectures, he rejected chauvinistic or hierarchical claims, telling an 1855 audience of black New York youths in New York that "the Negro race equal in every and all respects to the so-called Anglo-Saxon, the superiority of which [is] dinned so constantly in the public ear."[144] To his dismay, such ideas were even found in certain of his former Garrisonian associates who, as he complained in another 1857 speech, "talk of their proud Anglo-Saxon blood as flippantly as those who profess to believe in the natural inferiority of races."[145] He was acutely aware of the racial mixture that defined African-Americans in particular, and mounted powerful critiques of racial essentialism in his major lyceum-format lectures "The Claims of the Negro Ethnologically Considered" and "Our Composite Nationality," in which he argued for the "one-ness of the human race."[146] Even while embracing institutional understandings of an Anglo-American commons, therefore, he had little time for those who sought to exploit its purely racial implications.

However, in his speaking career he did find one productive use for a subtheme of this discourse. In venue after venue, he pointedly reminded American audiences that, under the "Norman yoke," the plight of their much-cherished Saxon looked an awful lot like the bondage from which he had escaped. "It will not be denied that the Anglo-Saxons are a fine race of men, and have done something for the civilization of mankind," he pointedly informed a Boston audience in 1862, "yet who does not know that this new grand and leading race was in bondage and abject slavery upon their own native soil."[147] As Christopher Hanlon has shown, the analogy between Saxon villein and African-American slave was part of a wider national trend for using politicized readings of archaic English history as templates for understanding contemporary quarrels.[148] "Douglass himself would pursue the homology over the course of two decades" following his return from Britain, Hanlon reveals, "tapping the transatlantic genealogies that had circulated through his national culture since at least 1850."[149] Douglass understood that both English and American audiences were apt to project their political aspirations for freedom back to the formative Anglo-Saxon period. This meant that he could strategically exploit the pride of Romantic racism, the rhetoric of freedom, and the profound confusion of terminology surrounding Norman, Saxon, and Anglo-Norman, and unravel what he saw as the contradictions of their historical reading. By taking Anglo-Saxonists at their word, he made their folkloric misconceptions part of his rhetorical arsenal.

The most memorable instance of such reasoning came in his famous January 1865 speech before the Massachusetts American Anti-Slavery Society, a group that he had not addressed for many years, and now returned to as the proud associate of President Lincoln. At Boston's Melodeon theater, he was called to the stage, and at the end of an of an impromptu speech, declared:

> I utterly deny, that we are originally, or naturally, or practically, or in any way, or in any important sense, inferior to anybody on this globe. This charge of inferiority is an old dodge. It has been made available for oppression on many occasions. It is only about six centuries since the blue-eyed and fair-haired Anglo-Saxons were considered inferior by the haughty Normans, who once trampled upon them. If you read the history of the

Norman Conquest, you will find that this proud Anglo-Saxon was once looked upon as of coarser clay than his Norman master, and might be found in the highways and byways of Old England labouring with a brass collar on his neck, and the name of his master marked upon it. You were down then! (laughter and applause) You are up now. I am glad you are up, and I want you to be glad to help us up also. (applause).[150]

Often anthologized as "What the Black Man Wants," the speech laid out claims not just for mere generosity but full equality and suffrage. In front of this New England audience, his cajoling invocation of Anglo-Saxonist slogans made that case by playing particularly effectually on the acutely racial self-esteem of his listeners, who the transcript records had already responded with sympathetic "(laughter)" to a line mocking the notion that "the Yankees are superior to us." Within the "(laughter and applause)" quoted above we might see further flickers of ironic recognition. First, at the conflict between his rhetoric of elevation and the literal positioning of performance, with Douglass speaking *down* from the platform of the Tremont Temple at his supposedly nonpareil audience. But also, more subtly, because the discourse of Anglo-Saxonism placed such emphasis upon a particular type of oratorical prowess. As we shall see from our forthcoming discussion of Thackeray, the approval implicit in references to an apparently "sturdy" or "candid" Anglo-Saxon aesthetic of succinct, brisk, vigorous expression was a ubiquitous feature of coverage of performance culture. If this powerfully direct and unadorned style was such a diagnostic of ancient English lineage, then the curt, paratactic closing lines of Douglass's appeal above seem to make their own stylistic argument for belonging and for the moulding of "coarser clay."

"The Margin Formerly Held by the Platform"

From this high point of engagement with British themes, Douglass's postwar speaking career is marked by growing disillusionment both with the ideals of the Anglo-American commons and with the medium of public speech.[151] This move away from transatlantic rhetoric was driven in part by Douglass's growing sense of disillusionment with British society and politics. In 1859 he had returned to England, in rather sudden and unexpected fashion, having had to flee the United States following the fallout from John Brown's raid on Harper's Ferry. This second trip was a far more muted affair than the first triumphant voyage, and he remained in the North of England and Scotland throughout. As he told audiences there and upon his return, he noticed two troubling new features of British life. The first was what he described to a Leeds audience as "the new and strange doctrine in England ... the doctrine of non-intervention," which he read as a closing-off of the Anglo-American affinities he had previously cherished.[152] The

second change was that he no longer felt it possible to make the "proud boas
fourteen years prior of being treated equally in Britain: "American prejudice
told his Newcastle audience, now "might be found in the streets of Liverpool a..u
in nearly all our commercial towns."[153]

Even the discursive connections that he had previously celebrated between the
two nations had proven their negative potential. Organs of British free speech,
he now found, were frequently also centers of anti-Americanism, and Douglass
found himself attacked by his former friend the British abolitionist George
Thompson, who gave speeches quoting passages from Douglass's lectures on his
previous trip in order to highlight his shifting positions on constitutional abolition.[154] Transatlantic publishing and performance circuits had also become to
Douglass a medium not just for liberal values but a route for proslavery propaganda and minstrel exhibits. In the place of his earlier metaphors that imagined
the voice of freedom heading west, Douglass began to speak of transatlantic contagion, and before a Bradford audience in January 1860 decried that "the moral
sense of this country [was] being corrupted by the influence of the system on the
other side of the Atlantic."[155]

Douglass's sense of disillusionment was exacerbated by British conduct during the Civil War. Following what he saw as the treacherous equivocations of
Westminster toward the Union, he began to soften his reliance on tropes of
Atlantic affinity. This growing estrangement was marked in several ways. For one
thing, after Tsar Alexander II's abolition of serfdom in Russia in 1861, Douglass
had other models than Britain to use in his Emancipation Day speeches.[156] After
Lincoln's own proclamation in 1863, it was possible to tell American audiences
that though "England set in motion a great moral tidal wave ... the abolition of
the slave, in the US, was an incomparably greater act."[157] There were also subtler
ways in which his Anglophilia was tempered. An example is how his lectures
began to qualify his respect for British oratory; by 1867 we find Douglass telling
a St. Louis audience, "I have listened to the eloquence of their noblest orators ...
I am free to say, without wishing to disparage the English Houses of Parliament
[that] ... our Senate is the superior."[158]

Douglass's postwar rhetoric therefore saw him move toward a broader form
of internationalism. In place of the strategic Anglophilia that had long been the
mainstay of his cultural politics, his thought increasingly emphasized instead
the unity of the global dispossessed. His growing engagement with the realities
of American and British imperialist expansion led him to a more global view
of issues of emancipation, racial equality, and citizenship. For instance, his
increased involvement in the Irish question also led him by the time of his 1880s
speeches to present the "poor, ragged, hungry, starving and oppressed" condition
of Ireland as a "standing menace to the power and glory of England."[159] In place
of the Anglo-Saxonism with which he had flirted earlier in his career, he now proclaimed to audiences merely that "the love of power is one of the strongest traits

in the Anglo-Saxon race."[160] His earlier laudatory idealizations of British society also gave way to more nuanced sketches that deconstructed myths of empire, echoing the "condition of England" bifurcations of Benjamin Disraeli or Thomas Carlyle in describing "two Englands ... distinct and separate" between the liberal, working nation and its conservative Establishment.[161]

Most fundamentally, Douglass moved from a strategic focus on the Anglo-American commons to a more decisively Africanist set of affinities and rhetorical reference points. [162] We can see this in action in his important and frequently repeated lyceum lecture "Our Composite Nationality," delivered from 1869 onward, which moved toward a more capacious global view of black diasporic identities. But the culmination of his Africanist development is best seen in the symbolic weight he came to attach to Haiti. He had written about the country repeatedly since the early 1860s, heralding its 1791–1804 revolution as instrumental to the nineteenth-century teleology of progress, with the destiny of its people a key theme of humanitarianism and international law. After he served the Harrison administration as consul general to Haiti between 1889 and 1890, the nation became the subject of the two last prominent speeches of his career, both delivered in Chicago in 1893: one before a mixed public crowd at the dedication of the World's Fair's Haitian Pavilion; the second before an African-American audience at the city's African Methodist Episcopal Church.[163] In those speeches, the Caribbean nation now took on the place that Britain had once held as the symbolic site from which "they struck for the freedom of every black man in the world.... the greatest of all our modern teachers."[164] In the lecture, England remains "foremost among the modern nations in commerce and manufactures," but the reduction of this estimation is made particularly sharp by its contrast with the land of Toussaint L'Ouverture, which "will remain in the forefront of nations, and, like the star of the North, will shine on and shine for ever."[165] Douglass's rhetoric had always been fluid. He had balanced shifting estimations of global power against an astute reading of the sympathies and appetites of his many audiences. And as his worldview, reformist agenda and understanding of identity politics shifted, so too did his symbolic repertoire. As Hanlon puts it, "The resolution of the slavery question relieved US thinkers somewhat of the importance of feeling English," and gave license to greater eclecticism of reference points.[166]

This softening of his transatlantic rhetoric was mirrored by his increased tendency to downplay his previous praise for the practices of the Anglo-American commons, in particular that of public lecturing. Douglass's relative valuation of speech and print fluctuated during his career. He had used the lecturing medium across various platforms as a powerful vehicle for black advancement, and for the dissemination of antiracist ideas. His energy on the Garrisonian and later the lyceum circuit had helped break down barriers between various forms of "lecturing," and between the social vanguard and middle-class respectability. Yet though it had helped him achieve prominence, the constraints of even unaffiliated lecturing had become ever more apparent. His shift to the role of editor in the late 1840s is therefore rightly seen as far more central to the second, broader phase of his development; not least because, as critics from Fanuzzi to Patricia McKee have argued, the liberating color-blindness of print allowed the period's African-American intellectuals to flourish by creating a freer disembodied subjectivity.[167] The medium of speech and the respect it commanded among American popular culture had certainly frequently failed him. Perhaps the most iconic incident occurred in December 1860 when a talk at Boston's Tremont Temple was broken up by a mob, and Douglass was beaten—events that led to his delivery of a famously strident impromptu plea for free speech while lecturing Faneuil Hall the following week.[168] The triumph of emancipation seemed to mark a diminished role for embodied performance. Douglass later recalled feeling "that I had reached the end of the noblest and best part of my life, the anti-slavery platform had performed its work and my voice was no longer needed."[169] The sentiments of his earlier rhetoric, in which institutions of national and transnational public voice held the potential to transcend political constraints, grew increasingly distant.

At the twilight of his career, however, we can see nostalgia for the power of the mid-Anglo-American platform creep into his rhetoric, a tone that helps us grasp what it had meant to him. In 1887 he delivered a public lecture in Washington, DC, devoted to his recent experiences on a purely touristic third visit to Britain with his wife. And in metarhetorical fashion, he reflected on the futility of the exercise:

> There is indeed, scarcely a ripple on the social, intellectual and political life of Europe which we do not almost instantly know and feel in America. Not only does it seem useless to make a voyage to Europe for such a purpose [educating fellow Americans], but useless to presume to enlighten an American audience by lecturing on the subject, and indeed I may say upon any other subject. The press is every day narrowing the margin formerly held by the platform, and is more and more assuming the office of lecturer, teacher and preacher. Our people are doing more with their eyes and less with their ears than formerly. They are reading more and hearing less. They are thinking more and speaking less.[170]

It was a striking and ambivalent elegy for the midcentury lecture hall. What had once stood as a symbol of vital cultural exchange has become redundant, leaving no space for group formation through the force of great oratory. The potency of the earlier moment stemmed from a combination of rarity, distance, and a national eagerness for British respect—elements diminished in the generations that followed, as overconnectedness diluted the romance and purchase of transatlantic commentary. The Atlantic reform lecture had never been as potent as in those years of Douglass's emergence, when his rise coincided with that of the lyceum and reformist lecture platforms. It had never held a "margin," or edge, as vigorous as during his own 1847 transformation on the stage of the Broadway Tabernacle. Yet our next chapter takes us directly back into that context. Tracing the "ripples" that spread from Emerson's lectures on the same theme will help us continue our investigation into the cultural role of the very "platform" that Douglass mourned.

[Handwritten marginal notes:]

→ lyceum as space of temperement cultivation.
→ passage from anti-est to conservative figure takes place on stage / in reception

Britain as Order   (Emerson in rel to pol + class struggles over Anglophobia)

— Media accounts of Emerson's full range of performance as the way communities piece together his aphoristic, undigestible style / pronouncements - Medium is message.
   ↳ creating performance style as a "laudable national synechdoche" / "an avator of national eloquence"

• Aestheticisation of his reformism into a national manner, by 1850.
   ↳ Scrutinising on his transAt return, "England."

• Balanced appraisal of Eng read as eulogy
   ↳ Balance is performed, metacommentary → difficulty of registering in lyceum environment.
   ↳ Emerson's performances allowed his cul nationalism to be misrecognized as praise for Br producing oppositional readings.

• Locating lyceum performance as a key venue for what has become characteristic Emerson "lit" style.

↳ Contextualising through class antagonisms surrounding performance of Britishness after Astor Place riot.
   ↳ selective interps of Emerson's studious balance provide "a potential glimpse of the antianist boisterousness of the city's performance culture." -105 showing that the point of reception was product of a cul in which readers wanted to hear the audience used the zeitgeist.
   ↳ Press using speech to politically shape pub sphere around Ang-Am commons. Herald's pos reading of his balance as response to Astor Pl.
      ↳ framing praise as cosmopolitan nationalism

• Ohio press reads mainly to distance itself from N.E. to produce its own Emerson as statement of regionalism rather than transAt rel.
• Conc: exploiting Lyceum stage's orientation towards cul compromise, Emerson was in turn read so as to fashion a conservative image. "Whig stewardship" reigning in "the more indulgent + violent strains of Anglophobia."

• Lyceum as middle ground in what he claims, departing from Levine, is the early beginnings of high/low cul split.
   ↳ Early middlebrow cul — m/c formation

Britain as Order

LISTENING TO RALPH WALDO EMERSON'S "ENGLAND"

On the corner of Nassau and Beekman Streets, the lecture room of Manhattan's Clinton Hall was filling up for the evening performance. After struggling to secure high-quality speakers during 1849, the Mercantile Library Association had scheduled an impressive cast of orators for the winter 1850 season, and such was the opening performer's popularity, organizers had been "strongly urged to choose another hall."[1] Complaints about the state of the city's lecturing facilities had been escalating of late, and Clinton Hall in particular was dismissed as "out of the way, too small and too uncomfortable."[2] Nonetheless, on the evening of Tuesday, 22 January 1850, a significant audience had begun to assemble, comprising several correspondents from the chief newspapers of the city. One recalled that the auditorium was "crowded to its utmost capacity"; another observed that "a large number were obliged to go from the door without obtaining admission"; a third wrote that even among those who gained entry, "many had to shift for accommodation."[3] The magazine writer Nathaniel Parker Willis was fortunate enough to get inside, but having arrived late,

> found the place crowded, and no chance of a near view of the speaker. The only foothold to be had was up against the farthest wall; and a row of unsheltered gas-lights blazed between us and the pulpit, with one at either ear-tip of the occupant, drowning the expression of his face completely in the intense light a little behind it.[4]

With this ecclesiastical tableau, Willis captures an atmosphere of almost messianic anticipation. The evening's performance was the first time many had seen this well-known, out-of-town orator, and expectation for intellectual, aural, and visual stimulation from the "pulpit" was intense.

Ralph Waldo Emerson's appearance at Clinton Hall was clearly a media event, yet to many in the audience the material he was to present was already familiar. He had agreed to deliver a piece performed several times in New England during the previous winter entitled "England," reports of which had appeared in both the American and the British press.[5] Though it was to prove one of his most popular lectures, its tone had surprised early audiences: its subject matter was less abstract than in his typical talks; and moreover, many heard it as a startlingly positive appraisal of British society for someone typically thought of as a cultural nationalist. Reporting on an early performance in Providence, Rhode Island, a Boston journalist informed readers that Emerson had "lain it on quite thick, I assure you," and his apparent eulogy to the miracle of British order and stability was widely censured as a provocatively reverent account.[6]

By contrast, of the reporters at Clinton Hall the following January, a number found much to commend in such provocation. The *New York Herald* commented on its "surprising epithets," "singular conjunctions," and "striking contraries of ideas."[7] In the *Home Journal*, Willis praised Emerson's mastery of "surprise" and his "very bold and fearless comment."[8] The *Albion* thought it possessed an admirably "bold, uncompromising love of truth, and a carelessness of consequences."[9] Such divergence of response was of course not unfamiliar to Emerson and, as we have seen from the case of Douglass, was not uncommon in discussions of the popular lecture circuit. However, the reception history of this particular performance offers instructive insights into the construction of Emerson's persona and into antebellum debates over the ideas of "order" contained within notions of both English society and the culture of deference toward it. The afterlife of this one performance helps us trace the development of lecturing as a force of polite middle-class immersion.

Since the operative meanings of lectures such as "England" were fashioned by the interpretive gestures of the print media, Emerson's full impact can be understood only by attempting to recapture the figure he struck both on the lyceum platforms and in the newspaper lecture columns of antebellum America.[10] The recent publication of his later lectures has generated renewed interest in Emerson the speaker, focusing on how these neglected pieces mark his intellectual growth.[11] In particular, the work of Mary Kupiec Cayton, Sallee Fox Engstrom, and Bonnie Carr O'Neill has demonstrated that an emphasis on issues of audience reception and the communal construction of meanings is particularly rewarding in the case of so copiously documented an individual as Emerson.[12] As his most recent editors argue, the Emerson of the platform is a figure whose cultural place "we are just now beginning to appreciate."[13] Newspaper lecture coverage was instrumental in establishing this significance, since, as Cayton maintains, the "impact" of his lecturing "may have depended less on what he intended than on what key communities of interpreters made of him."[14] The ways in which the listeners in the media articulated what they heard was often a consciously partial ideological process.

In this chapter, I pursue this line of inquiry to examine the traces of audience reception of "England" in two distinct settings: its Clinton Hall performance and its subsequent recital during appearances in Ohio in May 1850. This year was pivotal for Emerson, representing his final transition from secular preacher to a professional lecturer of national stature, reaching new audiences in both urbanized and newly settled America. Shorn of much of his troubling early radicalism, his cultural symbolism was in flux, available for audience manipulation and annexation. In what follows, I argue that reports of "England" in the Manhattan media performed such appropriation, using a reading drama of appraisal in the lecture as a useful shoring up of transatlantic affection in the wake of anti-British urban upheavals of the late 1840s. Tracing this process of refraction further, I then explore how subsequent responses to his Ohio performances demonstrate *appropriation* a pattern of resistance to the metropolitan interpretations, and an attempt to *Emerson* appropriate anew the resonance of Emerson's appraisal for Midwestern realities. *for geo + class*

This chapter offers a detailed account of the context, delivery, and conflict- *specific* ing readings of these Emerson performances. In doing so, it restates a running *ideological* theme of this book: that the lecture circuit, so often omitted from discussions of *purposes.* broader performance culture, needs to be reconnected to wider debates within the antebellum media concerning Anglo-American show practices, physicality, and manners.[15] Such reconstruction allows us to recapture a sense of how the press seized on both the "England" talk itself, and aspects of Emerson's performance style, making the discursive contests over thoughts voiced in spaces such as Clinton Hall a means of questioning and shoring up civic order and patriotic urban kinship.[16]

Deciphering Emerson the Lecturer

In Emerson, we confront the central cultural figure of the "mid-century explosion of American speech."[17] Synonymous with the lyceum and among its most enduringly popular speakers, he was present at the inception of the short-lived profession of the public lecturer, and his career roughly coincided with its rise and fall.[18] He is, argues Bode, simply "the only lecturer in the movement who could unhesitatingly be called great."[19] Such prominence means that, unlike the other orators in this book, we know a great deal about his platform activities thanks to his own copious journals, extensive biographical scholarship, and the sheer quantity of contemporary testimony regarding his speaking engagements.[20] More than any other performer, Emerson was also a theorist of the lyceum, recording his views of the platform circuit, the process of lecturing, and the relationship of audience and performer. He thus presents a unique opportunity for more thoroughly understanding the relationship of oratorical intent and audience response on the platform circuit.

Beyond the content and context of Emerson's lectures, the idiosyncratic visual and aural properties of his performances also merit detailed attention. It is equally vital that we develop an appreciation for the interpretive stances involved in accounts of these nontextual, sensory aspects of his platform art, and the degree to which accounts of his lecturing operate as ideologically freighted texts. As I have argued, lecture reports were often deeply felt and carefully artic-ulated responses to communal oral experience. As with the other performers in this book, the process of working up a concise literary response to Emerson the lecturer represented both an artful delay of interpretation and a channeling of audience reaction. However, the combined strategic elusiveness of his message and performance style renders such documentation especially valuable in the generation of cultural meanings.

Emerson developed an adversarial relationship to such reporting in response to its erratic entanglement of oral and print values and to what he saw as its finan-cially injurious theft of intellectual property.[21] Such opposition may have contrib-uted to his cultivation of an "unrecordable" idiom; both his notoriously elliptical style and his habit of rearranging pieces on the fly at the lectern seem at times spe-cifically designed to thwart such reporting.[22] By the mid-1850s he was perform-ing an average of eighty lectures a year, one of the most visible and gazed-upon literary speakers in the nation, with audiences attending partly out of a desire to sate their curiosity for spectacle. At the outset of the decade, however, Emerson was still sufficiently unfamiliar to remote communities—and to some extent to New York audiences—to represent a novel subject for discussion. His 1850 tour, and performances of "England" in particular, therefore, occasioned some of the most revelatory reports of his career.

As this book argues, lecturing was a conflation of intellectual and physical performance, with performers' costume, carriage, and gesture inviting interpre-tation as texts. For a figure as elusive as Emerson, such scrutiny acquired consid-erable significance and his appearance was often the focus of reports. As his first biographer, George Willis Cooke, maintained, "His voice and manner become a fine commentary on his written thought, giving to it new and unexpected mean-ings."[23] More than for almost any other speaker, accounts of Emerson's perfor-mances attempt to capture the man in full: voice, manner, and appearance. As a result, reports occasionally read as fictional sketches; one such account from Boston in 1854 began by observing,

> When Ralph Waldo Emerson stood up in the Tabernacle last night, one could have heard a pin drop. He had entered the hall with that shy, shrink-ing manner ... but when he began to speak, and his voice, rich and musical "to the ultimate degree" broke the silence with those well-commented sen-tences, the vast audience was hushed into a close attention.[24]

Here we encounter some characteristic and recurring tropes of reportage on Emerson's lectures: an emphasis on music, and his deceptively diffident physi-cality. His vocal properties and oral delivery were repeatedly described in musi-cal terms, both euphonic and discordant. Emerson himself often characterized his approach to lecturing in a comparable fashion, calling it "a panharmonicon combining every note on the longest gamut, from the explosion of cannon to the tinkle of a guitar."[25] Reports speak of his peculiarly compelling baritone, and the melodic nature of his oratory: an oral flow that, unlike the performances of Edward Everett or Daniel Webster, was hypnotic rather than pyrotechnic in character. It was a voice that writers repeatedly felt obliged to capture in their reports, cementing its place in the experience of Emerson's art. Margaret Fuller described it as "a grave body tone, full and sweet rather than sonorous, yet flexible ... the words uttered in those tones floated a while above us, then took root in the memory like winged seed."[26] Control and modulation of voice was a key part of the artifice of Emerson's performance practice, which seems for many to have bestowed new meaning on his words. In particular, observers commend his facility with what we might describe in musical performance as "ritenuto": the delay or deferral of expectation, creating an effect of suspense and spontaneity.

> Occasionally at the end of a sentence he would suddenly stop, for what seemed like a long time, and, with his eyes uplifted upon his audience, looking like one inspired. Everyone in the audience seemed to stop breathing, as if afraid to mar the solemn impression produced. Then another sentence would be commenced on another key; and, rising higher and higher, his voice would again drop to lower tones, like the solemn peals of an organ.[27]

Such musical comparisons often seem designed to disavow the place of conventional rational intent in Emerson's discourses, positioning them beyond conventional analysis. Aestheticizing his vocal properties in this way licensed a wider, potentially idiosyncratic range of interpretations of his message.

Second, as in the above reference to his "shy shrinking manner," Emerson's style was often described in terms of its paradoxical reserve. His physicality also attracted much attention in reports, a fact interesting in itself since the body is generally considered a topic frequently overlooked in Emerson's thought.[28] His *carte de visite* of 1852 presents a full-length portrait exhibiting what reports continually characterize as his conventional, sober New England attire, the epitome of bourgeois circumspection.[29] (See Figure 3.1.) Reports speak of an inexpressive, awkward figure of almost six feet, often caricatured, as in the famous Christopher Cranch illustration, as an angular ectomorph—an aspect that led Fredrika Bremer to term him "an animated icicle."[30] Both vocally and physically, Emerson represented a very distinct model from the exaggerated gestures and virtuoso vocal styling of American theatrical performers such as Edwin Forrest, or lyceum peers such as Oliver Wendell Holmes.[31]

Yet reports observe a paradox at work in these performances, a disjunction or interplay between Emerson's text and body: his words imparted vigorous ideas that were often threatening and disruptive; his body projected calm reason, even staidness. In his account of "England," Willis stressed the lack of correspondence between such a voice and Emerson's relatively unprepossessing body,

FIGURE 3.1 *Ralph Waldo Emerson, carte de visite, 1852*

a curious contradiction which we tried in vain to analyze.... What seems
strange is to hear such a voice proceeding from such a body. It is a voice
with shoulders in it, which he has not—with lungs in it far larger than his—
with a walk in it which the public never sees ... the want of correspondence
between the Emerson that goes in at the eye and the Emerson that goes in
at the ear.[32]

It was a performance style seemingly characterized by serenity and order, and
a kind of intoxicating self-possession. It presented a spectacle of composure
that communicated moral meanings, exemplifying both a Whig reformist stress
on self-control, and the kind of benign, cosmic indifference and insouciance
explored in his essay "Experience" (1844). It also carried implications of class: the

patrician body on display, in control of its faculties, and a social luminescence and poise similarly championed in "Manners" (also 1844).

One particularly intriguing property of Emerson's lecturing deportment, captured in the *carte de visite* and in the portrait painted in Edinburgh in 1848 by David Scott, was his use of his right hand. "His customary gesture," maintains Robert D. Richardson, "was to clench his right fist—knuckles upward, arm bent at the elbow—then to deliver a downward blow of the forearm, full of power bridled."[33] This compelling physical trait speaks to the level of artifice in Emerson's performance style. Of such quirks, his first biographer maintained that these oddities were not, "as has so often been said, cultivated, but the natural manner of the man ... the marks of a genuine simplicity and sincerity."[34] However, Emerson's self-consciousness, and his repeated delivery of particular pieces, seems to suggest a more considered, complicated method of almost theatrical preparation.

His use of the fist also embodies his adversarial conception of the lecturing process. By the 1840s, Emerson was conceiving of oratory as "an opportunity ... for painting in fire my thought & being agitated to agitate"; the lecture room was "the true Church of the coming time" into which audiences came "not knowing what shall befall them there, but uncommitted and willing victims to reason and love."[35] This lexicon of conflict and violence reveals a tendency to view the lyceum as an agonistic space of conflict and provocation. Each performance was a chance to transform the way in which listeners conceived of and conducted their lives, a chance to "agitate" audiences and thus alter their moral vision.

Emerson had earned a reputation as a gadfly of the lyceum, famous for his ability to exercise and exasperate listeners. As Bode states, "He did not entertain audiences; on the contrary, he sometimes irritated them."[36] Certain aspects of his performance were markedly oppositional: he offered willfully incoherent or contradictory messages; he took aim at audiences' fundamental beliefs; he customarily refused to offer closure, or obey traditional structures. Of his Clinton Hall lectures, a reporter in the *New Englander and Yale Review* paid him the period's customary compliment to contrarians and attention-seekers, considering him as a "sort of intellectual Sam Patch," the famous jumping daredevil.[37] Another report of his 1850 tour judged that "there never was any preaching more direct and pungent; more aggressive or more provoking."[38] Yet the escalation of national requests for lecture engagements through the 1850s and 1860s testifies to a surprising degree of audience receptivity.

The intent of Emerson's provocative approach was and remains hard to grasp. Comprehending his utterances, which regularly defy confident analysis even for modern readers equipped with full textual apparatus, was a problem infinitely more intractable to the audiences of his day. Listeners thus took away whatever they could understand or discern. In its rejection of linear neoclassical logic and its notion of "creative reading as well as his creative writing," his oeuvre seemed to invite, even endorse, divergent responses.[39] As this chapter will explore, reporting involved an often conscious process of *misconstrual* and *mishearing*. Accounts of Emerson the lecturer were a key means by which communities could annex their own version of his positions: on radicalism, reform, progress, the market, nationality, and modernity.

The process by which various constituencies and publications constructed Emerson's meanings was in fact a recognized contemporary phenomenon. Speaking of his Clinton Hall lectures, the *Christian Inquirer* observed in March 1850 that "the reviews, magazines, newspapers, foreign and domestic, have made it no small part of their business these few months past, to say their say about Mr. Emerson," observing shrewdly of this cacophony,

> Some must adore what others curse, and love what others hate, to keep the beam of things easy.... Mr. Emerson seems to be used in a good many places, as the wagon full of chain cables is used on board our steamboats, to trim ship. If the orthodoxy of a man is suspected, let him abuse Mr. Emerson; if his liberality is doubted, let him praise him.[40]

One example of such "use" of Emerson's lecturing was to present his performance style as a laudable national synecdoche. A theme that emerges from certain accounts of his performance is the paradoxically American—or at least representatively "New England" —nature of his performance. "We Yankees are thought to be fond of the spread-eagle style," observed James Russell Lowell, "and nothing can be more remote from that than this," before proposing: "What, then is his secret? Is it not that he out-Yankees us all?"[41] By 1850, Emerson was beginning to acquire the status of an avatar of national eloquence; his diffidence, insouciance, and self-possession were taken as symbols of a certain strain of "American" speech. It contained the peculiarly republican combination that Fuller characterized as "the union of an even rustic plainness with lyric inspiration."[42] Attendees of "England" in 1850 therefore justifiably wondered whether these qualities had survived his recent transatlantic exposure.

Above all, Emerson's lecturing projected a variety of cultural and moral values that combined to establish a paradoxical, peculiarly pliable celebrity. At the time of his bringing his "England" material to the platform, these projected values were beginning to coalesce. To attend an Emerson lecture in 1850 meant the excitement of proximity to an increasingly recognized native philosophical voice. With speakers such as Greeley, it still meant the associative frisson of reform, but in Emerson's case, it meant radical energy circumscribed in an almost neutered, aestheticized form. It afforded audiences throughout the nation the spectacle of Unitarianism, of New England intellectualism, oddity, and eccentricity. Moreover, it meant the opportunity to interpret, decipher, and scrutinize the character of one of the nation's most prominent moral critics. Having just returned from the seat of world power, and now a transatlantic celebrity, his verdict on the moral character of Britain was therefore highly anticipated. Following his trip to Europe and his troublingly pro-British lecture in Boston with interest, New York newspapers were eager to assess firsthand the extent to which this symbol of Yankee intellectual independence had been tainted—physically or mentally—by his global exposure.[43]

"England" as Affirmation of Balance

One of his most popular performances, "England" was delivered under varying titles dozens of times throughout the Northeast and Midwest during 1848–51.[44] An analytical consideration of British modernity and an extended reflection upon the question of "Why England is England," it represented an early version of the influential transatlantic vision of *English Traits* (1856).[45] That book, which shares with the lecture a similar elusive tone, has enjoyed a troubled and divided response in recent criticism. Commentators have variously regarded Emerson's apparently benign assessment of midcentury Britain as a maturation of his global vision; as an underhanded, disingenuous "double-cross"; or as an evasion of domestic sectional tensions.[46] Thanks to this upsurge in recent attention, we have enriched our understanding of Emerson's evolving response to transatlantic relations and Anglo-Saxon culture, but such consideration has to date neglected the gestation of these themes on the lecture circuit, and the light that can be shed by the complex history of audience response.

The "England" lecture represents an important moment for those who read Emerson's later career as a drift from utopian idealism toward the accommodation of industrial market capitalism.[47] During the 1840s, he had been moving from the enraptured idealism of his earlier work toward a benign skepticism and concern with the apprehension of social structures, and "England" was an expression of this new, urbane Emerson. Like *English Traits*, it remains a dissonant work within his canon: at odds with his often caricatured cultural nationalist agenda, an apparent shrinkage of vision and lowering of sights to terrestrial, mundane concerns. In addressing as its subject the most glittering of nations, it was also a seeming abandonment of his previous emphasis on "low," democratic subject matter.[48] However, compared to the other texts in this book its most striking formal feature was what Spiller and Ferguson have characterized as the "dispassionate depth and balance" of Emerson's middle period.[49] Just like his more celebrated "Fugitive Slave Law" address of the following year, "England" seems designed to be read as an expressive speech act that, unlike many of his earlier more elusive gestures, conveyed affiliation with particular social positions. To many, it sounded like a surprisingly affirmative gesture toward British society.

Though characteristically resistant to linear summary, "England" contained some key strands.[50] It purported to be an account of experiences gained on his recent lecture tour; like *English Traits*, it began with an impressionistic passage describing the visceral experience of British modernity, before interrogating the paradox of the nation's "success" through the question of "Why England

Is England." Emerson's idiosyncratic theories pointed to the temperate British climate, the strong diet, the presence of an aristocratic class, the history of racial mixing, and other intangible qualities such as English "pluck." Various anecdotal illustrations were introduced to support these arguments, and he concluded by denouncing prophecies of the nation's imminent decline. On the surface, at least, it was an affirmation of English modernity and supremacy, conveyed through a series of bold, counterintuitive statements.

In one sense, his choice of topic represented a compromise for the platform circuit—a presentation of accessible material, rich in personal anecdote. Of a comparable later lecture, "France" (1854), Emerson privately remarked that it was with such pieces that "he liked to reward the young people for good behavior during the other metaphysical lessons."[51] Since his British tour had been less profitable than he had anticipated, "England" was, of course, also a topic that might reliably offer financial reward. Writing to his brother William in August 1848, Emerson was "not without hope, first or last, to make the whole [British] Excursion pay itself."[52] Converting the excursion into a lyceum performance, he had attempted to do just this; he confirmed to William the following February that he had been "a hack of lectures ... the 'London Lectures' in Boston have been a tolerable success."[53] In some settings, it was a stand-alone lecture; in others it formed part of the "Conduct of Life" series; on at least two occasions it was used as a last-minute, impromptu replacement.

The genre of subject matter into which "England" fell was in fact not unprecedented for Emerson. In 1834, at the beginning of his platform career, he had delivered two travel accounts of Italy in various Massachusetts venues, complete with numerous visual aids.[54] In 1843, he had attempted a holistic treatment of a culture in a New York lecture series on New England, very much in the mode of his great mentor, Madame de Staël, whose *De l'Allemagne* was the most influential model to hand for such expansive cultural analysis.[55] However, as one might anticipate, the figure most instrumental in the development toward the lecture was Thomas Carlyle. "England" and *English Traits* were key documents in what has been termed the "public continuation of a private dialogue."[56] The aesthetic and conceptual approach of these "condition of England" writings was a catalyst for the development of Emerson the cultural observer: it is worth recalling that Carlyle also pointedly considered "The English" from an external point of view.[57] In "Self-Reliance," Emerson had famously argued against his culture's worship of travel, and in his correspondence with Carlyle had maintained "the view of Britain is excellent from New England."[58] Reading *Past and Present* seems to have been instrumental in an appetite to experience anew the compelling, evolving phenomenon of British modernity. However, Carlyle also presented an instructive model of what to avoid in such depictions. As expressed in his 1844 review of *Past and Present* in *Dial*, one of Emerson's central reservations about Carlyle's depiction was its lack of balance:

> It appears to us as a certain disproportion in the picture, caused by the obtrusion of the whims of the painter ... the habitual exaggeration of the

tone wearies whilst it stimulates. It is felt to be so much deduction from the universality of the picture. It is not serene sunshine, but everything is seen in lurid stormlights. Every object attitudinizes, to the very mountains and stars almost, under the refractions of this wonderful humorist, and instead of the common earth and sky, we have a Martin's Creation or Judgment Day.[59]

As a result, composure and evenness became the central principles of his depiction in "England."

The ostensible theme for the lecture was an attempt to account for Britain's historical greatness, but Emerson's approach is characterized by continual qualifications and a self-conscious register of cool analysis. Toward the beginning of the talk, Emerson announces:

Some of the causes of the historical importance of England, I shall enumerate. But I premise with this remark, that the praise of England is not that it has freed itself from the evils under which other countries labor, not that England has found out how to create wealth and power without the creation of poverty and crime,—No, for all have these griefs and England also; but, that England has with this evil produced, in the last five hundred years, a greater number of strong, wise, educated, and humane men,—a greater number of excellent and finished men, than any other nation.[60]

In almost legalistic, scientific diction, he speaks of the process of "enumeration," and treats "the praise of England" as an objective task of *epideictic* rhetoric: a willful but qualified choice. Emerson ultimately arrives at a positive assessment of Britain, but wishes to be understood as rendering a critical appreciation, and in the parenthetical aside above ("all have these griefs") is careful to implicate American society in contemporary social dilemmas.

Throughout the lecture, Emerson maintains an evenness of tone through qualifications ("once there was mysticism in the British mind ... now there is musty, self-conceited decorum" [165]) and caveats ("It is not to be disguised, however, that here is much in this English culture, so much prized at home, so much admired abroad ... built on wealth, built on trifles" [161]). Listeners repeatedly encounter the kind of metaphors of visual presentation and concealment used in his above Carlyle review, which serve as a metacommentary on his method of balanced appreciation. In a central later image of the lecture, such figurative language is revived as Emerson concedes that, "in drawing these sketches, I am well aware there is a dark side of England, which I have not wished to expose":

There are two Englands;—rich, Norman, Saxon, learned, social England,— seated in castles, halls, universities, and middle-class houses of admirable completeness and comfort, and poor, Celtic, peasant, drudging, Chartist England, in hovels and workhouses, cowed and hopeless. I only recognize this fact in passing. It is important that it be stated. It will not help us now to dwell on it.

England is the country of the rich. The great poor man does not yet
appear. Whenever he comes, England will fall like France. (164)[61]

Operating in this register of visual strategies allows him to explore the tension
between the twin demands of sober analysis and artistic representation. In this
passage—one of his rare gestures toward the grotesque idiom of Carlyle—we
receive the lecture's only glimpse of the ethical problems faced by British poverty,
a problem Emerson's journal entries record so vividly, and which Mann had so
graphically treated.[62] Interestingly, we also receive a racialized analysis of midcentury British social divisions. Christopher Hanlon has recently explored the
ways in which American writers of the antebellum period, south and north, drew
upon British history to present similar oppositional typologies of Norman and
Saxon, deriving legitimacy by analogue for domestic sectional divisions.[63] Here
Emerson complicates such a discourse by figuring the Celtic fringe of the nation
as an underclass socially, architecturally, and intellectually divorced from the
dominant union of Norman *and* Saxon.

But perhaps more revealing than the relatively conventional typologies artic-
ulated in this passage is Emerson's metacommentary on his own analysis: his
even-handed desire not "to expose" the "dark side"; that this "fact" should only
be recognized "in passing"; that "it will not help us now to dwell on it." At such
moments, we are provided with glimpses of the conscious modulation of a performance of interpretation. Presenting an exploration of British success is conceived of in terms of proportion, and of additions and "deductions," a term from
his *Dial* review that reappears at the end of the lecture: "With all the deductions
from the picture which truth requires, I find the English to have a thorough good
nature; they are a true, benign, gentle, benevolent, hospitable and pious race,
fearing God, and loving man." The balance that embodied his own approach
was, ultimately, a quality he commended in the English natural character—"a
certain balance of qualities in their nature, corresponding to what we call temper
in steel ... neither too cold, nor too hot; neither too swift, nor too slow" (162).
His stance of impersonal inquiry thus serves to mimic what he presents as the
"tempered" nature of English national character, a stylistic correlative to this
particular English "trait."

Emerson's piece was thus a broadside against excess, luridness, and hyper-
bole. It consisted of a series of consciously bold, subtly counter-intuitive
appraisals, but strove for dispassionate composure. Its criticisms of Britain
were real, but decorously voiced. In this way, "England" appears not as a
mere concession to popular taste, but rather a significant statement, in a
mature, confident, ethnographic register. However, as an oral performance,
it proved more problematic. For all of Emerson's figurative concern with
visual strategies—a medium of delayed effects, modification, and artful
"disguise"—these proved qualities hard to resolve in oral performance—
a medium of near-instantaneous apprehension of cumulatively unrolling

meanings. When Carlyle read reports of its 1849 Boston rendition, he wrote to Emerson in praise:

> Your beautiful curious little discourse (report of a discourse) about the English was sent me by Neuberg; I thought it, in my private hear, one of the best words (for *hidden* genius lodged in it) I had ever heard; so sent it to the *Examiner*, from which it went to the *Times* and all the other Papers: an excellent sly little word.[64]

Crucially, however, this verdict on its understated, "sly," "hidden" nature was often missed in its reception. It was a problem of comprehension particularly acute on the lyceum stage. Amid the unique, more obviously compelling properties of Emerson's performance, audiences risked missing his modulation and subtlety. Misunderstandings or mishearings of its balanced assessment of Britain reveal the disparity of intention and consequence in lyceum lecturing, since aspects of delivery made the piece appear more of a eulogy than it actually was.

Hearing "England" as Eulogy

Three moments in particular appear to have registered most deeply in lecture reports, the first of which was Emerson's opening passage. Though early performances seemed to have commenced with an impromptu, anecdotal introduction, the manuscript begins with what was to become the opening gesture—a striking paragraph that commences the experience of England in medias res:

> The traveler, on arriving in England, is struck at once with the cultivation. On every side, he sees the triumph of labor. Man has subdued and made everything. The country is a garden. Under that ash-colored sky, the fields are so combed and rolled, that it seems as if they had been finished with a pencil instead of a plough. The structures that compose the towns, have been piled by the wealth and skill of ages. Nothing is left as it was made. Rivers, hills, valleys, the sea all feel the hand of a master. The long habitation of a powerful and ingenious race has turned every rood of land to its best use, has found all the capabilities, all the short cuts, all the arable soil, all the quarriable rock, all the navigable waters; and the new arts of intercourse meet you everywhere, so that England itself is a huge mill, or hotel, or palais-royale, where all that man wants is provided within the precinct. Cushioned and comforted in every manner, the traveler rides everywhere, as on a cannon-ball, high and low, over rivers and towns, and through mountains, in tunnels of three miles and more, at twice the speed, and with half the shaking, of our trains, and reads quietly the *Times* newspaper, which again, by its wonderful system of correspondence and reporting, seems to have machinized the world for its occasion. (151–52)

In classical rhetorical terms, this is no standard exordium confirming the ethos and qualifications of the speaker, but rather an establishment of tone: admiring, fervent, and seemingly deferential. As an opening flourish, it unfolds a provocative catalog, almost a panegyric to the physical, technological, and temporal accomplishments of British modernity. It forcefully confronts the audience with an intemperate succession of superlatives ("wonderful," "in every manner," "ingenious," "best use," "all," "every," and "all man's wants"), and its first invocation of the possessive determiner "our" appears as merely part of a negative comparison with the quality and speed ("twice" as great) of British rail. One might say that the passage presents not mere approval, but a depiction of a Britain rich in political meanings; Emerson's admiration for the extent of English infrastructure and "cultivation" are expressed in a register redolent of Whig-inflected "internal improvements."[65] Above all, the passage's ebullient present tense constructions frame an unmistakable rhetorical argument: that the British nation requires confrontation as a contemporary fact, and not, as in his own famous early formulation in *Nature*, as the mere "dry bones of the past."[66]

What was the aural impact of this opening statement? The paragraph seems designed to enact the experience of arrival, mimics the intense rush of sensation, and assaults the ear with a breathless rush of enthusiasm. It has a rhythm of affirmation and mounting awe: twice, a succession of terse observations ("the country is a garden," "rivers, hills, valleys, the sea all feel the hand of a master") give way to an expansive catalog of achievements ("the long habitation of a powerful"). Their cumulative effect is registered by the "again," which precedes the closing praise of the "machinized" reality of the *Times*. The luxuriant periodic sentence from "long habitation [. . . to] within the precinct" almost exhausts the listener's capabilities of comprehension and stamina. Following such a passage, with its seemingly endless succession of mostly asyndetic clauses, involved a feat of endurance, a physical challenge for Emerson's audiences.

This staccato rhythm offers no sense of gradation between each successive observation, yet the opening line frames these as a narrative: an experience rendered in the abstract, universal third person of "the traveler." This invocation also represents an appeal to ethos, and implicitly secures subsequent gestures of interpretation as empirical observations experienced by the speaker. As Greeley will later achieve in his account of the Great Exhibition, Emerson locates his listeners in England, drawing in later passages on deictic spatial indicators ("Happy is the man who lives where life is cheap! Life is here in extremes; the traveler goes from show to show" [154]). These stylistic resources were an attempt to render the sensation of being in England itself, transporting his audience to imaginitively inhabit the place about which he speaks.

The passage is, moreover, a bravura performance of encapsulation and interpretation, in which Emerson's idiosyncratic use of aphorisms comes to serve a newly significant role. The lecture is studded with such gnomic verdicts and epithetical characterizations of English culture: "Every one of these islanders is an

island himself" (159); "The English mind has more breadth and cosmopolitanism, but has no ascending scale" (166). Yet the effects of this approach operate
at one remove from that of his typical discourses. A characteristic Emersonian
aphorism would tend to operate orally as a miniature objet d'art, a flash of insight
that audiences could judge against their own experience as it unfolded word by
word. Such flourishes were one of the main draws of Emerson's lectures; the invitation to assess each homely maxim's worth lent a sense of inclusiveness and participation to the process of interpreting his often obscure insights. In "England,"
however, the speaker drew on claims not to privileged insight but rather to privileged *experience*: how could audiences unfamiliar with European landscape
or society begin to assess the validity of his sweeping, magisterial verdicts on
English "cultivation"? As a result, the performance of "England" was distinctly
more assertion-led and tutelary than was typical of Emerson; perhaps even alienating in its didactic tone.

Considered in such a way, was this breathless, tightly wound opening as positive as it sounded? By means of explanation, we can turn again to Emerson's
analysis of Carlyle's *Past and Present,* which characterized the movement of the
latter's comparably aphoristic prose as a process of territorial advance:

> Carlyle is the first domestication of the modern system with its infinity of
> details into style.... This is the first invasion and conquest. How like an
> air-balloon or bird of Jove does he seem to float over the continent, and
> stooping here and there pounce on a fact as a symbol which was never a
> symbol before.

In "England," as later in *English Traits,* we see Emerson assume this "bird of Jove"
register, "pouncing" on British society in just such "sharper, simpler" terms. Like
Mann, he is explicit in his use of the epistemological synthesis of the bird's-eye
view. Emerson's approach is also confrontational, offering a succession of characterizations ("the country is a garden," "nothing is left as it was made") that
summarize the nation in strident, conclusive terms. Each aphorism appears to
flatter as it unfolds, but also subtly undermines. If we consider Lawrence Buell's
characterization of the "unmasking" process of the Emersonian aphorism, and
recall the Greek etymological root of aphorisms as a spatial process of "defining
boundaries," we begin to discern how these gestures engage in a process of literary and linguistic reverse-colonization.[67] The opening lines of "England" *capture*
the nation in successive acts of summary interpretation, akin to steps moving
outward from the shore of arrival. For every sensation that "strikes" the traveler,
Emerson's passage strikes back with an act of encapsulation, unveiling the realities of British society. In *Tait's Edinburgh Magazine* of 1848, in a piece reprinted
widely in the United States, this oratorical method was subjected to another
martial analogy: "[Emerson's] intellectual tactics somewhat resemble those of
Napoleon, as he aimed at, and broke the heart of opposing armies. Emerson loves
to grasp and tear out the trembling core of a subject, and show it to his hearers."[68]

The opening passage of "England" performed just such an act of invasion, but also acted as a challenge to his audience, for whom the "hidden" underside of his Janus-faced assessment was often obscured.

In the second key moment of the lecture, Emerson treated audiences to a fulsome celebration of British progress:

> In America, we fancy that we live in a new and forming country, but that England was finished long ago. But we find London and England in full growth. The towns are growing, some of them almost at the rate of American towns. Birkenhead opposite Liverpool, was growing as fast as South Boston. . . . Trafalgar Square was only new finished in April 1848. . . . The London University opens like our mushroom colleges at the West. . . . Everything in England bespeaks an immense and energetic population. (157–58)

These lines, recorded in several reports, are striking in their assertion of British growth, and their derisive rejection of predictions of expenditure and decline. He dismisses purveyors of such spread-eagle exceptionalism as possessed by mere "fancy." This rhetorical refutation is buttressed by extended empirical evidence, a catalog that again confronts the listener with the aggregate force of exemplar, amplified by the verb "bespeaks," which presents the process of cultural apprehension in sensory terms that Emerson's own oratorical performance serves to replicate. The first-person plural pronoun announces that this is a communal recognition, and casts the orator as a spokesman. Such a rhetorical appeal reinforces his argument that Britain needs to be confronted as a present-tense fact; not obsolete or undermined by technological and social pathologies. The passage thus served almost as a transatlantic inversion of his earlier hymn to American progress in "The Young American" (1844), and rang in some ears as a channeling of English triumphalism.[69]

In the final passage of the lecture, a refutation is once more introduced, invoking again the "fancy" of prophesying British decline:

> It is common to augur evil of England's future and to forbode her sudden or gradual decline under the loads of debts, and pauperism, and the unequal competition with new nations where land is cheap. (168)

The lecture then ends with a graphic *peroration* in the form of a vivid closing metaphor:

> But though she may yield to time and change, what a fate is hers! She has planted her banian roots in the ground, they have run under the sea, and the new shoots have sprung in America, in India, in Australia, and she sees the spread of her language and laws over the most part of the world made certain for as distant a future as the science of man can explore. (168)

With this image, Emerson resolves his implicit argument that English greatness could only persist and continue in the nation's "offspring." The image of the banyan tree is precise, being particularly notable for its aerial roots, offshoots that eventually grow more visible than the trunk. Nonetheless, the image is also characteristically elusive, and in performance the emphasis of the final line rests in part on the semantic finality of "certain," providing apparent closure to the topic of transatlantic relations. Irrespective of the ambivalence of the image, and its implicit confirmation of imminent New World supremacy, the line risked sounding to audiences like a cadence of prophetic certitude and resolution. It closed the piece with an trope heard by some as a defiant rejection of British decline; the zenith of an hour-long triumphal paean of unrestrained praise for Britain.

We can consider "England" as an instance of the dialectical aesthetic employed in Emerson's wider practice of portraiture: discourses that first elevate only to undercut. This was the strategy of his conflicted elegies to Thoreau and his aunt Mary Moody Emerson, and the dynamic of each portrait in *Representative Men*, in which his assessments are often deceptive and backhanded in their praise, resulting in a tone of subtle denigration.[70] As forcefully argued by Robert Weisbuch, this form of poisoned portraiture also lay at the heart of *English Traits*, but its outline was more readily discernible and its effect more readily comprehensible at the level of the shorter essay or lecture.[71] However, in the moment of oral rendition, much is lost to even dutiful ears, which often retain only the most vigorous, animated, or stark of passages. The lecture's reception history reveals how an understanding of this apparent hymn of praise to Britain led to a range of transparent, negotiated, and oppositional readings.

"England" and Astor Place

Emerson's January 1850 appearance was hotly anticipated by New York audiences and editors, not least because of the voyage that reports of early performances of "England" had already undertaken. The first review, of a rendition in Providence, Rhode Island, on 5 December 1848, had lamented its informality and narrative character:

> We had last night the pleasure of hearing Mr. Ralph Waldo Emerson lecture on the subject of England; in praise of which he could not say enough. He laid it on pretty thick, I assure you. The people here are terribly disappointed, as they had made up their minds to be enlightened upon transcendental philosophy and things belonging to super-terrestrial interests, instead of which they had only a plain chatty account of England, mostly extracts from Mr. Emerson's journal, including a description of his passage, the number of miles sailed each day, the length of the ship, height of

the mast, name of the captain &c &c. I presume that Mr. Emerson thought anything more intellectual would be thrown away upon such a benighted place as Newport.[72]

Though clearly referencing an early version of the lecture, this first report established the dual themes of response: surprise at its accessible style, and concern at its provocative nature. Following further performances in rural Massachusetts, the piece received its major urban debut before the Boston Mercantile Library Association at the Tremont Temple on 27 December.

A terse, concise précis of this performance appeared in the *Boston Post* on 29 December, and the *Tribune* reprinted the piece on 6 January 1849, commenting on his "strongly favorable impressions of the English character."[73] From there, Emerson's words began their progress through the national media, in various guises.[74] Notably, extracts were printed in the *Literary World* of 4 February under the heading "England From Two Points of View," and compared unfavorably alongside a piece from the *Union* magazine by Caroline Kirkland, who had a "strongly and singularly contrasted report of the condition and character of England."[75] In this piece, the view of the "Boston Philosopher" was dismissed as "fanciful," "rose-colored," and "idiosyncratic," "an English view of England"; while Kirkland's more scathing vision of British jealousies and military weaknesses was termed "shrewd" and "direct," offering "brown tints" from a "plain-spoken New Yorker." The *Christian Inquirer* of 10 February alluded to Emerson's lecture, alongside a similar talk by R. F. Hedge, as being unoriginal and insufficiently concerned with "the crushed and starving laborer."[76] *Holden's Dollar Magazine* printed extracts in its February and March editions, lamenting in the latter that Emerson had "generalized to a dangerous extent" in his rejection of British decline.[77]

By this time, the *Boston Post* report had found its way into hands of readers on both sides of the Atlantic. Through its *Tribune* version, the piece reached Carlyle, who promptly circulated it through the London press: the *Examiner* printed the Boston report on 10 March, and four days later the *Times* approvingly reprinted the piece under the heading "An American's Opinion of England."[78] Following this printing, it was the subject of some discussion in the British media during 1850—a discussion that was itself reprinted by papers back in the United States. Seemingly perturbed by Emerson's positive appraisal, John Stuart Mill wrote to Harriet Taylor, complaining of that "most *bête* and vulgar say [*sic*] by Emerson in a lecture in Boston about the English … it is hardly possible to be more stupidly wrong."[79] In August, the *Saturday Evening Post* (Philadelphia), which had dismissed the original lecture as "a rose-colored *coup d'oeil*," provided extracts from an anonymous deconstruction of the lecture by a "writer in a late English journal" under the heading "The Other Side of The Picture," arguing that, in its avoidance of British social inequalities, "the impression it produces is fallacious."[80] The circulation of these reports, and the polarizing controversy that they documented, helped build up a head of steam for its revival in New York the following January. By then, "England" was a prepackaged experience and a known quantity. It had earned the status of cultural event, on which the Manhattan cognoscenti intended to pronounce.

Emerson was entering New York City at a volatile time for civic and cultural life, and doubly so for public performances that took as their theme the discussion of British culture. In May 1849, the infamous "Shakespeare Riot" had taken place at the Astor Place Opera House, in which supporters of the American actor Edwin Forrest besieged the theater where the illustrious English actor William Charles Macready's *Macbeth* was to open on 7 May.[81] After several days of escalating unrest, culminating in tens of thousands of protesters in the streets around Astor Place, the city's Whig authorities sent the National Guard to quell the disturbance, resulting in twenty-five dead and 120 injured. Though the idiosyncratic origins of the event have led to the event being cast as a vaudevillian historical curiosity, it was nonetheless the deadliest civic disturbance of the early republic, and the urban divisions it revealed were stark.

As seen in chapter 1, the fissures of urban class politics found expression to an often surprising extent through reference to perceived adherence or rejection of British manners or cultural practices (see Figure 3.2). This frequently involved the imputation of supposedly antidemocratic values, with putative battle lines established between the bearing, carriage, and costume of demotic Democrats and effete, aristocratic, Eurocentric Whigs. In particular, the *New York Herald* regularly fueled such resentments, its editor James Gordon Bennett fully alive to the commercial rewards of playing to working-class anxieties and prejudice. During early 1849, the paper chronicled developments in urban culture in a language marked by vilification of "fashionable society," and the "coteries and cliques which make up our pseudo-aristocratic circles," castigating their antidemocratic, implicitly Whig, pro-British sentiments.[82] Inevitably, both tragedians' performances were read in terms of national synecdoches: Forrest as the authentic Everyman, overbearing and stridently demotic; Macready as haughty, introspective, and aristocratic.

However, the outpouring of xenophobic anti-British sentiment in Astor Place had sounded a note of alarm for the city's cultural and media elite. Publications such as the *Herald* grew conscious of the extent of their influence in fanning the flames of street-level resentment within the city, and the potential for further disturbance.[83] There was a broad sense of the wisdom of enforced austerity. Willis, himself chief among the tastemakers of the "aristocratic coteries" that routinely lambasted the *Herald*, wrote a considered "After Lesson of the Astor Place Riot" in the *Home Journal* on 26 May 1849, in which he rejected claims that it represented "the breaking out of a deep-seated hostility to England and Englishmen." He argued that it was, instead, a symptom of needlessly stoked class antagonisms, and he stridently argued for a more restrained, less ostentatious urban culture, earnestly warning that "WEALTH IN A REPUBLIC, SHOULD BE MINDFUL OF WHO ITS

FIGURE 3.2 *"Working men, shall Americans or English rule! in this city?" American Committee broadside, 1849*

LUXURIES OFFEND!"[84] Moreover, there was an increased degree of sensitivity over the treatment of British themes. Observing the affair with a mixture of concern and bemusement, the *Times* of London warned that the violent indignation of the Bowery Boys, "supplied as it is with so much anti-British material, is too likely to be repeated, unless all the good sense of the Union is exercised to extinguish it."[85]

Emerson's invitation to speak came from the Mercantile Library Association, whose lectures attracted an audience of the rising professional class and, for speakers as prominent as Emerson, the cream of the city's cultural elite. As a lecture-sponsoring organization, it competed with the Stuyvesant Institute and the Apprentices' Library, and like those institutions, had developed a prominently moral and literary character.[86] Of the crowd at Emerson's January 1850 engagements, the *Christian Inquirer* recalled "rarely having even seen so splendid a collection of cultivated people, gathered by any public lectures."[87] However, its membership drew upon an ostensibly working-class demographic of clerks and tradesmen, the very clientele the city's cultural elite were hoping to reclaim from the potentially disruptive influence of Anglophobic sentiment.[88]

Issues of class tension, and their refraction through perceived manifestations of exclusivity, elitism, and condescension, were thus at this point acutely central to the atmosphere of the city. Those who termed Emerson's appearance "bold" and "fearless" in part spoke to the risk of presenting such an affirmative version of British culture on the platform amid such a climate of agitation. Having followed his trip to Europe and his lecture in Boston with interest, New York newspapers could have been forgiven for their eagerness to assess firsthand the extent to which this speaker had been affected, tainted, or changed by his British experiences, and whether his success in London had compromised his style of performance and expression. An address with the contentious nation itself as its subject would surely provide fertile ground to test this theory. As a result, discussions of the Clinton Hall performance involved both coded recognitions of the author's risky treatment of British themes, and subtle attempts to "fix" the public meanings and cultural symbolism of his performance.

Endorsing "England"

It is useful to conceive of this process in terms of what Stuart Hall terms transparent, negotiated, and oppositional readings: secondary textual representations that, respectively, channel, mediate, or recode elements of any given performance.[89] Responses to "England" can be mapped onto this spectrum. A neutral report in Horace Greeley's *New York Tribune*, for example, was effectively transparent, merely providing a neutral account. The *Albion* and the *Home Journal*, however, offered more interpretive, negotiated readings, and the rhetoric of their accounts offered pointed commentaries on both message and performance style.

The *Albion* began with an extended commentary on Emerson's mode of presentation, observing how his impressions had

> undergone the scrutiny of a clear and singularly masculine intellect ... he
> contrived for an hour to enchain the closest attention of his hearers, and
> to wring from them marks of their approbation. These testimonies to the
> power of his simple eloquence, and to the justness of his conclusions were
> *wrung*, we say, from the listeners, because Mr. Emerson made no appeals
> to their own national and patriotic feelings—the shortest and surest road
> to the applause of a public meeting. On the contrary, there was an honest
> bluntness, a directness of purpose, a defiance, so to speak, of the prejudices
> of those around him, that argued a bold, uncompromising love of truth,
> and a carelessness of consequences, worthy of a philosophic mind.

The violent register here ("enchain," "wrung") approvingly emphasises both
Emerson's forceful counterintuitive ideas and the agonistic process of quelling
audience resistance. The means by which he "contrived" such "marks of approbation" is presented as a subtly dynamic process: a fusion of sincerity, insouciance, and dispassionate objectivity. As the distinction between lyceum and
"public meeting" suggests, this passage also represents a commentary on competing performance practices. His talk had been "masculine" both for its authoritative handling of ideas, and for avoidance of the crude xenophobic rhetoric of
the city's Anglophobic orators such as "Ned Buntline" or Mike Walsh, or the
physical more "native" performers such as Edwin Forrest.[90] Emerson's physicality, shorn of ostentation and bombast, is figured as a reclamation of the nature of
noble civic vigour.

The report then closed with an overwhelmingly favourable account of the lecture's concluding remarks:

> In concluding, Mr. Emerson touched upon the croakers and detractors
> from England's glory, assuring them that he saw no signs of her approaching fall from the lofty vantage ground that she occupies. Forced she may
> be by circumstances to contract the limits of her immediate sway; but she
> is indelibly impressed upon countless regions of the earth the genius of her
> laws, her institutions and her language. Yes, Mr. Emerson is right. Trim,
> as men and Time may, the ample skirts of her flowing garments, the great
> heart of England yet beats with undiminished vitality, and the generous
> blood of her sons yet courses with vigour through her veins.[91]

The passage adopts an analytical tone that overplays the linearity and prominence of Emerson's argument. His script, in fact, did even less than "touch upon"
theories of decline, as dismiss them in a single phrase. Here, the nuanced "banyan" image of cultural transfer is recast as a matter of indelible global "impress,"
presenting the lecture's finale as a simple gesture of confirmation of supremacy.
Ending with the outspoken affirmation of lineage as organ for the "sons" of

England, the passage cements its negotiated reading of Emerson's nuanced portrait as an act of Anglophilic affirmation.

Willis's sketch in the *Home Journal* was the most elaborate of all the published reports of the lecture; an account that, through subsequent reappearance and reprintings, helped to secure the popularity of this lecture.[92] A valuable document for the study of Emerson's platform style, its account was to condition the received public opinion of his Clinton Hall appearances. Willis was by 1850 a central chronicler of antebellum New York cultural life, a shrewd taxonomist of urban types, and an object of ridicule in the *Herald* (in which he routinely appeared as "Nincom. Poop. Willis"). Having become a national tastemaker through his journalistic portraits, he was an instrumental figure in the crystallization of American celebrity culture. In particular, having coined the phrase "upper ten" (a somewhat misunderstood term intended to refer to the nouveau riche metropolitan cultural elite), he had willingly become a divisive symbol of urban class strife.[93] his representation can be read in the light of an attempt to dampen the tensions he had helped to generate.[94]

After narrating Emerson's arrival at "crowded" Clinton Hall, he spent much of his sketch elaborating on the speaker's oddities of vocal expression and his use of "surprises." The report then largely skirts over the message of the lecture itself:

> We can only say of this Lecture on England, that it was, as all is which he does, a compact mass of the exponents of far-reaching thoughts—stars which are the pole-points of a universe beyond, and at the close of each sentence, one wanted to stop and wonder at that thought, before being hurried to the next. He is a suggestive, direction-giving, soul-fathoming mind, and we are glad there are not more such. A few Emersons would make the every-day work of one's mind intolerable.[95]

It is a document of respect for sheer force; the qualities ascribed are all coercive ("direction-giving, soul-fathoming"), suggestive of aphoristic generalizations almost tyrannical in their force. As with the *Albion* account, we get not the sense of a pleasurable aural experience, but a bold intellectual encounter with uncomfortable ideas.

Willis ended his piece with a paraphrase of the "banyan tree" passage, preceded with praise for the "very bold and fearless comments" that he offered "on the croaking that predicts the speedy downfall of England."[96] Such was the strength of the closing metaphor, argued Willis, that "Queen Victoria should name one of her children 'Emerson.'" The nature of Emerson's praise was therefore "fearless" in various senses: undaunted by the prospect of audience reproach, of the real danger of provoking violence in the immediate urban context, and of the risk that the grandeur of his generalizations be proved wrong and his prophecy thought ridiculous. In his summary, Willis deliberately seems to eschew Emerson's negative message, and instead the sense we take away from his negotiated reading is his exaltation of Emerson's benign cosmopolitan affirmation; and endorsement of his physical geniality as an exemplary, salutary cultural stance.

Recoding "England"

The final report, and in some ways the most intriguing, was that of the *New York Herald*. In 1850 the paper was not a regular supporter of the lecture circuit and often prophesied its imminent demise, which meant that to award its report of "England" front-page position next to daily "Theatrical and Musical" reviews was a significant move.[97] The lecture was thus presented as a curiosity, a newsworthy act, rather than a routine cultural event. The report opened with a concise but dense introductory sketch quietly inflected with commentary on matters of exclusivity and elitism:

> Mr. Emerson delivered a lecture on the above subject last evening. The room was crowded to its utmost capacity from curiosity to hear this gentleman's lecture who has deservedly acquired a high reputation for the originality, boldness, and some have said, the transcendentalism of his style and ideas. On entering the room and taking his place at the reading desk, Mr. Emerson was greeted with some applause and marks of public admiration. His appearance is pleasingly prepossessing, being modest, simple, and unostentatious, having in his countenance the marks of intellect and benevolence, and in his manners of the evidence of quiet gentility and good breeding.[98]

The tone is carefully modulated. While "deservedly" seems to convey a measure of respect, the wry reference to "transcendentalism" (still decidedly a pejorative in 1850), and the double-edged valences of "boldness" and "originality" betray muted scepticism. Similarly ambivalent is the emphasis on "curiosity" as the motive to "hear" him speak, a curiosity that resided as much in visual as aural stimulation.

Accordingly, the final sentence presents a full physical sketch, encompassing physiognomy, costume, and gesture. Placing such a nuanced pen portrait before an account of his words performed an implicit service for the reader. It suggested that the enigmatic nature of his potentially unruly utterances demanded comprehension through nonverbal signals. Only after such prior scrutiny were audiences thought equipped to assess the weight to attach to his "original, bold" discourse. Several of the terms here ("prepossessing," "ostentatious," "gentility," and "manners") operated in the 1849 New York media as freighted code words. Through such terms, the social text of the Emerson's lecturing body is scoured for its meanings, and ultimately found safe, sentient, and "benevolent," not the bearing of a supercilious aristocrat, nor a threatening reformist firebrand. "We do not shut our eyes," the paper had reported in June 1849, "to the fact that among the

[Astor] rioters there were a large proportion of youth, persons at that age when the temperament is most excitable." Emerson's quietly forceful performance style furnished an example of positive "temperament," counteracting more inflammatory anti-British oratory.[99]

His message itself is then conveyed in relatively neutral terms, reducing his argument to a tabulation of factors. However, the report closes with another vivid commentary on both performer and audience:

> It would be an impossible task to follow Mr. E in his eloquent and descriptive lecture. It abounded with scintillations of striking and original genius, with rare and surprising epithets and occasioned singular conjunctions of ideas and analogies. Herein his *forte* seems to lie joined with a power of vivid description and striking contraries of ideas. Singularly enough, though Mr. Emerson was loudly cheered at several striking passages, we remarked that the loudest and most animated cheering occurred at the mention of the name of Oliver Cromwell, proof positive that he was before an audience who sprang from the people of whom Oliver was one—the people who settled New England, and the people who decapitated a king—a deed for which Oliver and his companions were called regicides and who afterwards for asserting their right to independence and liberty were called rebels.[100]

Once again, conventional compliments sit amid other indicators of a more cautious tone. "Singularly enough" reprises "singular" in a way that suggests that Emerson was a victim of his own "singularity," a sense illustrated by the shift into audience response. Through the kinship of the forename "Oliver" the *Herald* seems to validate and claim affinity with the crowd's reaction. Since the reference to Cromwell in Emerson's script was minimal, and since no account of reaction occurs in any other report, the overemphasis here seems pointed.[101] What was at stake at this moment, and what does this record of equivocal vocal interaction achieve or make audible?

It implies, first, that audience reactions were therefore ultimately beyond Emerson's verbal control, that while his carefully calibrated "contrary" moments met with approval, it was to a passing historical allusion that his audience were most receptive. The *Herald* celebrates the means by which unpredictability of response overcame him; that the contingency of the lecture hall was just as "singular" as Emerson's own provocative message. Second, the energies that emerge through this moment offer a potential glimpse of the antiaristocratic boisterousness of the city's performance culture. During the week leading up to the lecture, the *Herald* had been running coverage of the trial of the Astor Place rioters, and reported rumours of another impending riot at the Italian Opera House.[102] As Willis's sketch had described it, Clinton Hall was a primitive, overcrowded auditorium, significantly downtown from the gentility of Astor Place. Through the resonances of the *Herald* report, and the sudden lexical intensification ("decapitate," "regicide," and "rebel"), we get a sense of the genuine "fearlessness" it may have taken to speak so provocatively in praise of Victoria's realm in such an arena.

Impossible though it may have been to "follow Mr. E" and his lecture, the *Herald* passage achieved just that, subtly recoding the meaning of his performance. Such mediation foreclosed the meanings of his words, refracting his appraisal through the ambivalent centripetal force of audience vocality, wresting control of the oral discourse from the speaker. One of the duties of lecture reporting, the *Herald* suggests, was the gauging of public response; scouring newspaper columns was the chief means by which the urban public not only "read," but also "heard" the character and mood of their own civic life. The *Herald* leaves readers listening not to Emerson, but to the clamour of antimonarchical rowdiness.

The mood and tenor of New York's cultural life had altered significantly between Emerson's Boston rendition of "England" and its performance at Clinton Hall. The marked difference in reaction to the two—consternation at the former; qualified embrace of the latter—serves to suggest a softening of attitudes among the city's cultural and media elite, and a realization that further ferment of anti-British rhetoric undermined rather than strengthened the goals of party politics. The episode shows how Emerson was used as part of a wider impulse toward the moral control of the young urban male, amid fear of unbridled Anglophobic sentiment. Since the Astor Place Riot, in particular, there was an awareness of the need for positive examples, even role models, in popular culture. "We do not shut our eyes," the *Herald* had reported in June 1849, "to the fact that among the rioters there were a large proportion of youth, persons at that age when the temperament is most excitable, when consequences least regarded, and offenses against law are most thoughtlessly committed." Emerson's judicious, impersonal appreciation of Britain furnished just such an example of positive "temperament," potentially counteracting the inflammatory anti-British oratory of figures such as Mike Walsh.[103] Various parts of Manhattan's media elite were prepared to use the example of Emerson's "fearless," "defiant" praise of England as a model for a renovated model of cosmopolitan nationalism.

"England" Out West

After performing "England" once more in Manhattan at the Hope Chapel on 26 March, Emerson was prepared to take the lecture further afield.[104] As he wrote to Carlyle later that year, "A letter from Cincinnati, signed by a hundred men, asking me to read lectures, drew me across the Alleganies [*sic*], for the first time."[105] Though Emerson was to become a familiar performer in these states during the coming years, in 1850 Ohio audiences were getting their first glimpse of this figure, and their first experience of a lecture about which they had read a great deal. As one might expect, less testimony survives from Ohioan performances of

"England," but those that do exist provide an insight into the distinct meanings it acquired as it traveled West.[106] A brief examination of these responses to his 1850 tour show an implicit rejection of the discursive ambitions of the metropolitan organs, an assertion of regional independence and interpretive autonomy.[107]

Its first Ohio performance was ultimately an accident. En route via steamship from Buffalo, a fire on the fifteenth forced him to dock at Cleveland, where the Cleveland Library Association invited him to stay and deliver a lecture in the city.[108] The fact that "England" was the chosen performance demonstrates Emerson's valuation of the lecture as an accessible, central statement. The Association hastily announced a free lecture by highlighting its premediated status as a literary artifact:

> Mr. Emerson lately delivered in New York City, his last course of lectures, of which the one selected for this evening was the most popular and applauded. The subject of it is England. We lately saw a review of this lecture in the *Eclectic Literary Magazine*, from the pen of one of our most polished American writers, lauding it very highly.

The two uncovered reports of its performance at Cleveland's Empire Hall are of limited value, exhibiting merely a courteous imperative to secure return bookings. "Clevelanders," one recorded, had "rarely heard any lecturer more captivating," and Emerson had "delighted a crowded hall—collected together at a few hours' notice—with his brilliant discourse" in what it praised as his "compact, nervous English."[109] Given the demographic makeup of much of 1840s Ohio, and especially northern centers such as Cleveland, one might read the midcentury lyceum system in terms of New England figures speaking to members of their own diaspora.[110] Emerson wrote in 1854 of having "found a population of Yankees out here, and an easy welcome for my Massachusetts narrowness everywhere."[111]

The social makeup of Cincinnati was altogether more complicated. In 1850 the city was caught between two aspirations: simultaneously "Porkopolis" and "Queen City of the West," brash commercial powerhouse and aspirant cultural center.[112] It was beset by anti-British tensions similar to those of New York. Anglophobic sentiment played a far more prominent role in official party politics, with Democratic politicians and orators such as Stephen Douglas and William Allen offering broadsides against British commercial policies and imperial designs on the North American continent.[113] Such sentiment was present in theatrical culture, and in the months leading up to his ill-fated 1849 appearance at Astor Place, Macready was attacked onstage in Cincinnati.[114] It was also present in the rhetoric of Cincinnati's cultural institutions, and the Young Men's Mercantile Library Association described its lecture-sponsoring activities in terms that spoke directly to anti-British aspirations: "It now remains for us, the young men of Cincinnati, to say ... whether we will meekly consent to wear the stigma applied to our profession by a British statesman, that our 'ledgers are our Bibles, and our gold is our God.' "[115]

However, the city's prevailing public culture was defined less by global tension than by the interregional imperative of civic boosterism, a "widely shared community vision with an ability to mobilize large segments of the population," that strove to promote and solidify the Midwest's incipient power, and encouraged particular hostility toward international competitors such as Britain, but also toward the cultural centers of the Northeast.[116] Nonetheless, the city's most prominent platform, the Mercantile Library Association, was attracting prominent eastern speakers: Horace Greeley had spoken on "Self-Culture" in November 1849 "before one of the largest audiences ever assembled" in the city.[117] Due to a relative lack of competing entertainments, speakers often drew the best elements of western towns; as the *Atlantic Monthly* recalled of the period in 1865, "At the West, the lecture is both popular and fashionable, and the best people attend it."[118]

Regardless of such demographic subtleties, a chief dynamic was the textual interplay of eastern and western media. Throughout the nation there was a measure of resentment at the hegemonic influence of the metropolitan media, and regional papers consciously sought to gainsay New York opinions and interpretations. Responding to Emerson's lectures presented an ideal opportunity for such self-definition. Following his Clinton Hall performances, the *Gloucester Gazette* (Massachusetts) spoke for many by remarking that "the Manhattanese are altogether wrong" in being "so dazzled by "the great eyeball"; he may have "gathered about him the most aristocratic audience ... but that does not influence his hearers in this place one iota."[119] By the time it reached the Midwest, "England" was a doubly prepackaged text, filtered through the copious reports and analyses of both its Boston and New York performances. By contrast, Emerson's lecture was used in Ohio as a means of distinguishing local response from eastern interpretation.

On 22 May, Emerson began his full scheduled course at the Universalist Church, and both the city's media and national reporters turned out to chronicle the event. The Cincinnati reporter for the Massachusetts *Salem Register* proudly described for eastern readers an atmosphere of anticipation at the opening of Emerson's lecture series, observing that "the town was on the tiptoe of 'look out' to see what kind of reception would be extended to him, what class of people would attend, and finally, what would be thought of him." In a sketch akin to the narrative approach of Willis, the correspondent recounted:

> Obtaining a near and comfortable seat we looked around to see who was in. The company was large, then, and numbered what is generally termed the select. By eight o'clock the spacious hall was well filled. Hon. Timothy Walker introduced Mr. Emerson to the audience, and instead of looking upon a man of fifty-five or sixty, which age was generally meted out to him by almost every body here, we made our *conges* to an urbane and quiet looking gentleman of apparently thirty-five. The eastern papers had said

much of Mr. Emerson, and we get an eastern mail every day. In these papers has been discovered something more than mere puffing for pay. True men have spoken of a true man, as we thought and we wanted the genuine staple woven into us—the more the better.[120]

A recurrent theme of responses to Emerson's lecture series was the attempt to distance Cincinnati interpretations from the representations of these "eastern papers."

In these earlier performances, some observers opposed what they perceived as condescension to western audiences. In his report on Emerson's opening address, "Eloquence," the editor of the *Daily Commercial* "remained long enough to hear him utter one unmistakable absurdity and left," lamenting the speaker's apparent ambition of "im*posing* upon the Western people, by means of his truly singular statements."[121] By contrast, others were relieved at his appearance, and the *Daily Cincinnati Gazette* observed,

> Judging Mr. Emerson's matter and manner, by the single lecture, we should write so differently of both, from what we have seen written by others that the same man could not be recognized as the subject of the several descriptions ... he is so far, in his intellectual and oratorical lineaments, from resembling the newspaper portraits above which we have at various times seen his name written, that we half incline to think the wrong man has come along, and attempted to play off a hoax upon us backwoods people.[122]

Seemingly with the representations of Willis and the *Herald* in mind, the report continued to argue that "if this gentleman has not mistaken himself for Mr. Emerson, Gothamite scribes have certainly mistaken Mr. Emerson for somebody else, and given descriptions of him which will not be recognized in this region."[123] "We were perfectly satisfied, by the Lecture of Wednesday evening," the *Salem Register* reporter declared, "that Mr. Emerson *was* Mr. Emerson, and 'nothing else,' and just as well satisfied that a great deal [of] nonsense has been written about him, by Gilfillan and others."[124] The region, the implication was clear, must "recognize" and define its own Emerson. The figure that confronted them on the platform of the Universalist Church was at once more muted and less controversial than eastern reports had led them to believe, but also more comprehensible, less radical. However, the response is ambivalent: Cincinnati audiences are simultaneously rejecting the hegemonic interpretive gestures of "Gothamite" scribes such as Willis, while essentially concurring with their assent.

Some observers went beyond mere assent in claiming Emerson's performance style and manner as "belonging" to the West itself. In seeking to define their own Emerson, Cincinnati reports seized upon aspects of his lecturing style that were seen as jarringly demotic in other contexts. In its opening review of his lecture course, the *Gazette* praised his "simple dignity and clear, well-knit common sense."[125] The review of his fourth lecture praised his performance style as

"exceedingly pleasing, and unpretending," and particularly valued that customary western virtue, an iconoclastic "sense of the ludicrous," which they thought
"even keener and more instantaneous than that of Senator Corwin," the Ohio
Whig.[126] "After all," the writer concluded, "so far as Mr. E has yet shown himself
before a Cincinnati audience, his most remarkable trait is that of plain *common
sense;* as good a quality as he can exhibit in this latitude, by way of introduction
to the respect and confidence of the people."[127] The *Salem Register* correspondent
even wryly informed his eastern readers,

> His style of speaking, as you well know, is not declamatory, is *not western,*
> and yet we hail him as a brother and one of us. He belongs to us as much as,
> if not more than, to you; for I can not help saying that there is, in the West,
> much more of deep, quiet thinking among the masses, than is expressed by
> their mouth-pieces.[128]

What sometimes surprised audiences in New York as the impetuous, daring insouciance of his performances, some valued in Ohio as true democratic
eloquence.

Divorced from the context of urban class conflict, "England" in Cincinnati
was less a story of transatlantic manners and party politics, and more one of
interregional rivalry. Nonetheless, the lecture's vision of transatlantic realities
could be expected to resonate for this community in distinct ways. If this region
represented the future of the republic, what should audiences make of the past?
If this representative of northeastern society was to gaze eastward to Britain
with such admiration, what did this mean for East Coast attitudes toward
the West? Particularly provocative aspects of the lecture, therefore, included
Emerson's reference to Britain as rivaling the West in growth and progress,
specifically the line regarding the growth of London University, which his lecture script stated as "growing as fast as our mushroom colleges in the West."
Emerson's verdict on such competition in "England" was therefore a matter of
civic pride.

Two Cincinnati responses to "England" help to flesh out this response. The
first was the private journal of future president Rutherford Hayes, at this stage
a fledging lawyer and one of the signatories of Emerson's invitation letter to the
Cincinnati Literary Club:

> Monday 27 [May]: This evening Mr. Emerson lectured on England. He gave
> England and Englishmen the highest place in the world's history. She has
> the best working climate, not too hot nor too cold; the best race of people—
> the mettle of the Danes, Norwegians, and Swedes, the Saxons and Britons,
> a good cross.... But the fault of England, if she has one, is her success
> is *material.* She has not mysticism, no faith, no soaring. The Americans
> have more versatility, and adaptedness; they are the people of the future.
> England is "mortgaged" to the past.[129]

It is an interpretation that places significantly more emphasis on the negative aspects of the lecture's depiction than that of the Boston or New York reports, perceiving the balanced critique at the heart of Emerson's dialectically balanced message. Here, one might also say that the qualities of "versatility" and "adaptedness" were qualities particularly celebrated as western virtues, and that the lecture was thus read as less of a hymn to Britain than a confirmation of imminent Midwestern ascendancy.

The *Daily Cincinnati Gazette* report of the lecture similarly highlighted the negative side of the picture:

> Mr. E's account of England and the English, devoted almost wholly to the personal traits of the people from the middle classes upwards, was one of the most graphic and interesting pieces of descriptive narration that we have ever listened to. But it was at the same time, a great deal more than this language would imply;—it was a profound view of the genius of England, a skilful analysis of the events and qualities that have given that nation its proud position as the leading power of the world, and a fair, independent, comprehensive estimate of the English people: their cleverness, their individualism, their unobtrusive habit, their "pluck," their nationality, and their present decline from old mystical and poetical characteristics, to material developments that make them less interesting to others and less great among themselves.[130]

The passage offers an uneasily gracious response to the lecture: it is courteous and respectful, praising the "skilful" and "fair" nature of his depiction, but strikes an odd note in its recollection of "descriptive narration" and a focus on "events," neither of which characterizes the lecture script. Various other choices of verbiage or tone suggest ambivalence. As the line "more than this language would imply" invites us to notice, the adjectives that precede it ("graphic," "interesting," and, especially, "descriptive") are relatively restrained, torpid characterizations. Framed in the most decorous of terms, the *Gazette* nonetheless chastised the absence of workers or Chartists from his analysis, much as had early critiques of its Tremont Temple performance.

Again, the account can be seen to establish a distinction with what New York reports represented as the lecture's "fearless" and positive message. Just as the *Salem Gazette* correspondent claimed Emerson's style as "Western," it seems likely that the typically "English" traits singled out in this report represent an aptly chosen inventory of "Western" characteristics: "cleverness," "individualism," "unobtrusive habit," and "pluck." This list can be read as a way of distinguishing natural western manners as possessing a plainer transatlantic affinity than the more ostentatious cultural style of the Northeast. But the most telling divergence from the "Gothamite" reports was the *Gazette*'s emphasis on Emerson's critique. Ending the tabulation of Emerson's "estimate of the English people" with the fact of "their present decline" undercuts all preceding qualities.

The resounding declarative final sentence presents British societal "decline" as the culminating feature: the most "profound" and valid of Emerson's observations. Again, this was an emphasis elided or obscured in the lecture's Clinton Hall reports.

Moreover, in its summary paragraph the *Gazette* report seems to hint that, far from the "bold" and "fearless" interpretations of its Clinton Hall performance, the lecture was felt to be routine rather than idiosyncratic. "We are pleased that Mr. Emerson has announced a second course," they added, hoping that "our people will get something more of what is *peculiar* in Mr. Emerson's mind, and philosophical views, than was obtained from the first course." The people of Cincinnati had been prepared by national reports to expect provocation, iconoclasm, and eccentricity. By contrast, we encounter surprise at its apparent conventional nature. Denying the presence of qualities of iconoclasm or surprise, the *Gazette* distanced its interpretive stance and agency from those that had spread word of the speaker's "fearless," "singular" qualities through national media. The situation of Cincinnati was not, after all, that of the "Gothamites" or "Manhattanese." In New York, what could be considered the positivity of Emerson's drama of appraisal was used to ameliorate urban class tensions. The example of Cincinnati reporting on Emerson's 1850 lectures shows that the Ohio media sought to distance itself from such remote, less palpable demands.

The Fate of Clinton Hall

There was some justification in interpreting "England" as a provocative tribute. The lecture inveighed against a "stable" or "stagnating" reading of Great Britain, offering a renovated, nuanced return to transatlantic admiration, rejecting an emotional reaction against British power in favor of a balanced appreciation of its worth. Emerson was inviting audiences to reform and reconsider the nature of their Anglophobic sentiments, demanding that they be mindful of transatlantic inheritance, and desirous of Anglo-American unity. Rejecting the gothic Anglophobia at large in much public discussion of Britain, Emerson's lecture was a call for re-engagement. Europe was presented not as it had been in "The American Scholar" as the "dry bones of the past": the United States was implicated, and must absorb and reform.

Different audiences and constituencies heard different things to admire, condemn, or put to work in this cultural stance. But Emerson was certainly a victim of his own laconic detachment and obscurity of oratorical style. Rather than a polemical or threatening reformer or firebrand, he had developed into a playful, witty, unpredictable, but ultimately potentially consensual voice. Moreover, his unprepossessing yet quietly forceful performance style embodied a functional cultural compromise. This chapter has shown the ways in which influential interpreters such as Willis in the *Home Journal* and the *Herald* embraced and helped to fashion this emerging, conservative, accommodating Emerson: while appropriating certain aspects of his iconoclasm, they welcomed the abandonment of his more radical 1930s persona in favor of a more moderate, temperate stance seemingly validating the cultural status quo.

The reception history of Emerson's "England" in 1850 allows us to glimpse the ways in which a culture of Whig stewardship attempted to shore up and rein in the more indulgent and violent strains of Anglophobia, and saw in Emerson's stance what Tamarkin has identified as the beneficial model of renovated deference by which "a renewed commitment to belonging could be learned from feelings for Britain."[131] Various constituencies saw that fear of Britain was irrational and dangerous, and Emerson offered a form of transatlantic conception that was salutary and beneficial.

These were not the only discourse communities to construct or appropriate Emerson's transatlantic vision to serve their own contexts. During the Second World War, the British Ministry of Information printed a stirring passage from the close of *English Traits* as a patriotic broadside that manipulated Emerson's terminology (replacing "England" with "Britain"), his pagination (capitalizing and centring his refrain to "Mother of Nations; Mother of Heroes"), and ultimately his message, which was stripped of its qualifications.[132] This episode attests to the longevity of the flexible propaganda value of his stance on Britain that Emerson first formulated in his "England" lecture. It is significant, moreover, that the passage originated in a closing chapter, "Speech in Manchester," that owed its force to an original oral context. Nineteenth-century nationalist discourse was constructed most powerfully through such print manipulation of speech events.

The malleability of Emerson's meanings, as his words reverberated elusively around the lecture halls of Manhattan and Cincinnati, demonstrates the unique capacity of oral performance to create a fluid dialectic between intention and consequence. It reminds us that it was in the very process of lecture reporting that most was at stake: one hour's worth of speech in Boston, New York, and Cincinnati meeting halls translated into a pliable, reusable succession of print inches. In midcentury oratorical culture, even as authoritative a figure as Emerson was regularly a victim of co-option and reappropriation. By 1850, he had metamorphosed from a powerful antiestablishment voice of reform to a figure of potential: the late, conservative Emerson, whom the press was instrumental in constructing.

As discussed earlier in this book, the lyceum offered a realm in which temperament could be cultivated. Lawrence Levine famously located the emergence of American high/low cultural distinction at the turn of the twentieth century, yet a plausible reading of the lyceum's rise might be that it represented a pragmatic middle ground between realms already engaged, by midcentury, in vigorous, unruly dispute.[133] Civic tensions over bodily control, audience conduct, and modes of attention coalesced to promote this self-consciously nonpartisan institution. In the North, but to a lesser extent in the antebellum South, lecture halls represented a neutralizing middle realm, a crucible in which collective habits of listening could be forged, and lyceum attendance duly became a <u>performance of middle-class identity.</u>

The context of the New York delivery of "England" provides an instructive closing vignette regarding this ascendancy of the popular lecture system during the 1850s. Following its damage in the riots, the Astor Place Opera House fell into decline, and observers advised its conversion to other uses; the *Herald* swiftly recommended that "the proprietors of Massacre Place Opera House convert it into a church—into a place for hearing sermons, and singing psalms, and making prayers."[134] (See Figure 3.3.) Fittingly, the Mercantile Library Association acquired the building in June 1850 and, following an extensive refit, reopened the building as the new Clinton Hall, with a lecture hall at the center—"a place for hearing sermons" of the secular variety championed by the city's Whig elites.[135] (See Figure 3.4.) Concerns over ventilation and lighting in the original venue in which Emerson spoke should be read in terms of this cultural agenda. Willis was celebrating not only the message, but also the medium: his account of attending "England" was a celebration of access, of egalitarianism, of democratic space.

The Clinton Hall that rose out of the ashes of the Astor Place Opera House symbolized a reorganization of urban space, <u>the ascendancy of middlebrow culture</u> through a medium that embodied aspiration ostensibly divorced from the troubling associations of elitism. Though it was to decline as a venue once more

FIGURE 3.3 *"Riot at the Astor-Place Opera-House, New York," Illustrated London News, 1849*

CLINTON HALL.

FIGURE 3.4 *"The New York Mercantile Library," Scribner's Monthly*

during the Civil War, while it retained its status as a lecturing platform it was a symbol of a crucial strain of northern civic nationalism. As the 1850s opened, this civic enthusiasm for the lecture circuit was reaching its zenith, encouraged by outlets such as the *Tribune*, whose editor was among many to follow Emerson by casting themselves as prophets in their lecture hall discussion of an Anglo-American commons.

|| – Performing as prophet; using Br as model of "Old World futurity" 117

    ↳ This performance fuses disciplines – soc sci + sentiment.

118 – "choreography of reform" – 118 → Performing spatial + temporal change (imagined futures)
Focussing on "metaphors of motion" as means of blending dry soc analysis + theatrical
sensation. → a form of "Whig oratory" – 120 A means of social + pol manipulation/
                                                               engineering.

• Mann + Greely use the theatricality of imagined TransAt excursions.

    ↳ Mann's gothic contrasts of detached + elevated vision of Br soc life + immersed
spectacle of poverty; "composite nature of reform." 127
                                            midC

    ↳ Both Mann + Greely assume role of prophet by adopting lang of "ascension + elevation"
    ↳ imagine Br as warning of poss future of Jacksonian Democracy (either through visions
of US difference from or worrying tendency towards Br trends).

{ 4 }

Britain as Prophecy

HORACE MANN, HORACE GREELEY, AND
THE CHOREOGRAPHY OF REFORM

Even when at its most solemn and serious-minded, popular lecturing was always a role-play medium. To educate a live crowd involved embodying the fruits of knowledge; expanding an audience's horizons involved personifying virtue. This was particularly true of those who came to the lectern with the aim of promoting social change. The most effective reformers were also performers with a developed sense of their own persona, with one foot in other forms of popular culture. Among those who took aspects of the Anglo-American commons as their subject, plenty of personae were available: the performers in this book posed variously in the lecture room as cosmopolites, gadflies, diplomats, or sentimen- *persona:* tal travelers. One of the most potent persona for the transatlantic reformer was *prophet* that of prophet. In the mind of antebellum reform, Britain represented a paradox of Old World futurity, with the result that for many commentators, the modernity of the Victorian age seemed to furnish lessons for the United States. Many progressive-minded writers, from socialists such as Margaret Fuller to peace movement protagonists as Elihu Burritt encouraged their readers to reflect on the condition of England as a means of predicting the future course of the cen- *England is* tury.[1] And several found the lecture hall an ideal place in which to bring their *future.* predictions to dramatic life.

The school reformer Horace Mann and the *New York Tribune* editor Horace Greeley were two prominent examples of this approach. Returning from a tour of Britain in 1845, Mann had argued that, in the streets of London, "we commune, as it were, face to face, with those great principles which bear the destinies of mankind in their bosom."[2] Five years later, Greeley returned from the 1851 Great Exhibition in London's Hyde Park, proclaiming that he had witnessed the future and brandishing his influential verdict, "The Crystal Palace and Its Lessons."[3] With a view to reaching the largest possible audience, both adapted their reflections for the lecture stage. They toured the United States over the course of the

...xt decade performing pieces that cast them as seers and oracles, using British futurity as a means of imagining starkly distinct national futures for the republic. In doing so, they transformed their findings into elaborate oratorical tours de force that reveal the blending of social science and sentiment in lecture hall reform rhetoric.

As recent work on nineteenth-century social movements in Britain and America has shown, melodrama and sensationalism were properties not just of the playhouse but also of diverse cultures of reform, in which activists fused rational and sensational appeals in order to make their case.[4] It was a theatricality sometimes evident in performance style, or in the use of visual aids such as the panorama. But it was just as marked on the level of rhetoric of and metaphor. We can see it emerging particularly clearly in oratory due to a dual dynamic of depiction: the need to place before audiences the social problems one intends to correct, before moving them toward an imagined remedy, all using spoken language alone. As a result, the rhetoric of social change habitually turned on twin metaphors of spatial and temporal motion, both of which took on new importance in live performance. The richness of the period's reform oratory rested on performer's ability to transform the passages of speech into simulated experiences, conjuring up vivid aural representations and transporting audiences into imagined political futures through what I describe in this chapter as the "choreography of reform."

In this chapter I explore how this choreography worked in the lectures of two of the period's most prominent Whig reformers. I show how transatlantic reformers transitioned nimbly, if sometimes incongruously, not only between print and public speech, but also between strikingly different discourses and registers. Both Mann and Greeley brought to the stage judgments about the value and future of an Anglo-American commons communicated through a language that consciously merged the austere approach of social investigation with the sensational excesses of lurid urban exposés.[5] One of the subtleties of this, I argue, was the role of metaphors of motion, in which the movement of identification between audience and speaker, and between community affiliation and independence, became the focus of rhetorical drama. As we have seen with the examples of Douglass and Emerson, reformist statements were choreographed in the press as part of a broader cultural conversation between sincerity and showmanship.[6] This chapter reveals further how the ambivalent choreography of lecture hall performances in print allowed the media to cast reformers as protagonists in what Julia Swindells has called the "grand theater of political change," and transform the meanings of their performances.[7]

Making Republicans in the Lecture Hall

Both Mann and Greeley were central to a late-Jacksonian nation-building moment in which Whig-leaning cultural elites saw potential in the lecture circuit's power for the shaping of citizens' sensibilities. Mann was one of the period's chief architects of American public education, the first secretary of the Massachusetts Board of Education, and one of the North's most eminent moral critics.[8] Faced with an industrializing New England and the influx of unskilled European immigrants, he championed Whig doctrines of social control that united strands of Romantic perfectionism into what he called a "science of moral economy."[9] The solution to the problem of universal white male suffrage, he thought, lay not in political reform alone, but in the provision of state education of the kind he had witnessed in Prussia during educational reconnaissance tours in Europe, and a network of common schools that would nurture a coming generation of informed, responsible, and self-aware republicans. As he declared in an 1840 lecture, "The passions of the multitude have gathered irresistible strength," and the remedy for Mann lay in a multilevel strategy of civic education whose rhetorical dynamics were clearly at work in his "Great Britain" performances.[10] Greeley was a far more idiosyncratic Whig and a considerably more outlandish figure. A generation younger than Mann, his rise from New Hampshire agricultural stock saw the vocation of printer transform his prospects as it had done Benjamin Franklin's, and he into a statesman-editor, founding the *New York Tribune* in 1841, and overseeing its rise during the following decades. As both a founding editor of the nation's most widely read newspaper, and an outspoken champion of diverse causes from vegetarianism to the international peace movement, Greeley sat at the heart of debates over the role of literacy, news, and the relationship of print to nationhood as a symbol of print's centralizing force.[11]

Both were quick to perceive the potential of lecturing to further their causes. The rise of the lyceum so closely coincided with Mann's political ascendance and his common-schools program that he was sometimes erroneously linked with its foundation. Though he had misgivings about the diffuse nature of the education it provided, dismissing the emerging format in an 1842 report as "too unsystematic and desultory," during the 1840s and 1850s he became as well known for his speaking career as for his congressional or educational work.[12] Tellingly, Mann tended to conceive of the print media in explicitly aural terms as "a vast sounding gallery" in which "from horizon to horizon every shout of triumph and every cry of alarm are gathered up and rung in every man's dwelling." Through both lecturing and press reports of his speeches he could achieve the "daily access to the public ear" that his reforms demanded.[13] Greeley was a strong supporter of lecture culture, though as one might expect from such a creature of print, was more skeptical about the limits of public speech. He repeatedly warned against the perilous allure of charismatic speakers, and in one of his own lectures dismissed oratory as "exhilarating fumes of liquor" and mere "bewildering gas."[14] Nonetheless, Greeley championed the lecture circuit in *Tribune* as a constitutive arena of northern life. In one of his dispatches from Hyde Park he had even suggested that, should a successive exhibition be held, the United States would be wise to offer up such civic institutions as the lyceum as symbols of its progress.[15]

In related ways, both saw the practical and intellectual aspects of lecture culture as a means of forging republic citizenry. "It may be an easy thing to make a
republic," Mann wrote in 1848, "but it is a very laborious thing to make republicans."[16] The lecture hall was an ideal crucible for this process. This dissemination
of republican values had multiple strands. Greeley saw a core attribute of lecturing to be its role as a social nexus, and a means of fostering cooperative habits
of listening and congregation.[17] A crucial element of this intercourse was that it
was to be cross-class, an endeavor he pursued by actively seeking out a working-
class audience for his talks. By his own admission, he preferred to speak in "popular Lyceums and Young Men's Associations, generally those of the humbler
class, existing in country villages and rural townships," and his 1855 biographer
describes the audiences for even his Manhattan speeches as having "decidedly
the air of a country audience. Fine ladies and fine gentlemen there are none. Of
farmers ... there are hundreds. City mechanics are present in considerable numbers."[18] From a more theoretical perspective, Mann was a committed believer in
the pedagogical powers of forceful rhetoric: the best kind of lecturing, he argued,
involved confronting audiences with positive and negative models. In a famous
formulation, he argued that the "innate" propensities of the republic must be
"bridled and tamed by our actually seeing the eternal laws of justice ... by our
actually feeling the sovereign sentiment of duty."[19] In particular, civic-minded
republicans could be created through confrontations not just with each other as
a public, but through oratory that revealed appropriate standards against which
to measure their lives.

As Howe and Holt argue, Mann and Greeley must be seen in terms of a distinct
tradition and aesthetic of Whig oratory.[20] Jacksonian Democrats saw the orator
as spokesman; their political opponents conceived of the same figure as potential prophet and guide. Conceiving of oratory as a means to establish control
over ungovernable reality and counteract the baser instincts of the crowd, Whig
speeches were frequently exhortatory and admonitory, aiming not to please but
to challenge and convert.[21] A typical patrician persona relied upon a necessary
illusion of disinterested statesmanship, the figure of the virtuous speaker locating and guiding listeners toward the true path of the republic. Inevitably, the
more explicitly partisan or patrician hard edges of this Whig style needed to be
smoothed down for a general lyceum audience. Speaking on ostensibly neutral
platforms, there was the need for instruction over persuasion; for the avoidance
of explicit party political content; for a focus on more *epideictic* or display rhetoric rather than a more recognizably political *deliberative* tone; and the need for a
statesmanship that was more belletristic than bellicose. As the rest of this chapter
reveals, this hardly precluded the subtle use of lecture appearances as political
occasions.

Mann's and Greeley's recourse to a topic as secure in its familiarity as transatlantic travel represented an ideal vehicle for Whig oratory, allowing them to
apply the wisdom of a comparative analysis of forms of global government, while

bridling and taming listeners through a confrontation of British modernity. In doing so, their rhetorical procedure relied not simply upon appeals to rationality but also on the creative choreography of multiple discursive levels of apprehension, analysis, and persuasion. Travel discourse has always had a powerful yet unresolved relationship to reform. Its subjects provide comparative frames that allow for the projection of alternative social structures, and above all an imaginative space in which American culture and society could be reconsidered. Travel texts are always both narrative and dramatic, in that the process of imagining these alternatives rests on dramaturgical representative techniques: not just arcs of personal development, but dialogue, characterization, plot, and motion through space. Narratives of travel enact a process of political understanding as a form of motion. As I shall explore, this can be traced through dramatic metaphors of elevation and perspective, between which audiences are guided, and whose implications accumulate to foster what speakers hope will be a revised political consciousness.

On the lecture stage this dramaturgical element was amplified in two important ways. In recounting experiences of travel, an imaginative space is brought alive on the platform and the orator assumes the role of choreographer: conjuring up a scene; placing the audience at vantage points; directing the tempo and vision; conducting their movement from one mode of apprehension to another. Garvey describes antebellum reform as "a structure of debate," and it was one that can be understood in terms of a range of movements through space; mobile perspectives achieved through grammatical forms, rhetorical conceits, or descriptive flourishes; directing and guiding a dramatic portrayal in ways suitable for an agonistic public sphere of dramatic forces.[22] It was the responsibility of reform lecturers to transport their audience with them on their voyage. Temperance reformers might transport audiences into taverns and tenements; abolitionists brought the realities of slave markets and plantations alive for awestruck crowds; anti-Catholic activists led listeners into the dark heart of licentious priestly residences. More subtly, on the platform, the imaginative space of projected travel scenes was brought into productive tension with the space of performance, and with the dramatic relation of spectator to audience. As the words of the speaker at the lectern bridged the gulf between their audience and the scenes described, orators relied upon metarhetorical connections between the social relations at work in the lecture hall and those of the projected spaces of travel, drawing listeners out of and back into the live moment of performance in ways that help inflect the political imagination of their textual journeys.

As with all reform rhetoric, this process relied upon the assumption of authority and legitimacy. In persuasive speeches that posed as instructive lectures, personal credibility and ethos took on acute and problematic importance. Successful reform went hand in hand with a perception of sincerity. With the reformist's visible condition of zeal and authenticity assessed as one might a theatrical performance, the question of speakers' personal ethos became central to their rhetorical reception. Yet by injecting reformist discourse with forms of affective dramatic technique, orators such as Greeley and Mann risked complicating the value of sincerity. It is not insignificant that the term *theatricality* enters the language at the onset of the period covered by this book as a specifically political concept through Carlyle's *French Revolution* (1838), as an antonym for "sincerity" evoking the use of the resources of drama as route to action.[23] In Greeley and Mann, we see a pair of performers exploiting the dramatic resources of visual language to urge audiences to accompany them on imaginary Atlantic excursions and particular understandings of the Anglo-American commons.

Bird's-Eye Rationalism

Mann composed the piece "Great Britain" following his return from his 1843 educational mission to Europe, performing it first during 1844–46 and reviving it again in the mid-1850s. It was based on a distinctive two-part structure: the first twenty minutes cataloged British cultural achievements before a second movement launched an outspoken critique of British educational failings.[24]

From the outset, the lecture asked listeners to suspend many of their habitual interpretive assumptions. After formal introductions by the evening's presiding officer, each delivery commenced not with a dramatic or descriptive exordium, but with a careful disclaimer that sets the analytic tone of the piece:

> My subject is Great Britain. I propose in the following lecture to give a bird's-eye view of British institutions and the spirit of British society, with their effects upon the condition of mankind.
>
> It is with no unkind or inimical feeling towards the mother-nation, that I select this theme. I repudiate the rule by which the ardor of man's love for his own country is to be measured by the fierceness of his hostility to others. The receptive spirit of philosophy and philanthropy asks only what is most effectious of the well-being of mankind—accepting whatever is good and rejecting whatever is bad, with equal impartiality. (1)[25]

The coolness of register here was in part an attempt to distance his words from the shrill Anglophobic "ardor" of the public discourse surrounding the current 1844 election campaign. But more broadly, Mann sought to construct an ideal reform persona. His script consistently disparaged the coarse, violent language of his evangelical counterparts, and from the outset he establishes his speaker's ethos as a disinterested analytic persona, balancing the "receptive" Anglo-Saxonist logic of "mother-nation" rhetoric against the empirical ambitions of social scientists such as Chadwick or Mayhew. Addressing the question of how "it is permitted that a nation so pre eminent in greatness" could simultaneously "be the most ignorant, the most debased, the most vicious, and of course the most suffering nation on earth," Mann offers not to "penetrate this awful mystery, but . . .

attempt to state the proximate causes as to convince you of the facts" (16). Reform is presented as a matter of cosmopolitan sincerity, and the lyceum as a crucible for sober reflection, in which the disposition of rational citizenship might be forged. Part of this was achieved on the level of language in a tone of cautious detachment: rather than persuade, the lecture promised simply to "enumerate" (11) and "take a sober and instructive view" (10) of British developments. Part of this was conducted through more explicit audience stewardship, urging his listeners: "Let us glance at the terrible displacement of crime" (13); and later, "I now invite your attention to some of the consequences of such social relations" (22).

The central spatial metaphor of the piece was, however, one of ascension and elevation. As in a number of Mann's other lectures, the drama of reform involves an analytical persona explicitly elevated above a given scene, in order for audiences to "behold" various ideas and patterns.[26] One contemporary observer recorded of this technique that Mann's speeches typically led audiences "high up the mountain so that they may see the Promised Land where the nations shall dwell in the good time coming."[27] Figuring the reform orator as omniscient viewing subject above partisan embroilment, this "bird's eye" rhetoric equates comprehensive understanding with panoramic vision, in a form that George Landow's study of nineteenth-century sage rhetoric calls the ecclesiastical revelation or "Pisgah Sight."[28] Such elevation had roots in both pedagogic theory and popular visual culture. On the one hand, it was part of Mann's commitment to the "exhibitory method" of Swiss educationalist Johann Pestalozzi, which stressed elaborate demonstration over mere explanation.[29] Equally it was also embedded in the representational and epistemological logic of midcentury visual culture, not least the social ambitions of the period's vogue for panorama and "bird's eye' lithographs, by which unruly urban fabrics were made comprehensible through unified depiction.[30]

Such elevation was of course choreographed into the power relations of the lecture hall context. As Mann's sentences unfold from elevated lectern to audience, the invitation for those below to assume a privileged vantage point and participate in "bird's-eye view" condenses the experiences of both lecture attendance and social reform into one apparent collaborative process, urging the assumption a unified civic vision. Yet for the most part this choreography of elevation reinforced power relations. Mann repeatedly disowned the authority of the seer throughout piece, claiming not to "attempt to penetrate this awful mystery" of British inequalities, but instead rather to modestly "state the proximate causes as to convince you of the facts" (16). But his bird's-eye view was nonetheless readily seen as a form of almost aristocratic Whig detachment, an imperious position above both the republic and Britain, and at one remove from both their respective claims and bonds of reciprocal audience connection.

The effects of the piece can therefore be read as the cultivation and projection of a patrician Whig persona. The fact that the lecture centered on a key diagnostic proposition—"What a man sees in England is a very good test of what he is"

(16)—made this theme of moral sensibility paramount. By framing the condition of Britain as a genre of inadvertent personal revelation, he invited his audiences to use the transatlantic imaginary as a way to evaluate the ethical commitments and interpretive strategies of all reformers. As in Carlyle's comparable mode, the lecture's force lay less in evidential appeals than in the dramatization of an act of perception. His experiences are presented as a dramatic descent into a British underworld, with his humanitarian response a testimony to his ethical selfhood, just as his performance of exemplary analysis enacted a republican sensibility. "Great Britain" implied also that this was the condition of equanimity afforded and legitimated as much through the extraordinary privilege and transatlantic experience as the authority of statistical information. And yet, for all that Mann promised a "sober and instructive" mode of analysis, certain other aspects of dramatic choreography owed as much to the more lurid strands of sensational coverage as to the austere sociology of governmental reports.

Gothic Contrasts

Mann's choreography involved navigating a series of stark opposites. In addition to a register of empirical investigation, his lecture drew heavily upon millenarian exposés and the expressive power of contrasts and dualities of popular sentimental nonfiction. As we have seen, the lecture's fulsome opening used an assumption of rapport between speaker and audience regarding shared regard for the cultural achievements of the "Mother Country" as a descent, and the shared regard for Britain and its glories as a body of knowledge. These first fifteen minutes offered a breathless hymn to the machine nation, its productive powers, its mobility, its locomotive quality, its "works of splendor—art, literature, museums, palaces" (2); "comforts, embellishments, luxuries" of the people (3). Mann's catalog runs through an "enviable and enduring" roster of "artists, scientists, philosophers and poets" and offers a panegyric to the globalized reach of British commodities. Mann's speech took listeners on an elaborate journey, with its point of embarkation the industrial-imperial sublime.

But even here this grandeur begins to take on an intriguingly gothic tone. Its most dramatic flourish takes the form of a simulated invasion, rich in ambivalent rhetorical effect:

> A dash of the minister's pen in Downing Street names a rendezvous, and from opposite sides of the globe, from all points in the earth's circumference, armies, munitions, fleets, may be seen running down convergent lines, to meet and to be present at the place and hour. The world to her is only what a parade-ground is to other nations.

From this fantasia of logocentric agency, Mann traces the force of British power outward from the pen to the very republic itself:

Now she is in the Mediterranean, sinking fleets at the mouth of the Nile or bombarding some city of Palestine. Now, when not suspected to be within a thousand miles, she comes like a night-robber, breaks open the gates of the Baltic, despoils a nation of its forces. Now she is *on* the Northern Lakes, mid-way across our continent—up the Potomac, *at* the gates, and *within* the gates, of the Capitol . . . all longitudes and sound are witnesses of her might.

It is a moment of embroiling rhetoric, with a stress on mutual susceptibility. Mann's manuscript underlining confirms the intended emphatic drama of such a moment of performance, with the speaker's incantatory constructions escalating audience anticipation of redcoats at the very lyceum door. Such hyperbolic rhetoric was characteristic of Whig commentators during 1844, who were dismissed in the Democratic press as "heavily engaged in painting war scenes," to dissuade the nation against its Texan and Oregon ambitions prompting British engagement.[31] Ultimately, the level of his comparison rises to the sacred, observing of Britain that "like the Almighty, the great deep is her pathway and the winds her chariot. Oh, would to heaven that she would imitate the Almighty in her beneficence as well as in her power!" (6–7).

Mann's drama then enters its second act. In a volte-face comparable to that of Douglass's "July Fourth" lecture, he turns his previous praise on its head to challenge such sentimental attachments, and to counsel for a turn away from the influence of Britain's error-strewn example. Turning to the topic of poverty and a statistical presentation of Britain's ills, Mann frames both through a flurry of statistics expressed in a violently sensationalist register. Describing the condition of British mines, he observes that "some of the child workers never see daylight for weeks" (11); that their condition "descends to infinite depths below common iniquity" (11); and that their "young lips are trained to profaneness and blasphemy" (31). At times, his illustrations approach the unsettling mode of Carlyle, as when recounting how "several instances have lately been detected, where parents have murdered their own children" (41). Such "bridling" imagery culminates in another rhetorical interrogation:

Whence comes this fearful debasement, these dreadful sufferings, this astounding guilt? They come from that sovereign spirit of selfishness and pride which reigns in the hearts of British rulers and governs the government.... Hence the manufacturers look upon the bones and fingers of children as they do upon iron and beans—as things created for their use.... Where children can be used, they are plucked by hundred and by thousands, like buds from the stalk of life; where they cannot be used, they are abandoned to storm or night and frost. (41–42)

Considerably heightened from comparable passages in his *Report*, the passage presents an almost cannibalistic industrialist class, figuring their utilitarian priorities as an alien value system.[32] Here, the familiar Carlylean notion of the degradation of spiritual selfhood under capitalism is expressed as a process of grotesque alchemy that underpins labor "turning minerals into gold."[33]

One particularly striking performance moment brought the very voice of the British poor alive to American audiences. Mann cites an interview with London street children that reads like a parodic catechism "from the last report of Her Majesty's Committee of Commercial in Education," mocking the ignorance and moral impoverishment of British youth:

> I take the following account of an examination of one of the schools in London, from the last report of Her Majesty's Committee of Commercial in Education:
> Who was Jesus Christ the son of?
> "Son of David"
> Who was Moses?
> "Son of Christ"
> Who was Adam?
> "Son of Abraham" (36)

The effect of estrangement presents their religious ignorance as threatening. The self-representational strategies of the British state become a performance text. Through this ironic interrogation, Mann brings the disconcerting sounds of debasement into the lecture hall, making what Carlyle famously captured as the "huge, inarticulate question" of the British poor "audible to every reflective soul" in the lyceum, where it hangs in the air, enunciated as an emblem of the effects and results of educational neglect.[34] Such passages might have been a technique for forging transatlantic sympathy, but such a response is repeatedly undercut. Mann aims to convince audiences of the impossibility of a connection, with language, morality, and religion all in peril under conditions of industrial modernity inextricably tied to physical decline.

The two-part structure is the lecture's most striking feature, and this divided portrayal played into multiple midcentury Anglo-American tropes. Its reliance on antithesis, and its dualistic vision of a pathologically divided British state, placed it squarely in the mainstream of popular party system rhetoric. Yet it also seems to play into the prevailing "two nations" rhetoric of Young England that would soon be popularized by Benjamin Disraeli's *Sybil* (1845). [35] In a more immediate but ambivalent fashion, it drew upon what we might call the "condition of England" diptych of sensationalist British writings. Texts such as Pierce Egan's *Life in London: Day and Night Scenes* (1821), Douglas Jerrold's *The History of St. Giles and St. James* (1841), and James Grant's *Lights and Shadows of London Life* (1842) involved rich dialectical response to the contradictions of Regency and Victorian modernity,[36] and there was a healthy transatlantic pirated readership for such texts in the periodical press.[37] The trope of gothic contrasts also became an American discourse in the hands of works such as Charles Edwards Lester's *Glory and Shame of England* (1842), an epistolary treatment of the same themes whose John Martinesque frontispiece captures an apocalyptic medley of icons as variously glorious and shameful as those in Mann's account.[38] Whether in print or on the stage, the compensatory and contradictory rhythm of a cultural code that Kate Flint has termed "part horrific investigation, part voyeuristic" text became an idiomatic analytical rhythm of the period.[39]

In place of the even-handed balance of Emerson's "England," therefore, Mann offered a fractured body politic composed of contradictory, incompatible impulses and desires.[40] Once again, the choreography of performance was crucial. With two vastly divergent "visions" rendered sequentially, the oral form took on the dynamic of a tragic descent as much as a process of recoil and withdrawal. As this sequence of contrasts unfolds temporally, it invites other analogies: to the panorama; to the movements of a musical composition; to the structure of sermonic form or a judicial pronouncement.[41] In classical oratorical terms, Mann's speech fused panegyric to philippic, with praise of British "glory" merely the *confutatio* or acknowledgment of counterarguments preceding the *narration*, or central thesis, of the nation's "shame." Judging from the press response, audiences walking home from Mann's series of gothic contrasts were conscious of their having experienced a hybrid mode. Drawing as heavily upon the sensationalist register and iconography of Jerrold and Lester as on the rationalist template of Chadwick, Mann's rhetoric reveals the composite nature of midcentury reform.

Greeley's Hyde Park Dramaturgy

Greeley had returned from serving as a juror at London's Great Exhibition enthused with the potential of industry and global cooperation, and toured the Northeast with a piece entitled "The Crystal Palace and Its Lessons." In presenting his own account of revelatory transatlantic experience, Greeley drew even more than Mann had done upon vivid modes of analysis and theatricality. This lecture represented a significant evolution from his earlier accounts of his time in London.[42] His letters home for the *Tribune* had been boisterously dismissive, but during his attendance at the Exhibition an undercurrent of reluctant respect emerged for the organizational and industrial achievements of the British. By the time he came to lecture on his experiences, he had become a convert to virtues of the Exhibition and strove to dramatize the reformist conversion experience he had seen in Hyde Park, presenting the paradoxes of Old World modernity in terms of an inclusive communal experience.[43]

After a brief introduction, he began the central movement of his lecture by "guiding" listeners in elaborate fashion through a description of the sensual experience of the Palace:

> There are doors on all sides, one or more devoted exclusively to the reception of articles for exhibition; one for Jurors in attendance on the Fair;

others for the Police, the Royal visitors, &c.; while the main entrances
for paying visitors are upon the south side, into the transept. But we will
enter one of the three or four doors at the east end, and find ourselves
at once in the excessive space devoted to contributions from the United
States. (8)

Over the course of this tour, the lecture script escorts the listener through successive present-tense tableaux ("before us are large collections of Lake Superior
Native Copper" [8]; "passing these ... we are confronted by abundant bales of
Cotton" [9]), periodically shifting into the second-person address customary to
travel guides ("as you pass laterally from the dazzling glories of the center aisle
... the fabrics of taste and adornment will greet you" [11]). Reveling in what Flint
has called the "geographical carnivalesque" of the Palace's layout, Greeley pointedly guides his listeners directly to the US exhibit, on the fair's eastern periphery,
bypassing the intended circuit through the western doors, which mandated initial
contemplation of the British sections.[44] From the American exhibit, the audience
is then guided "westward," crossing what he pointedly terms "the imaginary line
which here separates the United States from the nations of Continental Europe,
and look westward" (10). Audiences are then invited to consider the sensual over-
load of the Exhibition: "How magnificent the prospect! Far above is the sober
sky of canvas-covered glass, through which the abundant light falls gently and
mellowly. ... The aisle itself, farther than the eye can reach, is studded with works
of art" (11). After the sparse account of the American exhibit, here is the sensual experience audiences had come to hear, and continuing his playful theatrical idiom, he suggests a false ending, before extending the experience into three
dimensions: "And our journey is at an end. But no!—we have not yet mounted to
the upper story, whither four broad and spacious stairways in different parts of
the building invite us" (12).

This turn takes Greeley's audience up to the Exhibition's second floor, into the
space familiar from the popular illustration *The Interior of the Crystal Palaces,
viewed from the Gallery level*. It is an image whose contemplative male gaze
crystallizes the famous role of the Exhibition as arena for human observation,
and one that Greeley's script emphasizes as he directs his listener's own gaze
down toward the spectacle of European fabrics below the gallery in a significant
humanistic gesture:

But the eyes ache, the brain reels, with this never-ending succession of the
sumptuous and the gorgeous; one glimpse of sterile heath, bare sand, or
beetling crag, would be a sensible relief. Wearily we turn away from this
maze of sensual delights ... these we do not care to look upon again. MAN
is nobler than the works of his hands; let us pause and observe. Hark! the
clock strikes ten; the gates are opened; the crowds which had collected
before them begin to move. No tickets are used; no change given; it is a
"shilling day." (16)

As with the rhetoric of elevation familiar from Mann's treatment, Greeley uses the gallery level to lend authority to his appraisal. In one sense, this gallery vantage point serves as a figurative conception of the liminal American place in the global public sphere: at once part of, yet apart from, the European powers behind what he termed "the imaginary line" (10). But this turn to the crowd of visitors is a central moment in the dramatic structure and political meanings of the lecture. By dramatizing the rejection of the seductions of Old World luxury and plenty, the lecturer's stewardship guides listeners away from this threat and toward "this vast tide of life, which ebbs and flows beneath our gaze as we stand in the gallery," which Greeley claims as "the grand spectacle of all."

This precinematic touristic rhetoric was typical of tendencies in both 1850s culture and contemporary scholarship to read the Exhibition as dramatic spectacle.[45] To many at the time it seemed only fitting that the most suitable means of capturing its bizarre qualities was through the illusions of visual display. Other lecturers and performers delivered their own accounts of the fair, including P. T. Barnum, who had also been present in London, and whose widely exhibited *Moving Panorama of the World's Fair* prompted the *Boston Evening Transcript* to remark that "we need no longer trouble ourselves with asking questions of the happy fellows who visited London last year."[46] Though Greeley was a vocal critic of Barnum's culture of spectacle, his choreography of the event in the lyceum was part of a continuum with a range of competing performance events.[47] Whereas other adaptations tended to reduce the complexity of event to surface and spectacle, Greeley's choreography used the resources of language to direct perception and attention in the interests of explicit political goals of global commerce and international trade.

These strategies, working in tandem with other choreographed moments, helped to frame Greeley's description more subtly as a form of metacommentary drawing elaborate parallels between the spaces of Crystal Palace and lecture hall. First, Greeley's account centered on its status as an idealized forum of cosmopolitan interaction. Describing the Exhibition floor from the gallery, he paints for his audience an image of a liminal postnational space:

> The Civilized World here is strongly represented. America and Russia, France, and Austria, Belgium and Spain, have here their Commissioners, their Notables.... On every side sharp eyes are watching, busy brains are treasuring, practical fingers are testing and comparing. Here are shrewd men from the ends of the earth: can it be that they will go home no wiser than they came? (18)

The idealism of international cooperation and observation in Hyde Park becomes a theater of self-identification resembling that of Douglass's microcosmic mixed street scene. Despite its ethnocentric emphasis on the "Civilized World," his outspoken praise for the diversity of the Exhibition sits well alongside William Wells Brown's account of "the great deal of freedom" he had experienced as an

African-American in Hyde Park: "The prince and the merchant, the peer and the pauper, the Celt and the Saxon, the Greek and the Frank, the Hebrew and the Russ, all meet here upon terms of perfect equality."[48] Building on the above invocation, Greeley's second metarhetorical gesture in the final minutes of the piece turns to reflect on the potential of civic collectivity:

> As individuals, the few can do little or nothing; but as the State the whole might do much—every thing—for these poor, perishing strugglers. As I look out upon their ill-directed, incoherent, ineffective efforts to find work and bread, they picture themselves on my mind's eye as disjointed fragments and wrecks of Humanity—mere heads, or trunks, or limbs—(oftener "hands")—torn apart by some inscrutable Providence, and anxiously, dumbly awaiting the creative word, the electric flash, which can alone recombine and restore them to their proper integrity and practical efficiency.

As Greeley himself stares out over heads of audiences in small-town and city lyceums, he therefore allows himself to imagine an American miscellany. Listening audiences are encouraged to measure themselves against the Hyde Park multitude and the "vast tide of life" he has conjured up in their midst. Figuring collective power in the passage explicitly in terms of the "power to speak," he uses the symbolism of the unifying power of oratory to extend and reinforce the connection between institutions of speech and civic institutions of state expression such as the Crystal Palace. In this, and in his final metaperformative invocations—"'ere we meet again as workers"—the lecture repeatedly makes and unmakes a series of connections between the *spaces* of Crystal Palace and lecture hall, and the seas of faces, securing their implication into the lessons for labor, whose future he will outline by assuming the role of the lecturer-prophet.

Prophecy and Choreography

The second dimension of the choreography of reform lay in the establishment of modes of rhetoric that fused spatial and temporal movement. Orators such as Mann and Greeley put to work rhetorical techniques that moved audiences through a slide-show spectacle of British modernity, while also guiding them toward imagined endpoints. In so doing, they used the concept of an Anglo-American present to consider issues such as the teleology of nationhood and speeds of national development, asking audiences to contemplate what Mann called the "great principles" and "destinies of mankind" inherent in the fact of British modernity.[49] The handling of this process necessitated the assumption and construction of the rhetorical role of prophet, and the formulation of visions of an Anglo-American future conceived in spatial as well as temporal terms.

Mann's vision of the destiny of British society was uncompromisingly bleak. "A different spirit is now taking possession" of the British workers, he asserts in the final minutes of his script, "a spirit of envy towards the wealthy, of vengeance towards rules, of vandalism" (46). These dark premonitions are given shape in a closing Gothic architectural image:

> And here it is that Great Britain now presents the spectacle of a vast and lofty edifice whose burnished pinnacles and towers give back to sun and stars, splendor for splendor, whose midway walls and bulwarks are solid with adamantine strength, but whose basements and crypts—filled with shells and explosive magazines—are inhabited by madmen. (46)

In this tripartite architectural image, the aristocratic upper reaches of society maintain consonance with heavenly forces, giving "back to the sun and the stars"; middle-class stability and strength are figured as "adamantine"; and proletarian unrest is figured as literally explosive. The abjection of the toiling millions invoked throughout his speech is stripped of sympathy, and returns in the form of a prediction of upheaval. This infernal imagery prompts the series of questions that his material has yielded, relating to the demographic pressures of mass immigration:

> Shall this great lesson given in the providence of God be lost upon us? Shall all this suffering and crime of 20 millions of people bear no warning to our society, to prevent similar calamities for the hundred millions of people who will soon dwell in this broad land we inhabit? . . . Shall not the retribution of others be admonition to us? Or, must nation after nation rise up, to perform an infernal cycle of sin and suffering? (47)

Listeners are forced to conceive of this cyclical historicism—the "cycle of sin and suffering" and "retribution" of class warfare—as an acute dilemma for the republic as it "rises" to maturity.

Greeley engaged comparable themes of futurity through his own speculative and teleological question: how would the republic define itself historically? It was a note established in the flight of Romantic historicism with which the piece began:

> EACH age, each race, inscribes itself; with more or less distinctness, on History's dial. Nineveh, almost faded from our traditions of the world's infancy, revisits us in her freshly exhumed sculptures and in the vivid narrations of Layard. The Egypt of Sesostris and the Pharaohs survives no less in her pyramids and obelisks than in the ever-enduring records of Moses and Manetho.... The England of the last three centuries confronts us in the Bank—not a very stately nor graceful edifice, it must be allowed; but very substantial and well furnished—the fit heart's core of a trading, money-getting people. So we Americans of the Nineteenth Century will

be found in due time to have inscribed ourselves most legibly, though all unconsciously, on the earth's unfading records—how, or in what, time alone can tell. Perhaps a railroad over the Rocky Mountains, a telegraph across the Atlantic. (1)

The historical forces or Geist of nineteenth-century geopolitics and the "pervading spirit of enterprise generated by Commerce" of the Crystal Palace were presented as a dramatic challenge for the republic, a demand for comparable national "inscription." Breathing deep in what Michael E. Woods has called "the political economy of hope" of antebellum reform, Greeley sees British modernity as a guarantor of the republic's own future happiness.

As his speech progresses from the epideictic display rhetoric of his guided tour to the deliberative material of solutions and propositions, he adopts his own position as omniscient sage.[50] He gazes in Carlylean fashion "out upon" the poor of Britain and their "ill-directed, incoherent, ineffective efforts to find work and bread," toward an even more elevated prospect that establishes a parallel between "clarity" and "height" of vision:

> To my mind nothing is clearer than this—the immense strides and vast scope of invention and discovery during the last age, render morally certain the achievement of far more and greater triumphs during the like period just before us ... I doubt not that our children, looking back on that progress from heights whereof we can but vaguely dream, will honorably distinguish the World's Exhibition of 1851. (28)

Second, he predicts an imminent crisis for European monarchies. "It is time the World's Fair were closed, or this meager account of it," he argues, since "the year 1852 has sterner work in hand": namely, a "battle summer" in which "the skies are red with gathering wrath of nations." A series of European rules are cataloged, Greeley predicting their downfall amid a rising spirit of unrest that crucially does not include Britain. The prophecy of the downfall of European monarchy and the survival of the renovated rulers of London is presented as the "cheering truth" (29) and the dramatic culmination of Greeley's appraisal. The Great Exhibition became for Greeley what a recent collection has termed a "Victorian prism," allowing him to use transatlantic experience to ratify his evolving status as national oracle.[51]

In both cases, the power of Greeley's and Mann's lectures depended on their ability to inhabit the role of prophet imagined in terms of ascension and elevation. Throughout his piece, Greeley is careful to disavow this role, moderating his claims to insight through self-effacing deflations of his "crude and hasty suggestions" (2), and "this meager account" (31). In a cautious tone comparable to Mann's, he states his simple intention to "try to give some general notion of its character, by glancing at the more obvious details, so far as I, at this distance of time and space, may be able to recall them" (8). Nonetheless, the consciously polemical goal of the piece is as much a product of persona as persuasion. As with Mann's "bird's eye" positioning, Greeley secures this persona through constant reference to the spatial position, providing the platform for his closing prophetic gestures. Having ascended to this raised subject position for the dramatic climax of the epideictic section of the lecture, Greeley shifts to his deliberative reflections, alternating between observations intrinsic to the Exhibition hall, and those more extrinsic, messianic visions: "From our elevated and central position almost the entire length of this magnificent promenade is visible" (17). From his position in the gallery level, Greeley presents this simple vision of the industrious mass as "some prophetic premonition of the New Age dawning upon mankind" (18). He uses the rhetoric of revealed truth and insight to elevate by extension the position of the United States into one of unique privilege in world history.

Greeley's lecture is thus bookended by passages of prophetic vision, both of which are legitimized and secured by reference to his firsthand experience of the Exhibition. Often such moments are narrated in a continual present tense: "standing amidst this labyrinth of British machinery, this wilderness of European fabrics, I cannot but ask ..." (21). However, as the "lessons" continue, we gradually shift from present-tense deictic references to "here" to past-tense formulations using "there," as Greeley slowly modulates away from the gallery position: "These convictions are not new to me, but they were strengthened by weeks of earnest observation in the Crystal Palace" (22); "More and more was I there convinced" of the need for "combination of labor" (22). In this way, prophecy is figured as a form of external perspective. Greeley's subsequent travels in Europe were framed as providing this critical distance necessary to dispassionately analyze domestic American problems, while reinforcing his role as an arbiter of cultural prestige. Greeley derived the authority of his speech from his firsthand experience of Britain; his lecture rhetorically located access to truth in his authentic experience of the Old World.

The choreography of reform enacted through such rhetorical gestures helped give shape to the public's understanding of its Anglo-American past, and by extension its future, not least through the aggregation and implied comparison of these two cultures. For Greeley, the centripetal force of the Great Exhibition and its values of global intercourse suggested a future of growing cooperation between the British and American peoples. For Mann, the lessons could not have been more different. He asked audiences to simultaneously embrace Anglo-American identity and inheritance, while rejecting its excesses as symptoms of the past rather than the future. The central image of his lecture was one of "divergent paths" for the republic: a divergence between a failed social model that would generate an anarchic working class, and one whose education of the poor would secure the nation's future health. His "bird's eye" detachment ultimately counseled separation from uncritical affection for British society and culture, while his "sober and instructive view" revealed Britain's failings and rejected their claims to offer proper standards for American life. Moreover, his rhetoric was one of social and cultural contagion—of preventing the transfer of "mature, full-grown calamities" across the Atlantic.[52] In his hands, philanthropic discourse reinforced notions of the impossibility of mutual recognition, powerfully communicating to audiences how irretrievably backward British publics were by comparison with those that sat before him as he spoke in the auditoriums of the Northeast. It was a form of eastward-gazing demonization tinged with the exotic, and balanced with a nostalgic nod to a great yet faded past, reminiscent of the most pernicious undertones of European Orientalism and serving a not dissimilar rhetorical purpose, one captured in an 1846 Brooklyn report of the lecture, which reflects on the greater proximity of the British poor to "Hottentots and Patagonians" than to the American public.[53]

In both lectures, the performance of prophecy was amplified in the experience of live rendition. The very duration of a spoken performance served this end: lecturing as a process that unfolds over time was particularly crucial to the effect of Mann's piece, since the shape of his diptych or dual form enacted the process of a tragic fall. The narratology of medieval diptychs was typically eschatological, presenting a panel of the living, followed by the departed, and Mann's comparable process invited audiences to turn from the "glory" of Britain's past to the "shame" of its present.[54] Such a rhythm served to underscore a temporal distinction of American belatedness.

In both, too, this enactment of revealed prophecy underscores the crucial debts of the lecture form to the habits of nineteenth-century Protestant practice: both on one level enacted a Whig polemic; one another, a quasi-biblical dialectic resolving in the balance and harmony of vice and virtue.[55] Both drew upon the sermon form, using the lyceum as a mode of secular preaching.[56] The status of lyceum discourse as displaced religious reflection was never clearer than in the homiletic presentation of the "text" of social reality followed by the commentary of social analysis. Mann's piece ends in just such a homiletic and didactic manner, with the only real moment of direct address to the audience:

> You then who hope for fortune and have friends or children to inherit it; you who care to know by what hand the scales of justice are to be held and on what principles the honorable and the base are to be rewarded, you to whom the deeper sense of humanity and religion and the coming myriads of mankind mean something more than the shadows of a dream; you who stand at the angle of those divergent paths, whereof one leads to the depths of ruin, infamy and remorse, but the other to the heights of joy, renown and immortal blessedness—guide, guard, elevate, sanctify, the rising generation! (47–48)

What might appear as a generic extolment of youth also serves as an expression of impassioned warning. "Rise" here serves to connote both germination and flourishing, but also the negative processes of encroachment. This closing peroration for the "rising generation" is thus predicated on his fear of unchecked suffrage; the "coming myriads" refer not just to bodies from other shores, but also to those empowered by the Jacksonian franchise. And here, prophecy as a form of social control fulfills this historically sacred role through a secular setting. Mann's lecture bridles and subjugates his audience by using this powerfully symbolic representation of England as a regulatory force, holding up the nation as an irreconcilable antithetical model. It could by extension be seen to operate as a displaced jeremiad, reconfiguring the dramatic dualisms inherited from Calvinism in terms of an admonishment proceeding inductively from another society's failings. Greeley urged audiences forward; Mann counseled them back from an imagined brink. Both relied upon the spatial and temporal aspects of prophecy to imagine the Anglo-American commons as a live and urgent matter of immediate action.

Choreographies of Response

The role of the lecturer as clairvoyant was far from straightforward to negotiate. In 1858, thoroughly disillusioned with the vagaries of lecture culture, Thoreau declared in his journal that "audiences do not want to hear any prophets":

> They do not wish to be stimulated and instructed, but entertained. They, their wives and daughters, go to the Lyceum to suck a sugarplum. The little of medicine they get is disguised with sugar. It is never the reformer they hear there, but a faint and timid echo of him only. They seek a pass-time merely.[57]

With varying degrees of transparency, the "audience" of the print media helped police this distance between prophetic sound and the "echo" to which Thoreau refers. Press mediation made its own attempts to define the limits and meanings of the nonprint public sphere by choreographing their own representations of reform. In particular, by casting reformers almost as fictive protagonists and dramatis personae in the tapestry of national life, they exerted a powerful influence over perceptions of the sincerity or inauthenticity of reform culture. For Mann and particularly for the more ostentatious and elusive Greeley, these acts of media choreography played an often poorly understood role in dictating the terms on which their actions were understood.

Mann first performed "Great Britain" in 1844–46 before reviving it in 1853–55. Shifting responses to the lecture during its two periods of performance reveal various modes of media encoding. Whereas fellow Whig speakers such as Daniel Webster and Greeley tended to adopt flamboyant modes of self-presentation, 1840s images of Mann reveal a staid, stern appearance.[58] (See Figure 4.1.) Accounts of his oratory therefore focused on his forcefulness: one spoke of his "strong heart and strong hand"; another lamented that "he partakes of excessive zeal"; a third that he strove unduly "hard to produce an immediate

FIGURE 4.1 *Horace Mann, carte de visite, 1850*

impression."[59] Six feet tall and commanding in bearing, he represented the model of a Ciceronian orator—the man of public affairs equipped to give order to society—and his apparently stentorian presence can be read as expressive of a reform-physiology emphasis on regulation of the body. This acquired a new significance in "Great Britain," a central idea of which was that Old World modernity had affected a physical decline in the English poor. Mann's carriage can be seen to represent the counterexample of the patrician body on display, regulated and in control.

One typical response to "Great Britain" during Mann's first tour of the piece was the tendency to make explicit the unstated sources and traditions upon which his lecture drew. A report in the *Brooklyn Eagle* from January 1845, for example, reminded readers of the origins of his gothic contrasts with the au courant gesture of "in other words he led us through 'St. Giles and St. James,'" naming Grant's exposé, then being serialized in the *Living Age*.[60] Making such comparisons explicit reduced Mann's reformist representation to literary cliché, connecting his elevated mode of social analysis to this disreputable cultural counterpart. When Mann revived the lecture in 1853, his public profile had undergone a significant transition,[61] while the intervening years had also witnessed important shifts in the climate of North American perceptions of Britain. Following the apparent decline of Chartism and the triumphalism of the Great Exhibition of 1851, the nation seemed to have weathered the storm of internal collapse. Faced with this apparent new "age of equipoise," the specter of imminent British decline no longer served the simple moral function it once had for foreign observers, amid a new spirit of pragmatic, capitalistic cooperation between the two nations.[62]

The media's response to these new conditions of national debate can be atomized through one paper's intriguing choreography of a vivid moment of audience interaction. In the *New York Times* report of 10 March 1853, an account of "Great Britain" at the Broadway Tabernacle closed its report with a richly suggestive scene that served to complicate these meanings:

> At the conclusion of Mr. Mann's address, a gentleman from the gallery said he would like to say a word on the other side of the question. He was from the manufacturing districts, and could say that the statements made were exaggerated; that— ... The gentleman's voice was overpowered by a storm of sibillation.[63]

As with most accounts of audience interjection, the rhetorical effect is ambivalent. The recording of this kind of audience response in lecture transcripts was a stenographic characteristic of the fledgling *Times,* but the dramatic rendering of the scene marks it out as something more than a simple depiction of atmospherics. Aptly illustrating the transatlantic divisions explored in the previous paragraph, the "gentleman" duly appears to give "a voice against" Mann's account. This scene vividly recreates the sense of audience-hood of the 1850s circuit: the assembled public's apparently spontaneous adherence to the conventions of the lyceum suggests the persistence of an idea of a highly rarefied arena of lyceum oratory, in which disruptive acts such as these, though seemingly respectful, were nonetheless taboo, and a violation of sacred space. On the other hand, the "heckle" depicts Mann's reformist gesture as a live, urgent thing, and dramatizes the disciplinary function of the public sphere as a spectacle of confrontation and a staged controversy.

The *Times* voiced the heckle as a testimony to dissent, but did so equally with a view to circumscribe that dissent. Its playful typographical reproduction of the "sibillation" re-enacts a cathartic moment of democratic silencing. However, by framing his objection in terms of "the other side of the question" it also legitimizes a debate, and given the tone of the *Times's* recent coverage of Anglo-American affairs, the fictional scene it sketches can be read in several ways. On 12 March, two days after Mann's report, the *Times* printed an editorial entitled "England and America" that argued that, while talk of perfect Anglo-American amity was "excessive," the recent resurgence of Anglophobic rhetoric from demagogues such as Stephen Douglas was even more counterproductive to the spirit of commercial cooperation.[64] "It will be far more difficult than ever before," the paper declared, for those aiming "to create suspicion of [British] designs and dread of her purposes" or "stir up hostile distrust" amid the American public.[65] Since such "dread" was at least partly the effect of Mann's lecture, it seems possible to discern a genuine measure of ambivalence in the dramatic closure of the *Times* report. As if to confirm this, that day's edition also printed an extensive letter from the "gentleman" heckler from the Tabernacle, choreographing the workings of a public sphere centered on controversy as unresolved spectacle.[66]

Greeley's reception, on the other hand, was typically dominated by a fascination with his appearance, with reports habitually casting him as an outlandish figure.[67] "Reading" Greeley as a text was as creative and feverish an activity as it was in the cases of Douglass and Emerson, with reporters turning their focus on his demotic, willfully eccentric, "uncultured" appearance while attempting to gauge its apparent pretension or sincerity. In 1858, one commentator observed that "his careless, slipshod, slovenly way of dressing his person, has rendered him a man of mark and remark. His white hat and white coat have been immortalized, because they are ever worn and everlasting."[68] His lyceum costume in the 1850s was captured in Mathew Brady's 1851 daguerreotype and in the frontispiece of Parton's *Life of Greeley* (1855), both of which show the hat and notorious white coat that became shorthand for the editor in political cartoons of the period (see Figure 4.2).

The combined attributes of Greeley's costume, bearing, and vocal style represented a conscious class performance, and were often interpreted as such.[69] In 1861, two political opponents wrote in frustration of his "objectionable hat or the eccentric coat, or the affected drawl."[70] His disheveled appearance was one that Parton tellingly characterized as "elaborate disorder," a costume that "would be applauded on the stage as an excellent 'make-up.'"[71] His persona was in itself an eloquent symbol of the coming age of egalitarian republicanism, self-consciously at odds with the norms of the bourgeois public sphere. Attending a lyceum address by Greeley was not to submit to a stable, uncontroversial bearer of truth; it was to encounter one of the chief exemplars of a bracing, often troubling Jacksonian democracy.

Greeley's presence at the Great Exhibition had already been understood as a drama of sorts, and his excursion to Hyde Park occasioned a degree of comment regarding the potential transatlantic incongruity of his strange mode of dress. "Among the numerous representatives of the American press now in London is Mr. Horace Greeley," lamented the *Savannah Republican*. "The 'shocking old hat' and old 'white coat' do not give John Bull a very correct notion of our members of Congress."[72] Returning from London, ironic fears were even expressed that he may have potentially been changed by the experience. "The late Hon. Horace Greeley returned from his 'grand tour' of Europe," the *New York Mirror* wryly noted in September 1851. "What will Mrs. Grundy say, if we tell her that the philosopher of the *Tribune* comes back completely metamorphosed—with whiskers and mustache ... and long-waisted, short skirted black coat!"[73] His tour of the "Crystal Palace" pushed these aspects of his persona into relief, and encouraged the public to attempt to gauge any potential change.

FIGURE 4.2 *James Parton, The Life of Horace Greeley, frontispiece*

Greeley's self-presentation as triumphant returning juror, then, spoke to the confrontational aspect of this unruly, linen-coated prophet's involvement in the Exhibition. Responses to the lecture, with their emphasis on physical scrutiny, demand to be read in terms of the fresh symbolism that his "class performance" had acquired as the result of transatlantic experience. Given the complexity of the discussion surrounding the Great Exhibition, Greeley's meanings were doubly fraught. At the height of the Exhibition, the correspondent of the *Georgia Telegraph* wrote from London dismayed at how Americans were "gulled [by the] benevolent professions of England towards this country," pointing to the "real aim" of abolitionist "schemes to unsettle the relations of harmony" of North and South.[74]

Some reports can therefore be read in terms of a journalistic attempt to banish Whig reform as the realm of the outlandish.[75] Reporters' persistent focus on

Greeley's appearance and dress suggested an oppositional privileging of delivery over content. One report from Barre, Massachusetts, in January 1852 was particularly excessive in this regard, observing,

> We fancy [the auditors] were moved, as much as anything by curiosity to see the man of whom so much has been written, and whose journal penetrates into almost every village of the land. If Mr. Greeley were the denizen of some country town, he would not be regarded as anywise peculiar to his personal appearance and habits; but being a citizen of no mean city, it is natural that his want of "smartness" of cityish style, should have drawn down upon him the criticism of his compeers. Mr. Greeley is a taller man than we had supposed—he is, say, five feet ten. He walks and stands, stooping forward; the bump that erects the head is wanting. His head is large, with a bald patch over it from front to rear, which leaves his long flaxen hair straggling down the sides and back. . . . As to habiliments, we must say that Mr. G's hat was not in the latest style—it looked as though it had been out in a storm and had not been well cared for afterwards. That same old white overcoat protected his person, which was otherwise arrayed in garments worn rather *negligee*.[76]

In their almost phrenological intensity, such descriptions suggest a degree of irony that we might productively understand in terms of the complex cultivation of theatrical response. Tracy Davis's definition of the process of theatricalization in terms of "a spectator's dedoublement resulting from a sympathetic breach (active dissociation, alienation, self-reflexiveness) effecting a critical stance toward an episode in the public sphere" shows how such a response acts to introduce a mode of critical distance as a means of closing off debate.[77] Audiences are encouraged to reflect upon and evaluate the spectacle rather than the meditating on the substance of a lecturer's propositions.

One final example of reporter response, from a performance in Albany, New York, on 18 December 1851, shows how spectacle was also one of response and crowd dynamics. The day after Greeley's lecture, the *Albany Evening Journal* dramatized the remarkable scenes that greeted the speaker during the tour:

> For at least an hour and a quarter before the hour appointed for the lecture last evening, the crowd began to gather at the rooms of the Young Men's Association, and long before 8'o'clock, not only was every seat and aisle filled, but a large crowd stood around the entrance and stairway, apparently preferring rather to stand and be squeezed than to retire and lose the lecture. Hundreds were, however, obliged to leave, being unable to gain admittance. In common with the crowd, we went early, and during the hour we sat waiting, we were amused by an old Vermonter, who appeared to have ransacked all the newspaper files in the Union to find anecdotes of

Mr. Greeley. He treated us to some ten or fifteen good things, which he told in capital style.

The subject of the Lecture was "The Crystal Palace and Its Lessons." Mr. G. commenced by remarking that they could not expect from him a finished lecture, such as would be given them by Ralph Waldo Emerson, or any other of the distinguished lecturers who had the leisure for careful preparation. He, as a public journalist, engaged in the busy bustle of life, could do no more than devote an hour now and then to jotting down his ideas; and this lecture they would find little more than a superficial newspaper essay. But such was not the verdict of his audience. They deemed his lecture deeply interesting and sufficiently profound for all practical purposes.[78]

These lingering descriptions speak to intersection of celebrity, spectacle, and news in this overwhelmingly political state capital. Readers may well imagine that chief among the Old Vermonter's repertoire of stories were recent tales of Greeley's exploits in Hyde Park, and the transatlantic fame that had clearly swelled the "crowd ... squeezed" into the building to see this returning celebrity. In the telling account of his remarks, we also witness a form of cultural and aesthetic hierarchy being mutually negotiated by Greeley, the *Albany Evening Journal* and the YMLA audience. The report shows the lecturer disowning the craft of the lyceum lecture, but the audience's rejection of this self-criticism ("such was not the verdict of his audience") seems to place his discourse above the print media ("a superficial newspaper essay")—a verdict the report appears to willingly endorse. These and many other responses to figures such as Greeley help situate the activities of reformers as part of a culture of public and private entertainment.

Thanks to this choreography of response, reform prophecy was not limited to the public realm, but could also reach the most intimate of spheres. When Greeley's *The Crystal Palace and Its Lessons* was published in pamphlet form, one reformist journal advised in July 1852 that those "tired, discouraged, and sick of life" could do well, in their households, to "peruse or listen to the reading of this attractive Lecture ... a document imparting so much life, light, and energy."[79] By bringing the piece alive in this way in homes across the land, families could reimagine the dramatic movements of Greeley's London tour, and perhaps even reflect on its performance across the nation's stages. The scenes of Hyde Park became a world that readers could conjure up and reinsert themselves into, an Anglo-American commons brought alive in the parlor. This sense of the "light, and energy" of shared geography and shared traditions would find further expression in the years that followed, amid the remarkable scenes that would follow the arrival of William Makepeace Thackeray on the American lecturing stage.

Thackery

156 – Using his tour, in context of the copyright debate, as occaision not to protest but to promote a transatlantic readership, a version of the Ang – Am connexions.

⤷ At some time he used speech to monetize his words in the lit marketplace. Preparing his speeches for print w/ Am publisher.

throughout the book this is not a single network/value, but a discourse + means of value indyconcerl re lit audience + civic ideal.

⤷ Exploiting/selling an image of "global Englishness".

• Again the focus on reception as negotiation of method — Interpreted by Herald as anti-Irish. Turn his Anglo-Saxon attempt at cosmo into a nativism which they attack.

⤷ Speech making drawn into the debates policing the evt of assimilation + exclusion in urban N.E.

‖ lecture hall as "a flashpoint of 1850s urban pol" 162

166 – Thackery provokes Qs re rle of satire his openness clashing w/ civic ideas of lecturing as "social adhesive"

Britain and Kinship

WILLIAM MAKEPEACE THACKERAY
AS CULTURAL COMMONS

After disembarking from one of the new Bowery tramcars that rattled along Broadway, William Makepeace Thackeray made his way to no. 548 and entered the Unitarian Chapel. Millard Felt, the Secretary of New York's Mercantile Library Association, greeted him and began to show him round the space in which he was to speak the following night, 19 November 1852. As he inspected its cavernous interior, his response was a mixture of astonishment and bemusement. His companion, the British painter and writer Eyre Crowe, recorded:

> I shall not easily forget the author's expression of wonder when he looked athwart the long, dark, wainscoted benches, and saw the pillared nave and the oak pulpit. He seemed fascinated by the idea of his lay-sermonizing in this place. Then looking at the communion table, and appealing to Secretary Felt, he asked—"Would not the sacred emblems be removed from the altar?" Followed by the query: "Will the organ strike up when I enter?"[1]

What Crowe calls the space's "prevailing gloom" troubled the famous novelist's expectations. Thackeray's fascination was stirred by the combination of ecclesiastical solemnity and civic spectacle surrounding the assignment he had traveled from London to perform: the delivery of a series of mutedly satirical lectures on eighteenth-century English literature. The distance between the Chapel's faux-gothic atmospherics and the "mercantile" nature of his institutional hosts was as jarring as that between the gaudiness of the democratic republic and the belletristic repose of the Augustan world into which he planned to usher his listeners. These were a series of performances that he conceived in clear-eyed fashion as a straightforwardly commercial adventure, and he had written ahead to his New York publicist, James T. Fields, that he was "not afraid of any room in which my friends would think proper to hear me."[2] But his glimpse of his first Manhattan "room," with its fusion of civic and sacred space, suggested something else. It was the first of many indications over the next year that his appearance on the lecturing platform involved him standing in for a set of often contradictory cultural values.

Thackeray's two tours of the United States were among the most prominent mainstream entertainments of the decade. During the 1852–53 season he delivered a series of lectures, "The English Humorists of the Eighteenth Century," and returned for an even more extensive tour during 1855–56, speaking on the "four Georges" of the Hanoverian dynasty. His appearances became a ubiquitous feature of the press. As the *Literary World* put it in 1853, "Thackeray is in the wind, and American curiosity is on the scent."[3] Another magazine claimed the same year that "the delivery of these Lectures by Mr. Thackeray during the last winter constituted among us one of the most notable literary events which marked the season. In our principal cities, at least in the North, it was for a time the reigning fashion to read Thackeray, hear Thackeray, and talk Thackeray. It did not so much rain Thackeray as it poured."[4] When he spoke in Washington two presidents—the outgoing Millard Fillmore and his awaiting successor Franklin Pierce—were in attendance.[5] He was the subject of tempting overtures from P. T. Barnum to publicize him and make him part of a traveling show, an offer he declined.[6] His first tour took him through the Eastern seaboard, and into the South, and what one Boston paper called "Mr. Thackeray's clumsy graces and blundering charms of delivery" were repeatedly met with an almost rapturous response as a living symbol of an Anglo-American amity.[7]

Yet the idea of Thackeray taking to the platforms of the republic was also a strange proposition (see Figure 5.1). As Carlyle wrote to Emerson on hearing of the impending tour: "Thackeray is coming over to lecture to you; a mad world, my masters!"[8] City commentators shared surprise at the nature of his invite. "It is not the least interesting fact connected with this gentleman's appearance in America," remarked the *Tribune*, "that he comes on the invitation of the Mercantile Library Association," since it suggested that clerks of the city were now apt to "aspire to the culture of scholars and gentlemen ... decidedly it is a changed world which allows merchant's clerks, as a class, not only to enjoy, but actually to patronize such unquestionable luxuries as Mr. Thackeray."[9] "The old landmarks" of metropolitan life, the paper concluded, "seem indeed everywhere submerging."[10] The madness of the entrance of this global literary celebrity on the lecture circuit generated a dense body of material. To date, this historical record has been far less fully understood than the equivalent response to Dickens's American visits.[11] In what follows, I argue that these traces reveal a phenomenon that clarified important transformations in the ideals of lecture culture and the Anglo-American commons, one that this chapter attempts to explain in three ways.[12]

The first relates to the emergence of an idea of culture as adhesive force. As we saw in the previous chapter, lecture attendance was being actively promoted by the authorities of cities such as New York as one of the new "landmarks" of urban

FIGURE 5.1 *John Leech, "Mr. Micheal Angelo Titmarsh at Willis's Rooms," 1851*

life, through which forms of conduct, attention, and civic collectivity might be formed. The build-up to and reception of Thackeray's appearances helped make him both the representative of nineteenth-century tradition and literary prestige, and a mediator of English literary and cultural history for the Atlantic world. As I argue, both series of lectures represented attempts to reconfigure and offer a usable eighteenth century, and a literature and heritage belonging to all Anglophone readers. For American audiences, however, this was a shared tradition that Thackeray, as an Indian-born product of empire, embodied in fascinatingly contradictory ways. Building on the readings of Victorian "Englishness" in the work of Angelina Poon, Peter Sinnema, and Paul Langford, this chapter shows how the Thackeray of the platform offered a version of Englishness centered on shared values rather than place of birth.[13] His embodiment of a diasporic identity both resonated and jarred with various audiences in the patch-work republic of the 1850s, playing into American ethnic tensions resultant from British imperial legacies.

This sense of the author-lecturer as shared "luxury" also dovetailed with the dynamics of the midcentury copyright crisis. Thackeray's American ventures came a decade after Dickens's famous tour, and his notoriously unsuccessful campaign for an international intellectual property agreement. The presence of the author of *Vanity Fair* helped to revive this debate and bring an ongoing debate over the status of British books and ideas in North America into focus. As Paul Saint-Amour has argued, and Meredith McGill and Albert Clark have demonstrated in the American context, shifting understandings on international copyright must be seen as shadow forces in the history of literary production,[14] forces that Thackeray's twin roles as star performer and self-appointed cultural arbiter help to bring to the surface, allowing us to perceive anew the legal and political questions underpinning the rhetorical ideal of an Anglo-American liter-ary commons. The final lens through which this chapter approaches Thackeray's tours is that of the role of humor and geniality in indexing cultural divergence. As coverage of his performances reveals, the novelist who exposed power structures, challenged vested interests, and debunked aristocratic pretension fitted neatly within the dialogue of late Jacksonian and antebellum democratic politics. In particular, his lectures formed part of the transatlantic discussion of national comic styles: most specifically what Gregg Camfield calls the "rhetoric of geni-ality" as a means of rereading both the English past and the American present.[15]

Tightrope Walking

Immediately before departing to the United States in October 1852, Thackeray found evidence in a copy of the *New York Herald* in the reading room of the Liverpool Athenaeum that his imminent trip to the New World was not seen in a universally positive light. Under the heading "Another Cockney Character Coming Over," the paper dismissed the author as a snob and predicted that the only audiences he would meet would be "old-womanish societies," with an unpa-triotic zeal for "toadying" to foreigners. "There might be some excuse," the arti-cle conceded, "for our giving flattering receptions to such writers as Macaulay, Bulwer, Dickens, or even James of the 'solitary horseman' school, but as for feting Thackeray, it is ... ridiculous."[16] Among a variety of observers, the major con-cern was that, like Dickens before him, the novelist's real motivation was to accu-mulate material that would form the basis of travel book satire upon his return.

The genre of the transatlantic travel book was a notorious thorn in the side of early and Anglo-American cultural relations.[17] One part political and spir-itual pilgrimage, one part social satire, these books occupied a prominent if mostly unremarkable place in the literary landscape of both countries. While the

American part of the genre—from the essays of Washington Irving's *Sketchbook* (1819) through Harriet Beecher Stowe's *Sunny Memories of Foreign Lands* (1854)—typically adopted a fawning stance toward British sights, and while even more explicitly reform-oriented artifacts such as William Wells Brown's *The American Fugitive in Europe* (1855) and Elihu Burritt's *A Walk from Land's End to John O'Groats* (1864) still engaged positively with the lessons of the Atlantic voyage, the same was not true for British travelers to the New World. A sequence of seemingly mean-spirited accounts commencing with Frances Trollope's *Domestic Manners of the Americans* (1832) had culminated in the overt tone of disillusionment of Dickens's *American Notes* (1842). Some of these texts represent lasting archives of cultural analysis, but for the most part their popularity far outstripped the frequently formulaic nature of their observations. For English writers in particular, the apparent uncouthness, ill manners, and jingoism of the young republic seemed to confirm Old World superiority, and generated a rhetoric of the other nation as both freak show and troubling harbinger of human decline.[18] Trading in the narcissism of small differences, these books worked against notions of commonality, helping to disaggregate the two cultures through an imagery of misrecognition and dissonance.

Dickens's book in particular was widely seen in the United States as an unforgivable act of betrayal. His 1842 visit, and his subsequent rejection of everything he had once seemed to prize there, was remembered as an unreciprocated embrace. From a writer such as Thackeray, likewise synonymous with caricature and satire, a similar approach was widely feared. The *Cleveland Plain Dealer* advised all countrymen to be on their guard for this "bigoted and spiteful" satirist:

> It would be well for Americans to be a little on their guard, as to how they treat this man. They should lay aside their usual proneness to make gods of pigmies, keep Thackeray out of their private circles, and treat him just as if he was only Toddy Maloney from Cork ... go and hear him, but don't deify him, feast him, toast him and glorify him. Don't put the spectacles of vanity on him, he'll see crooked through the glasses of bigotry.[19]

Similarly, the *Brooklyn Eagle* warned upon the novelist's arrival that he had come "to lecture the Yankees and ... to collect material wherewith to charicature [*sic*] the American character, on his return to Cockneydom," and reminded readers that since his "chief merits as a writer consist in graphic portraiture [and] ... very keen sarcasm ... [he] will find ample material for their exercise in ridiculing the eccentricities of Americans, if they choose to make fools of themselves in lionizing such a mediocre individual on his arrival among them."[20]

Thackeray's American reputation was notably contradictory. For some, the caricaturist of *Vanity Fair* was simply an aristocratic apologist. John O'Sullivan's fiercely nationalist *United States and Democratic Review* labeled him "essentially an anti-republican," and readers were warned against succumbing to his ideology of prejudice and "rank": "don't prop the falling edifice of aristocratic pride. Let the building come down . . . you cannot delay its ruin at home, Mr. T;—do not put it into the heads of any Americans to erect another such framework here."[21] To others, however, the force of his satire suggested an entirely opposite tendency, toward an extreme critique of power structures. Thackeray's apparently universal and indiscriminate satirical agenda exhibited not misanthropy but a democratic impulse that was recognizably republican. This liberalist impulse behind his wit meant for the *New York Post* that it was "not the individual he exposes, but the social medium in which he has lived, the corrupt atmosphere, the perverted tone of sentiment, the frivolous ambitions, the consummate hypocrisies, which are the inevitable results of the existing social relations. In a word, Thackeray—without knowing it perhaps,—is the most tremendous Socialist of the day."[22]

At the heart of these conflicted expectations was the ambivalent concept and stance of "snobbery." An elaborate fixation with social distinction, assessment, and condescension was one of Thackeray's great themes, an attitude he had helped to codify through his *The Book of Snobs* (1848). The term was invoked in numerous contexts in the coverage of his American arrival. In outspoken critiques such as those of the *New York Herald*, it was used against both Thackeray himself and a fawning Anglophilic public, noting that

> in this country [he] has proved himself as great a literary snob as any described in his book. This writer has been vastly overrated on both sides of the Atlantic. Here, since his advent, he has been outrageously puffed up by the press, and like Dickens he will probably be courted and fawned upon by all the snobs of every circle.[23]

In similar terms, the *Daily Ohio Statesman* urged that "there be no 'snobbery' in receiving Mr. Thackeray, like the crazy displays made over Lind, Sontag and others."[24] Speaking of a reported confrontation between Thackeray and an overly zealous American patriot, the *Cleveland Herald* maintained that "it is such consequential snobbery as this, which gives visitors an impression that the American people, as a class, indulge in self-laudation; while among the education and intelligent, there is really as little of assumption and foolish pride as can be found anywhere."[25] This Midwestern sensitivity was part of a wider resistance of a discourse of civility; from a different perspective, some saw that attending his lectures might cure audiences of their own habits of false snobbishness. New York's *Evening Post* duly argued that Thackeray might even serve as antidote to the corrosive effect of such manner-consciousness, and it praised him as a "thorough, implacable, drastic enemy to the vast world of snobbery and humbug."[26]

For a British author of the 1850s, lecturing was a questionable choice that raised its own issues of snobbery. He nervously referred to himself as a performer in a "tight-rope exhibition," and this uneasy new role as "tight-rope dancer in ordinary to the nobility and the literati."[27] Its relationship to the public and to the market, and its proximity to the habits of the theater made it, as Thackeray himself recognized, less than "a seemly performance for an author" and he repeatedly spoke slightingly of his lectures to his friends as *"infra dig,"* partic-ularly in an American platform that conjured the associations of Barnum.[28] He first turned to the lecture platform in May 1851, delivering the series "Humorists of the Eighteenth Century" at Willis's Rooms in St. James's, news of whose prom-inence in the social calendar of the British capital had reached American shores. Though Carlyle's 1840 "Hero Worship" series provided a respectable precedent, the spectacle of such a major cultural figure lecturing in public was still a novelty in Britain, and curiosity meant that Thackeray commanded the most impressive audience yet. The crowd for his debut in Willis's Rooms boasted a mixture of London high society alongside the toast of the literary world, including Charlotte Brontë, who was scornful of the setting and fashionable audience, and Carlyle himself, who fidgeted through what he considered Thackeray's superficial and unimpressive remarks.[29] Accounts suggested a performer perhaps too much at his ease. The *Examiner* had damned the first talk with faint praise as having "sac-rificed much to effect."[30] Jane Carlyle complained privately that these speeches "are no great things—as *lectures*—but it is the fashion to find them 'so amus-ing'!"[31] Her husband took particular exception to Thackeray's ingratiatingly con-versational style, remarking, "I wish I could persuade Thackeray that the test of a great man is not whether he would like to meet him at a tea-party."[32] John Chapman, the noted freethinker publisher, was "much disappointed. The lecture was more like a long sermon than anything, and did not gain by being read."[33]

Having completed his London series, he then delivered the lectures at Oxford, Cambridge, Edinburgh, and Liverpool before taking them across the Atlantic the following year upon the completion of the novel *Henry Esmond*. By this point, coverage of the British performances had already reached the American press.[34] *Putnam's* had reported to American audiences that "the most notable of the aris-tocracy both by birth and of intellect were eager 'listeners.'"[35] Other accounts of half-empty lecture halls at his engagements in Liverpool were reported in a glee-ful manner. One particularly elaborate account from the London correspond-ent of the *New York Evening Post* ushered readers into this cardinal event in the London social scene:

> It was like a flash of lightning, then, from a dull November sky, when, cas-ually taking up the *Times,* I read that Mr. Thackeray was going to repeat one of his lectures on the wits of Queen Anne's reign, in a literary institu-tion not far from where I sojourned. Incontinently I caught up my hat and cloak, rushed as well as one could rush.[36]

The piece proceeded to describe the experience and the performer in the inten-sive terms that Thackeray would learn to be characteristic of the American press:

> He was a tall, brawny man, with a full face, clumsy abrupt manner, care-lessly dressed, his head turning grayish and with a quiet sagacious, and rather good-humored face. I should have said, without knowing him, that

he was a comfortable English gentleman and scholar and not a cynical philosopher. His voice was agreeable and distinct, but not loud, while there
was nothing of the orator in his manner. He merely read what he had to say,
as any well-educated man might read it, a little rapidly, and now and then
with a dry sarcastic interjection, as if it had just occurred. His emphasis
was often misplaced, and his modulations of voice unpleasant, while he
used no action.[37]

This account's intensive assessment provided a taste of both the attention that
was to come his way and the themes such coverage would engage: in particular, a
febrile combination of skepticism and expectation, and a sense of acute pleasure
in turning the forms of caricature wielded so fiercely in the great novelist's works
back on himself. Above all, perhaps, was the sense that this was a great social
phenomenon whose meanings could only be discerned through the approxima-
tion of the details of live encounter. As the *New York Times* put it, such "sketches
of his lectures in England . . . have sharpened the public eagerness to hear him."[38]
And it was not long before Americans could have their own chance to take their
measure of the man.

Representative Humorists: The 1852–53 Tour

Thackeray sailed from Liverpool to Boston on 30 October 1852, accompanied
by the painter Eyre Crowe as his secretary and research aide.[39] "Nobody is quiet
here" was his immediate positive response, and "no more am I—the rush and
restlessness please me."[40] Demand exceeded supply for tickets to his first run from
19 November to 6 December, and a second New York series was organized, on
top of four lectures at the Female Academy in Brooklyn, which began while the
other series was still being delivered. He then traveled to New York, where his lecture tour began, and then on through Philadelphia and Baltimore to Richmond.

The subject matter of his lectures had grown out of the process of historical
research into the Restoration and Augustan periods for his novel *Esmond* (1852).
The series presented a survey of the leading comic writers of the previous century,
offering entertaining assessment of Swift; Congreve and Addison; Steele; Prior,
Gay and Pope; Hogarth, Smollett and Fielding; and Sterne and Goldsmith.[41]
Stylistically, the pieces represented a curious mix of fictional sketch and scholarly research, and Thackeray often cast himself as someone who is trying on
roles, conjuring up historical figures in depictions that amounted to informed but
fanciful imaginative excursions. His appraisals were often stark and outspoken.
In talking of Swift, he was critical of the "caverns of his gloomy heart" and his
mistreatment of his wife, whose "laugh jars on one's ear after seven score years."[42]
Congreve was a "humorous observer, to whom the world seems to have no moral
at all"; Addison was praised for his "kind, serene, impartial humor"; Smollett was

"manly, kindly and irascible"; Fielding "may have had low tastes, but not a mean mind"; and in an encomium to Pope he saluted "the achieving genius, and do homage to the pen of a hero."[43] As performed in the United States, the series was concluded with a piece entitled "Charity and Humor" as a "supplement to the former lectures" that tied together the theme of the "righteous hatred of hypocrisy" latent in Thackeray's critical sensibility.[44]

These pieces were well suited to the lecture circuit, combining the attractions of literary prestige with biographical trivia. As a group portrait they formed part of a wider minigenre of lyceum entertainments, among which Emerson's *Representative Men* lectures were only the most well known.[45] Considering them as such, the *New York Times* claimed the lectures as "the most exquisite piece of biographical criticism and characterization we ever heard or read."[46] Moreover, they were part of a tradition of literary criticism on the 1850s stage, and, as with Oliver Wendell Holmes's "Lectures on the English Poets of the Nineteenth Century," and James Russell's 1855 series later published as *Lectures on English Poets*, Thackeray's pieces both traded in information and consciously worked to cement an Anglophilic popular taste.[47] It was well understood that Thackeray's treatment of this topic was a metacommentary on his own fame, and when he coyly suggested listeners "rank the present speaker among that class" of writers about whom he spoke, it was clear that he was making his own claim to the status within the tradition of comic men of letters.[48]

This expression of Anglophilic cultural capital was particularly well tuned to the desires and associations of 1850s audiences. Not only did they form part of a trend for discussions of Englishness, but they activated powerful nostalgia by presenting these authors repeatedly as part of a childhood inheritance: remarking of Addison, "Listen to him: from your childhood you have known the verses"; of Steele, that listeners receive "the expression of the life and of the time; of the manners, of the movement, the dress ... the old times live again, and I travel in the Old Country of England"; of reading Steele that "the past age returns ... the England of our ancestors is revivified."[49] In this way, his presentation was underpinned by the notion of the eighteenth century as a time of unified Anglo-American realities, and a refuge from the fractures and complexities of the nineteenth-century moment (see Figure 5.2).

Thackeray was fascinated by what he took to be an overwrought American obsession with the "lions" of the stage. However, in various ways his chosen topic, with its emphasis on the great men of literature and focus on reading personality, endorsed such an approach and licensed a kind of personalized pattern of response to him as a speaker and representative type. In the case of Thackeray, we might say such attention and such scrutiny was particularly relevant: a mode of sociocultural capture not entirely dissimilar from his own literary caricatures. His disposition and demeanor were much remarked upon. As Carlyle had written of Thackeray to Emerson in September 1853, there was something of a mismatch between his inner chaos and his outer calm: "He is a big fellow, soul and body; of

W^M THACKERAY. Boston. 1852.

AT THE MELODEON, BOSTON.

FIGURE 5.2 *Eyre Crow and Thackeray at the Melodeon Boston, 1853*

many gifts and qualities (particularly in the Hogarth line, with a dash of Sterne superadded), of enormous *appetite* withal, and very uncertain and chaotic in all points except his *outer breeding*, which is fixed enough, and *perfect*, according to the modern English style."[50]

While much focus stressed this aspect of sheer physicality, another strand seized on the deficiencies of his performance style. The *New York Courier and Enquirer* complained that "he in no way attempts the orator."[51] For the *New York Times*, "Mr. Thackeray's fascination lies wholly in what he says—nothing of it is due to the way in which he says it."[52] Recollecting the tour from old age, James Grant made the comparison with Dickens, noting how "the style of 'Boz' was that of the perfectly trained actor; of 'Titchmarsh' that of the accomplished gentleman amateur."[53] To the Boston *Courier*, he lacked "grace and elocutionary accomplishment. He seems to have studied Dr. Johnson's manners, and speaks in the same dogmatic style. He has no pity, no forgiveness and no charity to bestow upon an offender."[54] Some simply complained of his tendency to thrust his hands into his clothing as he spoke: "He scarcely makes a gesture, except an emphatic hiding of his hands in his pockets now and then, yet his listeners hang upon every word uttered. Mr. Emerson is the only one of our lecturers that we now recollect, who produces equal effects, with the same small apparent expenditure of means."[55] Others compared this unfavorably with the apparent style of his London performances in terms of the politics of his bearing, with *Putnam's* magazine recalling a generation later that "what especially amused an American was the apparent indifferent and nonchalant coolness of the lecturer, he seemed less deferential and more completely at his ease, more than when he repeated the same course to a *republican* audience at Dr. C's Church."[56]

More worrying were the ways in which his delivery worked against one of the key attractions of watching an English orator at work: to hear the English language rendered in all its authentic sonority. This expectation was incompatible with Thackeray's style. As the *Boston Evening Transcript* complained, for every passage that he read aloud, "Mr. T slurred it over abominably, in his reading."[57] However, to other minds, this artless performance was valuable. The *Tribune* saw this as something that suited the lecture circuit particularly well:

> His manner, without any oratorical pretensions, is admirably adapted to the lecture room. As a medium of instruction, it is far more graceful to the hearer than the more impassioned style, which is often adopted by our popular lecturers. The calm flow of his speech is so transparent that the sense shines through it without subjecting the mind's eye to too severe a trial. His voice is rich, deep, flexible and equally expressive of emotion and thought in his intonations—the words are delivered with that clean finish which so often distinguishes the cultivated Englishman.[58]

The calmness of this "perfectly unaffected" style was also noted by William Cullen Bryant for the *Boston Evening Post*, which observed, "The most striking features in his whole manner was the utter absence of affectation of any kind. He did not permit himself to appear conscious that he was an object of peculiar interest in the audience."[59]

A final strain of response turned the focus toward the audience, reading Thackeray's appearances explicitly in terms of what they signified about the host communities. Various cities used his talks to cement their reputations. One New England paper proclaimed that his Boston attendance and reception were "alike worthy of his distinguished reputation, and of the appreciating taste of our citizens."[60] The *Philadelphia North American* was similarly eager to stress how the attendance at his appearances there confirmed the "the literary and cultivation of the city."[61] Such an aspirational emphasis was indeed a theme that shone through key moments in his lectures: "Might I give counsel to any young hearer," he reflects in his lecture "Prior, Gay and Pope," "I would say to him, try to frequent the company of your betters."[62] To many, the prize of attending such events was the thrill of achieving precisely this kind of aspirational proximity. As the *New York Post* observed, upon the close of his performance, "Every auditor looked round to his neighbor, and nodded his head, as much as to say, *wasn't that capital?*"[63] In his final talk of this first tour, he spoke directly to the social symbolism of his performances as rituals of community, framing his task in terms of proving the existence of a literary audience in the United States:

> Long before I had ever hoped for such an audience, or dreamed of the possibility of the good fortune which has brought me so many friends, I was at issue with some of my literary brethren upon a point—which they held from tradition I think rather than experience—that our profession was neglected in this country; and that men of letters were ill received and held in slight esteem. It would hardly be grateful of me now to alter my old opinion that we do meet with good-will and kindness, with generous helping hands in the time of our necessity, with cordial and friendly recognition.[64]

And these themes of recognition and shared tradition were complicated and given added resonance by the broader context of the ongoing dispute over copyright.

Commons and Copyright

As *Putnam's* magazine noted after his first tour, "Mr. Thackeray's visit at least demonstrated that if we are unwilling to pay English authors for their books, we are ready to reward them handsomely for the opportunity of seeing and hearing them."[65] His visit played into the debate over intellectual property that had structured transatlantic literary life for the previous two decades. Two factors in particular complicate the meanings of his visit. By adopting a persona through his lectures as a mediator and custodian of the English literary tradition, he seemed to promote the validity of the idea of a shared tradition open to all. Second was the very fact that, as live performances, his utterances seemed to slip free of the constraints governing the entire copyright controversy. As a result of both, Thackeray perhaps unwittingly brought into sharp relief the legal and political questions underpinning the rhetorical ideal of an Anglo-American literary commons and our own critical methodology that Amanda Claybaugh has asked us to think of as a "new transatlanticism."[66]

Thackeray's tours were inescapably entangled within copyright controversies that had dominated Anglo-American relations during previous years. Because of an absence of international legal regulations and rights for authors, the reproduction and circulation of intellectual property in the form of pirated copies of British books was an entirely legal practice. It was also big business in the United States, where the resulting overflow of writings recycled from English presses vastly boosted readership for British authors while denying them royalties on this sizable secondary audience. Readers in both nations were enthusiastically consuming the same texts, but payment was a more complex matter. Far from simply being seen as a problem affecting British writers, this flooding of the North American market remained a serious obstacle to the commercial viability of native authors, and voices such as James Fenimore Cooper went further in 1842 in arguing that "adulation of foreigners, Englishmen in particular" was a severe block to the creation of a viable literary culture at home.[67] Attempts at legislation to address the situation during the preceding decade had raised hopes for British authors, and also catalyzed a debate among US publishers on the issues of international copyright, culminating in the unsuccessful Anglo-American copyright treaty supported by Fillmore and Pierce, rejected by the Senate in 1854.[68]

These issues had become front-page news during Dickens's visit to the republic a decade earlier. During his time in the United States, the novelist had lobbied Congress to ask that they recognize British copyright, only to have undercapitalized publishers argue that their future relied upon cheap imports. One feature of an ill-tempered public debate was the claim of a certain ideological hypocrisy in Dickens's efforts. "The very absence of such a law as he advocates," the *New World* magazine editorialized in 1842, "surely worked largely in his favor, not least since it carried the progressive message of his work to that class of his readers—the dwellers in log cabins, in our back settlements,—whose good opinion he says is dearer to him than gold and [to whom] his name would hardly have been known had an international copy-right law been in existence."[69] As McGill's account of the affair made clear, so alien was the culture of reprinting to Dickens "that he had difficulty comprehending why his vocal support for copyright posed a threat to his reputation."[70]

For his own part, Thackeray maintained a pragmatic view of these issues. He was certainly no stranger to the situation regarding his works, and in one amusing incident, stepping aboard a train in New York, the extent of this piracy became clear to him, as he heard a newsboy passing down the carriage shouting out his advertisement for the illicit "Thackeray's Works" he had to sell.[71] London press coverage ahead of his departure for the United States spoke to this awareness of the implications of these reading and publishing practices on the power relationships of an emerging globalized literary world:

> No Englishman who is looking for lasting fame among the Anglo Saxon race should forget that already the majority of his readers are found on this side of the Atlantic; and writers who have their eye fixed upon the future should, above all others, remember that in a humane and an enlightened age like this, any disrespectful or malignant word dropped against an entire nation will "return to plague its inventor."[72]

Clearly, one motivation of his trip was to take full financial advantage of the only way he could monetize this vast readership. Moreover, another motive for crossing the ocean was to liaise with the "pirates" directly, since, as John Sutherland puts it, the novelist, acknowledging that "half a loaf was better than no loaf, laughed and befriended the American publishers: James Fields in Boston, George Putnam in Philadelphia, and in New York the Appletons and the Harper Bros., who were the biggest pirates of them all."[73] Whereas Dickens had railed furiously, Thackeray was muted and diplomatic. He was aware of the dangers of alienating readers, and responded by making an agreement with Harper's, the "chief buccaneers" for the publication of his lectures in America, planning to hasten publication to forestall piracy.[74]

There is the wider sense, however, that Thackeray was attempting to fashion a collective shared tradition. The copyright dispute was understood in the antebellum period as a struggle between competing visions of a rapidly expanding marketplace. But it was also a conceptual issue about the shared traditions and discourses of two nations whose cultural divergence was matched on the level of feeling and affect. On the literal level, Thackeray saw the potential of this new scale and scope of readership. In the American preface to *Henry Esmond* (1852) he had touched on the question of American literary piracy, reflecting that "our names and writings are known by multitudes using our common mother tongue, who never had heard of us or our books, but for the speculators who have sent them all over this continent."[75] More broadly, he saw the lessons of this notion of commonality of readers: one that stretches beyond the nation, and a new conception of the public domain. He recognized the ways in which his role as custodian of the "English humorists" was helping to cement a transnational readership. If, as McGill argues, "antebellum ideas about intellectual property helped to produce a distinctive literary culture," then Thackeray duly saw the long-term potential in the influence a skewed market gave him to help promote a developing sense of commonality through celebration of the "common property" of literary tradition.[76]

His lecture tours introduced another dimension to these issues due to the uncertain legal status of spoken words.[77] Realizing that the American press mediation would likely transcribe his words and circulate them irrespective of consent, he took matters into his own hands and offered them for publication *[editing from speech]* immediately. He wrote to James Hannay on 21 October 1852, notifying him that "my Lectures are to be printed for fear of American pirates."[78] "Should no pirate carry my prize off," he later wrote to George Smith toward the end of November, "I shall even be able to give my lectures over again on my return to London before publishing them."[79] Reports repeatedly noted that Thackeray had forbade coverage, though others such as the *New York Times* capitulated given the conduct of their peers, noting, "As some of our contemporaries, however, have been less scrupulous in this matter to the entire defeat of the object which Mr. T. evidently designed to secure, we shall present an outline sketch of his lecture . . . little more than a dry skeleton."[80] Despite the fact that Thackeray made more money from lecturing during 1852 than from his published work, the role of these spoken pieces as artifact of shared experience was still uncertain. Audiences appeared to prize physical presence over even reproduced words.

The conceptual status or value of these pieces was certainly unclear from their very first performance in London. One Liverpool paper simply defined his task in terms of "appearing in public to deliver viva voce his ideas and opinions,"[81] while Forster reviewed them for the *Examiner* as "literary entertainment," and they stood at the crossroads of high and low cultures of display. However, the fundamental sense one gets from the body of response to his appearances was of his presence itself as commodity. There was a great deal of cultural capital attached to attendance. The question "'Have you heard Thackeray's lectures?,'" recalled the *Daily National Intelligencer*, "was among literary *quidnuncs* a question quite as important as the 'to be or not to be' of Hamlet. For to have heard them was 'to be,' and not to have heard them was 'not to be.'"[82] The *New York Tribune* tellingly referred to him as a "luxury," and with sensitivity to the claims of the whole nation, others complained that his visit must not be restricted like a "choice commodity" to the "happy few" of the Northeast. "If Jonathan has a cake, the whole family must come in for a share of it," they reasoned in January 1853. "Thackeray must make up his mind to a universal appreciation, north and south, east and west. There is no escape in our gregarious republic from this law of universal distribution."[83] This was a sense of common property and a duty to spreading this "Englishness"—this cultural product—as widely as possible, in ways that were to reveal the limitations of certain strains of the novelist's ideal of Englishness. As the *Charleston Courier* observed, the novelist was consciously trying to bind together an Anglophone commons that crossed sectional lines: "With an honest and manly sympathy, he recognized the literary affinities which bind the lecturer on such themes to his auditories . . . thousands of American friends."[84] In a sociocultural and legal sense, Thackeray was figured as common property as much as the literature about which he spoke. However, the importance of his two tours also lay in his embrace of the deeper "affinities" underpinning this shared commons.

Imperial Identities, Urban Politics

By speaking about English literature and history on the American stage, Thackeray also stood in for contentious forms of Anglo-American identity. At various points on his tour, there seemed to be willingness on the part of both performer and audience for embracing an expansive form of diasporic Englishness. A series of formulaic but revealing public statements help reveal the dynamics of this. At the close of his Brooklyn series, for example, the *Eagle* broadcast the host's spoken thanks to the lecturer for "the satisfaction we all felt in being carried back to the spring of pure English Lit, of which we were just as proud as Americans as was an Englishman."[85] Similarly, in his final Manhattan performance, Thackeray thanked the "gallant young patrons of the Mercantile Library Association, as whose servant I appear before you," and who eagerly passed a resolution celebrating the "more generous intercourse of thought between England and America," before the master of ceremonies added:

> Our honored guest has expressed himself as much pleased, at finding himself perfectly at home here, since we seem to live like every Englishman. Will he allow us to return the comparison, as we hope that it will not injure his standing at St. James's to have it said that he appears very much like a Yankee, likes what he likes, and thinks, writes, and speaks what goes to our hearts. That racy old English has to us the mother tone, and we rejoice to thank him in the free, glorious language which he brings to us in such purity, without stilted rhetoric or mawkish sentimentalism.[86]

On one level, such remarks were simply part of the empty rhetoric of lecture hall diplomacy. But the record of response reveals how the cultural work permeated far deeper. Englishman, Yankee, London clubland man of letters, and mercantile audience are presented as part of a continuum of Englishness, in the characteristic interpretive gesture of finding republican demotic candor in his purity of style. The appropriation of both literary tradition and Thackeray's Englishness was offered as an opportunity to reimagine and heal cultural dislocation. The act of hosting this celebrity author, and traveling with him through to the source of British literature, represented an elaborate ritual that smoothed the ruptures of half a century of divergent history.

But Thackeray's Englishness was also a product of his own theorization of a more explicit form of diasporic identity. In his first lecture on Swift, his manuscript defended the Anglo-Protestant dean's claim to inclusion in his survey through the assertion that "he was no more an Irishman than a man born of English parents at Calcutta is a Hindoo."[87] It was a rejection of the primacy of location over innate ethnic identity that was not lost on American ears. Nor was it left unacknowledged that this Indian-born author was referring at least in part to his own relationship to the tradition of which he spoke, and which his lectures represented a form of working through. Tellingly, one Manhattan paper reflected on this issue of complexity of origins when announcing his arrival, observing that "in a city in which the tides of men depart and are replaced with such rapidity, it may be interesting to briefly repeat that Mr. Thackeray was born in India in the year 1811."[88] Situating his remarks within a wider discourse of complicated diasporic and imperial identities, Thackeray's defense of ancestry suggested that more local elective affinities would be always secondary to the force of bloodline claims. The novelist appeared to have as much claim as his audiences to the sentiments and affections of legitimate Englishness.

And yet Thackeray's seemingly simple theory of identity politics proved ill-formed enough for its implications to spin free of his intent. As Lionel Stevenson points out regarding this first lecture tour, the choice of the English literary survey as a subject "had been congenial and yet perilous," since the politics of literary tradition ensured that some of his mixed audience were bound to find offense at some of his verdicts.[89] This offense takes us back into the world of Gotham's urban politics that loomed so large for Emerson in chapter 3, and emerged from a predictable media source. A running sore of his trip had been the continual attacks from the *New York Herald*, which ran a campaign against him both due to its temperamental disdain for English celebrity and as part of a circulation war with Greeley's *Tribune*, which had loudly supported his trip.[90] Writing to Mrs. T. F. Elliot and Kate Perry in early December 1852, he reported with relief that the press had treated him well, "with the exception of the *Herald*, which abuses me like anything."[91] The paper kept up its battering throughout his stay in New York, reprinting letters of complaint about the overcrowded seating and creating a miniscandal regarding the overselling of tickets for Thackeray's first appearances.[92]

The interesting aspect of this antipathy lies in the *Herald*'s own mediation of Thackeray's global Englishness in that increasingly mixed city. The paper was famously sensitive to the power of its Irish readership within the city and cultivated its political support. "It is well-known," observed the city's leading Celtic paper in 1853, "that the *Herald* has always ... espoused the cause of Ireland, and ably and effectively denounced the oppressions of her merciless tyrant."[93] Temperamentally disposed to criticize such Anglophile entertainments as the visit from a famous British novelist, the *Herald* was eagerly attuned to the elements of Thackeray's lecture on Swift that might be perceived as affronts to Irish-Americans, in terms of both its negative appraisal and its seeming dismissal of his national origins. Its initial notice for that performance observed that Thackeray's discussion "seemed to have been more peculiarly suited to the prejudices of an English audience, for whom it was at first perhaps exclusively intended," before it itemized the allegedly incendiary remarks upon the character of Irish culture.[94] Other papers described this lecture's content in neutral tones, and even captured its conciliatory even-handedness and the warmth with which it was greeted. The *New York Commercial*, for example, endorsed the relevant section in his first lecture, repeating Thackeray's claims:

The lecturer said that though Swift was born in Ireland, he was no more an Irishman than a man born of English parents in Calcutta was a Hindoo, and as further proof alluded to Swift's economy and the rudeness with which he served his friends. "No," said he, "the Dean was no Irismen [*sic*]—for no Irishman ever gave but with a kind heart and open hand" [Applause].[95]

It was Thackeray's intention, after all, neither to impugn the Irish national character nor to stress the particular Irishness of a literary figure he was claiming for the English tradition. And yet offense at his apparent condescension dogged the rest of his trip. "The Irishmen," he wrote home, "are furious and their press has been flinging hot potatoes at me."[96]

The most prominent of these hot potatoes was a second, more lengthy notice in the *Herald* under the title "Mr. Thackeray and Dean Swift," which offered more detail on the "outrageous" attacks made upon on the Irish writer and, by implication, an entire swathe of Manhattan's population. The novelist, the reviewer claimed, had "proved himself as great a literary snob as any described in his book" through his outrageous claims about Irish culture:

If this be English prejudice, because Dean Swift was born and educated in Ireland, and recommended the Irish people to burn everything that came from England except the coal, it is unworthy of the enlightened liberality of the present day, and far from creditable in a man who comes forward to administer instruction to the public in a course of lectures in this great and free country. He would have acted a wiser part if he altered a lecture originally composed for English audiences and adapted it to the large and comprehensive spirit of the people of the United States, who entertain no prejudices against a man in consequence of the place of his birth, and who cherish a more friendly feeling to the Irish than to any other people in the world.[97]

To guard against the imputation of national prejudice, Mr. Thackeray pretends that Dean Swift was not an Irishman, but an Englishman all through—that his character was too bad for an Irishman. The inference involved in this blunder is certainly not very complimentary to Mr Th's own country, the argument being that Dean Swift was a great scoundrel and therefore could not be a Celt, but must be a Saxon. It is true that Dean S was the son of English parents; but then he was born and brought up in Ireland, and like the Geraldines, he became "more Irish than the Irish themselves." As well might Mr. Th say that Andrew Jackson was not an American.[98]

As his biographer recounts, on one occasion when he was returning to his breakfast in his Manhattan hotel, he realized that six different people were reading the *Herald*'s latest unflattering account of his lectures, only to register his presence and hide their copies as he entered.[99] More than likely it is this piece that they hid. The piece was a comprehensive attack that attempted to dismantle the complex argument Thackeray had made regarding the claims of inheritance, parentage, and immigrant identity, while unraveling his logic of an idea of global Englishness. Placing the novelist's argument back within the context of anti-Irish condescension condemned both the "snob" Thackeray and the very act of administering education through public lectures, positioned squarely within the aristocratic vocabulary that proved so instrumental in the coverage of Emerson.

The story of this controversy included some strange twists. In the weeks following this outspoken attack on Thackeray, a retraction was placed in the *Herald* from a "Washington Correspondent," softening the paper's take on Thackeray and offering a positive view of his activities and lectures in the country. When it transpired that this retraction was published during a periodic absence of James Gordon Bennett, the paper's strident editor, some saw in the affair the hand of sinister pro-British elements. In particular, this did not escape the notice of the city's *Irish-American* newspaper, which took the *Herald* to task for its vacillations, arguing that "as soon as Mr. Bennett's back is turned upon NY, the cloven hoof of Yankeedom sticks out." In restating the "offense" Thackeray's lecture had "given to thousands of Irish-American subscribers and readers," it clarifies a number of the key complaints of the Irish against the ideas and values of the lecture:

> The snob Thackeray—as all know—delivered a lecture on Dean Swift, in which he did the grossest injustice to that great man and betrayed either an utter ignorance of his subject or a depraved desire to misrepresent. While some of the other papers ignorantly and toadyishly lauded the lecture, the *Herald* in the most gifted and powerful manner, scathingly analyzed it and showed its injustice. . . . Every Irish and American scholar with whom we conversed about it was delighted at its historical knowledge, its good taste, and appropriateness. Again; after the lapse of weeks a letter appeared in the *Herald* from "a Washington Correspondent" denouncing that article on TH [*sic*] as "ferocious" and containing an elaborate puff (unpaid of course) of that father of pretentious snobs. . . . In this connection we can come to no other conclusion than that the "Washington Correspondent" was written, for a co-operation, for Thackeray, or by himself. That Thackeray who . . . denounces one of the greatest patriots the world ever saw.

Thackeray's negative assessment of Swift was bad enough. However, by seeming to legitimize a viable form of Anglo-American identity and tradition, the novelist had also closed it off. The sectarian implications of his comments on national identity helped convince ethnic audiences that what already seemed to be a subtly nativist expression of Anglo-Saxon superiority was in fact an incitement to urban division. The throwaway nature of his critiques of Swift could not disguise the fact that Thackeray was attempting to police the boundaries of culture, control legitimate claims to literary tradition, and deny the very kinds of assimilationist principles on which the future of the public relied. Such expressions of Irish-American outrage were a performative protest against the rising tide of Anglo-Saxonism and its attendant exclusions. And since their complaint was based in part on Thackeray's apparent betrayal of the educational purity of the lecture circuit, it reveals the continuing role of lecture hall expression as a flashpoint of 1850s urban politics.

Navigating American Monarchism:
The Second Tour, 1855–56

By the early months of 1853 Thackeray had grown tired of the controversies and repetitive inauthenticity of the American platform. On 7 February he wrote home to London in anguish that "in another hour [I must begin] that dreary business of 'In Speaking of the English humorous writers of the last &c' . . . and the wonder to me is that the speaker once in the desk gets interested in the work, makes the points, thrills with emotion and indignation at the right place, & has a little sensation whilst the work is going on—but I can't go on much longer: my conscience revolts at the quackery."[100] Writing to Lucy Baxter in March 1853 he simply declared himself "lecture-sick, O Steward! Bring me a basin," and in April confessed by mail to his mother that "my conscience revolts against reading these old sermons over and over . . . and I have given up St. Louis and West, and declined Montreal."[101] Perhaps inevitably, however, the financial rewards had proven so alluring that two years later he found himself returning with a new series of lectures on the topic of the "four Georges" of the Hanoverian dynasty.

This second series was even more successful than the first financially, yet, if anything, more outspoken and risky than its predecessor. As the words of a song that was performed at a London banquet hosted by Dickens to mark Thackeray's departure declared: "*He's about to be crossing the surges / to tell all the Yankees about the Four Georges.*"[102] The hectoring pedagogy that this implies was a fraught proposition. The monarchical topic, and the fact that his stance on the Hanoverians in his pieces was often surprisingly hostile, led Thackeray to be more uncertain this time about its potential American response. Reporting on this impending departure for the United States, the *London Illustrated News* thought that the planned lectures were "admirably selected" for American audiences, but wondered aloud that "Mr. Thackeray must knuckle down a little to Jonathan or he will not draw the dollars in New York or Boston."[103] In the words of London's *Athenaeum* magazine, "The subject is a very good one for an English audience, for in England we have learnt to look back with very philosophic loyalty to the First Gentlemen of Europe . . . but the Americans will remember them with something fiercer than contempt";[104] not least because, in their estimation, "the good folks of that country are not always swift and sure in their appreciation of such delicate irony as Mr. Thackeray delights in."[105]

His tour this time was on a much broader scope, encompassing not just the major cities of the Northeast but taking him through the South to perform in New Orleans and Charleston.[106] In the words of one paper from the latter city, the British novelist was greeted as "an approved and well remembered visitor and friend."[107] The papers throughout the country guided readers with muted amusement through now familiar "clumsy graces and blundering charms of delivery," in one account; "perfect ease and manly naturalness" of his style in another; and elsewhere the "conversational" nature of his approach."[108] The pieces were generally praised as informative historical surveys, "less a lecture," in the words of the *New Orleans Times Picayune*, "than a graphically sketched panorama, the features of which passed before the eye in a brilliant procession."[109] The response was mixed, with alternating positive and lukewarm responses. As the *New York Evangelist* put it, where "the lectures delivered by Mr TH, the novelist, in his former visit to this country, were thought by some to approach, at least, the extreme verge of toleration," his new material went far further, and raised a number of new related problems of reception.[110]

The first issue was a certain moralistic opposition to the excesses of eighteenth-century life. As with the previous series, part of the appeal of the lectures lay in their apparently neutral refuge in the recent past, a period that the *Brooklyn Eagle* suggested "Mr. Thackeray thinks ... a more pleasant place than now."[111] But others saw his treatment of a more licentious and messy age as something of a moral liability. The *New York Evangelist* reflected that

> we are not surprised that some parents have already returned their tickets for the course, and some sensible women of our acquaintance decline attending the remaining lectures. We beg to inform Mr. TH that he has mistaken his auditors. We do not think it the best mode to improve the taste of the young of either sex, to give such prominence to this form of vice, even in the way of satirical and humorous descriptions of court pageantries and follies.[112]

Moreover, many inevitably bridled at the very topic. Adopting an ironic distance from the monarchical subject matter, the *Charleston Courier* argued that "the more you are disgusted on contemplating some pictures, the more directly do you testify to the success and achievement of the painter."[113] Nonetheless, the *New York Times* reporter found himself reflecting on "how precarious an institution, we could not help thinking, that depends upon the accidental features of character of one single individual."[114]

With its own long tradition of mistreatment at the hands of the British Crown, Boston might have been expected to demonstrate particular opposition. That city's *Advertiser* recorded "a very sympathetic (what the magnetizers call an *impressible)* audience" for the first appearance, and countered its muted support with the hope that "when Mr. T in due course comes to the 'third of the fools and oppressors called George' we shall expect to have that addle-headed monarch much cut up for his sins, and particularly for his shabby treatment of the port of Boston."[115] The city's *Post* was even more outspoken:

> I was prepared for disappointment, consequently, in Mr TH's lectures on the Georges; but he fell extremely far below my worst anticipations. He was dull, uninteresting, and sometimes vulgar, in each and all of his four lectures. He crossed three thousands miles of ocean to instruct us in the Augustan era of English history; but he has totally failed to do so.... He chose as his themes those contemptible topics which may be interesting to old ladies in the decline of life, as the gossip of mystic scandal over the tea-table.[116]

The composition of these lectures was testimony to Thackeray's increasingly pragmatic sensitivity to the need for deft handling of ideas of Anglo-American inheritance. His Georges lectures exist in two versions: the manuscript text from which Thackeray addressed his American audiences, and the text printed for British readers in 1861. As John Sutherland points out, "The differences are striking and systematic. The lectures that the Americans heard contain prominent diatribes against old-world royalty, aristocracy and the rank system generally. Many of these references are toned down or removed altogether for English readers."[117] In Sutherland's terms, Thackeray developed an "evasive strategy": throughout the lectures, wicked noblemen are presented as a shared foe of both middle-class Englishman and his American republican audience, aspects that were then toned down in the British publication. As one of his detractors had written in 1856: "No one succeeds better than Mr. Thackeray in cutting his coat according to his cloth: here he flattered the aristocracy, but when he crossed the Atlantic, George Washington became the idol of his worship; the "Four Georges" the objects of his bitterest attacks.[118] The *Georges* lectures marked with something of a return to Thackeray's radical past: his "hot-blooded, lord-baiting youth":[119]

> Here in America, your unfortunate education has deprived you of the benefit of understanding that great difference which existed, and even still exists in many parts of the European continent between the *Adel* or *noblesse*, and the common people. In a well regulated principality in Germany you may still see the army officered by a nobleman—at the theater the noble society sits apart from the citizen society; to be a merchant, a lawyer, a doctor, is still almost an eccentricity among persons of noble blood.[120]

The animus of the lectures, shown at its plainest in the suppressed passages, can be seen as a revival of the republican enthusiasm exacerbated by despair at the administrative incompetence shown in the Crimean War campaign. Thackeray was active in the Administrative Reform Association with Dickens, and used satire to back up his convictions.

This navigation of monarchism for an ostensibly republican audience was widely remarked upon. "There was," the *Philadelphia Inquirer* recorded, "a deep, honest, heartfelt tone of indignation in Mr Thackeray's voice when he dwelt on the 'evils of monarchy.' "[121] In fact, back in England, the *Albion* reported, "he has also been accused of designedly lowering the respect felt for the Royal Family under the impression that such a cause would be specially acceptable to Americans" in pieces "cooked up for the American market."[122] Whether or not the lectures bore this out, he certainly made some choices that support this claim. In his April series in Philadelphia, Thackeray changed his topic from the Georges back to the more straightforwardly appealing humorist lectures, an approach that appealed to one of the city's papers, rather than talk to audiences about what one paper called the "hideous figures of history."[123] As coverage of his New Orleans lectures put it, his talks seemed to place the concept of deference to the Crown in analytical perspective, and "dealt with the 'religion of loyalty' to royalty and its surroundings—its traditional superstitions which invest it with such strange potency."[124] Reports suggest that crowds were particularly affectionate toward the current queen. In New York, "At the passages referring to Queen Victoria especially, the response rose into enthusiasm."[125] At a St. George's Day event, Thackeray's most vocal recorded response followed the delivery of the following address:

> I honored her because she was a good wife, a good mother, an accomplished lady, and enlightened friend of art ... and it was pleasant to me, as an Englishman, making my tour through this country, and in repeating these words, to find the universal and cordial response by which they were received [Cheers].[126]

The *Albion* account records "the hearty, spontaneous and generous applause, with which an American audience receives an honest Englishman's tribute to the virtues of one whom his cordial nature loves, honors and respects."[127]

Just as on the previous tour, these events involved outspoken moments of seeming Anglo-American unity. At the close of the series in Manhattan, the *Albion* declared that "Mr Thackeray may henceforth consider himself a citizen of two countries."[128] "We thank Mr. Thackeray for these lectures. They cannot but bring the best things of England and of English feeling into finer communion with the American mind."[129] Furthermore, it was fitting that Thackeray also spoke at various St. George's Society events, reading "Humor and Charity."[130] Some reports presented Thackeray as the spectacle of the loyal subject and, somewhat at odds with his reputation elsewhere, as a lesson in patriotism:

> The efforts made to disparage Mr. Thackeray had the effect to stimulate the anxiety to listen to him, and the melody of his beautiful elocution, uttering at the end words of loyalty to the land and the institutions of his own country, fell pleasantly on the hearts of the most intelligent and cultivated audience that our undemonstrative community ever congregated.[131]

As Tamarkin has noted, this American monarchism meant that conservative British values could be celebrated safely through nostalgia and response to the

British past. Yet while it was a fetishization of kingship and authorship based on a fantasy of deference, it was a response with subtle consequences for cultural definition that we might trace through the theme of humor and satire.

Geniality and Independence

Throughout both of his tours, readings of Thackeray repeatedly returned to the question of the social function of satire. Critics were fascinated by the mixture of moral clarity and social insight promised by the novelist's unsparing comic derision, and the tightrope risks it involved. As we have seen, views on the politics of his satirical stance divided observers long before his arrival. A final fascinating aspect of his American lecturing career lies in how his commitment to candor, openness, and bold honesty conflicted with the public civic ideals of lecturing and the aspiration toward an Anglo-American commons as a social adhesive. On both tours, Thackeray was received as the sardonic caricaturist par excellence. A key question in discussion of his lectures was whether such humor formed a useful part of reading the world or of conducting public life. To an influential body of observers, his comic style came to represent a viable tradition of irreverent Englishness, with suggestive political value.

The ethical value of humor was the essential underlying theme of Thackeray's first series of lectures. His appraisals of the comic writers of the eighteenth century repeatedly advanced a humanist model of the role of the humorous writer as the master of multivalent collective affect. The key term here is the versatile label of "humorist." Attempting to unravel Thackeray's "comfortably imprecise" term, Robert Kiely argues for a dual attitude in which social criticism was deftly balanced against "brainless geniality or a tendency to conceal one's own vices while ridiculing those of others."[132] Thackeray's lectures, however, made clear an ethic of sentiment and social vision underlying his conception, opening the series by telling listeners that "the humorous writer professes to awaken and direct your love, your pity, your kindness—your scorn for untruth ... your tenderness for the weak."[133] At numerous points, he made clear that this was a tradition and a mode of humor within which he was consciously placing himself, and whose values he saw perpetuated in his own writings. "A literature man of the humouristic turn," he argued, "is pretty sure to be of a philanthropic nature."[134] In the final set piece lecture, "Charity and Humour," he positioned himself as mediator of the intertwined legacy of these two abstract forces, and looked back

> on the good which of late years the kind English humorists have done; and if you are pleased to rank the present speaker among that class, I own to an honest pride at thinking what benefits society has derived from men of our calling.[135]

Thackeray is clear-eyed about the value and virtue of what comedy achieves, and what he considers the correct and incorrect use of "tears" and emotion as a means of navigating between social conflicts and between different historical realities. He praised Dickens, for example, for his "innocent laughter and sweet and unsullied style," and his essays on the Augustan wits was in one sense a manifesto, reclaiming the careful balance of acerbic wit and compassion he saw in the urbanity of that age, and which he was attempting to revive in his self-image as a subtle, benevolent moralist.

As we have seen, therefore, the discourse surrounding Thackeray's tours helps clarify competing interpretations of satire's uncertain role in democratic life. On the one hand was the familiar sense of wariness with which he was anticipated, with the *Cleveland Plain Dealer* conceding, for instance, that "it is said that Thackeray intends to make a book on the manners and customs of the American people, when he returns from his present visit ... his satiric powers are superior."[136] From another perspective, however, these powers were welcomed by those who saw positive potential in submitting the life of the nation to external satiric critique. Hopes were expressed in the New York press, for example, that Thackeray might take up the indigenous modes of humor and offer "characteristic sketches of individuals he encountered in the southwest"; while the *Tribune* hoped that

> if he stay long enough with us, he will discover that we also put forth many legitimate provocations to satire, though hardly to satire of so bland a temper as his own. Our follies need not so much good-natured ridicule, as sorrowful and indignant reprobation, for they are not the mere *debris* and wreck of old manners which boast a lingering decency even in decay, but rather the brand new inventions of an underbred and prosperous vulgarity.[137]

With social habits and custom in flux, satire and the comedy of manners acquired a centripetal force whose regulatory function was promoted by much of the press during his two tours. As Emerson wrote to Carlyle on 10 August 1853, reporting on recent New York gossip, "Thackeray has made a good mark in this country by a certain manly blurting out of his opinion in various companies, where so much honesty was rare and useful."[138]

On the other side of the coin, questions of value were raised over whether this "great scandal-monger of the day" was simply an exponent of corrosive cynicism.[139] In his own lectures, Thackeray had drawn careful distinction between the benign comic modes of Goldsmith—"merciful, gentle, generous, full of love and pity"—and that of harsher satirists such as Swift or Sterne, the latter of whom was criticized as both a "coward" and "a great jester ... the foul's Satyr eyes leer out of the leaves constantly ... bad and wicked."[140] Responses to Thackeray navigated between these two poles, with concerns that his outbursts of moral indignation and ridicule steered his lectures too far toward the temptations of

xenophobic stereotype or the excesses of the discourse of gentility and urban condescension. For some modern critics this equated to a troubling and paradoxical
moral relativism. As D. J. Taylor has argued, "It is impossible to read Thackeray
for very long without being pulled up sharply by his matter-of-factness, his casual
acceptance of rogues and rascals, his delight in establishing that even the most
outwardly scrupulous people are still motivated by selfishness and vanity."[141]
Bayard Taylor maintains of Thackeray's problematic reception that "that which
he had written with a sigh was interpreted as a sneer."[142] The *Albion* magazine
reminded its readers in 1855 ahead of his second tour that "his genius was supposed to possess more of light than of warmth."[143]

One recurring idea that helped navigate between these two poles was the unifying concept of "geniality," a form of humor taken by various commentators
to possess a definite social and even democratic value. Proclaiming his arrival
in New York for his first tour, Henry James Sr. had gushed in the *Tribune* that
Thackeray was "the most thoughtful critic of manners and society, the subtlest
humorist, and the most effective, because the most genial, satirist the age has
known."[144] Gregg Camfield has argued for the self-consciously good-natured
form of "geniality" as a particularly important feature of antebellum life, whose
basis in genuine nonaggression rather than displaced or suppressed pugnacious-
ness made it exert a crucial force in sentimental and domestic fiction.[145] It was
seen as having both a pedagogic and a purgative role in urban society, as both an
antidote to undue enthusiasm and a route through urban and mercantile life. In
particular, it shone through in Thackeray's performances. Audiences primed to
expect a gloomy, cynical misanthropist were surprised by a genial figure of the
type best characterized in the terms the lecturer himself used in his "Charity and
Humour" piece as the "humorous preacher." It was a stance that he argued was
most apparent in the role of Dickens's *A Christmas Carol* as "a better charity sermon" than almost all writing of recent memory, possessed of exactly this "kind
light of benevolence."[146] And it was this carefully displaced religious energy—the
performative fusion of gentle caricature and moral vision—that helps explain
a great deal of Thackeray's contemporary appeal as celebrity of the lecture
platform.

In the midcentury context, these ethical dimensions to comic style were increasingly understood in national terms. Thackeray's attempt to celebrate a tradition
based on the figure of the humorist therefore coincided with and informed debates
over the attempt to define a brand of American humor. This was the period of the
emergence of Young American humorists such as Cornelius Mathews, and of disputes such as those between William Gilmore Simms and Evert Duychinck over
the viable politics of the role of the nineteenth-century comic.[147] There was profound ambivalence about the influence of the British comic mode. The not especially comically minded Emerson was to remark in *English Traits* (1856) how "the
English are a nation of humorists," balancing his misgivings about this almost

imperial comic assertiveness against the positive acknowledgment that "the wit and humour of England have taken the direction of humanity and freedom."[148] More commonly, the argument was made that the new conditions of the republic impelled new comic modes at one remove from what were seen as harsher and even aristocratic British satirical traditions; whereas tyranny bred satire, new freedoms were seen to engender divergent forms of humor.[149]

These national dimensions to comic impulses might therefore be understood in terms of the interplay of "independence" and "solidarity." This was a tendency that structured the humor of Thackeray's fiction and which can be viewed more broadly as among the key influences on his reception as a lecturer. Assessing the entirety of his first lecture tour in 1853, the *Democratic Review* used just these terms. "It has always been an easy thing to gain a reputation for independence, and the most facile method of all has been found in that cynicism of which Mr. Thackeray is by common consent the most eminent modern exponent."[150] His performances seemed to bring a host of traits together for his audiences: an unentangled comic bent, dedication to externality, willingness to operate beyond the realms of narrow national stereotype. At the beginning of his second tour, the *Albion* remarked that "Mr. Thackeray may henceforth consider himself a citizen of two countries."[151] More than many of his peers, Thackeray was an ideal transatlantic figure and committed to the ideals of Anglo-American cohesion—a position that these two formative tours helped to solidify. His experiences and reception in the Union helped to steer the function of modern authorship away from creativity toward not only the theatrical but also the symbolic functions of persona and performance.

Thackeray's pair of Augustan set-piece series were unlikely lecture hall successes. They held, in the words of the *Times* of London, "the merit of being the unillustrated lectures to cause a 'crush'" of popular hysteria.[152] And for the modern scholar, the ways in which they allowed him to stand in as a representative of a larger set of Anglo-American ideas help reveal the politics and limitations of the 1850s public sphere. Closer understanding of these notably successful oral discourses provides a key insight into both Thackeray's public presence and contemporary reputation; into the hybrid figure of the gentleman lecturer, and the mixture of quackery and comic preaching at the heart of the lecturing vocation. His relationship with his public shifted, and he was seized in various ways as an embodiment of a complicated shared tradition. "It has been a great triumph for Mr. Thackeray to have established this personal relation between himself and the admirers of his books," observed the *London Spectator* upon the novelist's return to England, "so that henceforth he speaks to them through his books, not as an abstraction, a voice issuing from a mask, but as a living man, and a friendly, companionable, accomplished, gentleman."[153] By embodying the abstraction of an Anglo-American commons, Thackeray helped reveal how the lecture circuit was structured by the same types of tensions.

- Popularisation of the form in years leading up to Civ War. Not above public figures but theatrical entertainers
  - ↳ but retention of Trans At subject matter. Sectionalism + war give the issues of cul unity new pol significance. → measuring health of the Union — risk of disintegration.
  - ↳ Gough + Moretz by [temperaning], testify to strength of Any Am unity (embodying rather than explaining, through their 'hyphenated idents)
  - 2) The popularisation was not the decline but broadening of the medium (democratization) — "popular cosmopolitanism"

- Lyceum as "a theatre of individualism + reinvention", anchoring "the rises of celebrity in the (19th" – re Moretz. 175
  - ↳ Charting the stage's (lecture) class vw + imbrication in the cul of celebrity
  - ↳ The tensions in Moretz's performance + reception, "reveals the increasingly porous boundaries between otherwise seemingly incompatible public registers of performance" 177 → show cul/celeb + lyceum.
    - • charting her self-fashioning, myth-making.
  - → does all this by lecturing on Am in Br / Br in Am.
  - • Using a hyphenated ident to embody negotiation of cul diff when stepping into the genre of performing Any Am commons.

- Gough – former alcoholic, turned temperance reformer.

188 – Reading Gough's vocal performance of Br diff as complex satire, which through embodiment seeks to est. sympathetic connection + attraction in face of diff.

- 195 – Move towards "ambiv acceptance of the troubling fact that the Any-Am commons had proved to be more cul construct than nat or pol reality" ← fracture of Civ War.

- Not just a decline, but negotiation of shifting Any-Am commons through a broad form of 'N. & civic nationalism' – 197
  - ↳ it still had vitality – Gough + Moretz as pre-cursor to its transformation into new cul form of perf.

{ 6 }

Britain and Wartime Unity

LOLA MONTEZ AND JOHN B. GOUGH
AS CULTURAL DIPLOMATS

On the stage of the cavernous new Brooklyn Academy of Music, a well-dressed bearded man of middling years reduces an audience of thousands to hysterics with his mimicry of cockney and upper-class English accents. Striding from stage left to stage right, he moves on to a series of impersonations of British parliamentarians. First he is Gladstone, now Disraeli, Palmerston, John Bright: each imitation greeted with raucous applause. Gesturing into the middle distance, he points at an imagined vision of Queen Victoria, ostentatiously bowing and sliding out of the way as her mirage carriage passes through the proscenium arch. The crowd howls with approval; hecklers urge the artiste on; in the pit a concert band sit in anticipation, ready to offer accompaniment at the slightest encouragement. It is the autumn of 1861 and the venue has already secured this star performer for a series of follow-up shows throughout the year. The man on stage is John B. Gough, one of the nation's most notorious and prominent orators, a British-born, Massachusetts-raised failed actor and ex-drunk who had found a second career during the 1840s as a lecturer against the evils of the drink. Having recently returned from a trip to his home country, he resumed lecturing in 1859 with new material intended to stimulate Anglo-American affinity. Tonight's lecture is titled "Street Life in London," and Gough closes it with a heartfelt plea for transatlantic unity: "In the troubles that now surround our country," he declares, "the sympathy of England is precious; would that both countries could be brought nearer in their interests." The "immense audience" explodes in a standing ovation, the band throws itself into "God Save the Queen" followed by "Yankee Doodle," and "for five minutes it seemed as if every one of the 3,500 people who crowded the building joined in the cheering and clapping of hands."[1]

One year earlier, in halls from Kentucky to Chicago, an equally unlikely performer had been voicing similar pleas for transatlantic understanding. This was Lola Montez, the Irish actress, dancer, and courtesan, famed for her "Spider

Dance"—an elaborate erotic tarantella in which she mimed discovering spiders in the folds of her dress and hurling them into the crowd. Since the 1840s she had confounded crowds in the great cities of Europe, Australia, and both coasts of America, and had become celebrated as one of the great beauties of the age. Tales of her romantic entanglements amid the elite of European high society had made her a byword for louche nomadic glamour.[2] She had long ago forged her own imaginary Spanish persona. Now, like Gough, she had reinvented herself once more as a popular lecturer. Reporters in Pittsburgh thought her "singular and sharp-tongued"; in Baltimore "brilliant and facetious"; in Boston she was called "the queen of the lecture room."[3] For three years until her early death in 1860, she paced the lecture platforms on both sides of the Atlantic with a repertoire of pieces that strove to explain the Anglo-American world to itself. On the American platform she most often spoke to the theme "John Bull at Home," in which she concluded a series of wry observations of British social foibles by proclaiming that "England and America ... are fast becoming more and more united. If Americans would visit England, and Englishmen America more frequently, less discontent and rivalry, and greater harmony would exist."[4] Just like Gough, her topic held audiences transfixed. One memoirist recalled of her 1859 appearance at Mozart Hall in New York that "when the great blue eyes grew scintillant with smiles, and the electric voice in most exquisite intonations vibrated through the great hall in these words—'I hope none of you will accuse me of abusing the English,'—every reputed sin of the speaker was forgotten, and the audience, unconsciously, yet perfectly, seemed to pass within the sphere of her control."[5]

Both Montez and Gough found themselves, at precisely the same time, reimagined as popular lecturers, and speaking to audiences about Anglo-American unity. Taken together, their arrivals on the lecture circuit highlight the profound changes at work on the lyceum platform in the years before the Civil War. For one thing, the range of speakers was diversifying rapidly. Whereas the 1840s platform had been dominated by those with credentials from public life or the academy, a new generation of lecturers renowned primarily for their engagingly theatrical performance styles emerged. Figures from the worlds of theater and dance could now reimagine themselves as stars of the lecturing platform. Gough's success in particular demonstrates the radical evolution in the types of performance considered suitable for the lecture hall stage. Popular lecturing had always been, as Donald Scott put it, "a form of intellectual theatricality," with its success predicated on the challenge it posed to the theater.[6] But the genre-blending creativity of Gough's Brooklyn Academy performance shows that the boundaries between educational lecture, playhouse, and revival meeting were now more blurred than ever. The new popular appetite for theatrics seemed to have eclipsed the lofty educational and civic ideals of the Holbrook lyceum.

Yet as Gough's and Montez's choice of subject suggest, the old lecture-hall mainstays merely persisted in new forms. Like Mann, Emerson, and Douglass before them, both offered lectures on transatlantic affairs, drawing upon first-hand testimony—and crucially, both did so at a key moment for Anglo-American relations. As the secession crisis escalated and the Civil War erupted, the Union looked to its relationship with Britain as a means of guaranteeing its future. Theoretical issues of cultural unity and identity were now freighted with existential economic and military implications, and northern lecture halls became a forum through which to assess the health of an Anglo-American commons whose disintegration might prefigure that of the Union itself.

In this final chapter, I reanimate the moment of overlap between Gough's and Montez's performance careers to make two arguments. First, I reveal how these two performers used the authority of their hyphenated identities to pose as cultural mediators, reassuring audiences of the strength of Anglo-American unity. Whereas in previous examples, American audiences wanted the Atlantic world *explained* to them, now they wanted it *embodied*—an appetite that these two transatlantic performers satisfied in multiple ways. Certainly, on one level their lectures offered simple escapist entertainment during turbulent times; but as I will show, their interest rests in the use they made of a powerful and some-what counterintuitive comedy of recognition and dissonance. In Montez's caustic lampooning of the English, and even more clearly in Gough's mimicry of the voices of London, we can see a complex comic celebration of this opposition. As Montez put it in her lectures, "We often laugh at the eccentricities of those we love the best," and this dynamic helped transform these events into elaborate rituals of transatlantic loyalty, conducted both on the stage and in print.[7] Both orators informed audiences that the differences between these two nations were greater than ever before, yet also offered the cathartic view that a common thread persisted and mutual understanding was possible. The public's staged acceptance of misunderstandings, ironies, and difference as part of an Anglo-American togetherness, I will argue, offered a pattern of loyalty that provided one model of counteracting the deterioration of the Union.

My second broad thesis is that, rather that embodying a medium in decline, these increasingly theatricalized events were part of a lecture culture with an enlarged civic mission. To some contemporaries and to early chroniclers of the lyceum, the new appetite for celebrity represented by the advent of performers such as Montez and Gough was lamented as a "natural influx of mediocrity into the field," which diluted the medium's original civic mission.[8] This is a view that still tends to pervade accounts of the period. But properly considered, this moment represented the broadening of the medium beyond its initial elite scope, ushering in a diverse range of voices spanning gender, class, and racial backgrounds. The lectures of Gough and Montez, and the response they elicited, marked not the exhaustion of an Anglo-American commons but its democratization, embodying a taste for popular cosmopolitanism both as a middle-class leisure activity and as a ritual of identity. Reading such performers in this way rescues them from their reputation as mere larger-than-life curiosities, and reclaims them as figures whose skillful navigation of cultural hierarchy helped redefine the potential of celebrity in midcentury Britain and America.[9] Moreover, it places them as focal points of tremendous cultural energy within a moment of national crisis in which popular cultural forms such as the lecture were conscripted into the broader debates around the meanings of loyalty, disunion, and national identity.

Montez's New "Character"

Lola Montez's turn to the lecture stage was merely the last roll of the dice in one of the nineteenth century's more remarkable life stories.[10] She was born Eliza Rosanna Gilbert in Sligo, Ireland, in 1821, the daughter of a British army officer and Irish mother, and spent her itinerant upbringing between Scotland, England, and India. At sixteen she eloped with a lieutenant to Calcutta, divorced him within five years, reinvented herself as "Lola Montez," an exiled dancer from Seville, and introduced her infamous "Spider Dance" to the music halls of London in 1843. Most agree that she was a notoriously inept dancer, but her raven-haired beauty and boisterous charisma transformed her into an unlikely star of the European stage, and propelled her through a series of affairs with powerful and influential men. In Bavaria in 1846 she met King Ludwig I, who fell hard for her, took her as his mistress, and awarded her the title of Countess of Landsfeld, only to be forced to abandon her when, amid the European unrest of 1848, her presence became controversial enough to threaten his rule. Thanks to these events, Montez was now an international celebrity, a status she was quick to exploit on the stage of London and the New World, taking her act to New York in 1851 and playing herself in *Lola Montez in Bavaria*, a dramatization of her life (see Figure 6.1). After a tour of California, during which she remarried and briefly owned a gold mine, she embarked upon an unsuccessful tour of Australia in 1855. The following year she returned to settle in the United States as a citizen, and toured as a lecturer for three seasons before suffering a stroke and passing away in Manhattan in January 1861.

At the point that she embarked on her lecturing career Montez had been one of the Atlantic world's most famous women for over a decade. She danced professionally for the last time in Buffalo, New York, in July 1857 and in the same month gave her first performance as a public lecturer in Hamilton, Ontario, speaking on the topic of "Beautiful Women." Soon seemingly settled on a promising new career, Montez sailed east across the Atlantic in late 1858 for a season on the British Isles circuit. In cities from Cork to Wolverhampton and Edinburgh she spoke on a range of new topics, some of which one might have expected, such as "Comic Aspects of Fashion" and "Strong-Minded Women," but also others that marked a less predictable foray into cultural criticism.[11] Within a few years, her reputation and public persona had transformed. The *Boston Post* argued of her September performances that she "talks vastly better than she dances," and

CARICATURE OF LOLA MONTEZ'S DEPARTURE FOR AMERICA

FIGURE 6.1 *Caricature of Lola Montez's departure for America, 1852*

the *New York Herald* ranked her alongside Greeley and Edward Everett as one of the "principal lecturers of the day."[12] At the height of her fame as a lecturer, she could command more in fees than Dickens would for his readings a decade later.

This short-lived career on the lyceum stage is the most unexpected and least understood twist in the Montez story. It receives short shrift in most accounts of her life, often acting merely as a tragicomic coda. Yet much greater attention is merited for what it tells us about the rise of celebrity in the nineteenth century and the changing status of the lecture medium as a theater of individualism and reinvention. Montez's lecture years remain something of a mystery. As Bee Wilson has recently put it, Montez was "a dancer who couldn't dance and a Spanish temptress from county Sligo. She was a fake: the world knew it, and so did she."[13] My interest in this chapter is to think through what exactly she was "faking" in turning to the lecture platform and embracing the role of cultural ambassador, and what this might tell us about both performer and audience alike.

It is possible to read Montez's turn to lecturing in at least three key ways. First, it was a straightforward bid for respectability. As she declared in her first autobiographical lecture in New York, "The right of defining one's position seems to be a very sacred privilege in America, and I must avail myself of it, in entering upon the novel business of the lecture."[14] The platform itself helped her achieve this goal, as she was able to exploit the residual moral weight of lecturing to redefine her public persona. For years she had been the target of popular ridicule, the tone of which is captured in the lyrics of an 1850 London broadside ballad: "Lola Montes was a merry dame / Young and gay, and up to snuff / She carried on a

pretty game / One man for her was not enough."[15] Renouncing the stage for the
lecture hall went hand in hand with her apparent religious conversion as a way of
underlining her new status and seriousness. The figure she presented on the platform was described by one observer as "considerably chastened," with Montez
"dressed in exquisite taste, black velvet not low in the neck."[16] There was a dash
of feminist assertion about such a transformation. In her lecture "Beauty," she
argued that a woman "must possess merit. She must have accomplishments of
mind and heart," and lecturing became a means by which to prove herself as a
more substantial figure.[17] This was something that audiences seemed to recognize, meeting with "applause and laughter" her arch claim in one New York lecture to "the pleasure, so inestimable to every woman, of speaking out her mind."[18]

Her aspirational effort was at least partly successful, judging by the coverage
she received. In her first appearances in upstate New York, the *Buffalo Express*
struck a note that would be often repeated when it declared it "difficult to over-
come prejudices that have been created in this country regarding the name of
the lecturer … but if the mind will only entertain Lola Montez as a lecturer, her
success must be complete."[19] In a double-edged reference to her upward ethical
trajectory, the *Boston Herald* welcomed "the eccentric Lola Montez in her new
assumption of character as a public lecturer."[20] The *Philadelphia Press* similarly
trumpeted "a new, and we are glad to say, a very respectable phase in the career
of that celebrated woman … a triumph, a practical assertion of the *supremacy
of mind*," in place of erotic spectacle.[21] Yet as the *London Evening Journal* noted,
audience motivation may have been less than worthy:

> Nine-tenths of the ladies and gentlemen who thronged last night to St. James's
> Hall did not go there to hear the lecture, but to look at the lecturer … , not
> because they care one straw about her views on American or Yankee society
> but because they wished to get a surreptitious peep behind the scenes of the
> "demi-monde," and to behold, without fear of losing caste, one who played no
> inconsiderable part in the world of non-respectability.[22]

To some her mere presence on lecture programs symbolized the unwelcome
changes that had overtaken the form. Speakers were now chosen and valued for
their celebrity status; spider dancers as educators were a standing affront to the
apparent dignity of this formerly genteel arena.

A second way to understand Montez's lectures is to see them as part of a continuum of multiple performances. In her debut lecture she had maintained that
it was "not a pleasant duty for me to perform," and yet her career can be read as
series of provocative performances, in which the stance of the "popular lecturer"
was as much of a kind of stock character in its own right as anything else.[23] Since
the late 1840s, numerous burlesques and plays had taken her as their subject,
and when she dramatized herself in *Lola Montez in Bavaria* she flitted between
the roles of dancer, politician, countess, revolutionary, and fugitive. ("I sym-
pathise with the actresses who were forced to take part in such stuff," reported

one reviewer.)[24] Her old and new roles would continue to overlap in the public consciousness for the remainder of her career, a dynamic made palpable when her lectures in New York's Mozart Hall in March 1859 ran alongside a German-language performance of the *Bavaria* material at the Stadttheater.[25] So adept had she become at navigating the contradictions between her old and new personas that she merged her new roles, attending the rival production and erecting her table on the stage to deliver the lecture "Comic Aspects of Love" as a finale to the performance.[26] To confuse matters even more, the very same month a hoax lecturer promised to deliver a billed lecture on the topic "Lola Montez and Her Fancies" at the Stuyvesant Institute, but failed to show, leaving the audience to heckle the hall's owners and demand refunds.[27] Whether as dancer, actress, or lecturer, her place in show culture reveals the increasingly porous boundaries between otherwise seemingly incompatible cultural registers and categories of performance.

A final means of reading Montez the lecturer is to view her turn to the platform as the final in a lifelong series of efforts at personal mythmaking. Throughout her career Montez had played an active role in the fashioning of her own myth. She had published her memoirs first in Paris in 1850, and further biographies were published in German the following year.[28] The lecture hall was simply a new means to fashion the myth of Lola, a task she began with two autobiographical lectures in New York, pieces that were delivered in third person, and which were characteristically riddled with half-truths.[29] From the outset of her career, Lola Montez had taken particular care to cultivate ambiguity surrounding her origins: experience had taught her that, like the layers of performance she habitually adopted and discarded, national character was merely a matter of surface peculiarities. Central to this theme was her adoption and rejection of multiple accents. The *London Era* newspaper described her "speaking earnestly and distinctly, with the slightest touch of a foreign accent that might belong to any language from Irish to Bavarian."[30] Others simply thought she sounded French.[31] Some American newspapers were unwilling to support Montez's own mythmaking and aimed to expose her "true" origins. When one Cleveland paper rehearsed the claim that she was in fact "Betty Watson," a dancer at penny shows in Ireland, it was attacked by its rival paper, which called such allegations "fabricated imbecility," deeming it completely proper that "this magnificently gifted woman seeks to earn, in a praiseworthy manner, a living in this land of the free."[32]

My particular interest lies in how Montez attempted to translate her hyphenated status into a viable analytical persona, reinventing herself as a cultural commentator and ambassador. The preamble for her lecture about England laid out her credentials using a commonplace argument for cosmopolitan relativism:

> My love of traveling has led me to an acquaintance with almost every nook
> and corner of the habitable globe, and yet in looking back upon that expe-
> rience, I am unable to call to mind any real national differences which do

no chime with that Scriptural declaration that the *Supreme* "hath made of one blood all nations of men." The general characteristics of human beings are the same everywhere. Their passions may differ in degree, but they are of kindred quality.[33]

Montez now aimed to translate such experience into a position of rhetorical authority. In the preface to her published *Lectures of Lola Montez* she was promoted as "a political character" and reimagined as a liberal hero for her "support of popular rights" during her time at the Bavarian court.[34] Whether what some have called the "boudoir politics" of her Bavaria period truly qualified her for this role is debatable, but she was eager to stress that "on foreign politics she has clear ideas, and has been treated by the political men of the country as a substantive power"[35] Her own fusion of American, European, and British imperial identities and experiences would allow her to counteract what she called "forlorn stories . . . of either prejudiced or incompetent observers."[36] Her aim in discussing comparative national character was, as quoted by one Irish newspaper, "to talk about [England and America] as they are, not as they have been misrepresented by Mr. Dickens, Mr. Mackay, Mr. Thackeray, and others, who have 'done them.'"[37] And her set-piece lectures aimed to do so most compellingly via their dry comic tone.

The Dance of Cultural Arbitration

Montez had two parallel repertoires of sociopolitical lectures: in Britain she spoke to the themes of "America and Her People," "Emigration in America," and "American Slavery"; back in the United States, her topic was "John Bull at Home."[38] She had begun her tour of the British Isles in Dublin in late 1858, and as the *New York Herald* put it exactly a year later, having "lately returned from a visit to Europe, where she dissected American life, American customs, and American peculiarities, for the edification of English audiences," her new material "reversed the picture by presenting a New York audience with a detailed and humorous view of English peculiarities."[39] Formally, the pieces were undisciplined and rambling, and largely avoided personal investment or anecdote in favor of what she called in a letter to the *Herald* a more objective stance of "fair and truthful portraiture" of both countries.[40] Yet they were at their most intriguing when they abandoned such restraint, and indulged what one reviewer for a Virginia newspaper thought to be her "sarcastic strain" of intercultural humor.[41]

Her new pieces were certainly unrestrained in their pointed commentary. The lecture on slavery made an apology for bondage, and argued against interference in other nations' affairs. Back in America she was eager to lay bare the hypocrisy of the English "meddling with abolitionism . . . while they were at the same time fostering the cruel system of coolieism, and committing atrocities on the poor natives of India, the horrors of which it was impossible to convey."[42] No admirer of democracy, she saw the American Revolution as reversible, and that the "step from such a republic as America to such a Monarchy as England would be neither a long nor a difficult one."[43] On the topic of mass immigration, she argued that the volatile movement of people was destructive to republics:

> Whenever a foreign population flocks into a country faster than it can be assimilated or absorbed by the native element, the work of national disintegration commences, and this has been already going on, for at least ten years in America.... The tendency of Republics is inclined always towards anarchy.... During my seven years residence in that country, my head has been dizzy watching the young Republic whirling round upon the outer edge of Anarchy.[44]

At moments such as these, Montez's was both surprisingly outspoken and willfully melodramatic, thrilling audiences with lurid prophecy: "The greatest question that concerns America is that of Emigration. While she is busying herself with a thousand little isms, which are really based only in the plots and counterplots of scheming politicians, this mighty question is rolling down upon her with tremendous velocity.[45]

However, more interesting and far subtler was Montez's use of humor as a means of navigating Anglo-American distance and commonality. Speaking to Irish and English audiences about the foibles of the New World, she drew laughs by comparing American religion to drunkenness, mocking the language through which religious experience was communicated:

> Nothing can equal the ecstasy of their devotions. With many denominations, prayer is a sort of agony of delight or fit of ecstasy, with which the judgment has little to do as it has with a victim of delirium tremens. They carry on precisely as though they believed they were about to take an express railroad train to glory; and as though they were going to heaven in a painted balloon. To be without excitement in religion is to be considered as having no religion at all. To become religious is called "getting religion," a thing which they get, or catch, as suddenly, or as accidentally as they get the measles, mumps, or influenza. And a religion thus got or caught of course holds on to the patient about as long as the influenza or measles would do.[46]

This was the familiar comedy of manners and affect that had entertained the reading public for at least a generation. Montez's spin on it was frequently commonplace but was also shot through with asides wafting a sexual suggestiveness that may have only been apparent in performance, particularly where her manuscript underlinings reveal point of emphasis: "Practically I am afraid there is as much, if not more *free love* in the older countries of Europe as in America, but the Americans have beat you in reducing the thing to a science, and as they do by everything else; organizing it into a *creed* or an *ism*."[47]

The comedy of affectionate recognition was at its most effective back in the United States, where Montez seemed particularly at home speaking of the English in the third person. The title under which the talk was frequently billed ("John Bull at Home") was instructive. It placed her squarely within the more playful "national character" school of cultural analysis, suggesting both the tradition of Charles Mathews's and James Hackett's theatrical pieces of the 1820s, and the idiom of Gilray's caricatures for *Punch*.[48] To Montez, "John Bull" represented a string of contradictory traits whose coiled comic potential lay in drawing out the very words out in performance toward the final laughter line: "The British character itself is a mixture of Britons, Romans, Scots, Danes.... this driving, swelling, pompous, meddling, fearless, working, trading, bigoted, self-opinionated character—An Englishman." Perhaps her most ironic and complex use of such comedy was the lecture's wry critique of the English settlement of the New World:

> The way in which the New Englanders wrested their lands from the possession of the aborigines was so entirely English that we cannot cease to laugh at it, although our hearts are grieved at its cruelty. Their English sense of justice must of course have some valid excuse for exterminating the Indians and seizing their lands, so I have heard that they met in solemn convention and accompanied the whole thing by resolutions, in something like the following fashion—"Resolved—that this land is the Lord's. Resolved—that we are the Lord's people. And therefore, this land belongs to us!" And they took it. Nothing could have been more English than that.[49]

It was a way of talking both about the hypocrisy of her audience's ancestors and, perhaps, about the later hypocrisies of the English regarding the subject of slavery. Reports of this moment in Montez's performance reveal it as a key laughter line, its insistent and increasingly pointed repetition of "English" draining the term of its normative power as a marker of civilization. By a very different route, Montez's rhetoric arrived at the same critique as Native American lecturer William Apess's famously strident "Eulogy to King Philip" (1836), a satiric denunciation of Anglo-Saxon rapacity and Lockean legal claims that drew humor from the ambiguity between theft, appropriation, and legitimate possession. It was also a self-reflective gesture, directed at least implicitly toward the comparable "solemnity" of the lecture hall "conventions" and crowds that Montez now faced as an intellectual equal: a performative public sphere based on practices of lecture hall morality and Protestant collectivism was not too far from those that underpinned the seizure of the colonies. It was her task in her new role as cross-cultural arbitrator to peel away those layers of solemnity and cant, to present a more truthful and faithful image of the Anglo-American past, present, and future.

Such humor was placed in the service of a message of reassurance and unity. On both sides of the Atlantic she stressed points of shared habits: the mutual love of money and commerce; the performance repertoires that both countries had in common. "England may be justly proud that she has given birth to a child such as America," she told audiences in Britain.[50] To listeners in the auditoriums of America she confirmed that "John Bull at home in England and Jonathan at home in New England are the same sort of beings variously modified by local habitudes and institutions."[51] Her key task seemed to be that of reassurance. She aimed to comfort American listeners that "the people of England were entirely free from those ridiculous ideas of America which they were popularly supposed to entertain."[52] In her very person, she seemed to embody reassuring ideas about transatlantic differences, suggesting the miraculously transformative power of emigration and travel. Amid escalating tensions between North and South and between London and Washington, Montez fashioned a new persona as both gadfly and guarantor of Anglo-American unity, trying to use her hyphenated identity to promote ideals of kinship through the same kinds of shared humor that Thackeray had come to represent.

As she proclaimed nightly to her American audiences, which at Washington in January 1860 included senators, ambassadors, and Vice President Breckenridge, "We only laugh at the eccentricities of those we love best."[53]

Yet her success was only ever partial. Press response to her brand of sociopolitical prophecy reveals widespread reluctance on the part of media commentators to entirely embrace the seriousness of Montez's new role. Her pseudoanthropological pieces met with a lukewarm response compared to the easier charms of her discussion of beauty or strong women. The *Chicago Daily Journal* complained in tone at least that "her talk could more properly be styled a gossipy discourse than a lecture."[54] Reports from her Bradford, Yorkshire, performance observed that while "this notorious lady possesses a remarkably clear and distinct utterance . . . the substance of the lecture was all bunkum."[55]

The *London Morning Star* was muted about her "lively and somewhat immethodical commentary on English and American character."[56] To some, the very genre of transatlantic commentary was rather old hat. The *Era* lamented the talk as "decidedly didactic rather than diverting. With most of the characteristics mentioned as illustrative of the peculiarities of each country, we must presume the majority of her hearers had, in the course of their reading or experience, become already acquainted."[57] "There was no attempt to weave into the subject a few threads of personal interest," complained the *London Morning Advertiser*, "no mention of any incident that had happened to herself in any part of the American continent and no anecdote reminiscence that might have enlivened the dissertation in any way. The lecture might have been a newspaper article, the first chapter of a book of travels, or the speech of a long-winded American ambassador after a Mansion House dinner."[58] Moreover, some viewed her new role as cultural ambassador as simply a shrewd business move: the painted woman turned confidence trickster. "In this country she abuses the English, and when in England, she turns round and gives the Americans 'hark,'" complained a Virginia paper. "Lola cares more for the 'dimes' than for anything else."[59] By the time of her death she was not alone in attempting such Anglo-American diplomacy on the lecture circuit, since the similarly hyphenated John B. Gough was already touring the country with pieces that went even further in the attempt to use comedy to bring the Atlantic world together.

Gough's London Voices

Gough was the most famous temperance reformer of his era: a failed actor, ballad singer, and reformed alcoholic who became legendary for his passionate and theatrical oratory championing the salvation of abstinence (see Figure 6.2). Beginning in the early 1840s, his lectures on the evils of drink managed, in the words of an early biographer, to "hold audiences breathless on both sides of the Atlantic for nearly half a century."[60] The temperance cause took him to Britain in 1857, and, following a three-year stay, he returned to the United States at the end of the decade ready to take his career as a public speaker in a new direction. As an early biographer recorded:

> The professional season of 1860–61 witnessed a new departure on Gough's part. Until now he had spoken invariably upon temperance. He was suffering, in body and mind, from this "harping on one string." He realized the need of variety in his labors if he would preserve his health and continue his usefulness.

"After prolonged consideration," the account continues, "Mr. Gough consented to prepare a lecture on 'Street Life in London'—a taking caption [sic] and a topic upon which he could speak *con amore*."[61] English-born but Massachusetts-raised since the age of ten, Gough took pride in his transatlantic origins, and now opted to directly address this dual identity in pieces that offered irreverent and entertaining descriptions of the eccentricities of diverse slices of British life. He had transitioned from chronicler of addiction to interpreter of place. Gough tested his fresh material at the New Haven Library Society on 21 November 1860, and the following spring took his "London" reflections on tour. Soon he expanded his repertoire to include the related talks "Here and There in England," "London at Night," and "Life in London," pieces that would prove among his most popular in the decades that followed.[62] Between 1860 and the mid-1870s Gough delivered these British-themed lectures hundreds of times throughout the Northeast, Midwest, Canada, and California.[63]

These new pieces offered a lighthearted diversion from his customary reformist addresses, but Gough also saw the shift to more populist themes as a way to continue his "usefulness," as a promoter of Anglo-American unity. Introducing

FIGURE 6.2 *Daniel Macnee, John B. Gough, engraved by Edward Burton, 1855*

his new material in Philadelphia in May 1861, reports record Gough declaring that "he should count himself happy if, by anything he said, these lectures he might contribute to bind England and America more closely together. He felt proud of his birth as an Englishman, and of his adoption as an American."[64] Coming in the wake of Montez's performances, Gough offered material that was in many ways comparable assessments of British and American society designed to promote public understanding. Like Montez, he did so through an ambivalent mixture of satire and endearment. But his performances were both more complex and elaborate in form, and were also debuted at a historical moment that sharpened the urgency of such subject matter.

The secession crisis and outbreak of Civil War marked the most fraught time in a generation from the relationship between the United States and Britain. As the Palmerston administration in London appeared to vacillate in its support for the North during the early years of the conflict, many in the northern states grew angered and dismayed. As his asides in his lectures made clear, Gough was acutely aware of the ways in which this had made his material newly political. As he repeatedly told audiences, his aim was to temper wartime Anglophobic feeling in East Coast cities and persuade audiences of the goodwill and support of the peoples of Britain. Like Montez, he posed as a guarantor of union, and a galvanizer of the Anglo-American commons, suggesting that despite the growing distance between the two cultures, points of commonality still existed. What is fascinating, however, is the paradoxical manner in which these efforts at unifying were attempted, through a dynamic that pulled in two opposing directions: first, making transatlantic cultural distance more palpable through forms of comic mimicry that often exoticized his British subject matter; second, beckoning the two cultures together by encouraging audiences to join him in lavish declarations of loyalty to the monarchy and to Parliament. The remainder of this chapter examines how this worked by focusing on three locations—Brooklyn, Manhattan, and Philadelphia—with particularly complicated relationships to Britain, the war, and the Lincoln administration.[65] By tracing Gough's performances of his "London" material in these locations shifted in subtle fashion, we receive a fascinating glimpse into how transatlantic tensions registered on the texture of wartime lecture culture.

Gough's "London" pieces were far from traditional lyceum fare. As his first biographer claimed, he "had little ambition ... to take rank upon the literary lecturers of the day," and his pieces were more one-man theatrical shows than earnest treatises.[66] They were closer to playhouse than almost any lecturer encountered so far in their ostentatious mingling of sentimental and comic registers, moving within sentences from "hilarity" to moments "startling in their earnestness"—a fusion that reports suggest "completely carried away the audience."[67] Moreover, his lectures were essentially "monopolylogues," or sequential impressions, the form long associated with the Regency period British actor Charles Mathews, and which, in his own fashion, Charles Dickens would also bring to the postbellum American circuit.[68] "In the course of an address Gough enacted a dozen parts, with such fidelity that the last seemed the best," the same biographer tells us, offering up "more a succession of dramatic representations in which the author is the "star" actor of every part, than a succinct discourse."[69] His act had always relied upon a peculiarly embodied style, confronting audiences with elaborate simulations of his own past drunkenness that were by turns comic, threatening, and harrowing. And during the second half of his platform career, Gough drew upon the same resources of body and mimicry to conjure up the realities of London.

As an experienced actor and gifted mimic, Gough was able to reconceive the role of lecturer as impersonator, illustrating his arguments and observations through direct caricature. This was partly a matter of physical slapstick, as shown in a March 1861 performance in Philadelphia:

> Mr. Gough next took up a Jack of all trades ... at night he turned "wagabone," by "hacting hat a thehatre," taking the part of "doing the hind legs of a heliphant." The mode in which he did this was ocularly demonstrated by the lecturer walking across the stage *à la* the hind legs of an elephant, the audience heightening the managerial effect by roaring in the most abandoned laughter.[70]

However, beyond such vaudevillian physical feats, vocal imitations still formed the heart of these lectures. A report from Brooklyn the month before records how the speaker then gave us accounts of the different classes and seemingly different races of people who inhabit London, and also imitated their language, from the distorted use of the letter 'h' by the Bow-bell cockney, to the r-excluding exquisite of Regent and Bond streets. In thieves' slang he was at home, and showed the many of old English words have been conserved in this villainous dialect. He also described the tricks of London street merchants and thieves; and touched on fairs, holidays and amusements. He also came out strong on London criers, which he imitated with a naturalness that convulsed the house with merriment. Phrases of London industry, from the "mudlark" to the "cats-meatman" were touched on, and the speaker gave accounts of amusing tavern signs to be seen about the city.[71]

As he guided listeners through the streets of the city, his manipulations of his vocal tract and articulators became resonant shorthand for recognizable places. Audiences were transported to Regent Street and Pall Mall by Gough's soft bilabial fricatives ("vewy good") and aspirate onset ("horator"); his dropped consonants ("'appiness") delivered them to the slums of St. Giles and Bethnal Green.

In Gough's new pieces the impersonations took in all classes of Londoner, casting his satirical voice both up and down the social rank. At a repeat performance in Brooklyn the following week,

> Mr. G related a variety of incidents which came under his observation. His account of the habits and the ways of the little Arabs of the London streets was very racy; as a mimic, Mr. G has few superiors, and he reproduced the slang and manner of representatives of all grades of London life, singing as coster-monger, "cabbages, and cauliflowers," and imitating with admirable truthfulness the language and gait of the exquisite young men who are so "dooedly well dwessed" and patronize so liberally the "opewa." These are things that are not reportable, for they require Mr. G's admirable acting to give them the piquancy they have as related by him.[72]

On the stage of the Brooklyn Academy of Music a stratified society comes to life through a series of sonic and visual mnemonics. Reports suggest that audience members who prized their knowledge of London types clapped and cheered the mention of particular groups. Though impossible to recreate, a sense of this phonological mimicry can be derived from passages in Gough's autobiography, where the eccentricities of elevated British pronunciation are similarly treated:

> Another chairman, who aspirated his H's, and put them hon when they hought to be hoff, and took them hoff when they hought to be hon ... said "Ladies and gentleman, hi wish to hintroduce the horator of the hevening. He comes from the hother side of the Hatlantic ... hour transatlantic horator."[73]

Using such techniques, Gough's vocal abilities allowed him to encompass seemingly the whole strata of the British capital, populating it with voice, bringing the pages of Dickens or George Reynolds to life. The successive impersonations leveled the class distinctions of the metropolis into one continuum of comic voice. This aspect of Gough's performance was on one level simply of a piece with a popular fixation with accent games on the American stage. Though it might have been rare on the more conventional end of the lecture circuit, this entertainment was the lifeblood idiom of the midcentury stage. Nonetheless, Gough's incorporation of such material into the mode of the popular lecture involved forcing a certain pedagogic rationale upon what in other hands might have been mere raucous merriment. His framing above allows us to see a range of deeper cultural issues at work.

One key aspect was the fascination with linguistic divergence. Of the many transformations of the Anglo-American commons that energized the period covered by this book, one of the more notable took place within the throat, through incremental but significant metamorphosis of accent. Through the Revolution both nations inhabited relatively parallel acoustic worlds, and into the 1790s, New York naval officers reported difficulties in distinguishing American and English sailors.[74] By the middle of the next century, however, resemblance had given way to discord. In the popular imagination, transatlantic distinctions in accent became a matter of fascination and comment. The midcentury fascination with vocal fidelity was not simply the narcissism of small differences, but also registered the extent to which the American speech patterns were moving away from other cognate dialects of English. Such matters were of particular relevance to the cultural life of increasingly polyglot East Coast cities. Gough's accents served as equivalent geographic and class mnemonics for urban milieu in which immigration had created an enormous amount of spoken variation. Beyond the visual comedy, therefore, lay a humor based on the violations of grammatical and phonological norms, and on the broad traditional comedy of malapropisms, through which Philadelphians, New Yorkers, and Bostonians could measure their own vocal rectitude.

The details of Gough's handling of his "London" material shows that this was not just about sound but about language. We can situate their appeal within the popular American awareness that Britain was increasingly distinct not just aurally but linguistically. The discussion in his lectures of exotic slang mirrored debates over linguistic divergence that were typically framed in terms of advance, regression, and degeneration.[75] We can see the increasing linguistic self-awareness of the period, expressed in such artifacts as John Bartlett's influential *Dictionary of Americanisms* (1848), surfacing in the sonic playfulness of Gough's *linguistic* performance, in ways that prefigure the rise of the local color dialect sketch. As *self-* suggested in the reference of the Brooklyn report above to older forms of English *awareness* having "been conserved" in London street dialect, Gough's depictions also spoke *of the period* to the idea of British vernacular as a museum piece, an object of study for its historical idiosyncrasies. Gough presents the poor of London, and, by extension, British culture itself, as simultaneously unsettlingly modern and ossified exhibit, a disturbing repository of the past. Each lecture framed his impersonations through earnest descriptions in which he inhabited the role of British social investigative ethnographer, presenting London's poor in a stratified hierarchy. The *Philadelphia Press* mediated this for its readers, noting how "the philological and ethnological peculiarities of London" made it "almost impossible to believe that the city was not composed of several nationalities, so different were the various divisions in this respect.[76] "Street Life in London" was presented as a tableau of unfamiliar slang and dialect, in which the lecturer exoticized these bizarre sonorities as those of a seemingly alien race. Gough freely recycled tropes of racial stratification from respectable sources such as Mayhew but also more sensationalist accounts such as James Ewing Ritchie's *Night Side of London* (1857) that offered similar characterizations of the nomadic "alien" race of the British poor.[77] In this way, Gough presented not only a personal experience of the city but also channeled a condition-of-England discourse, appropriating the rhetoric by which urban writers exoticized their own dispossessed.

Of most interest, however, is Gough's role himself as embodied performer, a role that might be understood through reference to the comparable dynamics of his temperance speeches. In these earlier lectures, Gough had represented the popular orator as metaphysical interpreter. His talks on the evils of drink served to bridge chasms of experience and render comprehensible distinct psychological and social states: sobriety and inebriation; respectability and destitution; propriety and scandal. The kinds of "experience" speeches that temperance reformers such as those known as the Washingtonians specialized in were frequently dramatizations of physical transformation. In the words of Ian Tyrrell, this often involved the embodiment of stark contrasts on the part of the performer:

> The contrast between past degradation and present respectable condition which the reformed man presented on the stage carried tremendous dramatic force. The stark alternatives—poverty then, respectability now— were embodied in the person of the reformed man.[78]

Gough's accent-switching embodied a similar physical truth: the transatlantic transformation as reversible process. His effortless transition between multiple accents burlesqued the notion of fixed states or identities, suggesting that such distinctions were mutable, artificial accidents of vocality alone. In his impersonations, and in the texts that strove to capture them, his oral identity involved its own kind of Anglo-American traffic and exchange, summoning up an authentic inner British voice nightly for the entertainment of listeners.

Yet it was a sound that resonated in contradictory ways. In David Reynolds's study of antebellum "dark reform," he has encouraged critical caution regarding the nuanced effects of Gough's reform speeches. Such oratory, he points out, was heavily reliant upon complex levels of irony and complicity on the part of both audiences and performers. As a result, all was not what it seemed in a reform culture based on a perverse and prurient fascination with the very sins those involved claimed to want eradicated.[79] Just as Gough's temperance addresses can be read in terms of a mixture of attraction and repulsion, something similar seems to have been at work in the interplay between recognition and dissonance in his "London" material. On the simplest possible level, they were pure satire. By putting on British voices he rendered potentially intimidating distinctions or alarming differences laughable and harmless. But in the larger context of what he was trying to achieve with his wartime lectures, irreverence may have simply been one step on the way to fuller and more sympathetic connection. By stripping away layers of accumulated deference and hostility, Gough was able to encourage his audiences to see themselves as part of an even stronger Anglo-American alliance. To show this at work, we can turn to two moments from his performances in which he managed to elicit striking expressions of transatlantic unanimity.

Swearing Allegiance to Parliament and Queen

Just as Greeley had done with his oratorical tour of the Crystal Palace, Gough's accounts of London also aimed to offer the simulation of travel. These lectures were sometimes marketed as part of the circulation of cultural capital, with the *Philadelphia Inquirer* recommending them for prospective transatlantic visitors: "The opportunity should not be lost to gain information of so useful a character, especially to those who design visiting the English metropolis."[80] For the vast majority who couldn't make the trip, Gough's words offered a virtual guide. In 1861 one Boston paper advised potential audiences that his descriptions were such that it was "as though a listener had been on the spot and seen in person that of which he has only been told."[81] As we have seen, some of these spots included the slums of St Giles and the grandeur of Regent Street. But perhaps the most memorable moments of his performances were when he placed listeners in Hyde Park and the House of Commons, and used evocative descriptions and mime to encourage audience identification with the institutions of monarchy and Parliament.

In the second of the lectures in Gough's new repertoire, "Lights and Shadows of London Life," he ushered audiences into a vividly described summer's morning amid the beau monde of Hyde Park. As he would do in other of this London pieces, he offered a series of surprisingly sympathetic apologias for a misunderstood aristocracy, and described the glamour of their attire. The climax of the scene came with a dramatic account of the arrival of Queen Victoria's carriage passing through the park, a moment that typically appeared to have been met with an enthusiastic vocal and sometimes musical response. In Philadelphia in February 1861, the *Press* recorded that "when he introduced Victoria in the train, and uttered the sentiment 'God Bless England's Queen!' the audience responded with marked applause. Republicans as we were, he said, the people could not help saying 'amen!' to this prayer."[82] Of the same performance, the *Inquirer* recorded that "his eulogy of the Queen brought down the house with hearty applause."[83] An account of the same moment in a Brooklyn performance the following month allows to examine the dynamics at work more closely:

> Carriages are driving five abreast, and seated in them are the fairest and proudest of England's daughters, and every hand is raised for it is her, Majesty Queen Victoria (Applause). Respect for higher classes is a strong feeling in England; respect to the head of government is always shown, but when the head of the nation is a woman, a wife and a mother, and one who in those relations is a worthy example to others, is it any wonder that John Bull gets red in the face as he shouts:
> "Send her victorious
> Happy and glorious
> Long to reign o'er us,
> God save the Queen!"
> The audience applauded as loudly as the most devoted subjects of the Queen of England ever did, and the orchestra helped out the enthusiasm by playing the English national anthem.[84]

Gough presented the spectacle of the monarchical sublime at its most femi-
nine and decorous. A seemingly unaccountable or alien sentiment ("respect for
higher classes") is rendered comprehensible and intimate through an emphasis on shared values of domesticity and female virtue, emotively itemizing
Victoria's societal roles. In doing so, Gough subtly guides listeners toward models of deference based as much on domestic values as on assent to socioeconomic
hierarchies.

American monarchist sentiment was reaching something of peculiar climax
during these years. Gough was speaking in the wake of the feverish reception
that had greeted the 1860 visit of the Prince of Wales to the United States, an
event that seemed to offer much needed escapism for an otherwise distracted
and troubled country. The sentiments that underpinned such an unlikely
embrace, and that lay behind the scenes of response to Gough's invocation of
Victoria above, were nuanced and subtle. The remarkable scenario we glimpse
in the Brooklyn report does not mean these Brooklyn listeners all suddenly
became "the most devoted subjects" of monarchy. Rather, that by making
seemingly incompatible structures of feeling comprehensible to one another,
Gough has found common ground, and encouraged listeners to join him in
a familiar ceremonial ritual on their own terms within a theatrical space of
license and freedom. As Paul Downes has argued of early American monarchism, democratic rhetoric of the type we see in the accounts above ("republicans as we were . . .") was never entirely able to divest itself of reliance upon
the "worthy example" of monarchy and admiration for the patterns of loyalty
it commanded.[85] But what is even more clear here, following the reading of
Anglophilia offered by Tamarkin, is that at the moment of secession, public
fixation with the pageantry of the English state was a way of performing a
potent form of loyalty and cultural strength.[86] Contained within such seemingly paradoxical scenes as those above in Philadelphia or Brooklyn, we might
see a renewal of filial piety, one that Gough offered up as a viable model for the
shoring up unity in the wartime Union.[87] Inevitably, however, such sentiments
were only ever partially embraced. A report from another Philadelphia performance the following year gives us quite a different response, when a "man
in the parquet circle, clad in the uniform of an army officer," shouted over the
heads of an audience rising to leave that Gough's praise of Victoria "might be
applauded in Philadelphia; but if they were uttered in the West, where *we* had
done the fighting, the man who uttered them would be spit upon, and damned
and sent to hell!"[88]

The second of Gough's set-piece descriptions aimed to animate similar institutional camaraderie by guiding audiences through Westminster. In a sequence ide-
ally suited to his mimetic gifts, he adapted the well-known passage from *Sketches
by Boz* where Dickens offered an immersive diorama of the House of Commons,
in order to reel off a series of irreverent pen portraits of prominent politicians.[89]

Reporting on a March 1861 Brooklyn performance, the *Eagle* recorded what Gough made of such a scene:

> The lecturer suggested that we stand for a while in the House of Commons, some afternoon. It is now 4 o'clock in the evening, and as members pass in singly, we have a goodly opportunity of observing them. The assembly comprises England's most potent men. Do you see that youthful looking elder gentleman, very spirited in his bearing, with a flower in his button-hole, and another rolling about his lips? That is Lord Palmerston, the Premier of England.[90]
>
> ... This man who now comes along, makes you look at him, with his hook nose and deep grey eye and thin face covered with hair. His tall sinewy form startles you as he glides by you: he is a poet, novelist, orator and statesman—rich and full of fame. He is Sir Edward Bulwer-Lytton.
>
> Look what a contrast is the *next man*, dressed in Quaker garb, square built, with a face of a decided [*sic*] yet mild expression. He looks as a man of business, and so he is, for that is one of the members for Manchester, John Bright (Loud applause).[91]

His descriptions varied in length in each performance, but always followed a repeating rhythm: a rich description of an unnamed character laced with intriguing detail, whose identity is theatrically revealed at the end of the sentence. The choreography of their imaginary sight-lines ("see, there comes his rival") converts his audience into an intimate community of observers. The irreverent tone of these *Punch*-like caricatures nods toward satire, but here cloaked beneath an essentially conciliatory process that humanizes Parliament, eliciting audience recognition and acceptance of proxy representation by these emblems of a foreign democratic body. This response is witnessed not least in response to the figure of Bright, whose long-standing advocacy for the United States earned him profound affection across the Atlantic, and whose name duly received the loudest cheers in each hall in which Gough brought him to life.

It is possible of course that the loud outpourings of affection that Gough elicited at these events represented mere social display or harmless ironic indulgence. As this book has been keen to stress, lecture halls were always spaces of mutual performance and thus an ideal arena in which to be seen flaunting one's loyalties and transnational affections in ways that might have no meaningful broader purchase. However, just as Gough's moral project in his temperance lecturers was to convince and persuade listeners of the righteousness of sobriety, a similarly evangelical tone persists in these "London" pieces. Through description and evocation [Gough offered audiences the chance to feel like participants in London life and swear allegiance to its institutions.] With that aim in mind, and with the national conflict escalating, he repeatedly connected the fate of the American republic to that of the teleology of British endurance. "It will be an evil

day for religious and civil liberty, and for the general progress of Europe," ran a
stirring line toward the end of his "London" piece, "when the enemies of Great
Britain shall have their hope realized, and her silver light shall be robbed of its
luster and grow dim."[92] In Philadelphia in 1861 he fleshed this out using Thomas
Babington Macaulay's famous image of the New Zealander amid the ruins of a
post-British world:

> The lecturer described that London which a traveler, a philanthropist, or
> an inquisitive American would see ... and said that it would be a dark day
> for liberty in Europe if Macaulay's fancy could be realized, and 'the trav-
> eler from New Zealand' could stand in the broken arches of London Bridge
> and view the wild ruins of St. Paul's.[93]

Whereas numerous American commentators had conscripted the "New
Zealander" trope as part of jeremiads predicting British decline, Gough's broader
emphasis on transatlantic unity makes it into a symbol of the threats to Anglo-
Saxon civilization, threats that might be met through public pledges of mutual
support.[94]

Wartime Fractures

These rituals of allegiance allowed for the working through of the many evolving
contradictions of Anglo-American identity at a moment of potential national rup-
ture. However, as the conflict progressed, and domestic attitudes toward British
conduct toward the wartime Union sharpened, a number of the tensions written
into the above scenes—between monarchy and republicanism; between deference
and irreverence—began to unravel. Among the fascinations of Gough's wartime
tours of his "London" pieces is that his material shifts in meaning as the events
of the war unfold. From early 1861 onward, reports show that he used his talks
as versatile opportunities for unscripted political commentary on the evolving
Anglo-American situation. At first, his asides were laudatory, and formed part
of his broader ambition toward cultural unity, but as the conflict unfolded we
can trace on the part of performer and audiences alike, an emotional and political trajectory from wholehearted enthusiasm for British society to a much more
qualified and chastened assent.

An extended moment from a report of his second Brooklyn appearance in
February 1861 reveals the tone of his renditions early in the conflict:

> He (Mr. G.) had spoken in Great Britain one hundred and fifty times, and
> he never spoke of Bunker Hill that it was not responded to by a cheer; he
> never spoke of the Declaration of Independence that it was not received
> with applause. There were Americans in this house who were present when
> in Exeter Hall he spoke of the people of these colonies who tracked the

snow with their blood in their efforts to throw off what they believed to be a thraldom from their shoulders, and that vast audience sprang to their feet and honored them with round after round of cheers (*applause*).

In the troubles that now surround our country, the sympathy of England is precious; would that both countries could be brought nearer in their interests. On Friday last he felt proud of the fact that he was an Englishman born and an American by adoption, when he saw the devotion of the people to the old flag—the glorious stars and stripes. (*The immense audience cheered for several minutes, and the orchestra struck up the "Star Spangled Banner," when they ended enthusiasm grew wilder than ever. Someone in the body of the house shouted out, "Don't be afraid, go on," and thus encouraged, "Yankee Doodle" was given.*)[95]

Readers are presented with a scene rich in ritual and political theater. Gough's account of his British reception offers a nuanced version of British public opinion and confirms to his 3,500-strong Brooklyn audience the apparent existence of substantial pockets of sympathy among the mechanic's institutes and, as his reference to Exeter Hall seems to attest, British abolitionists. This metarhetorical gesture revives the trope of Atlantic voice so prominent in Douglass, and uses the same continuity of speech venues, only to inflect them further as symbols of conflict and rebellion. His pointed affirmation of shared sentiment, of the republic being "honored" with applause, confirms a degree of mutual respect—an account that itself elicits "applause" and we might say deftly completes a circuit of public assent that reaches beyond the sectional dispute to broader questions of identity and legitimacy.

The dynamics of the New York press and the valence of public displays of loyalty also complicate and enrich this scene. During the first months of 1861, the *Brooklyn Eagle* emerged as the most prominent of northern antiwar "Copperhead" outlets, channeling a measure of the strong antiwar sentiment of the New York City area, only for its editor Henry McCloskey to be forced to resign after publication of a false proclamation by Lincoln during March.[96] On 17 April a mob forced a display of Union support from the paper, and in August it was found guilty, alongside the *New York Daily News,* of a grand jury charge of disloyalty for attacks on the war effort, and its distribution privileges suspended.[97] These background forces and the paper's eagerness for European mediation in the early part of the year lend new meaning to the *Eagle*'s promotion of Gough's vision of transatlantic affinity as a sentiment compatible with its own goals for British mediation to end the war.

By November that year, an even greater degree of "musical unity" was reportedly achieved: "Long continued applause greeted the orator when he ceased to speak, during which the band struck up 'God save the Queen' followed by the 'Star Spangled Banner', playing the audience out of the house."[98] The only comparable urban gatherings that could conceivably have involved public juxtaposition of these two pieces would have been ceremonies for such ethnically British societies as the "Sons of St. George" or the "Sons of St. Andrew."[99] However, these performances in late 1861 also allowed Gough to express growing frustration and disillusionment at the delay in British military support.

This sense of frustration seems to emerge through isolated, seemingly impromptu expressions, as when here again in Brooklyn he offered a justifiably gloomy response to several months of heavily circulated Fleet Street abuse of the Union:[100]

> The lecturer, in good terms, denounced the London *Times*, whose influence was paramount in England. A more mercenary and unprincipled journal could not exist. Its articles were all made to order, to be used or rejected as the directory might see fit. The feelings of the masses in England are with us, and we shall receive their sympathies in this our struggle, but the aristocracy are against us.[101]

This disenchantment also began to inflected Gough's London material in other more subtle ways. One intriguing example is the development of his presentation of the "Great Stink" of 1858, an environmental crisis for the British capital in which a particularly hot summer rendered the River Thames even more noxious than usual, almost forcing a shutdown of Parliament. Gough found mobile political use for his account of the events and its implications. At Manhattan's Cooper Union in March 1861, for instance, he used the event as a rhetorical volley against the "traitors" of the Confederacy:

> the odor sometimes upon the deliberations of Parliament, by which the members were driven from their seats, he said, "I would to Heaven, when traitors get together to plot, some river Thames would *stench* them out" [Enthusiastic applause long continued].[102]

Of the same performance, the *Tribune* recorded that Gough could not even finish his above observation to the "two or three thousand auditors," since the "the rest was lost in the tumult of applause with which the sentiment was greeted."[103] These dual associations serve again to further Gough's argument for Anglo-American amity, since Britain, too, had encountered and successfully weathered periods of comparable "treachery" and crisis as that now faced by the Union. Over the years of the war his account gradually acquired a more straightforwardly antiparliamentary tone, such that by the time he took it to San Francisco in 1871, audience derision was directed toward the unpopular tenants of the House of Commons, where the "repulsive stench" forces a scene in which Parliament was "compelled to adjourn by the loathsome smell. The Thames got the best of it. [Laughter]. There was an intruder that they could not give into the custody of the Sergeant-at-arms."[104]

When Gough revived these lectures in the final months of the war, this sense of dismay at the shortcomings of British support and diplomacy had become even more pointed. In a March 1865 Brooklyn revival of "London," Gough had sharpened his critique and introduced a note of despondency:

> Mr. Gough launched a Philippic against England for her conduct towards this country during the rebellion, and cited the arts of that country to the Sepoys during the Hindoo mutiny as evidence of her hypocritical conduct in dealing with the United States.
>
> Before bringing his oration to a close, he expressed his conviction that the public sentiment of England was antagonistic to this country. As he retired, he was greeted with applause.[105]

Moving toward the kind of Anglophobic rhetoric more associated in the period with firebrands such as William H. Seward, we see fractures in the Anglo-American commons, exemplified by Gough's portrayal of a British nation no longer stratified on class lines but now by a broader, unitary "antagonism" to Union interests.[106] Unlike other observations based on firsthand experience in 1850s England, this closing "conviction" rested, like that of his audience, purely on his apprehension via the media of the course of British diplomacy. Even though claims of blanket "antagonism" were now for the most part unjustified following the eventual recognition and support of the Palmerston government, these moments of performance are testament to the limits of a popular vein of Anglo-American sympathy whose wave had crested in the early years of the war.[107] The governing tone of these lectures by 1865 was one of ambivalent acceptance of the troubling fact that the Anglo-American commons had proved to be more cultural construct that military or political reality. At a Brooklyn revival of "Life in London" in 1865, Gough was reported to have declared

> to all of them of the Anglo-Saxon race, on the face of the globe [that] there was not a city, so interesting as London. Their fathers came from there, the archives of their race were treasured there, and as they crossed the Atlantic, London held out the fraternal hand bidding welcome to the stranger. He had enjoyed largely the friendship and hospitality of the English people, and as Cowper said of England, he would say: "London, with all thy faults, I love it still."[108]

As Gough vocalized and embodied the eccentricities of London street life in these pieces, he aimed to encourage a version of the Anglo-American commons whose mixture of mutual mockery, irreverence, and respectful recognition would guarantee its survival as a useful cultural alliance. Here in 1865, we see a conclusion that registers the disappointments of the war years and present a more muted sequel to the histrionic gestures of unity four years before. Hours of performance when the fate of the Union seemed to lie in Gough's voice box, in the vigorous transformations of his transatlantic larynx.

Cables and Registers

In the words of the *New York Times* in 1861, he "laid an Atlantic cable from the 'streets of London' . . . to New York, and established a telegraph office in the heart of every listener."[109] The metaphor was resonant in several important respects. Listening to Gough lecture and inhabit the voices of London provided a form of aural link, a telegraphic means of listening to the primal, authentic sounds of the British capital. The apparent fervor and enthusiasm with which his rhetorical experiments were greeted also harked back to the similarly wild public reaction to the opening of the cable in 1858. More importantly, it spoke to a sense of fractured communication, since the cable had been workable for only a few months, and through the war years lay dormant in disrepair.[110] Through their coverage of mediating figures such as Gough, however, media outlets such as the *New York Times*, we might say, wished a channel of communication back into action, and a re-energized, re-engaged cable was an effective image for his attempt to address continental dislocation and ruptured understanding. Yet as Montez pointed out in her own pieces, the cable metaphor could also be a source of satire. As a London paper reported of her 1859 lecture, she connected "the gullibility and excitability of the Americans, individually and nationally" to their "rejoicings over the momentary success of the Atlantic cable, contrasting with the apparent apathy of the English people with the 'galvanic delight' of the Yankees."[111]

At first sight, Montez and Gough seem to embody what many have seen as the decline of lecture culture as it headed into the 1860s. In that reading an essentially literary, austere model of community education gave way around the Civil War to one of ephemerality and flamboyant showmanship. It was a shift that James Perrin Warren, for instance has mourned as one from "a process marked by intellectual and emotional reciprocity," to one of more disengaged "spectatorship."[112] A sense of these changes was certainly already being felt keenly at the time. In an 1859 satirical article, the comic writer and fledgling lecturer Artemus Ward conjured up a fictional character who railed against the threat the lecture hall now posed to the theater and music hall: "*The Show Bizniss, which Ive stroven to ornyment, is bein usurpt by Poplar Lecturs, as thay air kalled, tho in my pinion thay air poplar humbugs.*"[113] To those on the other side of the divide, it was more a case of the theater encroaching upon lyceum values. For Josiah Holland in 1865 it was a case of "the admission of buffoons and triflers to the lecturer's platform"; to Thomas Wentworth Higginson in 1868 it meant that "with the name 'lyceum' is also passing away the 'lyceum lecture.'"[114]

Clearly, the decision of performers such as Gough and Montez to turn to the mainstream lectern, and the decision of lecture-sponsoring committees to consider them suitable fare, represents a waypoint on the trajectory from the didactic solemnity of the early Holbrookian lyceum to postwar "show bizniss." The ease with which Montez was able to transition from dance to melodrama to oratory, and the success that Gough found with pieces were essentially one-man theatricals demonstrates the way in which lecture hall performance values were increasingly part of a broader continuum of cultural events. However, rather than marking a simple decline these factors brought a reimagined civic function. *Lecturing the Atlantic* has explored what it meant for an emblem of northern civic nationalism such as the popular lecture to host performances that explored questions of a shifting Anglo-American commons.

The chapters of this book have shown that the midcentury platform was an arena in which performers, audiences, and print commentators could stage nuanced and compelling cultural gestures. By the postbellum period, lecturing was simply becoming a richer and more complicated cultural form. The lecture hall was now a form not simply for didactic pedagogy or for spoken essays, but for innovative rhetorical modes and uncategorizable performances, all of which deserve greater recognition in the history of Anglo-American popular culture. The unorthodox transatlantic arbitration of Gough and Montez offers an intriguing paired example. Both testified to the growing distance between two national cultures, and in their own ways both argued for a form of future coexistence through laughter and reinvention. Just as with the other orators before them, it was to be a cultural continuity grounded on ideals of public speech. The Anglo-American commons was, in Montez's terms, a matter of the "the true identity of language, literature, and institutions, which bind the two nations together."[115] A bond that had the lecture hall at its heart.

200 – Notes formation of Am Studies + eulogy for lib pub cul → he could more explicitly explore the boundaries between "the problematic yet seductive myths of the (19th) lecture hall."

{ Epilogue }

Our twenty-first-century understanding of lecture culture has been conditioned by the priorities of three distinct moments of interpretation. The first of these took place in the final decades of the nineteenth century, as a series of commentators cast their gaze back fifty years to the height of the lyceum boom.[1] From that vantage point several offered wistful elegies for what they saw as the intensity and cultural power of a lost form. One recalled in 1895 that "the platform for a time was omnipotent. Its rise was rapid and startling. Free speech was demanded by freemen, and the response was 'you shall have it,'" before noting that, while the lecture might still be visible in American life, its "work is done. The lyceum rose to great power and fell away and practically died, inside a single quarter century."[2] Another rhapsodized nostalgically about a phenomenon that had helped weave tougher a decentralized republic, reflecting that the fact that "we are now intellectually almost one country and not several differing provinces, has stripped lecturers of something of the glamour that attached to that which is foreign."[3] For these and for other fin de siècle observers, the lecture culture of the 1840s–1860s represented an intellectual tradition whose heroism in the face of major issues had effected genuine cultural change.

Far from a cultural vacuum being left in its place, however, the postwar lecture platform was resurgent. Lyceum events became far more evenly spread across the republic, and speakers were now far more likely than before to be women. Lecturer's activities were far more fully integrated into a broader cultural and theatrical entertainment sector, and speakers drew in increasingly sophisticated ways on techniques of visual and show culture. During decades stretching from that of Anna Dickinson, Helen Potter, and Mark Twain to that of Oscar Wilde, the lecture hall model transitioned slowly but surely into other forms, including the world of Chautauqua in the North and tent shows in the South.[4] This was, to be sure, a far more commercialized and mature market "system," with enterprising agencies such as the Redpath Bureau emerging as dominant forces in who spoke and what was heard. Yet as with so many other supposed turning points, the transition point of 1865 can be misleading: popular lectures did not disappear as a space for education or critical cultural engagement. Thanks to a growing body of scholarship on this period, it is no longer obligatory to take the late-century elegists at their word regarding what they almost universally termed the "decline" of the lecture.[5]

In opting to focus on the antebellum years of this world, *Lecturing the Atlantic* sought not to discount the cultural importance of later trends, but to focus in a deliberate manner on a more explicitly literary moment in lecturing's history, when the tensions between worlds of reform, politics, and literary production were at their height and might most productively be grasped. In doing so it has hoped to act in dialogue with the second major period of intensive interpretation of the lyceum, that of the postwar birth of American studies. In this 1950s moment, the celebration of antebellum lecture culture in the studies of Carl Bode and David Mead can be seen as part of broader debates both within and beyond the academy over the fate of public culture, national wholeness, and the prospects for democratic participation. To these interpreters, the organic unity at work in the antebellum lecture hall served its own moral lesson. Just as we might read a lament for the passing of national regional distinctiveness into the elegies for the lyceum of the 1890s, a form of liberal consensus was also clearly at work in the postwar romantic claims made for the enduring power of the lecture halls of a hundred years previously.

The third phase of interpretation is our own, one that has begun to understand lecturing as just as much a *new media* phenomenon as it was *social.* As advances in broadcast, connective, and social media come of age in the first decades of the twenty-first century we can recognize some of the origins of our own habits of interaction and perception in the ferment of the antebellum media. As Augst has argued, "our contemporary media ecology continues to be organized by cultural economies that first emerged" at the same moment as the lyceum.[6] As our understanding of media history develops, we can continue to find our own types of nostalgia and fascination in prior forms of public dialogue. Interdisciplinary methods and new critical priorities promise that we shall discover new complexities and truths beneath the problematic yet seductive myths of the nineteenth-century lecture hall. An ideal perhaps most compellingly captured in 1870, when George William Curtis conjured up memories of how "every evening, from November to April, hundreds of thousands of persons were gathered in halls, larger or smaller, from the Penobscot to the Mississippi ... and the sublime beauty of a great ideal shone nightly into thousands of hearts all over the land."[7]

{ NOTES }

Note on the Terminology of "England" and "Britain"

1. For the evolution of such nomenclature, see Catherine Hall, *White, Male and Middle-Class: Explorations in Feminism and History* (London: Polity Press, 1992).

2. Linda Colley, *Britons: Forging the Nation (1707–1837)* (New Haven: Yale University Press, 1994); Paul Langford, *English Identified* (Oxford: Oxford University Press, 2000); Peter Mandler, *The English National Character: The History of an Idea from Edmund Burke to Tony Blair* (New Haven: Yale University Press, 2007).

3. Langford, *English Identified*, 12.

Introduction

1. Key works in what might be termed a "new orality" in American literary studies include James Fliegelman, *Declaring Independence: Jefferson, Natural Language and the Culture of Performance* (Palo Alto, CA: Stanford University Press, 1993); Christopher Looby, *Voicing America: Language, Literary Form, and the Origins of the United States* (Chicago: University of Chicago Press, 1997); Sandra Gustafson, *Eloquence Is Power: Oratory and Performance in Early America* (Chapel Hill: University of North Carolina Press, 2000); Peter Gibian, *Oliver Wendell Holmes and the Culture of Conversation* (Cambridge: Cambridge University Press, 2001), 16. For a critical survey of such work, see Gustafson, "American Literature and the Public Sphere," *American Literary History* 20.3 (2008): 465–78. Further treatments of this sonic theme from a more historical perspective include Kenneth Cmiel, *Democratic Eloquence: The Fight over Popular Speech in Nineteenth-Century America* (Berkeley: University of California Press, 1991); Mark M. Smith, *Listening to Nineteenth Century America* (Chapel Hill: University of North Carolina Press, 2001); Carolyn Eastman, *A Nation of Speechifiers: Making an American Public after the Revolution* (Chicago: University of Chicago Press, 2009).

2. In pursuing this bifurcated sense of "commons" I follow the division sketched by Elizabeth M. Dillon, *New World Drama: The Performative Commons in the Atlantic World, 1649–1849* (Durham, NC: Duke University Press, 2014), v–vii; and as explored in Lewis Hyde, *Commons as Air: Revolution, Art and Ownership* (New York: Farrar, Straus and Giroux, 2010). This book was also informed by the related usage in Michael Hardt and Antonio Negri, *Commonwealth* (Cambridge: Harvard University Press, 2009).

3. Christopher Hanlon, *America's England: Antebellum Literature and Atlantic Sectionalism* (Oxford: Oxford University Press, 2012), 1.

4. The generation of public sphere scholarship that has flourished in the wake of the English translation of Jürgen Habermas's *Structural Transformation of the Public Sphere* (1989) has offered multiple refinements and challenges to the idea of the early republic as a moment of flourishing for rational-critical discourse. Key contributions to this Americanist

debate include Michael Schudson, "Was There Ever a Public Sphere? If So, When? Reflections on the American Case," in *Habermas and the Public Sphere*, ed. Craig Calhoun (Cambridge, MA: MIT Press, 1992), 143–63; Lauren Berlant, *The Queen of America Goes to Washington City: Essays on Sex and Citizenship* (Durham, NC: Duke University Press, 1997); and Mike Hill and Warren Montag, *Masses, Classes and the Public Sphere* (London: Verso, 2000). For a more literary perspective, see Nancy Ruttenburg, *Democratic Personality: Popular Voice and the Trial of American Authorship* (Stanford, CA: Stanford University Press, 1998); and Jennifer Greiman, *Democracy's Spectacle: Sovereignty and Public Life in Antebellum American Writing* (New York: Fordham University Press, 2010).

5. Recent discussions of the importance of a structure of North Atlantic feeling for the development of the early republic are Leonard Tennenhouse, *The Importance of Feeling English: American Literature and the British Diaspora, 1750–1850* (Princeton, NJ: Princeton University Press, 2007); Elisa Tamarkin, *Anglophilia: Deference, Devotion and Antebellum America* (Chicago: University of Chicago Press, 2008), xxvii; and Hanlon, *America's England*. For discussion of the material networks of nineteenth-century reform, see Amanda Claybaugh, *The Novel of Purpose: Literature and Social Reform in the Anglo-American World* (Ithaca, NY: Cornell University Press, 2007).

6. Frederick Douglass, "The Lecturers," *Frederick Douglass's Paper*, 13 January 1854.

7. Ralph Waldo Emerson, journal entry, 5 July 1839, in *Journals and Miscellaneous Notebooks of Ralph Waldo Emerson*, 15 vols., ed. William H. Gilman et al. (Cambridge, MA: Harvard University Press, 1960–), 7:224.

8. George William Curtis, "Editor's Easy Chair," *Harper's Monthly*, April 1855, 695.

9. Henry David Thoreau, *A Week on the Concord and Merrimack Rivers*, ed. Robert F. Sayre (New York: Library of America, 1985), 86.

10. Examples of such elegies include E. P. Powell, "Rise and Decline of the New England Lyceum," *New England Magazine* 17.6 (February 1895): 720–37; Mark Lee Luther, "The Bygone Lyceum," *Dial* 25 (1 November 1898): 291–93; and Thomas Wentworth Higginson, "American Audiences," *Atlantic Monthly*, January 1905, 38–44.

11. Given its cultural prominence and interdisciplinary relevance, there has been surprisingly little modern scholarly attention to lecture culture in general. The two foundational modern studies of the lyceum clustered around the postwar period: Carl Bode, *The American Lyceum: Town Meeting of the Mind* (1956; reprint, London: Feffer & Simmons, 1968); C. David Mead, *Yankee Eloquence in the Middle-West: The Ohio Lyceum, 1850–1870* (East Lansing: Michigan State College Press, 1951). A series of articles by Donald Scott from the early 1980s also greatly expanded our understanding of lecture culture: Scott, "The Popular Lecture and the Creation of a Public in Mid-Nineteenth-Century America," *Journal of American History* 66 (1980): 791–809; Scott, "Print and the Public Lecture System 1840–1860," in *Printing and Society in Early America*, ed. William L. Joyce et al. (Worcester, MA: American Antiquarian Society, 1983), 278–99; and Scott, "The Profession That Vanished: Public Lecturing in Mid-Nineteenth-Century America," in *Professions and Professional Ideologies in America*, ed. Gerald Grierson (Chapel Hill: University of North Carolina Press, 1983), 12–28. The most comprehensive recent exploration is Angela Ray, *The Lyceum and Public Culture in the Nineteenth-Century United States* (East Lansing: Michigan State University Press, 2005). For a survey of current work on the same ground, see Tom F. Wright, ed., *The Cosmopolitan Lyceum: Lecture Culture and the Globe in Nineteenth-Century America* (Amherst: University of Massachusetts Press, 2013).

12. Scott, "Popular Lecture," 809.

13. Ray, *Lyceum and Public Culture*, 2.

14. See, for example, the discussion of lecturing's relation to reform activism in T. Gregory Garvey, *Creating the Culture of Reform in Antebellum America* (Athens: University of Georgia Press, 2006).

15. F. O. Matthiessen, *American Renaissance: Art and Expression in the Age of Emerson and Whitman* (Oxford: Oxford University Press, 1941), 23.

16. Lawrence Buell, *Emerson* (Cambridge, MA: Harvard University Press, 2003), 23. For important discussions of nineteenth-century public speech, see Looby, *Voicing America*; Thomas Augst, *The Clerk's Tale: Young Men and Moral Life in Nineteenth-Century America* (Chicago: University of Chicago Press, 2003); Eastman, *A Nation of Speechifiers*.

17. Wright, *The Cosmopolitan Lyceum*, 7.

18. "Lecture, n.," 4, *OED Online*, September 2014.

19. As will become clear, my interest is less in the clearly demarcated oral event of the kind sketched by Donald Scott and Carl Bode than in a range of oratorical events that passed themselves off as lectures, or were defined in a form recognizable as lecture content. But I sometimes range beyond this framework to compare "lectures" proper with other oratorical events, in order to explore the nature of the dynamics between them.

20. Bode, *The American Lyceum*.

21. Thomas Augst, "Humanist Enterprise in the Marketplace of Culture," in Wright, *The Cosmopolitan Lyceum*, 223–40.

22. See Trish Loughran, *The Republic in Print: Print Culture in the Age of U.S. Nation Building, 1770–1870* (New York: Columbia University Press, 2007).

23. "Mr. Thackeray in America," *Fraser's Magazine*, December 1852.

24. Jack Goody, *The Domestication of the Savage Mind* (Cambridge: Cambridge University Press, 1977); Walter J. Ong, *Orality and Literacy: The Technologizing of the Word* (London: Routledge, 1982).

25. Ong, *Orality and Literacy*, 157.

26. George William Curtis, "Editor's Table: Lectures and Lecturing," *Harpers New Monthly Magazine*, December 1856, 122.

27. For a discussion of this material as "orature" see Oz Frankel, "The State between Orality and Textuality," in *Cultural Narratives: Textuality and Performance in the United States before 1900*, ed. Sandra M. Gustafson and Caroline F. Sloat (South Bend, IN: Notre Dame University Press, 2009), 276–96.

28. Debates over orality and literacy in American studies have seen proponents of print-centric views of modernity pitted against those who urge us to focus more on the history of voice. Yet "forms of the talking mind" such as lyceum speech texts make this divide dissolve somewhat. Warner has recently argued against the notion of a separate category of "orality" as misleading, insisting that we think instead of "performance and print" in the early republic as "densely laminated together," proceeding as a parallel "set of intermedial relations." See Michael Warner, "What Is a Sermon?," University of Pennsylvania Libraries A.S.W. Rosenbach Lectures in Bibliography for 2009, "The Evangelical Public Sphere," http://repository.upenn.edu/rosenbach/2/ (accessed 20 August 2014); Gustafson, *Eloquence Is Power*, xvii.

29. "Places of Public Amusement," *Putnam's Monthly* 3.14 (February 1854): 141.

30. This book ranges across various methodologies. First, my archival emphasis shares with book history an interest in the social locations of culture and the material processes

of publication. It involves the compilation of institutional documentations and artifacts, as well as the textual and media traces of individual performances, including manuscripts, broadsides, and published versions, in addition to a copious number of lecture reports and accounts. Moreover, my approach shares with rhetorical and communication studies the explicit endeavor of reanimating communicative artifacts of print and speech. Above all, however, this is a literary project. In what follows, I employ the methods of literary and rhetorical analysis to the textual traces of lecture performance. In doing so, I develop strategies for bringing such analysis into the lecture hall, hovering close above the language of both original text and subsequent reports, teasing out ambiguities and tensions, remaining alive to the instrumentality and agency of both oratory and reportage.

31. At various points, considering the performance aspects of lyceum culture I also draw upon dramaturgical approaches to social negotiations in the work of Erving Goffman, the ritual aspects of social drama in Victor Turner, and the construction of social identities through performance in the more recent work of Peggy Phelan. See Erving Goffman, *The Presentation of the Self in Everyday Life* (New York: Doubleday, 1959); and Victor Turner, *Dramas, Fields, and Metaphors: Symbolic Action in Human Society* (Ithaca, NY: Cornell University Press, 1974). For more recent investigations see Peggy Phelan and Jill Lane, eds., *The Ends of Performance* (New York: New York University Press, 1998).

32. For the fullest articulation of this concept of historical "new media" see the essays in Lisa Gitelman, ed., *New Media, 1740–1915* (Cambridge, MA: MIT Press, 2003). For its relevance to the context of the lyceum, see Augst, "Humanist Enterprise."

33. Kenneth Burke, *Language as Symbolic Action* (Berkeley: University of California Press, 1966), 44–46.

34. On Dickens, most biographers have explored his two transatlantic visits in detail, most recently Michael Slater, *Charles Dickens: A Life Defined by Writing* (New Haven: Yale University Press, 2009); for discussion of his lecturing specifically, see Amanda Adams, *Performing Authorship in the Nineteenth-Century Transatlantic Lecture Tour* (Farnham: Ashgate, 2014). For Wilde in America see Michele Mendellsohn, "Notes on Oscar Wilde's Transatlantic Gender Politics," *Journal of American Studies* 46.1 (February 2012): 1–15; and Roy Morris, *Declaring His Genius: Oscar Wilde in North America* (Cambridge, MA: Belknap Press of Harvard University Press, 2013).

Chapter 1

1. Anon., "Lectures and Lecturers," *Putnam's Monthly*, March 1857, 317.

2. For my understanding development of nationalisms in the early American public sphere, I am indebted to the following works: David Waldstreicher, *In the Midst of Perpetual Fetes: The Making of American Nationalism, 1776–1820* (Chapel Hill: University of North Carolina Press, 1997); Elizabeth Maddock Dillon, *The Gender of Freedom: Fictions of Liberalism and the Literary Public Sphere* (Stanford, CA: Stanford University Press, 2004); and Michael Warner, *The Letters of the Republic: Publication and the Public Sphere in Eighteenth-Century America* (Cambridge, MA: Harvard University Press, 1990). For the cultural nationalism of the antebellum print media, see Sheila Post-Lauria, "Magazine Practices and *Israel Potter*," in *Periodical Literature in Nineteenth-Century America*, ed. Kenneth M. Price and Susan B. Smith (Charlottesville: University Press of Virginia, 1995), 116–27.

3. Anon., "Lectures and Lecturers," 321.

4. See Scott, "Popular Lecture," 791.

5. Hanlon, *America's England*, 1.

6. Josiah Holbrook, "Association of Adults for Mutual Education," *American Journal of Education for the Year 1826*, vol. 1 (Boston: Wait, Greene, 1826), 594.

7. Holbrook, "Association of Adults," 594.

8. For these figures, see Mead, *Yankee Eloquence*, 1–6; Ray, *Lyceum and Public Culture*, 77–101.

9. For the complicated overlaps involved in this range of organizations and institutions, see Bode, *The American Lyceum*, 241–42.

10. "Popular Lecturers," *Boston Daily Evening Transcript*, 29 October 1855.

11. "Editorial: Popular Lecturers," *Cambridge Chronicle*, 10 March 1860. See also earlier complaints over market saturation of lecturers in the New York market in "New York Correspondent of the Atlas," *Boston Daily Atlas*, 14 March 1856.

12. Bode, *The American Lyceum*, 132.

13. J. G. Holland, "The Popular Lecture," *Atlantic Monthly*, March 1865, 363; Scott, "The Profession That Vanished," 10–12; for a discussion of the composition of this new professional body, see Lewis Perry, *Boats against the Current: American Culture between Revolution and Modernity, 1820–1860* (Oxford: Oxford University Press, 1993), 173–85.

14. Anon., "Lectures and Lecturers," 318.

15. "Lecturers," *Times* (London), 9 November 1815, quoted in Linda Ferreira-Buckley, "Scottish Rhetoric and the Formation of Literary Studies in Nineteenth-Century England," in *The Scottish Invention of English Literature*, ed. Robert Crawford (Cambridge: Cambridge University Press, 1998), 95.

16. "The Rise and Progress of the Franklin Institute," *American Mechanics' Magazine*, February 1826.

17. George B. Emerson, *An Address, Delivered at the Opening of Boston Mechanics Institution, February 7, 1827* (Boston: Hilliard, Gray, Little, and Wilkins, 1827).

18. There has been far less scholarship on British lecturing than on the American context. Most studies have tended to come from the perspective of the history of adult education, including Thomas Kelly, *A History of Adult Education in Great Britain* (Liverpool: Liverpool University Press, 1962). More recent important work includes Diarmid Finnegan, "Geographies of Scientific Speech in Mid-Victorian Edinburgh," in *Geographies of Nineteenth-Century Science*, ed. David N. Livingstone and Charles W. J. Withers (Chicago: University of Chicago Press, 2011), 153–77; and Jon Klancher, *Transfiguring the Arts and Sciences : Knowledge and Cultural Institutions in the Romantic Age* (Cambridge: Cambridge University Press, 2013).

19. See Robert Chambers, "Mechanics Institutes," *Papers for the People*, vol. 3 (Philadelphia, 1857); and Robert John Morris, *Class, Sect, and Party: The Making of the British Middle Class. Leeds, 1820–1850* (Manchester: Manchester University Press, 1990).

20. James Boswell, *Life of Samuel Johnson*, ed. L. F. Powell, 6 vols. (Oxford: Clarendon Press, 1964), 4:92.

21. Michael Russell, *View of the System of Education at Present Pursued in the Schools and Universities of Scotland* (Edinburgh: John Moir, 1813), 95.

22. See Thomas Devine, *Glasgow: Beginnings to 1830* (Manchester: Manchester University Press, 1995), 340–41.

23. For the enduring importance of ideas of "orality" in Scottish culture of the eighteenth and nineteenth centuries, see Penny Fielding, *Writing and Orality: Nationality, Culture and Nineteenth-Century Scottish Fiction* (Oxford: Clarendon Press, 1996).

24. John Parsell, "Memoir of John Anderson," *Glasgow Mechanics Magazine*, no. 127, 1825.

25. For a discussion of Birkbeck's career as an institution-builder, see Thomas Kelly, *George Birkbeck: Pioneer of Adult Education* (Liverpool: Liverpool University Press, 1957).

26. "On Public Lectures on Works of Imagination at Literary Institutions," *Blackwood's Edinburgh Magazine*, November 1819.

27. Rev. Bennie, "Stirling School of Arts," *Glasgow Mechanics Magazine*, no. 87, 1825.

28. Birkbeck's organization was satirized as the "Steam Intellect Society" in Peacock's *Crotchet Castle* (1831).

29. Bode, *The American Lyceum*, 3.

30. From a Scottish studies perspective, Penny Fielding's work on "orality" and national identity in nineteenth-century Scottish literature provides a fascinating and useful way into this.

31. On the elocutionary revolution, see Fliegelman, *Declaring Independence*, 28–35.

32. Henry Brougham, "Scientific Education of the People," *Edinburgh Review* 41 (October 1824).

33. The most prominent of these include East Lothian émigré John Witherspoon at Princeton, Edinburgh-trained Benjamin Silliman at Yale, and William Russell, founding editor of the *American Journal of Education*. See Franklin E. Court, "The Early Impact of Scottish Literature in North America," Crawford, *Scottish Invention*, 134–63.

34. See Eastman, *A Nation of Speechifiers*; see also James Perrin Warren, *Culture of Eloquence: Oratory and Reform in Antebellum America* (University Park: Penn State University Press, 1999).

35. Daniel Boorstin, *The Americans: The National Experience* (New York: Random House, 1965), 276.

36. Henry Tuckerman, "Review of Robert C. Winthrop, *Addresses and Speeches on Various Occasions*," *North American Review* 75.157 (October 1852).

37. "Public Lectures," *New World*, 14 October 1843.

38. Bode, *The American Lyceum*, 31.

39. "Interesting Lectures in Boston," *New Bedford Mercury*, 2 November 1838.

40. "Popular Lecturing," *Christian Review*, 1 April 1850.

41. Charles Dickens Jr., "Lyceum and Lecturing in America," *All the Year Round*, n.s. 5 (1871): 317–21.

42. Ong, *Orality and Literacy*, 158.

43. Looby, *Voicing America*, 3.

44. Ray, *Lyceum and Public Culture*, 7.

45. Ronald Zboray, *A Fictive People: Antebellum Economic Development and the American Reading Public* (Oxford: Oxford University Press, 1993), 34.

46. Thomas Wentworth Higginson, "The American Lecture-System," *Littell's Living Age*, 4 April 1868, 630.

47. The limited state of scholarship on the southern lecture culture means that narratives of southern oratorical culture must be speculative. Key issues relating to the cultural context

are treated in Jonathan Daniel Wells, *The Origins of the Southern Middle Class, 1800–1861* (Chapel Hill: University of North Carolina Press, 2004).

48. "Mr. Thackeray's Lectures," *Charleston Courier*, 9 February 1856.

49. Michael O'Brien, *Conjectures of Order: Intellectual Life and the American South*, vol. 2 (Chapel Hill: University of North Carolina Press, 2004), 421.

50. "Newspapers Better Than Lectures," *Easton Gazette* (Pennsylvania), 17 December 1842.

51. Ronald J. Zboray and Mary S. Zboray, *Everyday Ideas: Socioliterary Experience among Antebellum New Englanders* (Knoxville: University of Tennessee Press, 2006), 112.

52. Meredith McGill, *American Literature and the Culture of Reprinting, 1834–1853* (Philadelphia: University of Pennsylvania Press, 2002), 107.

53. James Carey, *Communication as Culture: Essays on Media and Society*, rev. ed. (New York: Routledge, 2008), 4.

54. George William Curtis, "Editor's Table," *Harper's Monthly*, December 1860.

55. Carey, *Communication as Culture*, 41.

56. Isabelle Lehuu, *Carnival on the Page: Popular Print Media in Antebellum America* (Chapel Hill: University of North Carolina Press. 2000), 151.

57. "Dr. Dewey's Lectures," *Charleston Courier*, 13 March 1855.

58. "Frederick Douglass's Lecture," *Peoria* (Illinois) *Transcript*, quoted in *Frederick Douglass's Paper*, 11 March 1859.

59. "The Lectures," *Alexandria Gazette*, 12 January 1854; "College Students," *Cambridge Chronicle*, 10 May 1851.

60. "Mobocracy," *Flushing* (New York) *Journal*, quoted in *Frederick Douglass's Paper*, 27 July 1849. The question of how the people should participate in events such as popular lectures was also present in texts that projected the necessary conditions of debate in a rational society. Kasson traces in this period the disciplining of spectatorship, with concerted efforts to replace rude, noisy crowds with silent, disciplined public audiences. John Kasson, *Rudeness and Civility: Manners in Nineteenth-Century Urban America* (New York: Hill and Wang, 1990), 243–50.

61. Thomas Wentworth Higginson, *Part of a Man's Life* (Boston: Houghton & Mifflin, 1905), 83.

62. Frequently cited instances include Cicero's frustration with the transcriptions of Tiro, and the lines of Ausonious to his transcribers: "Come young and famous reporter, prepare the tablets … you fix my ideas on your tablets long before they are worded." For a nineteenth-century discussion of this incident see Isaac Pitman, "Phonography," *Popular Lecturer* 1 (1856): 120. For the role of oratory in newspaper editorial culture see Henry E. Birdsong, "James Gordon Bennett and the *New York Herald*," PhD diss., University of Wisconsin–Madison, 1925.

63. "The Audience: A Lecture by O.W. Holmes," *New York Times*, 3 December 1853.

64. McGill, *Culture of Reprinting*, 13.

65. "Horace Greeley and His Lecture," *Portland* (Maine) *Weekly Advertiser*, 3 April 1849.

66. See Albert J. Clark, *The Movement for International Copyright in Nineteenth-Century America* (Washington, DC: Catholic University of America, 1960). The early 1840s debate on lecture reporting is rehearsed in "Reporting Lectures," *Boston Daily Advertiser*, 7 December 1841. See also Richard A. Ek, "A Historical Study of the Speechmaking at Cooper Union, 1859–1897," PhD diss., University of Southern California, 1964, 85.

67. *New York Evening Post*, quoted in "Reporting Lectures," *Boston Daily Advertiser*, 7 December 1841.

68. *New York Commercial Advertiser*, quoted in "Reporting Lectures," *Boston Daily Advertiser*, 7 December 1841.

69. For example, lecturing in Massachusetts in 1850, the anthropologist and Egyptologist George Gliddon promised journalists attending his lecture and panorama that "a 'Reporter's Ticket' and a desk close to the stage, [would] be furnished to each of the Boston daily Papers." "Lands sacred & classical . . . ," broadside advertisement (Philadelphia: United States Job Printing Office, Ledger Building, 1850), American Antiquarian Society.

70. For Thackeray's resistance to transcription see "We are forbidden to report the lecture," "Mr. Thackeray's First Lecture," *Boston Daily Atlas*, 8 December 1855; for Emerson's practical and aesthetic resistance to reportage see Ralph L. Rusk, *The Life of Ralph Waldo Emerson* (New York: Scribner, 1949), 382–83.

71. "Mr. Thackeray's Lecture," *Boston Daily Atlas*, 8 December 1855.

72. Stuart Hall, "Encoding/Decoding," in *Media and Cultural Studies: Keyworks*, ed. Meenakshi Gigi Durham and Douglas Kellner (London: Wiley-Blackwell, 2006), 174–76.

73. James L. Machor, *Reading Fiction in Antebellum America: Informed Response and Reception Histories, 1820–1865* (Baltimore: Johns Hopkins University Press, 2011), 31.

74. Jay David Bolter and Richard Grusin, *Remediation: Understanding New Media* (Cambridge, MA: MIT Press, 2000), 26.

75. Charles Dickens to Henry Brougham, Baltimore, 22 March 1842, quoted in McGill, *Culture of Reprinting*, 114.

76. "Sketches of Lectures, Lecture and Lyceums," *Albany Evening Journal*, 4 November 1853.

77. Anon., "Lectures and Lecturers."

78. George William Curtis, "Editor's Easy Chair," *Harper's Monthly*, May 1870, 919.

79. "The Humbug Lecture System," *New York Herald*, 5 October 1859.

80. Ralph Waldo Emerson to Thomas Carlyle, 8 April 1856, *The Correspondence of Emerson and Carlyle*, ed. Joseph Slater (New York: Columbia University Press, 1964), 89.

81. "Lyceum Lectures: Their Abuses and Dangers," *Christian Reflector*, 19 March 1846.

82. "Places of Public Amusement," *Putnam's Monthly* 3.14 (February 1854): 141.

83. George William Curtis, "Editor's Easy Chair," *Harper's Monthly*, January 1862.

84. See Scott, "Popular Lecture," 791.

85. "The Lecture Season," *New York Tribune*, 4 January 1853.

86. Moses Coit Tyler, "How They Manage Their Lectures in England," *Putnam's Monthly* 13.13 (January 1869): 99.

87. Josiah Holbrook, "Brighton Lyceum." *The Family Lyceum* 1 (17 November 1832).

88. "Public Lectures," *New World*, 14 October 1843.

89. Margaret Fuller, "Entertainments of Past Winter," *Dial*, July 1842.

90. Ronald J. Zboray and Mary Saracino Zboray, "Nineteenth-Century Print Culture," in *Oxford Handbook of Transcendentalism*, ed. Joel Myerson, Sandra Harbert Petrulionis, and Laura Dassow Walls (Oxford: Oxford University Press, 2010), 103. For evidence of recorded personal response, see in particular the evidence for female audience members' written responses to lecture culture collated in Zboray and Zboray, "Women Thinking: The International Popular Lecture and Its Audience in Antebellum New England," in Wright, *The Cosmopolitan Lyceum*, 42–66.

91. Holland, "The Popular Lecture," 362.

92. "Lectures and Lecturers," *New York Times*, 1 September 1854.

93. Joan Shelley Rubin's *The Making of Middlebrow Culture* (Chapel Hill: University of North Carolina Press, 1992) provides a useful counterpoint to the classic discussion in Lawrence Levine, *High Brow / Low Brow: The Emergence of Cultural Hierarchy in America* (Cambridge, MA: Harvard University Press, 1988), by formulating a longer perspective on the development of middlebrow practices.

94. Fuller, "Entertainments of Past Winter."

95. Vern Wagner, "The Lecture Lyceum and the Problem of Controversy," *Journal of the History of Ideas* 15.1 (January 1954): 121.

96. Quoted in Mead, *Yankee Eloquence*, 133.

97. John Weiss, *Life and Correspondence of Theodore Parker* (New York: Appleton, 1864), 432.

98. "American Literature and Reprints: Our Quadrennial Election and Its Influence on Books," *Putnam's Monthly Magazine of American Literature, Science and Art* 8.48 (December 1856): 655.

99. "Oliver Wendell Holmes—the Audience," *New York Times*, 3 December 1853.

100. Greiman, *Democracy's Spectacle*, xi.

101. Buell, *Emerson*, 23.

102. Nancy Fraser, *Rethinking the Public Sphere: A Contribution to the Critique of Actually Existing Democracy* (Milwaukee: University of Wisconsin–Milwaukee, Center for Twentieth Century Studies, 1990), 6.

103. Charles Sellers, *The Market Revolution: Jacksonian America, 1815–1846* (Oxford: Oxford University Press, 1991), 365.

104. "It is all political, and political because politics have been now visibly swept into the realm of morals, where, properly considered, they always are." George William Curtis, "Editor's Easy Chair," *Harper's Monthly*, January 1862, 24. For lists of 1860s topics, see Wagner, "Problem of Controversy."

105. "Chapter of Wants: Extracted from an Unpublished 'Book of Human Nature,'" *Washington Reporter*, 5 March 1856.

106. George William Curtis, "Editor's Easy Chair," *Harper's Monthly*, January 1862.

107. Henry D. Thoreau, *A Week on the Concord and Merrimack Rivers*, ed. Carl F. Hovde, William L. Howarth, and Elizabeth Hall Witherell (Princeton, NJ: Princeton University Press, 2004), 100.

108. The most prominent such controversy surrounded Phillips on slavery. Phillips was banned in 1842 and 1845—see P. W. Stoddard, "The Place of the Lyceum in American Life," MA thesis, Columbia University, 1932.

109. Henry D. Thoreau, journal entry, 16 November 1858, in *The Heart of Thoreau's Journals*, ed. Odell Shepard (New York: Dover, 1961).

110. Thoreau, journal entry, 16 November 1858.

111. See Scott, "Popular Lecture," 793.

112. Oliver Wendell Holmes, *The Professor at the Breakfast Table* (1850), 146. In a particularly well-documented survey of this argument, Vern Wagner states that "the Lyceum was free, yes, not *to* but *from* the current reform ideas of the age . . . free from the taint of violent proposals," Wagner, "Problem of Controversy," 121.

113. For a good survey of the last twenty years of critiques of Habermas's public sphere, see Greiman, *Democracy's Spectacle*, xi.

114. For Habermas on strategic action, see Jürgen Habermas, "Discourse Ethics: Notes on a Program of Philosophical Justification," in *Moral Consciousness and Communicative Action*, trans. Christian Lenhart and Shierry Weber Nicholsen (Cambridge, MA: MIT Press, 1990), 43–50.

115. *The Collected Works of Ralph Waldo Emerson*, ed. Robert E. Spiller et al., 10 vols. (Cambridge, MA: Belknap Press of Harvard University Press, 1971–2013), 2:192.

116. For a discussion of this aspect of the "travel lecture" genre and a survey of its most important topics, see Tom F. Wright, "The Results of Locomotion: Bayard Taylor and the Travel Lecture in Nineteenth-Century America," *Studies in Travel Writing* 14.2 (2010): 111–34.

117. Wendell Phillips, "The Lost Arts," Boston, Boston Public Library, MS Phillips 1862; later version reprinted in Wendell Phillips, *Speeches, Letters and Lectures* (Cambridge, MA: John Wilson, 1891), 365–83.

118. See Garvey, *Creating the Culture*, 74–80; Amy E. Hughes, *Spectacles of Reform: Theater and Activism in Nineteenth-Century America* (Ann Arbor: University of Michigan Press, 2012); Greiman, *Democracy's Spectacle*.

119. Kenneth Burke, "Terministic Screens," in *Language as Symbolic Action*, 44–60.

120. Holland, "The Popular Lecture," 367.

121. Burke, "Terministic Screens."

122. Oliver Wendell Holmes, "English Poets of the Nineteenth Century," course in 1853; Edwin Percy Whipple, *Lectures on Subjects Connected with Literature and Life* (Boston: Ticknor and Fields, 1850); James Russell Lowell, *Lectures on English Poets* (Cleveland: Rowfant Club, 1897).

123. Scott, "Popular Lecture," 803. See also Wright, "The Results of Locomotion."

124. See David Chapin, *Exploring Other Worlds: Margaret Fox, Elisha Kent Kane, and the Antebellum Culture of Curiosity* (Amherst, MA: University of Massachusetts Press, 2004).

125. For Henry Clapp's lectures see David S. Reynolds, *Walt Whitman's America: A Cultural Biography* (New York: Knopf, 1995), 670–72.

126. George William Curtis, "Editor's Easy Chair," *Harper's Monthly*, May 1870.

127. These political meanings were amplified by the multiple threats the old colonial power seemed to pose. As Sam Haynes puts it, for observers in the early republic, "The British lion took on a wide range of threatening guises: an industrial hegemon bent on destroying domestic manufactures . . . a banking colossus . . . an evangelical slavery movement that had set its sights on the abolition of American slave labour . . . a government in London that seemed to be co-ordinating these various activities with masterful precision." Sam Haynes, *Unfinished Revolution: The Early American Republic in a British World* (Charlottesville: University of Virginia Press, 2010), 2.

128. Paul Giles, *Virtual Americas: Transnational Fictions and the Transatlantic Imaginary* (Durham, NC: Duke University Press, 2002), 38.

129. Tennenhouse, *Importance of Feeling English*, 10.

130. Nathaniel Hawthorne, *Our Old Home: A Series of English Sketches* (Boston: Ticknor & Fields, 1863).

131. Horace Mann, "Great Britain," undated manuscript, Boston, Massachusetts Historical Society; Ralph Waldo Emerson, "The Anglo-Saxon Race" (1852), in *The Later Lectures of Ralph Waldo Emerson, 1843–1871*, ed. Ronald A. Bosco and Joel Myerson, 2 vols. (Athens: University of Georgia Press, 2001), 1:9; "Mr. Thackeray and His Lectures," *Albion*, 1 December 1855.

132. For such celebrations of communal ancestry, see Tamarkin, *Anglophilia*, 70.

133. Andrew Chamberlin Rieser, "Lyceums, Chautauquas, and Institutes for Useful Knowledge," in *Encyclopedia of American Cultural and Intellectual History*, vol. 3, ed. Mary Kupiec Cayton and Peter W. Williams (New York: Charles Scribner's Sons, 2001), 354.

134. Higginson, "The American Lecture-System," 630.

135. Fraser, *Rethinking the Public Sphere*, 6.

136. See Edward G. Parker, *The Golden Age of American Oratory* (Boston: Whittemore, Niles and Hall, 1857); Lawrence Buell, *New England Literary Culture: From Revolution through Renaissance* (Cambridge: Cambridge University Press, 1986), 139; Anon., "Ancient and Modern Eloquence," *Littell's Living Age*, 3 May 1851. See also Eastman, *A Nation of Speechifiers*.

137. "German Lyceums," *American Annals of Education* 6 (1836): 476. The foundational coverage of African-American lyceums can be found in Dorothy B. Porter, "The Organized Educational Activities of Negro Literary Societies, 1828–1846," *Journal of Negro Education* 5.4 (October 1936): 555–76. On lyceums founded and run by African-Americans, see Leonard P. Curry, *The Free Black in Urban America, 1800–1850* (Chicago: University of Chicago Press, 1981), esp. 147–73, 204–8; Porter, "Organized Educational Activities"; Benjamin Quarles, *Black Abolitionists* (New York: Oxford University Press, 1969), 102–6; Exploration of lecturing among black literary societies is found in Elizabeth McHenry, *Forgotten Readers: Recovering the Lost History of African American Literary Societies* (Durham, NC: Duke University Press, 2002). For work on black orator, see Carla Peterson, *"Doers of the Word": African-American Women Speakers and Writers in the North (1830–1880)* (New York: Oxford University Press, 1995); and Shirley Wilson Logan, *We Are Coming: The Persuasive Discourse of Nineteenth-Century Black Women* (Carbondale: Southern Illinois University Press, 1999). For emerging work on the African-American lyceum, see Britt Rusert, "The Science of Freedom: Counter-archives of Racial Science on the Antebellum Stage," *African American Review* 45.3 (Fall 2012): 291–308; Bjorn Stillion Southard, "The Liberia Lyceum and the Transatlantic Contestation of Black Citizenship, 1838–1850," presentation at "Popular Knowledge, Public Stage" conference, Alexandria, VA, 24–26 September 2015.

138. Franklin Pierce Inaugural Presidential Address, 4 March 1853, http://www.inaugural.senate.gov/swearing-in/event/franklin-pierce-1853 (accessed 1 March 2016).

139. "Lecture by Thomas F. Meagher—Australia," *New York Times*, 26 November 1852.

140. "Ireland in 48," quoted in Michael Cavanagh, *Memoirs of General Thomas Francis Meagher* (Worcester, MA: Messenger Press, 1892), 424.

141. Henry Watkins Allen, the future governor of Louisiana, quoted in Gary R. Forney, *Thomas Francis Meagher: Irish Rebel, American Yankee, Montana Pioneer* (Ennis: G.R. Forney, 2003), 69; Robert G. Athearn, *Thomas Francis Meagher: An Irish Revolutionary in America* (Boulder: University of Colorado Press, 1947).

142. New Orleans delivery of "Ireland in 48," quoted in Cavanagh, *Memoirs of General Meagher*, 339.

143. Cavanagh, *Memoirs of General Meagher*, 337.

144. "Lectures on Irish Orators," San Francisco Musical Hall, 24 January 1854, quoted in Forney, *Thomas Francis Meagher*, 71.

145. Bryan McGovern, *John Mitchel: Irish Nationalist, Southern Secessionist* (Knoxville: University of Tennessee Press, 2009), 150. See also James Quinn, *John Mitchel* (Dublin: Historical Association of Ireland by University College Dublin Press, 2008), 64.

146. John Mitchel, *Memoir of Thomas Devin Reilly: A Lecture Delivered by John Mitchel, in the Tabernacle, New-York, on Dec. 29th, 1856* (New York: P.M. Haverty, 1857), 3.

147. David Brundage, *Irish Nationalists in America: The Politics of Exile, 1798–1998* (Oxford: Oxford University Press, 2016), 81.

148. These pieces were collected in Henry Giles, *Lectures and Essays on Irish and Other Subjects* (New York: D. & J. Sadier, 1869). For accounts of his lecturing see Mead, *Yankee Eloquence*, 62–68.

149. Henry Giles, "The Spirit of Irish History," in *Lectures and Essays*, 9.

150. Henry Giles, "Irish Born Citizens," in *Lectures and Essays*, 156.

151. George Catlin, *George Catlin's Notes of Eight Years and Residence in Europe* (London: George Catlin, 1848).

152. Kate Flint, *The Transatlantic Indian* (Princeton, NJ: Princeton University Press, 2009), 21.

153. Quoted in Philip Gura, *The Life of William Apess, Pequot* (Chapel Hill: University of North Carolina Press, 2015), 339. See also Todd Vogel, *Rewriting White: Race, Class, and Cultural Capital in Nineteenth-Century America* (New Brunswick, NJ: Rutgers University Press, 2004), 40.

154. William Apess, "Eulogy on King Philip," in *On Our Own Ground: The Complete Writings of William Apess, a Pequot* (Amherst: University of Massachusetts Press, 1992), 280.

155. Gura, *Life of William Apess*, xvi.

156. Apess, "Eulogy on King Philip," 310.

157. Matthew Frye Jacobson, *Whiteness of a Different Color* (Cambridge, MA: Harvard University Press, 1999), 4. The scholarship on whiteness in American studies includes David Roediger, *The Wages of Whiteness: Race and the Making of the American Working Class* (New York: Verso, 1991); Theodore Allen, *The Invention of the White Race*, vol. 1: *Racial Oppression and Social Control* (London: Verso Books, 1994); Noel Ignatiev, *How the Irish Became White* (New York: Routledge, 1995); Shannon Jackson, "White Noises: On Performing White, on Writing Performance," *TDR* 42.1 (1998): 49–65; Alexander Saxton, *The Rise and Fall of the White Republic: Class Politics and Mass Culture in Nineteenth-Century America* (London: Verso, 2003); Mary F. Brewer, *Staging Whiteness* (Middletown, CT: Wesleyan University Press, 2005).

158. "Lecture—the Moral and Social Aspect of Africa," *Chicago Tribune*, 1 May 1863.

159. See Theda Perdue, ed., *Cherokee Editor: The Writings of Elias Boudinot* (Athens: University of Georgia Press, 1996), 68–80; for Apess's speaking career see Mark J. Miller, "'Mouth for God': Temperate Labor, Race and Methodist Reform in William Apess's 'A Son of the Forest,'" *Journal of the Early Republic* 30.2 (Summer 2010): 225–51.

160. See discussion of Aggasiz's 1847 naturalism lectures in John Evelev, *Tolerable Entertainment: Herman Melville and Professionalism in Antebellum New York* (Amherst: University of Massachusetts Press, 2006), 135–38.

161. See Susan Branson, "'Barnum Is Undone in His Own Province': Science, Race, and Entertainment in the Lectures of George Robins Gliddon," in Wright, *The Cosmopolitan Lyceum*, 151–67.

162. Charles Sumner, *The Question of Caste: Lecture* (Boston: Wright & Potter, 1869).

163. See Wright, "The Results of Locomotion." For a defence of Taylor's lyceum career, see Peter Gibian, "The Lyceum as Contact Zone: Bayard Taylor's Lectures on Foreign Travel," in Wright, *The Cosmopolitan Lyceum*, 168–202.

164. "Indian Historical Lectures," Nicholson Henry Parker lecture broadside, 1853, Edward Ayer Collection, Newberry Library, Chicago.

165. Journal entry, 12 April 1849, in Samuel Longfellow, *Life of Henry Wadsworth Longfellow: With Extracts from His Journals and Correspondence* (Chicago: Sequoyah Books, 2003), 178.

166. *Richmond Southerner* and *New York Herald*, quoted in "Kah-ge-ga-gah-bowh . . . at Lyceum Hall, Old Cambridge," broadside, 1849, Boston, American Antiquarian Society.

167. Christopher Mulvey, *Transatlantic Manners: Social Patterns in Nineteenth-Century Anglo-American Travel Literature* (Cambridge: Cambridge University Press, 1990), 110.

168. See Mulvey, *Transatlantic Manners*, 110–11 and 160–61.

169. "Mr. Thackeray in America," *Fraser's Magazine*, December 1852.

170. Anon., "Lectures and Lecturers," *Putnam's Monthly*, March 1857.

171. "Lecture by Mr. Lane," *New York Tribune*, 19 December 1845.

172. "The State of England," *New York Tribune*, 17 March 1856.

173. See Stephen Fender, *Sea Changes: British Emigration and American Literature* (Cambridge: Cambridge University Press, 1992).

174. John O'Sullivan, introduction, *United States Magazine and Democratic Review* 1.1 (1837).

175. Robert J. Walker, *Letter of Mr. Walker, of Mississippi, Relative to the Annexation of Texas* (Washington, DC: Washington Globe, 1844), 11.

176. This was a dialectic that was prominently explored in the fiction published in such journals as the *Democratic Review*. See Sohui Lee, "Anti-Democratic Habit of Feeling: Nationalism and the Rhetoric of Toryism in O'Sullivan's *Democratic Review*," *Romantic Circles* (November 2006), https://www.rc.umd.edu/praxis/sullenfires/lee/lee_essay. html (accessed November 2016).

Chapter 2

1. *New York Express*, quoted in "Flavour of the New York Press," *National Anti-Slavery Standard*, 20 May 1847.

2. "American Anti-Slavery Society," *New York Inquirer*, quoted in "The Spirit of the New York Press," *National Anti-Slavery Standard*, 27 May 1847.

3. "Anniversaries—Anti-Slavery Society," *Christian Inquirer*, 15 May 1847.

4. "New York Correspondent," *Baltimore Sun*, 20 May 1847.

5. "Anniversaries—Anti-Slavery Society," *Christian Inquirer*, 15 May 1847.

6. "The Anti-Slavery Societies," *New York Herald*, 13 May 1847.

7. "Country, Conscience and the Anti-Slavery Cause," 11 May 1847, in *The Frederick Douglass Papers*, series 1: *Speeches, Debates, and Interviews*, ed. John W. Blassingame and John R. McKivigan (New Haven: Yale University Press, 1979), 2:59. Further references to this edition are cited as *FD* and include volume and page numbers.

8. Waldo E. Martin, *The Mind of Frederick Douglass* (Chapel Hill: University of North Carolina Press, 1984), 40.

9. Martin, *Mind of Frederick Douglass*, 199.

10. Fionnghuala Sweeney and Cody Marrs have made related arguments regarding Douglass's cosmopolitan commitments. See Fionnghuala Sweeney, *Frederick Douglass and*

the Atlantic World (Liverpool: Liverpool University Press, 2007); Cody Marrs, "Frederick Douglass in 1848," *American Literature* 85.3 (September 2013): 464.

11. "The Lecturers," *Frederick Douglass's Paper*, 13 January 1854.

12. Robert Fanuzzi, *Abolition's Public Sphere* (Minneapolis: University of Minnesota Press, 2003).

13. This is true of Fanuzzi and also the coverage of abolition in Garvey, *Creating the Culture*.

14. See John G. Whittier, *Life and Letters of John Greenleaf Whittier*, ed. Samuel T. Pickard (Boston: Houghton, Mifflin, 1894), 297–300.

15. R. J. M. Blackett, *Building an Antislavery Wall: Black Americans in the Atlantic Abolitionist Movement, 1830–1860* (Baton Rouge: Louisiana State University Press, 1983), 17.

16. See Audrey Fisch, *American Slaves in Victorian England: Abolitionist Politics in Popular Literature and Culture* (Cambridge: Cambridge University Press, 2000), 19–24.

17. See Denis Brennan, *The Making of an Abolitionist: William Lloyd Garrison's Path to Publishing the Liberator* (Jefferson, NC: McFarland, 2014), 163.

18. Henry Mayer, *All on Fire: William Lloyd Garrison and the Abolition of Slavery* (New York: Norton, 2008), 100.

19. Mayer, *All on Fire*, 101.

20. Frank Kirkland, "Enslavement, Moral Suasion and Struggles," in *Frederick Douglass: A Critical Reader*, ed. William Lawson and Frank Kirkland (Oxford: Blackwell, 1999), 121.

21. See Amos Phelps, *Lectures on Slavery and Its Remedy* (Boston: New-England Anti-Slavery Society, 1834).

22. Blackett, *Building an Antislavery Wall*, 16.

23. "English Necrophilism," *New York Express*, quoted in the *Anti-Slavery Standard*, 1 July 1847.

24. Blackett, *Building an Antislavery Wall*, 15.

25. "Letter from Edinburgh," *Liberator*, 28 August 1840.

26. William Wells Brown, *The American Fugitive in Europe: Sketches of Places and People Abroad* (Boston: Jewett, 1855), 30.

27. Mayer, *All on Fire*, 350–51.

28. "L. Sabine Poem," *Liberator*, 27 November 1846.

29. For the prehistory of his idea of "demonic speech" see Gustafson, *Eloquence Is Power*, xv.

30. *New York Express*, quoted in *National Anti-Slavery Standard*, 12 February 1846.

31. *Oswego* (New York) *Daily Advertiser*, quoted in *National Anti-Slavery Standard*, 29 October 1846.

32. Frederick Douglass to Horace Greeley, 15 April 1846, in *The Frederick Douglass Papers*, series 3, vol. 1: *1842–1852*, ed. John R. McKivigan (New Haven: Yale University Press, 2009), 61.

33. See Cynthia S. Hamilton, "Frederick Douglass and the Gender Politics of Reform," in *Liberating Sojourn: Frederick Douglass and Transatlantic Reform*, ed. Alan Rice and Martin Crawford (Athens: University of Georgia Press, 1999), 80.

34. Fisch, *American Slaves*, 70.

35. See Bacon and McClish, "Reinventing the Master's Tools"; and McHenry, *Forgotten Readers*.

36. Orators such as Sojourner Truth, Frances Ellen Watkins Harper, Sarah P. Remond, and James McCune Smith all emerged as prominent representatives of burgeoning black self-expression. The best introduction to the black oratorical tradition and survey of its prominent texts is Philip S. Foner and Robert J. Branham, *Lift Every Voice: African American Oratory, 1787–1900* (Tuscaloosa: University of Alabama Press, 1998). See also Richard W. Leeman, *African-American Orators: A Bio-Critical Sourcebook* (Westport, CT: Greenwood Press, 1996).

37. See Blassingame's discussion of coverage of African-American speeches in "Editorial Method," *FD* 1:lxxvii.

38. "Orators and Oratory," *Liberator*, 29 October 1852, in Foner and Branham, *Lift Every Voice*, 231.

39. For example, in Martin, *Mind of Frederick Douglass*, 106.

40. One discussion of Douglass that does justice to this shift is Angela Ray, "Frederick Douglass on the Lyceum Circuit: Social Assimilation, Social Transformation?," *Rhetoric and Public Affairs* 5.4 (Winter 2002): 630.

41. "Life and Times of Frederick Douglass," in *The Frederick Douglass Papers*, series 2: *Autobiographies*, ed. John W. Blassingame, John R. McKivigan, Peter P. Hinks, Joseph R. McElrath, and Jesse S. Crisler (New Haven: Yale University Press, 1999), 413.

42. "God's Law Outlawed," Manchester, NH, 24 January 1854, *FD* 2:454–60.

43. "Editorial Correspondence," *Frederick Douglass's Paper*, 3 February 1854.

44. See Ray, "Frederick Douglass on the Lyceum Circuit," 630.

45. "What Have the Abolitionists Done?," *Frederick Douglass's Paper*, 8 December 1854.

46. "Proceedings of the National Council of the Colored People," New York City, 8–10 May 1855, *FD* 3:59.

47. "The Lecturers," *Frederick Douglass's Paper*, 13 January 1854.

48. "What to the Slave Is the Fourth of July," Rochester, 5 July 1852, *FD* 2:368.

49. "American Slavery Is America's Disgrace," *Sheffield Times*, 25 March 1847, *FD* 2:9.

50. See Frederick Douglass, *American Slavery: Report of a Public Meeting Held at Finsbury Chapel, Moorfields, to Receive Frederick Douglass, the American Slave, on Friday, May 22, 1846* (London: unknown publisher, 1846) and "American Slavery, American Religion, and the Free Church of Scotland," London Finsbury Chapel, 22 May 1846, *FD* 1:269.

51. "I Am Here Advocating Rights for Ireland," 14 December, Washington, DC, *FD* 5:276.

52. Claybaugh, *The Novel of Purpose*, 119.

53. See Fanuzzi, *Abolition's Public Sphere*, 120.

54. "Farewell Speech to the British People," 30 March 1847, London Tavern, *FD* 2:23.

55. The oration is introduced by the words, "Mr Douglass rose amid loud cheers . . ." in Frederick Douglass, *My Bondage and My Freedom* (New York: Miller, Orton and Mulligan, 1855), 417; see "American Slavery," *Newburyport Herald*, 19 June 1846.

56. "My Slave Experience and My Irish Mission," 5 December 1845, Belfast, *FD* 1:93; "Slavery, the Free Church, and British Agitation against Bondage," 8 August 1846, Newcastle, *FD* 1:339; see also "England Should Lead the Cause of Emancipation," 23 December 1846, Leeds, *FD* 1:485.

57. "American Slavery, American Religion, and the Free Church of Scotland," London Finsbury Chapel, 22 May 1846, *FD* 1:269.

58. Frederick Douglass, *Life and Times* (1881) in *The Frederick Douglass Papers*, ed. John W. Blassingame et al., series 2: *Autobiographical Writings*, vol. 3 (New Haven: Yale University Press, 2012), 232.

59. Wendell Phillips and Francis Jackson, *Twentieth Annual Report, Presented to the Massachusetts Anti-Slavery Society, by Its Board of Managers, January 28, 1852: With an Appendix* (Boston: publisher not identified, 1852), 46.

60. "My Slave Experience and My Irish Mission," 5 December 1845, Belfast, *FD* 1:93.

61. Faye Halpern, *Sentimental Readers: The Rise, Fall, and Revival of a Disparaged Rhetoric* (Iowa City: University of Iowa Press, 2008), 60–62. See also Sarah Meer, *Uncle Tom Mania: Slavery, Minstrelsy and Transatlantic Culture in the 1850s* (Athens: University of Georgia Press, 2005), 8–12.

62. Kwame Anthony Appiah, *The Honor Code: How Moral Revolutions Happen* (New York: Norton, 2010).

63. Henry Colman, quoted in Allison Lockwood, *Passionate Pilgrims: The American Traveler in Great Britain, 1800–1914* (New York: Cornwall, 1981).

64. Douglas Jerrold and Blanchard Jerrold, *Specimens of Douglas Jerrold's Wit: Together with Selections, Chiefly from His Contributions to Journals, Intended to Illustrate His Opinions* (Boston: Ticknor and Fields, 1858), 135.

65. Thomas Carlyle, "Discourse on the Nigger Question," *Fraser's Magazine* 40 (December 1849): 670–79; Ralph Waldo Emerson, *The Letters of Ralph Waldo Emerson*, 10 vols. (New York: Columbia University Press, 1939), 4:87.

66. Samuel S. Cox, *Eight Years in Congress, from 1857–1865: Memoir and Speeches* (New York: D. Appleton, 1865), 126.

67. Hiram Fuller, editor of *New York Mirror*, quoted in Lockwood, *Passionate Pilgrims*, 232.

68. Reverend Daniel C. Eddy quoted in Lockwood, *Passionate Pilgrims*, 213.

69. "A Day, a Deed, an Event, Glorious in the Annals of Philanthropy," Rochester, NY, 1 August 1848, *FD* 2:142.

70. "Significance of Emancipation in the West Indies," Canandaigua, NY, 3 August 1857, *FD* 3:199.

71. "Slavery and the Irrepressible Conflict," 1 August 1860, Geneva, NY, *FD* 3:371; Douglass to Garrison, 29 September 1845, in *The Frederick Douglass Papers*, ed. John McKivigan et al., series 3: *Correspondence*, vol. 1 (New Haven: Yale University Press, 2009), 56; "A Sentimental Visit to England," Washington, DC, 22 September 1887, *FD* 5:273.

72. See in particular William Wells Brown's dramatization of lecture attendance in Coventry in *An American Fugitive in Europe*, in which he attends a lecture by civic gospel reformer George Dawson at the Coventry Mechanic's Institution. Brown, *American Fugitive in Europe*, 226.

73. Percy Howard, "The Passing of Exeter Hall," *Civil Service Observer* 13.5 (May 1907). See also Finnegan, "Geographies of Scientific Speech," 160.

74. Tunde Adeleke, "Afro-Americans and Moral Suasion: The Debate in the 1830's," *Journal of Negro History* (Spring 1998): 140.

75. John McKivigan, *Abolitionism and American Reform* (New York: Garland, 1999), 297.

76. "Monarchies and Freedom, Republics and Slavery," Bristol, 1 April 1847, *FD* 2:56.

77. "Reception of Douglass at the Belknap-Street Church, Boston," *Liberator*, 21 May 1847.

78. "Reception of Frederick Douglass by the Colored People," *New York Tribune*, quoted in *Liberator*, 21 May 1847.

79. "Colonizationist Measures," New York City, 24 April 1849, *FD* 2:164.

80. "The Rights of Colored Citizens," *Liberator*, 25 February 1842.

81. "William Wells Brown Lecture: I Have No Constitution," Store St Music Hall, London, 27 September 1849, quoted in *Liberator*, 2 November 1849. See in particular Brown's account of the Great Exhibition and the tolerance of London crowds in *An American Fugitive in Europe* (London: Gilpin, 1852), 200–220.

82. "Street Life in Europe," *Cambridge Chronicle*, 23 December 1854. The Houghton Library's folder accompanying the manuscript of his lecture "Street Life" contains a multitude of clippings on these themes, relating to Great Britain, Scotland, and France, suggesting a desire to keep matters topical. Wendell Phillips Papers, 1555–1882 (MS Am 1953), Houghton Library, Harvard University.

83. "Wendell Phillips on European Street Life," *Brooklyn Eagle*, 22 February 1860.

84. "Country, Conscience and the Anti-Slavery Cause," 11 May 1847, New York City, *FD* 2:59.

85. "Speech of Frederick Douglass," *New York Tribune*, 13 May 1847.

86. "Letter from New York Correspondent," *National Era*, 20 May 1847.

87. "New York Correspondent," *Baltimore Sun*, 20 May 1847.

88. "Keene," *New Hampshire Sentinel*, 20 May 1847.

89. Mayer, *All on Fire*, 372.

90. "Country, Conscience and the Anti-Slavery Cause," 11 May 1847, New York City, *FD* 2:59.

91. *New York Sun*, quoted in "Flavour of the New York Press," *National Anti-Slavery Standard*, 20 May 1847.

92. "New York Correspondent," *Baltimore Sun*, 20 May 1847.

93. "Correspondence of the Courier," *Charleston Courier*, 19 May 1847.

94. For this terminology, see Ifeoma Nwankwo, *Black Cosmopolitanism: Racial Consciousness and Transnational Identity in the Nineteenth-Century Americas* (Philadelphia: University of Pennsylvania Press, 2005).

95. "Revolution of 1848," Rochester, 27 April 1848, *FD* 2:115; at an 1849 Burns Night meeting in Rochester he pronounced in wry, self-aware fashion that "although I am not a Scotchman, not the son of a Scotchman (perhaps you will say, 'it needs no ghost to tell us that') … a Scotch heart throbs beneath these ribs." "Robert Burns and Scotland," Burns Night Festivities, Rochester, NY, 1849, *FD* 2:147; see Greg Crane, *Race, Citizenship, and Law in American Literature* (Cambridge: Cambridge University Press, 2002), 87–99.

96. "Abolitionist Measures of American Churches," 30 May 1849, *FD* 2:198.

97. "Love of God, Love of Man, Love of Country," Syracuse, 28 October 1847, *FD* 2:103.

98. William McFeely, *Frederick Douglass* (New York: Norton, 1995), 108; Mayer, *All on Fire*, 372.

99. Lloyd Pratt, "'I Am a Stranger with Thee': Frederick Douglass and Recognition after 1845," *American Literature* 85.2 (2013): 247–72.

100. Ross Posnock, *Color and Culture: Black Writers and the Making of the Modern Intellectual* (Cambridge, MA: Harvard University Press, 1998), 9.

101. Henry L. Gates, *The Signifying Monkey: A Theory of Afro-American Literary Criticism* (New York: Oxford University Press, 1988), 83.

102. Richard Powell, *Cutting a Figure: Fashioning Black Portraiture* (Chicago: University of Chicago Press, 2008), 66.

103. James Russell Lowell quoted in Robert T. Oliver, *The History of Public Speaking in America* (Boston: Allyn and Bacon, 1965), 248.

104. Both quoted in "American Anti-Slavery Society," *New York Evangelist*, 13 May 1847.

105. "Letter from New York Correspondent," *National Era*, 20 May 1847.

106. Tamarkin, *Anglophilia*, 200.

107. "The Anniversary Week," *New York Tribune*, 13 May 1847; Thomas Wentworth Higginson, *Contemporaries* (Boston: Houghton and Mifflin, 1899), 266.

108. Walker, *Letter of Mr. Walker*, 11.

109. *New York Sun*, quoted in *Baltimore Sun*, "Anti-slavery in New York," 15 May 1847.

110. Daphne Brooks, *Bodies in Dissent: Spectacular Performances of Race and Freedom, 1850–1910* (Durham, NC: Duke University Press, 2006), 3.

111. Tamarkin, *Anglophilia*, 194.

112. Fisch, *American Slaves*, 88.

113. Quoted in McFeely, *Frederick Douglass*, 133.

114. Thomas Wentworth Higginson, *American Orators and Oratory* (Cleveland: Imperial Press, 1901), 87; "Douglass," *Washington National Era*, 28 July 1853.

115. Stauffer, *Black Hearts of Men*, 158–60.

116. Frederick Douglass to Thomas Auld, 8 September 1848, in *Frederick Douglass Papers:* series 3: *Correspondence*, 1:313.

117. *Life and Times of Frederick Douglass* (1881) in *Frederick Douglass Papers*, series 2: *Autobiographical Writings*, 3:312.

118. See Monica L Miller, *Slaves to Fashion: Black Dandyism and the Styling of Black Diasporic Identity* (Durham, NC: Duke University Press, 2009), iv–x.

119. Jane Marsh Parker, *In Memoriam: Frederick Douglass* (Philadelphia, 1897).

120. "Douglass," *Philadelphia Evening Bulletin*, 18 October 1855.

121. John B. Chandler, *Concord* (NH) *Herald of Freedom*, 13 June 1845.

122. Anon., *Abolition Fanaticism in New York: Speech of a Runaway Slave from Baltimore at an Abolition Meeting in New York, Held May 11, 1847* (Baltimore, 1847).

123. Jesse Hutchinson Jr., "Fugitive's Song" lithograph (Henry Prentiss: Boston, 1845).

124. "New York Correspondent," *Baltimore Sun*, 20 May 1847.

125. "Anti-Slavery Society," *New-York Sun*, quoted in "The Spirit of the New York Press," *National Anti-Slavery Standard*, 27 May 1847.

126. James McCune Smith, in Frederick Douglass, *Frederick Douglass: Autobiographies* (New York: Library of America, 1994), 107.

127. As Ifeoma Nwankwo notes, it is particularly absent from his first *Narrative*. Nwankwo, *Black Cosmopolitanism*.

128. "Slavery, the Slumbering Volcano," Shiloh, NY, 23 April 1848, *FD* 1:163; "Emancipation Is an Individual, National and International Responsibility," *London Patriot*, London, 18 May 1846, *FD* 1:260.

129. *Hampshire Independent*, 20 January 1855.

130. "Slavery and the Irrepressible Conflict," 1 August 1860, Geneva, New York, *FD* 3:368.

131. "Colonizationist Measures," Anti-Colonization meeting, 24 April 1849, New York City, *FD* 2:163.

132. For the culture surrounding 1 August celebrations, see J. R. Kerr-Ritchie, *Rites of August First: Emancipation Day in the Black Atlantic World* (Baton Rouge: Louisiana State University Press, 2007); W. Caleb McDaniel, "The Fourth and the First: Abolitionist Holidays, Respectability, and Radical Interracial Reform," *American Quarterly* 57 (March 2005), 129–51.

133. "Darkydom Powwow at Poughkeepsie," *New York Herald*, 3 August 1858.

134. "Pioneers in a Holy Cause," Canandaigua, NY, 2 August 1847, *FD* 2:70.

135. "Pioneers in a Holy Cause," *FD* 2:70.

136. "Slavery and the Irrepressible Conflict," 1 August 1860, Geneva, NY, *FD* 3:368.

137. "A Day, a Deed, an Event, Glorious in the Annals of Philanthropy," Rochester, NY, 1 August 1848, *FD* 2:133.

138. "Significance of Emancipation in the West Indies," Canandaigua, NY, 3 August 1857, *FD* 3:199.

139. Most often associated with Adam Smith and William Robertson. A useful summative discussion of stadial ideas is found in John G. A Pocock, *Barbarism and Religion*, vol. 2: *Narratives of Civil Government* (Cambridge: Cambridge University Press, 2005), 342–65.

140. "Significance of Emancipation in the West Indies," Canandaigua, NY, 3 August 1857, *FD* 3:199.

141. "Haiti and the Haitian People," Chicago, 2 January 1893, *FD* 5:534.

142. "A Friendly Word to Maryland," 17 November 1864, Baltimore, *FD* 4:47.

143. Harriet Beecher Stowe, *Uncle Tom's Cabin, or Life among the Lowly* (Boston: Jewett, 1852), v.

144. "Advice to Black Youth," 3 February 1855, New York City, *FD* 3:4.

145. "Significance of Emancipation in the West Indies," Canandaigua, NY, 3 August 1857, *FD* 3:203.

146. "The Claims of the Negro Ethnographically Considered," 12 July 1854, Western Reserve College, Ohio, *FD* 2:501.

147. "Black Man's Future in the Southern States," 5 February 1862, Boston, *FD* 3:502.

148. Hanlon, *America's England*, 41–56.

149. Hanlon, *America's England*, 43.

150. "What the Black Man Wants," Boston, 26 January 1865, *FD* 4:65.

151. A useful record of this period of Douglass's speaking career is George A. Hinshaw, "A Rhetorical Analysis of the Speeches of Frederick Douglass during and after the Civil War," thesis, University of Nebraska, 1975.

152. "Britain and the Abolition of Slavery," Leeds, 9 December 1859, *FD* 3:321.

153. "British Racial Attitudes and Slavery," Newcastle-Upon-Tyne, 23 February 1860, *FD* 3:340.

154. "The American Constitution and the Slave," Glasgow, 26 March 1860, *FD* 3:346.

155. "The Present Condition of Slavery," 6 January 1860, Bradford, *FD* 3:313; see also "British Racial Attitudes and Slavery," 23 February 1860, Newcastle, *FD* 3:339.

156. See, for example, references to Russia in "Slavery and the Irrepressible Conflict," 1 August 1860, Geneva, NY, *FD* 3:370.

157. "Great Britain's Example Is High, Noble and Grand," 6 August 1885, Rochester, *FD* 5:196.

158. "Sources of Danger to the Republic," 7 February 1867, St Louis, *FD* 4:165.

159. "The Decision Has Humbled the Nation," 22 October 1883, Washington, DC, *FD* 5:117.

160. "I Am Here Advocating Rights for Ireland," 14 December 1887, Washington, DC, *FD* 5:276.

161. "I am Here Advocating Rights for Ireland," *FD* 5:276.

162. Sweeney, *Frederick Douglass*, 3.

163. Glen McClish, "Frederick Douglass and the Consequences of Rhetoric: The Interpretive Framing and Publication History of the 2 January 1893 Haiti Speeches," *Rhetorica* 30.1 (Winter 2012): 37–73.

164. "'Haiti and the Haitian People," 2 January 1893, Chicago, *FD* 5:506.

165. "'Haiti and the Haitian People," *FD* 5:506.

166. Hanlon, *America's England*, xi.

167. Fanuzzi, *Abolition's Public Sphere*, 83; see similar arguments made in Lindon Barret, *Blackness and Value: Seeing Double* (Cambridge: Cambridge University Press, 1999); and Patricia McKee, *Producing American Races: Henry James, William Faulkner, Toni Morrison* (Durham, NC: Duke University Press, 1999).

168. "A Plea for Freedom of Speech," 9 December 1860, Boston, *FD* 3:421.

169. "Life and Times of Frederick Douglass" (1881) in *Frederick Douglass Papers*, series 2: *Autobiographies*, 292.

170. "My Foreign Travels," 15 December 1887, Washington, DC, *FD* 5:278.

Chapter 3

1. Mercantile Library Association of New York, *Annual Report*, 1850.

2. "City Items—Lecture Rooms and Ventilation," *New York Daily Tribune*, 12 December 1849; Mercantile Library Association of New York, *Annual Report*, 1851.

3. "Lecture on England at the Mercantile Library," *New York Herald*, 23 January 1850; "Mercantile Library Lecture," *New York Daily Tribune*, 23 January 1850; "Mr. Emerson on England," *Literary World*, 2 February 1850.

4. Nathaniel Parker Willis, "Emerson," *Home Journal*, 2 February 1850.

5. Uncovered New England reports include "Newport R.I. Correspondence," *Boston Evening Transcript*, 11 December 1848; "England: Mercantile Library Lectures," *Boston Post*, 29 December 1848; and "The English and American Character," *Hartford Courant*, 20 January 1849. The lecture was reprinted in New York as "Mr. Emerson on England," *New York Tribune*, 6 January 1849, and subsequently discussed extensively in several articles, including "England from Two Points of View," *Literary World*, 20 January 1849; "The Durability of England and Englishmen," *Holden's Dollar Magazine*, February 1849 and March 1849; and "The Other Side of the Picture," *Saturday Evening Post*, 18 August 1849. It was discussed in the London media in "Emerson on England," *London Examiner*, 10 March 1849; and "An American's Opinion of England," *Times* (London), 14 March 1849.

6. "Newport R.I. Correspondence," *Boston Evening Transcript*, 11 December 1848.

7. "Lecture on England," *New York Herald*, 23 January 1850.

8. Willis, "Emerson."

9. "Mr. Emerson's Lecture on England," *Albion*, 26 January 1850.

10. Recent discussions of Emerson's platform career include Mary Kupiec Cayton, "The Making of an American Prophet: Emerson, His Audiences, and the Rise of the Culture Industry in Nineteenth-Century America," *American Historical Review* 92.3 (1987): 597–620; Cayton, *Emerson's Emergence: Self and Society in the Transformation of New England, 1800–1845* (Chapel Hill: University of North Carolina Press, 1992); Sallee Fox Engstrom, *The Infinitude of Private Man: Emerson's Presence in Western New York, 1851–1861* (New York: Peter Lang, 1997); Augst, *The Clerk's Tale*, 114–57; and Bonnie Carr O'Neill,

"'The Best of Me Is There': Emerson as Lecturer and Celebrity," *American Literature* 80.4 (2008): 739–67.

11. Emerson, *Later Lectures.*

12. Cayton, "Making of American Prophet"; and Cayton, *Emerson's Emergence*; Engstrom, *Infinitude of Private Man*; O'Neill, "Best of Me Is There"; and Nicole H. Gray, "The Sounds and Stages of Emerson's Social Reform," *Nineteenth-Century Literature* 69.2 (September 2014): 208–32.

13. "Emerson the Lecturer," in Emerson, *Later Lectures*, 1:xviii.

14. Cayton, "Making of American Prophet," 599.

15. The lyceum is notably absent from Rosemarie K. Bank, *Theater Culture in America, 1825–1860* (Cambridge: Cambridge University Press, 1997).

16. Much of the analysis that follows is influenced by the discussion of midcentury attitudes to Britain in Tennenhouse, *Importance of Feeling English*; and Tamarkin, *Anglophilia.*

17. Gibian, *Oliver Wendell Holmes*, 16.

18. See Scott, "The Profession That Vanished."

19. Bode, *American Lyceum*, 221.

20. Most notably Albert J. von Frank, *An Emerson Chronology* (New York: Hall, 1994); William Charvat, *Emerson's American Lecture Engagements: A Chronological List* (New York: New York Public Library, 1961); and see *Emerson: An Annotated Secondary Bibliography*, ed. Robert E. Burkholder and Joel Myerson (Pittsburgh: University of Pittsburgh Press, 1985).

21. See Rusk, *Life of Emerson*, 382–83.

22. See Emerson, *Later Lectures*, 1:xxiv–xxv; James Russell Lowell, "Emerson the Lecturer," in *My Study Windows* (Boston: Osgood, 1874), 379.

23. George Willis Cooke, *Ralph Waldo Emerson: His Life, Writings and Philosophy* (Boston: Osgood, 1881), 256–69.

24. "Ralph Waldo Emerson," *Boston Evening Transcript*, 11 March 1854.

25. Emerson, *Later Lectures*, 1:47–48.

26. Margaret Fuller, "Review of Emerson's Essays: Second Series," *New York Tribune*, 7 December 1844.

27. Anon., "A Series of Letters Published in the Gazette of Stapleton, NY," quoted in Cooke, *Ralph Waldo Emerson*, 258.

28. See Buell, *Emerson*, 92.

29. Kasson, *Rudeness and Civility*, 119–21.

30. See Frederick DeWolfe Miller, *Christopher Pearse Cranch and His Caricatures of New England Transcendentalism* (Cambridge, MA: Harvard University Press, 1951); Bremer quoted in *Boston Evening Transcript*, 11 March 1854.

31. See Barnet Baskerville, *The People's Voice: The Orator in American Society* (Lexington: University Press of Kentucky, 1979), 13; and Reynolds, *Walt Whitman's America*, 155–59.

32. Willis, "Emerson."

33. Robert D. Richardson Jr., *Emerson: The Mind on Fire* (Berkeley: University of California Press, 1995), 195.

34. Cooke, *Emerson*, 256–69.

35. Emerson, *Journals and Miscellaneous Notebooks*, 9:71; Emerson, *Later Lectures*, 1:47–48.

36. Bode, *American Lyceum*, 221.

37. Daniel March, "Popular Lectures," *New Englander and Yale Review*, 8 May 1850, 186–202. For Patch's symbolic valence in midcentury America, see Paul Johnson, *Sam Patch: The Famous Jumper* (New York: Hill and Wang, 2004).

38. "Mr. Emerson's Lectures," *Christian Inquirer*, 13 April 1850.

39. "The American Scholar," in *Collected Works*, 1:58.

40. "Mr. Emerson's Lectures," *Christian Inquirer*, 13 April 1850.

41. Lowell, *My Study Windows*, 380.

42. Fuller, "Review of Emerson's Essays."

43. Fuller, "Review of Emerson's Essays."

44. Statistics drawn from Charvat, *Emerson's American Lecture Engagements*; and Frank, *An Emerson Chronology*, 224–310. The lecture was also performed during 1848–51 under titles such as "Why England Is English" (e.g., Concord, December 1848), and "England and the English" (e.g., Cleveland, May 1850). Later performances under titles such as "English Influence in Modern Civilization" (e.g., Philadelphia, January 1854) and "Characteristics of English Civilization" (e.g., East Boston, March 1854) represent separate texts from the lecture as performed during the earlier period.

45. The Houghton Library manuscript of "England" is reprinted in *Later Lectures*, vol. 1; and in *The Selected Lectures of Ralph Waldo Emerson*, ed. Ronald A. Bosco and Joel Myerson (Athens: University of Georgia Press, 2005).

46. Responses that emphasize the book's underhanded, disparaging assessment of Britain include Robert Weisbuch, *Atlantic Double-Cross: American Literature and British Influence in the Age of Emerson* (Chicago: University of Chicago Press, 1986), 21–25; and Richard Bridgman, "From Greenough to 'Nowhere': Emerson's *English Traits*," *New England Quarterly* 9.4 (1986): 469–85. Studies that treat the work as an evasion of the escalating sectional crisis include Philip L. Nicoloff, *Emerson on Race and History: An Examination of "English Traits"* (New York: Columbia University Press, 1961); and William Stowe, *American Abroad: European Travel in Nineteenth-Century American Culture* (Princeton, NJ: Princeton University Press, 1994), 74–101. Recent work that synthesizes these readings includes Susan Castillo, "'The Best of Nations': Race and Imperial Destinies in Emerson's *English Traits*," *Yearbook of English Studies* (2004), 100–111; and Christopher Hanlon, "'The Old Race Are All Gone': Transatlantic Bloodlines and English Traits," *American Literary History* 19.4 (2007): 800–823.

47. See, for example, Sacvan Bercovitch, "Emerson, Individualism, and the Ambiguities of Dissent," in *Ralph Waldo Emerson: A Collection of Critical Essays*, ed. Lawrence Buell (Englewood Cliffs, NJ: Prentice Hall, 1992), 101–34; Christopher Newfield, *The Emerson Effect: Individualism and Submission in America* (Chicago: University of Chicago Press, 1996).

48. Stanley Cavell, *Emerson's Transcendental Etudes*, ed. David Hodge (Stanford, CA: Stanford University Press, 2003), 23–24.

49. Emerson, *Collected Works*, 1:161.

50. The Houghton Library manuscript of "England" is reprinted in *Later Lectures*, vol. 1; and in *Selected Lectures*.

51. Ralph Waldo Emerson to Lidian Emerson, *Letters*, 9 vols. (New York: Columbia University, 1966), 5:40; "France" is reprinted in *Later Lectures*, vol. 2.

52. Ralph Waldo Emerson to William Emerson, 3 August 1848, *Letters*, 4:103.

53. Ralph Waldo Emerson to William Emerson, 3 August 1848, *Letters*, 4:132.

54. James Eliot Cabot, *A Memoir of Ralph Waldo Emerson*, 2 vols. (Boston: Mifflin, 1888), 1:227–28; see also Charles T. Congdon, *Reminiscences of a Journalist* (Boston: Osgood, 1880), 34–35.

55. A series of five lectures, reprinted in Emerson, *Later Lectures*, vol. 1; Madame de Staël, *De l'Allemagne*, trans. Henry Weston Eve (Oxford: Clarendon Press, 1906).

56. Kenneth Marc Harris, *Carlyle and Emerson: Their Long Debate* (Cambridge, MA: Harvard University Press, 1978), 5.

57. For Carlyle's use of an external perspective, see in particular the chapter "The English," Thomas Carlyle, *Past and Present*, ed. Chris R. Vanden Bossche (Berkeley: University of California Press, 2005), 159–66.

58. Ralph Waldo Emerson to Thomas Carlyle, 30 October 1840, *Correspondence of Emerson and Carlyle*, 283.

59. Ralph Waldo Emerson, "Carlyle's 'Past and Present,'" *Dial* 4.1 (1844): 99.

60. Emerson, *Selected Lectures*, 155. Subsequent references in parentheses.

61. Emerson, *Later Lectures*, 1:164.

62. Notably his entries on Liverpool 1847, particularly the passage beginning, "I look at the immense wealth and the solid power concentrated and am quite faint; then I look in the street at the little girl running barefoot through the rain." In Emerson, *Journals and Miscellaneous Notebooks*, 10:245.

63. Hanlon, "Old Race," 801–4.

64. Thomas Carlyle to Ralph Waldo Emerson, 19 April 1849, *Correspondence of Emerson and Carlyle*, 453.

65. Daniel Walker Howe, *The Political Culture of the American Whigs* (Chicago: Chicago University Press, 1979), 20–21.

66. Emerson, *Collected Works*, 1:58.

67. Buell, *Emerson*, 56 and 83.

68. George Gilfillan, "Popular Lectures—No. II: George Dawson," *Tait's Edinburgh Magazine*, May 1848, 279; reprinted, for example, in "Lecture To-Night," *Milwaukee Daily Sentinel*, 6 February 1854.

69. "The Young American," in Emerson, *Collected Works*, 1:217–47.

70. "Mary Moody Emerson" and "Thoreau," in Emerson, *Collected Works*, vol. 7. For an assessment of this approach, see Buell, *Emerson*, 92.

71. Weisbuch, *Atlantic Double-Cross*, 275–76.

72. *Boston Evening Transcript*, 11 December 1848.

73. "England: Mercantile Library Lectures," *Boston Post*, 29 December 1848; "Mr. Emerson on England," *New York Tribune*, 6 January 1849.

74. E.g., "The English and American Character," *Hartford Courant*, 20 January 1849.

75. "England from Two Points of View," *Literary World*, 20 January 1849.

76. "Rev. F. H. Hedge," *Christian Inquirer*, 10 February 1849.

77. "The Durability of England and Englishmen," *Holden's Dollar Magazine*, February 1849 and March 1849.

78. "Emerson on England," *London Examiner*, 10 March 1849; "An American's Opinion of England," *Times* (London), 14 March 1849.

79. John Stuart Mill to Harriet Taylor, 14 March 1849, in *The Collected Works of John Stuart Mill*, ed. Francis E. Mineka and Dwight N. Lindley, 33 vols. (Toronto: University of Toronto Press; London: Routledge and Kegan Paul, 1972), 14:22. His editors

comment: "What JSM objected to most in Emerson's lecture is difficult to determine: it may have been the praise of English culture ("they surpass all others in general culture— none are so harmoniously developed") or of English individuality ("each man is trained to mind his own business. Personal eccentricities are allowed here, and no one observes them. Each islander is an island himself, reposing in quiet and tranquil waters"). *Collected Works*, 14:22 n. 1.

80. "The Other Side of the Picture," *Saturday Evening Post*, 18 August 1849.

81. The summary draws upon Richard Moody, *The Astor Place Riots* (Bloomington: Indiana University Press, 1958); and Nigel Cliff, *The Shakespeare Riots: Revenge, Drama, and Death in Nineteenth-Century America* (London: Random House, 2007). See Samuel W. Haynes, "Anglophobia and the Annexation of Texas: The Quest for National Security," in *Manifest Destiny and Empire*, ed. Haynes and Christopher Morris (College Station: Texas A&M University Press, 1997), 115–45.

82. Anon., "Shakespeare Readings and Fashionable Vulgarity," *New York Herald*, 23 April 1849.

83. See Moody, *The Astor Place Riots*, 86–96; and Thomas N. Baker, *Sentiment and Celebrity: Nathaniel Parker Willis and the Trials of Fame* (Oxford: Oxford University Press, 1999), 108–10.

84. Nathaniel Parker Willis, "After-Lesson of the Astor-Place Riot," *Home Journal*, 26 May 1849.

85. Anon., "America," *Times* (London), 29 May 1849, reprinted as Anon., "The English View of the Riot," *New York Herald*, 16 June 1849.

86. Speakers for the 1849–50 winter season had included six lectures by Henry Giles on "Don Quixote" and Horace Mann on "Advice to Young Mercantile Men." The association also specialized in narratives of travel and global culture: W. H. C. Hosmer had spoken on "Scottish Song" in December 1849, and the performances that were to follow Emerson's "England" and "London" in January included Rev. W. Ware, "Florence," and Rev. George W. Bethune, "Holland and the Hollanders." Mercantile Library Association, *Annual Report*, 1850, 24–25.

87. "Mr. Emerson's Lectures," *Christian Inquirer*, 13 April 1850.

88. Of 2,974 members in 1850, 2,805 described themselves as "clerks." New York Mercantile Library Association, *Annual Report*, 1850, 24; see also Augst, *The Clerk's Tale*, 118–21.

89. Hall, "Encoding/Decoding," 174–76.

90. See Cliff, *The Shakespeare Riots*, 196–210.

91. "Mr. Emerson's Lecture on England," *Albion*, 26 January 1850.

92. Printed first in the *Home Journal* of 2 February 1850, it was excerpted in the *Boston Evening Transcript*, 4 February 1850; it was subsequently published in Willis, *Hurry-Graphs: Sketches of Scenery, Celebrities and Society* (New York: Scribner, 1851), 189–92.

93. See Baker, *Sentiment and Celebrity*, 101–4.

94. See Baker, *Sentiment and Celebrity*, 101–4.

95. Willis, "Emerson."

96. Willis, "Emerson."

97. The *Herald* was mocked for its jeremiads in Anon., "Lectures and Lecturers," *Putnam's Monthly*, March 1857, 317.

98. *New York Herald*, 23 January 1850.

99. For *Herald* quote see Cliff, *The Shakespeare Riots*, 237. For discussions of anti-British oratory, see Robert Ernst, "One and Only Mike Walsh," *New-York Historical Society Quarterly* 36 (1952): 43–65.

100. *New York Herald*, 23 January 1850.

101. The reference in Emerson's script was as follows: "The fabulous St. George has never seemed to me the patron saint of England; but the scholar, monk, soldier, engineer, lawgiver, Alfred ... he is the model Englishman. They have many such in their annals. Cromwell is one." *Later Lectures*, 1:163.

102. For example, Anon., "Trial of the Astor Place Rioters," *New York Herald*, 17 January 1850; and Anon., "Interesting Opera News: Another Riot or *Emeute* Expected," *New York Herald*, 19 January 1850.

103. See Cliff, *The Shakespeare Riots*, 237; and Ernst, "One and Only Mike Walsh."

104. "City Items," *New York Tribune*, 26 March 1850.

105. Emerson to Carlyle, 2 August 1850, *Letters*, 4:224.

106. Newspaper reports of Emerson's May 1850 Ohio engagements are as follows: "Ralph Waldo Emerson," *Cleveland Daily Plain Dealer*, 16 May 1850; "Ralph Waldo Emerson," *Daily Commercial Gazette* (Cincinnati), 21 May 1850; "Emerson's Lectures," *Daily Commercial Gazette*, 22 May 1850; "The Spirit of the Times," *Daily Commercial Gazette*, 24 May 1850; "Mr. Emerson's Lecture," *Daily Commercial Gazette*, 30 May 1850; "Emerson in Cincinnati," *Salem Register*, 3 June 1850.

107. Mead, *Yankee Eloquence*, 1–15; and Louise Hastings, "Emerson in Cincinnati," *New England Quarterly* 11 (1938): 444.

108. See *Cleveland Herald*, 16 May 1850; *Cleveland Daily Plain Dealer*, 16 May 1850; Mead, *Yankee Eloquence*, 26–27.

109. *Cleveland True Democrat*, 18 May 1850; and Hastings, "Emerson in Cincinnati," 444.

110. Mead, *Yankee Eloquence*, 22–23.

111. Ralph Waldo Emerson to Lidian Emerson, February 1854, quoted in Bode, *American Lyceum*, 34.

112. See Walter Glazer, *Cincinnati in 1840: The Social and Functional Organization of an Urban Community during the Pre–Civil War Period* (Columbus: Ohio State University Press, 1999), 8–10.

113. See Haynes, "Anglophobia," 120; and Yonatan Eyal, *The Young America Movement and the Transformation of the Democratic Party, 1828–1861* (Cambridge: Cambridge University Press, 2007), 67.

114. Moody, *The Astor Place Riots*, 80.

115. Young Men's Mercantile Library Association of Cincinnati, *Annual Report*, 1850, 23.

116. Glazer, *Cincinnati in 1840*, xi.

117. Young Men's Mercantile Library Association of Cincinnati, *Annual Report*, 1850, 12. However, speakers for the association were not all northern: on transatlantic topics, Alexander Campbell of Virginia had spoken in December on "The Anglo-Saxon Language—Its Origin, Character and Destiny." Nor were Anglocentric themes the only topic of interest: the 1851 course included an address, "Memories of the German Father-Land," that would seem to speak more to the rising northern European population.

118. Holland, "The Popular Lecture," 366.

119. "The Lyceum," *Gloucester Telegraph*, 3 March 1850.

120. *Salem Register*, 3 June 1850.

121. *Daily Commercial Gazette* (Cincinnati), 21 May 1850, quoted in Hastings, "Emerson in Cincinnati," 443.

122. *Daily Commercial Gazette*, 22 May 1850.

123. *Daily Commercial Gazette*, 22 May 1850.

124. *Salem Register*, 3 June 1850.

125. *Daily Commercial Gazette*, 22 May 1850.

126. *Daily Commercial Gazette*, 24 May 1850.

127. *Daily Commercial Gazette*, 24 May 1850.

128. *Salem Register*, 3 June 1850.

129. *Diary of Rutherford B. Hayes*, ed. Charles R. Williams, 5 vols. (Columbus: Ohio State Archaeology and History Society, 1922), 1:304.

130. "Mr. Emerson's Lecture," *Daily Commercial Gazette*, 30 May 1850.

131. Tamarkin, *Anglophilia*, xxvii.

132. Emerson, *Collected Works*, 5:171.

133. Levine, *High Brow / Low Brow*.

134. Anon., "The Public Amusements," *New York Herald*, 29 May 1849.

135. See Anon., "The New York Mercantile Library," *Scribner's Monthly*, February 1871; and Augst, *The Clerk's Tale*, 261–64.

Chapter 4

1. See, for example, Fuller's commentaries for the *New York Tribune*, collated as Margaret Fuller and Arthur B. Fuller, *At Home and Abroad* (Boston: Crosby, Nichols, 1856).

2. Horace Mann, *Report of an Educational Tour in Germany, and Parts of Great Britain and Ireland* (London: Simpkin, Marshall, 1846), 403.

3. Horace Greeley, *Glances at Europe: In a Series of Letters from Great Britain, France, Italy, Switzerland, Etc., during the Summer of 1851* (New York: Dewitt & Davenport, 1851).

4. Claybaugh, *The Novel of Purpose*; Garvey, *Creating the Culture*; Julia Swindells, *Glorious Causes: The Grand Theater of Political Change, 1789 to 1833* (Oxford: Oxford University Press, 2001); Elaine Hadley, *Melodramatic Tactics: Theatricalised Dissent in the English Marketplace* (Stanford, CA: Stanford University Press, 1995).

5. Horace Mann on Great Britain—January 29 1845," Concord Free Public Library, "Concord Lyceum Records 1828–1879," Microfilm Reel 1, 1. Subsequent page references in parentheses.

6. For this interplay of sincerity and prurience, see David S. Reynolds, *Beneath the American Renaissance: The Subversive Imagination in the Age of Emerson and Melville* (New York: Oxford University Press, 2011), 70–73.

7. Swindells, *Glorious Causes*, xi.

8. See John L. Thomas, "Romantic Reform in America, 1815–1865," *American Quarterly* 17.4 (1965): 656–81; Daniel Walker Howe, *The American Whigs: An Anthology* (New York: John Wiley, 1973), 148–58; Howe, *Political Culture*, 36–37; Howe, *Making the American Self: Jonathan Edwards to Abraham Lincoln* (Cambridge, MA: Harvard University Press, 1997), 158–67. See also Merle Curti, *The Social Ideals of the American Educator* (Paterson, NJ: Pageant Books, 1959).

9. For Mann's intellectual heritage, see Howe, *Making the American Self*, 158–67; and Curti, *Social Ideals*.

10. Horace Mann, "What God Does, and What He Leaves for Man to Do, in the Work of Education," *Lectures on Education* (Boston: Fowle and Capen, 1845), 158.

11. "Horace Greeley," *Barre Patriot*, 23 January 1852.

12. Horace Mann, "Report for 1842," in Horace Mann and Mary T. P. Mann, *Life and Works of Horace Mann* (Boston: Walker, Fuller, 1865), 137.

13. Jonathan Messerli, *Horace Mann: A Biography* (New York: Knopf, 1972), 177.

14. "The Emancipation of Labor," in Horace Greeley, *Hints towards Reforms* (New York: Harper and Brothers, 1850), 14.

15. Greeley, *Glances at Europe*, 290; see also "The Popular Lecture Season," *New York Tribune*, 20 September 1855.

16. Horace Mann, "Report for 1848," in Mann and Mann, *Life and Works*, 689.

17. "The Lecture Season," *New York Tribune*, 4 January 1853; "Horace Greeley," *Barre Patriot*, 23 January 1852.

18. "The Emancipation of Labor," in Greeley, *Hints towards Reforms*, 7; James Parton, *The Life of Horace Greeley, Editor of the "New York Tribune"* (New York: Mason, 1855), 190.

19. Horace Mann, "The Necessity of Education in a Republican Government," in *Lectures on Education*, 125.

20. See Michael Holt, *The Rise and Fall of the American Whig Party: Jacksonian Politics and the Onset of the Civil War* (Oxford: Oxford University Press, 1999), 120; and Howe, *Political Culture*, 36–37.

21. James Jasinski, *Sourcebook on Rhetoric: Key Concepts in Contemporary Rhetorical Studies* (Thousand Oaks, CA: Sage, 2001), 237.

22. Garvey, *Creating the Culture*, 10.

23. Carlyle remarks of the "symbolic action" through which political conduct is uttered that "by act and word he strives to do it; with sincerity, if possible; failing that, with theatricality." Thomas Carlyle, *The French Revolution: A History*, in *Centenary Edition of the Works of Carlyle*, ed. Henry D. Traill (Cambridge: Cambridge University Press, 1907), 47.

24. "Horace Mann on Great Britain—January 29 1845," Concord Free Public Library, "Concord Lyceum Records 1828–1879," Microfilm Reel 1.

25. Horace Mann, "Great Britain," undated manuscript, Boston, Massachusetts Historical Society, Mann Collection, Microfilm Reel 31.53, 1. Subsequent page references in parentheses.

26. See, for example, Mann, "The Necessity of Education," 119–20.

27. George W. Bungay, *Crayon Sketches and Off-Hand Takings* (Boston: Stacy and Richardson, 1852), 22.

28. George Landow, *Elegant Jeremiahs: The Sage from Carlyle to Mailer* (Ithaca, NY: Cornell University Press, 1986), 66–67.

29. See Mann, "A Historical View of Education," *Lectures on Education*, 262; and Thomas, "Romantic Reform in America," 658–60.

30. See Kasson, *Rudeness and Civility*, 72–74.

31. "The Oregon Question," *Brooklyn Eagle*, 6 March 1844; see also Holt, *Rise and Fall*, 232.

32. Its original formulation occurs in Mann, *Report of an Educational Tour*, 407.

33. For a typology of the Carlylean grotesque, see Landow, *Elegant Jeremiahs*, 73–76.

34. Carlyle, *Past and Present*, 20.

35. Andrew W. Robertson, *The Language of Democracy: Political Rhetoric in the United States and Britain, 1790–1900* (Ithaca, NY: Cornell University Press, 1995), 30; and Robertson, "'Look on This Picture . . . and on This!' Nationalism, Localism, and Partisan Images of Otherness in the United States, 1787–1820," *American Historical Review* 106.4 (2001): 1263–80.

36. Douglas Jerrold, *The History of St. Giles and St. James* (Boston: Redding, 1847), i.

37. Jerrold, "St. Giles and St. James," serialized in *Littell's Living Age*, from 22 February 1845 to 5 September 1846.

38. "The Shame of England," *United States Democratic Review* 10.43 (1842): 89. For example, Anon., "Review of Lester's Book on England," *New York Review*, January 1842; British reviews included "The Glory and Shame of England. By C. Edwards Lester," *Monthly Review* 1.1 (1842); and extensive excerpts in Anon., "The Glory and Shame of England by an American," *Times* (London), 25 December 1841, and Anon., "The Glory and Shame of England by an American. Continued," *Times*, 31 December 1841.

39. Kate Flint, ed., *The Victorian Novelist: Social Problems and Social Change* (Oxford: Routledge, 1987), 131.

40. See Boyd Hilton, *A Mad, Bad and Dangerous People? England, 1783–1846* (Oxford: Oxford University Press, 2006), 579–81.

41. See, for example, the discussion of public pressure in David Nasaw, *Schooled to Order: A Social History of Public Schooling in the United States* (New York: Oxford University Press, 1981).

42. These were published as Greeley, *Glances at Europe*.

43. See *Times* (London), 15 May 1851, 5; Anon., "Brother Jonathan at the Fair," *Punch*, 24 May 1851, 209; *Punch*, 7 June 1851, 236; Frederick Saunders, *Memories of the Great Metropolis: or, London from the Tower to the Crystal Palace* (New York: Putnam, 1852), 41.

44. Kate Flint, "Exhibiting America: The Native American and the Crystal Palace," in *Victorian Prism: Refractions of the Crystal Palace*, ed. James Buzard, Joseph W. Childers, and Eileen Gilloly (Charlottesville: University of Virginia Press, 2007), 174.

45. Rosemarie Bank, for example, has read the American presence at the fair, and the subsequent 1853 New York Crystal Palace, as a form institutional, staged performance. Bank, *Theater Culture in America*, 167–90.

46. *Baltimore Sun*, 24 January 1852; Anon., "Moving Panorama of the World's Fair," *Boston Daily Evening Transcript* (reprinted from the *New York Mirror*), 12 February 1851; Anon., "Revolving Mirror of the Crystal Palace and World's Fair," *Boston Daily Evening Transcript*, 30 January 1852.

47. Anon., "Disgusting Exhibitions," *New York Daily Tribune*, 22 September 1853.

48. William Wells Brown, *Three Years in Europe; or, Places I Have Seen and People I Have Met* (Boston: Jewett, 1852), 211.

49. Mann, *Report of an Educational Tour*, 403.

50. For current definitions of epideictic, see Jasinski, *Sourcebook on Rhetoric*, 209–13. Examples of recent work on epideictic in American studies include Cindy Koenig Richards, "Inventing Sacagawea: Public Women and the Transformative Potential of Epideictic Rhetoric," *Western Journal of Communication* 73.1 (2009): 1–22.

51. Buzard, Childers, and Gilloly, *Victorian Prism*, 9.

52. Buzard, Childers, and Gilloly, *Victorian Prism*, 265.

53. "City Intelligence," *Brooklyn Eagle*, 16 January 1846.

54. *Grove Encyclopedia of Decorative Arts*, 1:315.

55. For the centrality of harmony and balance to Whig faculty psychology, see Howe, *Political Culture*, 76–77.

56. Robert H. Ellison, *A New History of the Sermon: The Nineteenth Century* (Leiden: Brill, 2010), xx.

57. Thoreau, journal entry, 16 November 1858, in *Heart of Thoreau's Journals*.

58. See Holt, *Rise and Fall*, 22.

59. James Spear Loring, *The Hundred Boston Orators* (Boston: Jewett, 1852), 603; Bungay, *Crayon Sketches*, 21; Evert Duyckinck, *Cyclopaedia of American Literature: Embracing Personal and Critical Notices of Authors* (New York: Scribner, 1856), 224.

60. "City Intelligence," *Brooklyn Eagle*, 16 January 1846. It was featured most recently in "St. Giles and St. James," *Littell's Living Age* 8.87 (10 January 1846).

61. First, he had become a truly national public figure, having spent 1848–52 in Congress, before a failed 1852 bid for governor of Massachusetts on a Free Soil ticket terminated his political career.

62. A term revisited in Martin Hewitt, *An Age of Equipoise? Reassessing Mid-Victorian Britain* (London: Ashgate, 2000).

63. *New York Times*, 10 March 1853.

64. "England and America," *New York Times*, 12 March 1853.

65. "England and America," *New York Times*, 12 March 1853.

66. "Hon. Horace Mann's Lecture upon Great Britain," *New York Times*, 10 March 1853. All of these elements were also revealed by a series of responses to the same Tabernacle performance that the *Independent* magazine printed during the spring and summer of 1853. "Our Correspondence," *Independent*, 28 April 1853. See also David Stevens, "England," *Ohio State Journal*, 17 January 1855.

67. Parton, *Life of Horace Greeley*, 347.

68. Putnam, *Science and Art*, 228.

69. For examples during 1849, see "The Hon. (We Beg Pardon) Horace Greeley," *Trenton State Gazette*, 2 April 1849; and Anon., "Vermont Politics—Horace Greeley—the Railroads," *Boston Daily Atlas*, 30 August 1849.

70. Andrew Oakley Hall and Joseph Hoxie, *Horace Greeley Decently Dissected: In a Letter on Horace Greeley, addressed by A. Oakey Hall to Joseph Hoxie, Esq.* (New York: Ross & Tousey, 1862), 30.

71. Parton, *Life of Horace Greeley*, 331.

72. Anon., "Greeley in London," *Savannah Daily Republican*, 27 May 1851.

73. *New York Mirror*, quoted in Anon., "At Home," *Kalamazoo Gazette*, 12 September 1851.

74. Anon., "The World's Fair—the Object of It, Abolition—the South," *Georgia Telegraph*, 24 June 1851.

75. Lecture reports used in this chapter are as follows: "Public Lecture: Horace Greeley," *Trenton State Gazette*, 5 December 1851; "Mr. Greeley's Lecture," *Trenton State Gazette*, 6 December 1851; "Horace Greeley," *Albany Evening Journal*, 19 December 1851; "The Crystal Palace and Its Lessons," *New York Times*, 1 January 1852; "Greeley's Crystal Palace," *Barre Patriot*, 23 January 1852; "Horace Greeley's Lecture," *Barre Patriot*, 23 January 1852; "Miscellany: The Crystal Palace and Its Lessons," *Barre Patriot*, 7 May 1852; Anon.,

"Notice: Crystal Palace and Its Lessons by Horace Greeley," *Water-Cure Journal and Herald of Reforms* 13.6 (1852).

76. "Horace Greeley," *Barre Patriot*, 23 January 1852.

77. Tracy C. Davis and Thomas Postlewait, *Theatricality* (Cambridge: Cambridge University Press, 2003), 145.

78. *Albany Evening Journal*, 19 December 1851.

79. Anon., *Water-Cure Journal and Herald of Reforms*, 19 July 1852.

Chapter 5

1. Eyre Crowe, *With Thackeray in America* (New York: Charles Scribner's Sons, 1893), 45.

2. William Makepeace Thackeray to James T. Fields, 29 November 1852, in *The Letters and Private Papers of William Makepeace Thackeray*, vol. 3, *1852–1857* (London: Oxford University Press, 1946), 191.

3. "Thackeray in America—His Books, Lectures, and the Man," *Literary World*, 15 January 1853.

4. "Notes on New Books," *Daily National Intelligencer*, 14 July 1853.

5. Lionel Stevenson, *The Showman of Vanity Fair: The Life of William Makepeace Thackeray* (New York: Russell & Russell, 1968), 272.

6. Stevenson, *Showman of Vanity Fair*, 263.

7. "Mr. Thackeray's First Lecture," *Boston Daily Atlas*, 8 December 1855.

8. Thomas Carlyle to Ralph Waldo Emerson, 25 August 1852, Ralph Waldo Emerson to Thomas Carlyle, 30 October 1840, *Correspondence of Emerson and Carlyle*, 540.

9. "Thackeray," *New York Tribune*, 13 November 1852.

10. "Thackeray," *New York Tribune*, 13 November 1852.

11. The discussion in this chapter relies upon the following sources. (1) Prearrival reports: "Thackeray and Brother Jonathan," *Daily Ohio Statesman*, September 17, 1852; "Thackeray," *New York Times*, 21 October 1852; "Thackeray's Lectures," *New York Times*, 3 November 1852; "City News and Gossip," *Brooklyn Eagle*, 9 November 1852. (2) 1852 sources: "Mr. Thackeray' Lecture," *New York Tribune*, 20 November 1852; "Thackeray's Lectures," *New York Times*, 20 November 1852; "Mr. Thackeray's Manner of Lecturing," *Brooklyn Eagle*, 20 November 1852; "Mr. Thackeray's Lecture," *New York Times*, 22 November 1852; "Thackeray in New York," *Baltimore Sun*, 22 November 1852; "Thackeray in New York" (reprints from *Commercial Advertiser, New York Post, Courier and Enquirer*), *Baltimore Sun*, 22 November 1852; "Mr Thackeray and Dean Swift," *New York Herald*, 22 November 1852; "Thackeray's Lecture" (reprints from *New York Times, New York Post, New York Mirror*), *Richmond Enquirer*, 26 November 1852; "Thackeray Lecture," *New York Post*, 27 November 1852. (3) 1853 sources: "Thackeray at the Academy," *Brooklyn Eagle*, 17 December 1852; "Thackeray in Boston," *Boston Evening Transcript*, 6 December 1852; "Mr. Thackeray's Lecture," *Boston Evening Transcript*, 22 December 1852; "Affairs in and about the City," *Boston Daily Atlas*, 22 December 1852; "Mr Thackeray—Congreve," *Boston Evening Transcript*, 24 December 1852; "Thackeray in Boston," *New York Times*, 27 December 1852; "Thackeray in Boston," *New Orleans Times Picayune*, 31 December 1852; "Mr Thackeray— Steele," *Boston Evening Transcript*, 29 December 1852; "Thackeray," *Cleveland Plain Dealer*, 31 December 1852; "The *Herald* Jumping Jim Crow: Thackeray, English Influence at the

New York Press," *Irish-American*, 25 December 1852; "Thackeray in America—His Book, Lectures, Man," *Literary World*, January 1853.

12. Slater, *Charles Dickens*, 176–200.

13. See Angelina Poon, *Enacting Englishness in the Victorian Period: Colonialism and the Politics of Performance* (Aldershot: Ashgate, 2008); Peter Sinnema, *The Wake of Wellington: Englishness in 1852* (Athens: Ohio University Press, 2006). For a survey of ideas relating to the development of English national identity see Langford, *Englishness Identified*.

14. McGill, *Culture of Reprinting*; Paul Saint-Amour, *The Copywrights: Intellectual Property and the Literary Imagination* (Ithaca, NY: Cornell University Press, 2003); see also Susan Eilenberg, "Mortal Pages: Wordsworth and the Reform of Copyright," *English Literary History* 56.2 (1989): 351–74; Clark, *Movement for International Copyright*.

15. Gregg Camfield, *Necessary Madness: The Humor of Domesticity in Nineteenth-Century American Literature* (New York: Oxford University Press, 1997). See also John Bryant, *Melville and Repose: The Rhetoric of Humor in the American Renaissance* (New York: Oxford University Press, 1993).

16. "Another Cockney Character Coming Over," *New York Herald*, 18 September 1852.

17. Kathleen Burk, *Old World, New World: The Story of Britain and America* (London: Little, Brown, 2007).

18. Robert Frankel, *Observing America: The Commentary of British Visitors to the United States, 1890–1950* (Madison: University of Wisconsin Press, 2007).

19. "America—Cockney Thackeray," *Cleveland Plain Dealer*, 31 December 1852.

20. "City News and Gossip," *Brooklyn Eagle*, 9 November 1852.

21. "Thackeray," *United States Review*, March 1853.

22. "A Sketch of Thackeray," *New York Evening Post*, 12 November 1852.

23. "Mr Thackeray and Dean Swift," *New York Herald*, 22 November 1852.

24. "Thackeray and Brother Jonathan," *Daily Ohio Statesman*, 17 September 1852.

25. "Thackeray's Greeting," *Daily Cleveland Herald*, 15 August 1853.

26. "A Sketch of Thackeray," *New York Evening Post*, 12 November 1852.

27. William M. Thackeray, *The Letters and Private Papers of William Makepeace Thackeray*, vol. 2, collected and edited by Gordon N. Ray (London: Oxford University Press, 1945), 773.

28. Quoted in Stevenson, *Showman of Vanity Fair*, xx.

29. See also Simon Heffer, *Moral Desperado: A Life of Thomas Carlyle* (London: Weidenfeld and Nicolson, 1995), 301.

30. Quoted in Stevenson, *Showman of Vanity Fair*, 234.

31. Quoted in Stevenson, *Showman of Vanity Fair*, 234.

32. Quoted in Ann Monsarrat, *An Uneasy Victorian: Thackeray the Man, 1811–1863* (New York: Dodd, Mead, 1980), 250.

33. Stevenson, *Showman of Vanity Fair*, 234.

34. "Mr. Thackeray's Lectures," *Albion*, 14 June 1851.

35. "Mr. Thackeray's Lectures," *Putnam's*, December 1869.

36. "A Sketch of Thackeray," *New York Evening Post*, 12 November 1852.

37. "A Sketch of Thackeray," *New York Evening Post*, 12 November 1852.

38. "Thackeray," *New York Times*, 3 November 1852.

39. Eyre Crowe recorded his impression in *With Thackeray in America* (New York: Charles Scribner's Sons, 1893).

40. Quoted in Catherine Peters, *Thackeray: A Writer's Life* (Stroud: Sutton, 1999).

41. Published in speedy fashion as William Makepeace Thackeray, *English Humorists of the Eighteenth Century: A Series of Lectures* (New York: Harpers, 1853).

42. Thackeray, *English Humorists*, 48.

43. Thackeray, *English Humorists*, 163.

44. Thackeray, *English Humorists*, 168.

45. Ralph Waldo Emerson, *Representative Men: Seven Lectures*, ed. Wallace E. Williams and Douglas E. Wilson (Cambridge, MA: Belknap Press of Harvard University Press, 1987).

46. "Thackeray's Lectures," *New York Times*, 20 November 1852.

47. See "Lectures on the English Poets," *New York Times*, 31 November 1853; Lowell, *Lectures on English Poets*.

48. Thackeray, *English Humorists*, 168.

49. Thackeray, *English Humorists*, 94, 76.

50. Thomas Carlyle to Ralph Waldo Emerson, 9 September 1853, *Correspondence of Emerson and Carlyle*, xx.

51. *New York Courier and Enquirer*, quoted in "Thackeray in New York," *Baltimore Sun*, 22 November 1852.

52. "Thackeray's Lectures," *New York Times*, 20 November 1852.

53. James Grant Wilson, "Thackeray's First Lecture in New York," *New York Times*, 1 December 1901.

54. *Boston Courier*, quoted in "Thackeray in Boston," *New Orleans Times Picayune*, 31 December 1852.

55. Thackeray's Lectures, *New York Post*, 27 November 1852. See also "Mr. Thackeray's Manner of Lecturing," *Brooklyn Eagle*, 20 November 1852.

56. "Mr. Thackeray's Lectures," *Putnam's*, December 1869.

57. "Mr. Thackeray," *Boston Evening Transcript*, 29 December 1852.

58. "Mr. Thackeray's Lecture," *New York Tribune*, 20 November 1852.

59. "A Sketch of Thackeray," *New York Evening Post*, 12 November 1852.

60. "Affairs in and about the City," *Boston Daily Atlas*, 22 December 1852.

61. "Mr Thackeray," *Philadelphia North American*, 17 January 1853.

62. Thackeray, *English Humorists*, 145.

63. "A Sketch of Thackeray," *New York Evening Post*, 12 November 1852.

64. Thackeray, *English Humorists*, 268.

65. "Thackeray in America," *Putnam's Monthly* 1.6 (June 1853): 638.

66. Amanda Claybaugh, "Toward a New Transatlanticism: Dickens in the United States," *Victorian Studies* 48.3 (2006): 439–60. See also Weisbuch, *Atlantic Double-Cross*.

67. Quoted in Robert McParland, *Charles Dickens's American Audience* (Lanham, MD: Lexington Books, 2012).

68. For an account of this history see Clark, *Movement for International Copyright*.

69. *New World* editorial, 12 February 1842.

70. See McGill, *Culture of Reprinting*, 110.

71. Stevenson, *Showman of Vanity Fair*, 262.

72. "New York Correspondence," *Times* (London), December 1853, quoted in "Thackeray: A Weak Attack: A Strong Defence," *Albion*, 17 December 1853.

73. John Sutherland, *Thackeray at Work* (London: Athlone Press, 1974), 121.

74. See Peter L. Shillingsburg, *Pegasus in Harness: Victorian Publishing and W.M. Thackeray* (Charlottesville: University of Virginia Press, 1991), 93–98.

75. Stevenson, *Showman of Vanity Fair*, 266.

76. Saint-Amour, *The Copywrights*.

77. See this discussion in Richard Pearson, *W.M. Thackeray and the Mediated Text: Writing for Periodicals in the Mid-Nineteenth Century* (London: Ashgate, 2000), 151.

78. Thackeray to James Hannay, 21 October 1852, *Letters and Private Papers*, 3:232.

79. Thackeray to George Smith, 26 November 1852, *Letters and Private Papers*, 3:xx.

80. "Mr. Thackeray's Lecture," *New York Times*, 22 November 1852.

81. "Thackeray Lecture in Liverpool," *New York Times*, 21 October 1852.

82. "Notes on New Books," *Daily National Intelligencer*, 14 July 1853.

83. "Thackeray in America—His Books Lectures, and the Man," *Literary World*, 15 January 1853.

84. "Thackeray," *Charleston Courier*, 2 January 1856.

85. "Thackeray Lecture," *Brooklyn Eagle*, 17 December 1852.

86. "Mr. Thackeray's Closing Lecture in New York," *Boston Daily Atlas*, 16 December 1852.

87. Thackeray, *English Humorists*, 8.

88. Quoted in "Thackeray," *Nebraskan*, 27 February 1856.

89. Stevenson, *Showman of Vanity Fair*, 235.

90. D. J. Taylor, *Thackeray* (London: Chatto and Windus, 1999), 332.

91. Thackeray to Mrs. T. F. Elliot, and Kate Perry, 7 December 1852, *Letters and Private Papers*, 3:505.

92. "Letters to the Editor—Thackeray," *New York Herald*, 15 December 1853.

93. "The Herald Jumping Jim Crow: Thackeray; English Influence at the New York Press," *Irish-American*, 25 December 1852.

94. "General," *New York Herald*, 20 November 1852.

95. *New York Commercial Advertiser*, quoted in "Thackeray in New York," *Baltimore Sun*, 22 November 1852.

96. Thackeray to Mrs. T. F. Elliot and Kate Perry, 7 December 1852, *Letters and Private Papers*, 3:505.

97. "Mr Thackeray and Dean Swift," *New York Herald*, 22 November 1852.

98. "Mr Thackeray and Dean Swift," *New York Herald*, 22 November 1852.

99. Stevenson, *Showman of Vanity Fair*, 264.

100. Thackeray to Mrs. T. F. Elliot and Kate Perry, 7 December 1852, *Letters and Private Papers*, 3:505.

101. Quoted in Taylor, *Thackeray*, 343.

102. *London Athenaeum*, quoted in "Thackeray's Lectures," *Wisconsin Free Democrat*, 7 November 1855.

103. "London Illustrated News—Thackeray," *Brooklyn Eagle*, 10 September 1855.

104. *London Athenaeum*, quoted in "Thackeray's Lectures," *Wisconsin Free Democrat*, 7 November 1855.

105. *London Athenaeum*, quoted in "Thackeray's Lectures," *Wisconsin Free Democrat*, 7 November 1855.

106. Uncovered sources for the second tour include the following. 1855: "Lectures," *Brooklyn Eagle*, 10 September 1855; "Mr Thackeray's Lectures" (reprint of *New York Evangelist*), *Vermont Chronicle*, 3 November 1855; "Mr. Thackeray's First Lecture," *Albion*,

3 November 1855; "Thackeray's Lectures," *Wisconsin Free Democrat*, 7 November 1855; "Mr Thackeray's Lectures," *New York Times*, 6 November 1855; "An Omission," *New York Times*, 10 November 1855; "Thackeray's Second and Third Lectures," *Albion*, 10 November 1855; "Thackeray, English Emigrants and American Orphans," 24 November 1855; "Mr. Thackeray and His Lectures," *Albion*, 1 December 1855; "Thackeray's Lectures" (reprint of New York correspondence of *Boston Post*); *Liberator*, 7 December 1855; "Mr. Thackeray's First Lecture," *Boston Daily Advertiser*, 8 December 1855; "Mr Thackeray's Lecture," *Boston Daily Advertiser*, 10 December 1855. 1856: "Mr. Thackeray's Last Lecture," *North American and US Gazette*, 9 January 1856; "Mr Thackeray's Lectures," *Charleston Courier*, 1 February 1856; "Mr. Thackeray's Lectures," *Charleston Courier*, 9 February 1856; "Thackeray" (reprints from New York papers), *Nebraskan* (Omaha), 27 February 1856; "Thackeray," *New Orleans Times Picayune*, 8 March 1856; "Thackeray in New York—His Lecture on George 1," *Philadelphia Inquirer*, 11 March 1855; "Mr. Thackeray's Return," *Philadelphia North American*, 7 April 1856; "Thackeray's Speech at St George's Day," *Boston Daily Atlas*, 28 April 1856; "Thackeray," *New York Times*, 14 May 1856. However, he was to reverse his assessment, having spent a great deal of time with the author during this New York stay. Writing to Emerson after his departure, he lambasted the baffling philosophically incurious Thackeray, who "could not see beyond his eyes and has no ideas, and merely is a sounding board against which his experiences thump and resound: he is the merest boy." Quoted in Stevenson, *Showman of Vanity Fair*, 265.

107. "Mr. Thackeray's Lectures," *Charleston Courier*, 1 February 1856.

108. "Mr. Thackeray's Lecture," *Boston Daily Advertiser*, 8 December 1855; "Thackeray in New York," *Philadelphia Inquirer*, 3 November 1855; "Mr. Thackeray's First Lecture," *Charleston Courier*, 2 February 1856.

109. "Thackeray," *New Orleans Times Picayune*, 8 March 1856.

110. Quoted in "Mr Thackeray's Lectures," *Vermont Chronicle*, 3 November 1855.

111. "Mr Thackeray—George III," *Brooklyn Eagle*, 21 November 1855.

112. Quoted in "Mr Thackeray's Lectures," *Vermont Chronicle*, 3 November 1855.

113. "Mr. Thackeray's Lectures," *Charleston Courier*, 9 February 1856.

114. "Mr. Thackeray's Lectures," *New York Times*, 6 November 1855.

115. "Mr. Thackeray's Lectures," *Boston Daily Advertiser*, 8 December 1855.

116. "New York Correspondent of the Boston Post," quoted in "Thackeray's Lectures," *Liberator*, 7 December 1855.

117. Sutherland, *Thackeray at Work*, 100.

118. Edmund Yates, *Town Talk*, June 1858; see Thackeray, *The Letters and Private Papers*, vol. 4, ed. Gordon N. Ray (London: Oxford University Press, 1946), 89–106.

119. Sutherland, *Thackeray at Work*, 100.

120. William Makepeace Thackeray, "George I Lecture," Pierpont Morgan Library, New York City.

121. "Thackeray in New York," *Philadelphia Inquirer*, 3 November 1855.

122. "Mr. Thackeray and His Lectures," *Albion*, 1 December 1855.

123. "Mr Thackeray's Return," *Philadelphia North American*, 7 April 1856.

124. "Thackeray," *New Orleans Times Picayune*, 8 March 1856.

125. "Mr. Thackeray's Lectures," *New York Times*, 6 November 1855.

126. "Thackeray's Speech at St George's Day," *Boston Daily Atlas*, 28 April 1856.

127. "Thackeray's Second and Third Lectures," *Albion*, 10 November 1855

128. "Mr. Thackeray and His Lectures," *Albion*, 1 December 1855.

129. "Thackeray's Second and Third Lectures," *Albion*, 10 November 1855.

130. "Thackeray and English Emigrants," *Albion*, 24 November 1855.

131. "Mr. Thackeray's Last Lecture," *North American and US Gazette*, 9 January 1856.

132. Robert Kiely, "Victorian Harlequin: The Function of Humor in Thackeray's Critical and Miscellaneous Prose," in *Veins of Humour*, ed. Harry Levin (Cambridge, MA: Harvard University Press, 1972), 148.

133. Thackeray, *English Humorists*, 6.

134. Taylor, *Thackeray*, 280.

135. Thackeray, *English Humorists*, 160.

136. "Thackeray," *Cleveland Plain Dealer*, 31 December 1852.

137. "Other Notices," *New York Times*, 14 May 1856; "Thackeray," *New York Tribune*, 13 November 1852.

138. Ralph Waldo Emerson to Thomas Carlyle, 10 August 1853, *Correspondence of Emerson and Carlyle*, 543.

139. "Thackeray," *United States Review*, March 1853.

140. Thackeray, *English Humorists*, 256.

141. Taylor, *Thackeray*, 281.

142. Bayard Taylor, "William Makepeace Thackeray, by One Which Knew Him," *Atlantic Monthly* 9 (March 1864): 372.

143. "Mr. Thackeray's First Lecture," *Albion*, 3 November 1855.

144. Stevenson, *Showman of Vanity Fair*, 262.

145. See Camfield, *Necessary Madness*, 66–70. See also Bryant, *Melville and Repose*.

146. Thackeray, *English Humorists*, 296.

147. Camfield, *Necessary Madness*.

148. Emerson, *Collected Works*, 5:81.

149. Bryant, *Melville and Repose*, 48.

150. "Thackeray," *United States Review*, March 1853.

151. "Mr. Thackeray's First Lecture," *Albion*, 3 November 1855.

152. *Times* (London), 21 January 1857.

153. *Spectator*, 11 June 1853.

Chapter 6

1. "Gough on Street Life in London," *Brooklyn Eagle*, 26 February 1861.

2. Bruce Seymour, *Lola Montez: A Life* (New Haven: Yale University Press, 1996); Lola Montez, *Lectures of Lola Montez* (Philadelphia: T.B. Peterson and Bros, 1858).

3. "Lola Montez," *Baltimore Sun*, 27 January 1860; "Mm. Montez," *Pittsburgh Post*, 7 February 1860; "Lola Montez Lectures," *Boston Post*, 6 March 1860.

4. Lola Montez, "On England," Harvard Theater Collection, LM lecture manuscripts.

5. Mary Clemmer Ames, *Outlines of Men and Women* (New York: Hurd and Houghton, 1873), 126.

6. Scott, "Popular Lecture," 806.

7. "John Bull at Home," *New York Times*, 16 December 1859.

8. Luther, "The Bygone Lyceum."

9. Montez's place in historiography is still based on the kind of tabloid innuendo that characterized her fame during her lifetime. In particular, see the prurient tone evident in James F. Varley, *Lola Montez: The California Adventures of Europe's Notorious Courtesan* (Spokane, WA: A.H. Clark, 1996) or James Morton, *Lola Montez: Her Life and Conquests* (London: Portrait, 2008). The key exception is the detailed biographical treatment offered by Seymour, *Lola Montez*. Far more work has been done on Gough. Most prominently, David Reynolds has placed him within the tradition of ethically questionable "dark reform" whose ambivalent appeal lay in prurient fascination, while Thomas Augst has reclaimed him as central to midcentury life-writing, abolitionist rhetoric, and constructions of masculinity. Reynolds, *Beneath the American Renaissance*, 67–69; David S. Reynolds, "Black Cats and the Delirium Tremens," in *The Serpent in the Cup: Temperance and American Literature*, ed. David S. Reynolds and Debra J. Rosenthal (Amherst: University of Massachusetts, 1997), 27; John W. Crowley, "Slaves to the Bottle: Gough's Autobiography and Douglass's Narrative," in *Serpent in the Cup*, 115–35; Thomas Augst, "Temperance, Mass Culture and the Romance of Experience," *American Literary History* 19.2 (2007): 297–323; Thomas Augst, "A Drunkard's Story: The Market for Suffering in Antebellum America," *Common-place* 10.3 (April 2010).

10. The following account comes mainly from Seymour, *Lola Montez* with some additions from Morton, *Lola Montez*.

11. Seymour, *Lola Montez*, 381–83.

12. "Lecture: Lola Montez," *Boston Post*, 2 September 1857; "Lola Montez Lecture," *New York Herald*, April 1860.

13. Bee Wilson, "Boudoir Politics," *London Review of Books*, 7 June 2007.

14. Lola Montez, "Autobiography Part 1," in *Lectures of Lola Montez, Countess of Landsfeld* (New York: Rudd and Carleton, 1859), 11.

15. "John Bull and His Rhubarb," broadside, London, 1850, National Library of Scotland.

16. George Clinton Densmore Odell, *Annals of the New York Stage*, vol. 7 (New York: Columbia University Press, 1931), 293; Thomas Gunn, Diaries, vol. 9, p. 67, 1857, Missouri History Museum.

17. Lola Montez, "On Beauty," in *Lectures of Lola Montez, Countess of Landsfeld*, 77.

18. "Lola Montez Lecture," *New York Herald*, April 1860.

19. "Lola Montez," *Buffalo Express*, 3 August 1857.

20. "Madame Montez," *Boston Herald*, 9 October 1857.

21. "Lola Montez on Beauty," *Philadelphia Press*, 9 November 1857.

22. "Lola Montez Lecture," *Evening Journal* (London), 7–8 April 1859.

23. Lola Montez, *Autobiography and Lectures of Lola Montez. With C. Chauncy Burr* (London: Gilbert, 1858), 7.

24. Quoted in Horace Wyndham, *The Magnificent Montez: From Courtesan to Convert* (New York: Hillman-Curl, 1935), 120.

25. "Lola Montez Lectures at the Stadt Theater—Her Enthusiastic Reception by the Germans," *New York Times*, 10 March 1859.

26. "Lola Montez Lectures at the Stadt Theater."

27. "Lola Montez and Her Fancies—by David Wemyss Jobson," *New York Times*, 18 March 1859.

28. Eduard de Mirecourt, *Lola Montès* (Paris: J.P. Roret et cie, 1850); Lola Montez, *Memoiren von Lola Montez, Gräfin von Landsfeld, aus dem Französischen übertragen von Ludwig Fort* (Grimma: Druck und Verlag des Verlags-Comptoirs, 1851).

29. Montez, "Autobiography Part 1," 11.

30. *Morning Advertiser* (London), 8 April 1859.

31. Odell, *Annals of New York Stage*, 293; Thomas Gunn, Diaries, Vol. 9, p. 67, Missouri History Museum, 1857.

32. "Lola Montez's Lecture," *Cleveland Daily Herald*, 13 February 1860;

33. Montez, "On England."

34. Montez, "Autobiography Part 1," 8.

35. Bee Wilson, "Boudoir Politics," *London Review of Books*, 7 June 2007; Montez, "Autobiography Part 1," 8.

36. Lola Montez, "On England."

37. *Galway Vindicator*, 24 November 1858, 2.7.

38. The manuscripts of "On Emigration" (1858), "America and England Compared" (1858), and "On England" (1859) are all preserved in Harvard Theater Collection.

39. "Lecture by Lola Montez," *New York Herald*, 19 December 1859.

40. Quoted in Seymour, *Lola Montez*, 250.

41. Unknown report, quoted in "Lola Montez," *Daily Intelligencer* (Wheeling, VA), 19 December 1859.

42. Montez, "On England."

43. Montez, "On Emigration."

44. Montez, "On Emigration."

45. Montez, "On Emigration."

46. Montez, "England and America Compared."

47. Montez, "England and America Compared." Emphases are Montez's own.

48. Winnifred Morgan, *An American Icon: Brother Jonathan and American Identity* (Newark: University of Delaware Press, 1988), 41.

49. Montez, "On England."

50. Montez, "England and America Compared."

51. Montez, "On England."

52. Montez, "On England."

53. Montez, "On England." For accounts of this Washington performance, see Seymour, *Lola Montez*, 389.

54. "Lola Montez," *Chicago Daily Journal*, 29 March 1860.

55. "Lola Montez," *Era* (London), 16 January 1859.

56. "Lecture of Lola Montez on English and American Character," *Morning Star* (London), 8 April 1859.

57. "Lola Montez," *Era* (London), 10 April 1859.

58. *Morning Advertiser* (London), 8 April 1859.

59. Quoted in "Lola Montez," *Daily Intelligencer* (Wheeling, VA), 19 December 1859.

60. Carlos William Martyn, *John B. Gough: The Apostle of Cold Water* (New York: Funk & Wagnall, 1894), xiii.

61. Martyn, *Apostle of Cold Water*, 212.

62. The American Antiquarian Society holds manuscripts for "Life in London," "London at Night," "Street Life in London," and the general lecture entitled "Here and There in Britain." During the next decades, these lectures were advertised and recorded under a host of roughly similar names, including "London Street Life," "Lights and Shadows of London Life," and "London by Moonlight." Reports indicate that sections from various lecture were, on occasion, conflated into one "London" performance.

63. Gough estimated that he delivered 6,064 lectures between 1843 and 1869, of which one-quarter were his nontemperance (i.e., mainly "London") material. *The Autobiography of John B. Gough* (New York: Bill, Nichols, 1870), 544.

64. *Philadelphia Press*, 16 May 1861.

65. Gough's fastidious documentation of his career in personal scrapbooks of newspaper cuttings has left us with a record of a lyceum career almost unmatched for any performer in its detail. In particular, "Diary of Lecture Engagements" and "Scrapbook of Newspaper Clippings," John B. Gough Papers, American Antiquarian Society, Worcester, MA, 2 vols., both undated. The main reports drawn on in this chapter are "John B. Gough at Musical Fund Hall Last Evening," *Philadelphia Press*, 16 October 1860; "John B. Gough's New Lecture," *New York Daily Tribune*, 16 February 1861; "Mr. John B. Gough's Lectures," *Philadelphia Inquirer*, 18 February 1861; "John B. Gough at the Academy of Music Last Evening," *Philadelphia Press*, 19 February 1861; "Local Intelligence: Mr. Gough on London Street Life," *Philadelphia Inquirer*, 19 February 1861; "Local Intelligence: Mr. Gough on London Street Life," *Brooklyn Eagle*, 19 February 1861; "Lecture by John B. Gough on Street Life in London—Crowded House and Extraordinary Enthusiasm," *Brooklyn Eagle*, 26 February 1861; "Mr. Gough on the Streets of London," *New York Times*, 16 March 1861; "John B. Gough at the Academy of Music—Lecture upon London his Experience," *Brooklyn Eagle*, 1 April 1861; "Gough at the Academy of Music," *Brooklyn Eagle*, 16 April 1861; "Mr. Gough's Farewell Lecture at the Academy, on Thursday Evening," *Philadelphia Press*, 16 May 1861; "John B. Gough's Second Lecture under the Auspices of the YMCA of This City," *Brooklyn Eagle*, 6 November 1861; "John B. Gough at the Academy of Music," *Philadelphia Press*, 14 March 1862; "Mr. Gough's Second Lecture at the Academy of Music," *Philadelphia Press*, 17 March 1862; "Mr. Gough's Non-temperance Lectures," *Philadelphia Press*, 6 May 1862; "John B. Gough at the Academy of Music—the Great Metropolis," *Brooklyn Eagle*, 4 April 1865. Further reports are identified in subsequent notes.

66. Gough, *Autobiography*, 525.

67. "Gough's Lecture," *Troy Daily Times*, 12 December 1861. For Gough's mingling of registers, see also Martyn, *Apostle of Cold Water*, xiii–ix.

68. See Don B. Wilmeth and Tice L. Miller, eds., *Cambridge Guide to American Theater* (Cambridge: Cambridge University Press, 1996), 253. See Paul Schlicke, *Dickens and Popular Entertainment* (London: Allen and Unwin, 1985), 234–41.

69. Martyn, *Apostle of Cold Water*, xiii; *Philadelphia Press*, 16 October 1860.

70. "Lights and Shadows of London—John Gough," *Philadelphia Press*, 16 March 1861.

71. "Local Intelligence: Mr. Gough on London Street Life," *Brooklyn Eagle*, 19 February 1861.

72. "Lecture by John B. Gough on Street Life in London—Crowded House and Extraordinary Enthusiasm," *Brooklyn Eagle*, 26 February 1861.

73. Gough, *Autobiography*, 334.

74. Richard M. Hogg, general ed., *Cambridge History of the English Language*, 6 vols. (New York: Cambridge University Press, 1992–2001), 6:71.

75. For arguments for the advance of American English, see George Perkins Marsh, *Lectures on the English Language* (New York: Samson & Low, 1860), 667–69.

76. *Philadelphia Press*, 19 February 1861.

77. James Ewing Ritchie, *Night Life in London* (London: William Tweedie, 1857), 200.

78. Ian R. Tyrrell, *Sobering Up: From Temperance to Prohibition in Antebellum America, 1800–1860* (Westport: Greenwood Press, 1979), 164.

79. Reynolds, *Beneath the American Renaissance*, 67.

80. *Philadelphia Inquirer*, 18 February 1861.

81. "A Boston newspaper," quoted in *Philadelphia Inquirer*, 18 February 1861.

82. "John B. Gough at the Academy of Music Last Evening," *Philadelphia Press*, 19 February 1861; see also "John B. Gough's Second Lecture under the Auspices of the YMCA of this City," *Brooklyn Eagle*, 6 November 1861.

83. "Local Intelligence: Mr. Gough on London Street Life," *Philadelphia Inquirer*, 19 February 1861.

84. *Brooklyn Eagle*, 26 February 1861.

85. See Paul Downes, *Democracy, Revolution, and Monarchism in Early American Literature* (Cambridge: Cambridge University Press, 2002).

86. Tamarkin, *Anglophilia*.

87. Tamarkin, *Anglophilia*, 58.

88. *Philadelphia Press*, 17 March 1862.

89. Charles Dickens, "Parliamentary Sketch," in *Sketches by Boz Illustration of Everyday Life and Every-Day People* (Philadelphia: Lea & Blanchard, 1839), 86–87.

90. *Brooklyn Eagle*, 1 April 1861.

91. *Brooklyn Eagle*, 1 April 1861.

92. *Brooklyn Eagle*, 26 February 1861.

93. *Philadelphia Inquirer*, 19 February 1861.

94. See David Skilton, "Contemplating the Ruins of London: Macaulay's New Zealander and Others," *Literary London Journal*, March 2004. See also Ledru-Rollin's *De la décadence d'Angleterre* (1850), much discussed and derided during the years of Gough's British sojourn in Britain.

95. *Brooklyn Eagle*, 26 February 1861.

96. See Stephen L. Vaughn, *Encyclopedia of American Journalism* (New York: CRC Press, 2008), 68–69; see also Roman A. Schroth, *The "Eagle" and Brooklyn: A Community Newspaper, 1841–1855* (New York: Greenwood, 1974), 65–68.

97. Vaughn, *Encyclopedia of American Journalism*, 69.

98. *Brooklyn Eagle*, 6 November 1861.

99. For example, "63rd Anniversary of the St. George's Society," *New York Herald*, 24 April 1849; or "The Scottish Societies," *Philadelphia Press*, 2 December 1861, both of which record similar juxtapositions of national anthems.

100. Duncan Andrew Campbell, *Unlikely Allies: America, Britain and the Victorian Beginnings of the Special Relationship* (London: Hambledon Continuum, 2007), 144–46.

101. *Brooklyn Eagle*, 6 November 1861.

102. *New York Times*, 16 March 1861.

103. *New York Tribune*, 16 February 1861.

104. "John B. Gough—Lights and Shadows of London Life," *San Francisco Bulletin*, 19 May 1871.

105. *Brooklyn Eagle*, 4 April 1865.

106. Campbell, *Unlikely Allies*, 147–49.

107. Gladstone's hostility expressed in his speech of October 1862; see Campbell, *Unlikely Allies*, 152.

108. *Brooklyn Eagle*, 4 April 1865.

109. "Mr. Gough on the Streets of London," *New York Times*, 16 March 1861.

110. See Tom Standage, *The Victorian Internet* (New York: Berkeley, 1998), 81–84.

111. "Lecture of Lola Montez," *Sun* (London), 8 April 1859.

112. Warren, *Culture of Eloquence*, 16.

113. Artemus Ward, "The Show Business and Popular Lectures" (1859), in *The Complete Works of Artemus Ward*, part 7 (New York: G.W. Dillingham, 1898), 121.

114. Higginson, "American Lecture-System," 634; Holland, "The Popular Lecture," 366.

115. Montez, "On England."

Epilogue

1. Powell, "Rise and Decline"; Luther, "The Bygone Lyceum"; Edward Everett Hale, "Lectures and Lecturers," in *Modern Eloquence*, ed. Thomas B. Reed, vol. 4 (Philadelphia, 1901), xxiv.

2. Powell, "Rise and Decline," 737.

3. Luther, "The Bygone Lyceum."

4. See Andrew Rieser, *The Chautauqua Moment: Protestants, Progressives, and the Culture of Modern Liberalism* (New York: Columbia University Press, 2003); Charlotte M. Canning, *The Most American Thing in America: Circuit Chautauqua as Performance* (Iowa City: University of Iowa Press, 2007).

5. See, for example, the essays on late nineteenth-century topics in Wright, *The Cosmopolitan Lyceum*.

6. Augst, "Humanist Enterprise," 223.

7. George William Curtis, "Editor's Easy Chair," *Harper's Monthly*, May 1870, 919.

{ INDEX }